# CASTE AND LIFE NARRATIVES

# Caste and Life Narratives

*edited by*

S. SHANKAR
CHARU GUPTA

PRIMUS BOOKS
*An imprint of Ratna Sagar P. Ltd.*
Virat Bhavan
Mukherjee Nagar Commercial Complex
Delhi 110 009

Offices at CHENNAI LUCKNOW
AGRA AHMEDABAD BENGALURU COIMBATORE DEHRADUN GUWAHATI HYDERABAD JAIPUR JALANDHAR KANPUR KOCHI KOLKATA MADURAI MUMBAI PATNA RANCHI VARANASI



*First published in India 2019*

ISBN: 978-93-5290-875-2 (hardback)
ISBN: 978-93-5290-876-9 (POD)

Published by Primus Books

Laser typeset by Mithu Karmakar
mithu.karma@gmail.com

*for*

ROHITH VEMULA

# CONTENTS

Acknowledgements ix

1. "My Birth Is My Fatal Accident": Introduction to Caste and Life Narratives
*S. Shankar and Charu Gupta* 1

Literary Lives

2. Speaking Self, Writing Caste: Recovering the Life of Santram BA
*Charu Gupta* 19

3. The Dalit Personal Narrative in Hindi: Reflections on a Long Literary Lineage
*Tapan Basu* 47

4. Tamil Dalit Literature: Aesthetics, Politics, and Life Narratives
*Parthasarathi Muthukkaruppan* 66

5. Bending Biography: The Creative Intrusions of "Real Lives" in Dalit Fiction
*Laura R. Brueck* 79

Lives in Visual and Performance Cultures

6. *Periyar* as a Biopic: Star Persona, Historical Events, and Politics
*Swarnavel Eswaran* 97

7. Affective Returns: Biopics as Life Narratives
*Bindu Menon* 120

8. Caste Life Narratives, Visual Representation, and Protected Ignorance
*Y. S. Alone* 144

9. Mangala Bansode and the Social Life of Tamasha: Caste, Sexuality, and Discrimination in Modern Maharashtra
*Shailaja Paik* 173

LAW, SOCIETY, AND NARRATIVES OF THE SELF

10. Brahmanical Activism as Eco-Casteism: Reading the Life Narratives of Bindeshwar Pathak, Sulabh International, and "Liberated" Dalits
*Mukul Sharma* 205

11. Invisibility of "Other" Dalits and Silence in the Law
*Sumit Baudh* 228

OUT OF INDIA

12. Stories of Dalit Diaspora: Migration, Life Narratives, and Caste in the US
*Shweta Majumdar Adur and Anjana Narayan* 253

13. Caste in Japan: The Burakumin
*June A. Gordon* 274

SELECT BIBLIOGRAPHY 297

NOTES ON EDITORS AND CONTRIBUTORS 301

INDEX 305

# ACKNOWLEDGEMENTS

Since the origin of the volume as a mere idea three years ago, the two of us have exchanged hundreds of emails, collaborated on every aspect of it, and have had many spirited conversations around caste and life narratives. In this journey, we got tremendous encouragement and inspiration from many colleagues, friends, and fellow travellers.

At *Biography*, as a special issue of which this volume began, we would like to thank the co-editors Cynthia Franklin, Craig Howes, and John Zuern for their expert knowledge of life narratives, unstinting support at every step, and extreme generosity. Thanks are also due to Stan Schab, then senior editor; and Anjoli Roy, then managing editor. *Biography* made it possible for all the contributors to come together at the University of Hawai'i at Mānoa in Honolulu for an intense and enriching three-day workshop in 2016, which helped us shape the volume in profound ways. We wish to acknowledge S. Charusheela, scholar and friend, who is not a contributor, but who in her eagerness flew out from Seattle to participate in the workshop.

The cover art for this volume is by Sudharak Owle and a debt of gratitude is owed to him for his kind permission, and to Y.S. Alone for facilitating our communication. Thanks too to Mari Yoshihara, who made time for advice at a key moment.

Finally, the contributors of this issue have themselves inspired us with their thought provoking ideas and readings. We thank them for making this collaborative project such a pleasure and such a success.

S. Shankar
Charu Gupta

# 1

# "MY BIRTH IS MY FATAL ACCIDENT"
## Introduction to Caste and Life Narratives

S. SHANKAR AND CHARU GUPTA

This book foregrounds "caste" and "life narratives" as reciprocally generative sites of serious study. We begin with the notion that the conjunction of a social phenomenon called "caste" with a genre of representation called "life narratives" deserves special scholarly attention. We are not the first to bring caste and life narratives together in this manner. As the essays collected here as well as the Selected Bibliography attest, this volume builds on previously existing work. We acknowledge such work while proposing that the essays here are unprecedented in the range of languages, archives, cultural traditions, and subgenres engaged, as well as in the kinds of theoretical discussions launched. Through these essays we hope to accomplish a twofold task: bringing discussions of caste to the scholarly study of life narratives and, reciprocally, foregrounding a nuanced and critical awareness of life narratives in explorations of caste.

In our own work, both of us have grappled with caste in the context of India in different ways. Shankar is a novelist and a literary and cultural critic, who in his 2012 book *Flesh and Fish Blood: Postcolonialism, Translation, and the Vernacular* explores the rich potential of vernacular literary expressions for representations of caste, with a particular focus on Tamil literature, including Dalit Tamil literature. He underlines how vernacular materials were often politically progressive. Part of his argument critiques postcolonial theory as presently configured. He also engages with caste in detail in his forthcoming novel, *Ghost in the Tamarind.* Charu is a feminist historian who in her 2016 book *The Gender of Caste: Representing Dalits in Print* brings together two complex markers of difference and inequality by rethinking the history of caste from a gendered perspective and by exploring its inextricable connections with popular culture, with a particular focus on Hindi print material of colonial North India. She argues that caste and gender are not only constitutive of the social; caste is central to how gender is reproduced. Our scholarly interests have cohered around how to historicize issues of embodiment and personhood from diverse regional and temporal frames. In different ways, both of us have a deep interest in how one might find caste in life narratives and how caste narratives may resist easy incorporation into dominant domains of academia or the "universal."

Life narratives have long been a constitutive archive and a performative mode for the oppressed. For example, Houston A. Baker remarks, "The locus classicus of Afro-American literary discourse is the slave narrative" (31). The slave narrative bears witness to the life of the slave. For similar reasons to do with witnessing, the experiences of some castes (some "caste-lives," in one potent formulation) have proven of especial interest to scholars. Generally, these have been Dalit ("untouchable") or Dalitbahujan ("lower caste") lives. In India, life narratives have been central to the recent boom in Dalit writings in the vernacular, particularly in Marathi, Hindi, and Tamil, which provide Dalits a means for declaring their own subjective agency. Various forms of life narratives—autobiography, *testimonio*, diary, confessional poetry, biopics—have been critical in testifying to the breadth and ferocity of caste oppression *and* for articulating a language of caste dissent and protest. While life narratives on and of caste raise questions of political inequality, they also underline the complex and subtle manner in which everyday lives and their retellings are sites for the social reproduction of a hegemonic caste order, as well as an enabling ground for the development of practices of resistance.

This book, then, acknowledges the unique status of Dalit and Dalitbahujan perspectives (of anti-caste radicals like Phule, Periyar, and Ambedkar, for example) in shaping a field of study such as "Caste and Life Narratives"; at the same time, the volume takes to heart that caste is not the lived reality of Dalits and Dalitbahujans alone and, accordingly, proceeds from the notion that the critical study of caste cannot be their burden alone. An "upper caste" Bania (such as M. K. Gandhi, touched on in Laura Brueck's essay in this volume) has as much a "caste life" as a Dalit. While not all "upper caste" life narratives acknowledge caste as directly as Dalit life narratives do, they nevertheless remain marked, even in their silence, by caste. Indeed, it has been argued (by M. S. S. Pandian, for example, in *Brahmin and Non-Brahmin: Genealogies of the Tamil Political Present*) that such silence is itself a mark of caste privilege—after all, is not the ability to ignore caste in itself a mark of privilege?

In this context, a useful distinction can and should be made between Dalit Studies and what we might term Critical Caste Studies. The former is the study of Dalit archives and lives, the latter the critical and interrogative study of any aspect of culture marked by caste. An analogy might be drawn here with the study of race in the United States. African American Studies is not the same as Critical Race Theory, though the former might offer an indispensable animating force to the latter. In a thoroughly racialized society like the United States, the critical study of race cannot be the burden of African Americans alone, and so it is with caste. Critical Caste Studies is vitally animated by Dalit Studies but is not coterminous with it. Additionally, a Critical Caste Studies acknowledges the existence of caste structures across the world (in Japan, for example, as indicated in June Gordon's essay) without in any way minimizing the virulence of caste within South Asia. Human Rights Watch offers this broad definition of caste in a global context:

> Caste is descent-based and hereditary in nature. It is a characteristic determined by one's birth into a particular caste, irrespective of the faith practiced by the individual. Caste denotes a system of rigid social stratification into ranked groups defined by descent and occupation. Under various caste systems throughout the world, caste divisions also dominate in housing, marriage, and general social interaction—divisions that are reinforced through the practice and threat of social ostracism, economic boycotts, and even physical violence.

A Critical Caste Studies might take as its purview this view of caste even as it learns from the exciting work within Dalit Studies.

In the context of India (with which caste is most often associated and with which all the essays in this collection save one are concerned), "caste" is the ubiquitous term for a form of social organization based on a mishmash of associated ideas of hierarchy, (notional) profession, ritual ideas of purity, endogamy, and (Hindu) scriptural stricture. Put in other words, "caste" is a protean category of social difference and a system of inequality based on hierarchy and heredity, ideologies of contamination, and stigmatization and exclusion (Bannerjee-Dube; Dirks 3–18; Bayly 1–96, 144–86; Shankar, *Flesh* 29–36). Caste is at one and the same time economic (in that it has consequences for how wealth is distributed), political (how power is distributed), and social (how status is assessed). It would be a mistake to think that the ways in which these three dimensions of caste map onto one another are predictable and uniform—a Brahmin priest in a village might, for example, be higher in social status than an economically more affluent landlord (as indeed made evident in the anticaste crusader Periyar's life, explored in Swarnavel Eswaran's essay). At the same time caste is not without its specificities, such that generations of scholars have found a relatively coherent object of study in it. This is why in some respects it seems, as V. Geetha and S. V. Rajadurai have suggested, that caste might be more usefully termed the "varna-jati complex" (xiii). The terms "varna-jati complex" and "caste" describe the same social phenomenon from different vantage points—the former from that of the vernacular and the latter from that of the transnational (Shankar, *Flesh* 34). *Varna* and *jati* are two terms commonly found in Indian languages denoting caste. *Varna* is a more abstract and scriptural term indicating the four broad groups into which castes are supposed to be divided (Brahmin, Kshatriya, Vaishya, and Shudra, with the *varna*-less "untouchables" or Dalits regarded as outcaste outsiders); while *jati* is a more locally situated and ethnographically relevant category, varying in its hundreds, if not thousands, across the length and breadth of not only India but the whole of South Asia. Ishita Banerjee-Dube underlines that the *varna*-model represents a "book view of caste," while the *jati*-model signifies a "field-view" or the actual reality of caste (xvii).

As with caste, so too with life narrative, which is a similarly imprecise term for modes of depicting a life. In this collection we intend the term to cover a variety of modes of representing "actual lives" in whole or in fragments—in autobiographies, biographies, memoirs, ethnographic interviews, nonfictional references within fiction, biopics, legal testimonies, art work, memoirs, Facebook posts, blogs, confessional poetry, and, lastly and most tragically, a suicide note. In using this term, we sometimes stretch the meaning of the word "narrative." We deploy life narratives in a generically fluid and wide variety of ways, as we wish to include not only biographies and autobiographies, but indeed to recognize the multiplicity of subgenres in which lives are narrated. It has seemed to us better to use the term "life narrative" rather than such alternative terms as "life writing" or "life representation" (not all texts are written, after all; and representation seems at once too theoretically loaded and vague a term). "Life narrative" has seemed the best of the terms on offer because more often than not, as an object of study, a life offers itself to us in some (fragmentary or otherwise) narrated form.

Life narratives are distinguished by their peculiar claims of authenticity established through a division between the fictional and the nonfictional. These claims of authenticity are, of course, unstable and continually negotiated, as Philippe Lejeune argues through the related notions of an autobiographical pact, the referential pact, and the readerly contract. Taken together, these ideas suggest both the insistence of life narrative genres (to expand the point beyond Lejeune's focus on autobiography) on a referential reality that exists separate from the text and the difficulty of articulating the difference between such a reality and that of, say, a novel. Recognizing a similar difficulty, Leigh Gilmore and G. Thomas Couser explore the ways in which life narrative genres may be said to be in a referential relationship to actual bodies, disabled, gendered, or otherwise. In the context of caste, these referential considerations, and the question of who "the contract" or "the pact" is with, are posed with a specificity to which it is essential to attend. With whom does Gandhi contract in writing his (nationalist) autobiography *The Story of My Experiments with Truth*? And who does Bama have in mind in her Dalit autobiography *Karukku* (discussed in Parthasarthi

Muthukkaruppan's essay)? Both Gandhi and Bama are Indian writers, albeit separated by language, period, gender, and caste. How, then, does Gandhi's contractual relationship with his reader relate to Bama's with hers? Such questions, which are not amenable to easy answers, are at the heart of this collection.

The life narrative genres engaged in this collection vary, often reflecting the disciplinary positioning of the contributing author. When we were making our selections for this volume, we were keen that the essays address how caste identities are imprinted and challenged in different genres of life narratives. We also hoped to start crossdisciplinary conversations on the subject between the humanities and the social sciences. We believe that juxtaposing essays from different disciplinary contexts can in itself help us in foregrounding differences of methodologies and epistemologies and in contextualizing some of the trends we witness in our fields of study. We were further interested in foregrounding diverse languages, regions, modes, and time periods, including the colonial and postcolonial. Finally, we were keen to extend our analysis to include communities other than Hindu (to see how caste is represented in Christian life narratives, for example); the Indian diaspora, an often neglected area of study; and regions where similar structures of inequality can be discerned and where race, for example, may be juxtaposed to caste.

The twelve essays that we have chosen—and that then underwent intense discussion amounting to a kind of peer review, including at a three-day workshop convened in Honolulu—thus represent a range of disciplines and methodological perspectives. The disciplines represented include art criticism, education, film studies, history, law, literary criticism, management studies, and sociology. In making our selections, we sought a diversity of languages, regions, genres and themes, and identities and personae:

### *LANGUAGES*

- Hindi: Laura Brueck, Tapan Basu, Charu Gupta
- Japanese: June Gordon
- Malayalam: Bindu Menon
- Marathi: Shailaja Paik
- Tamil: Swarnavel Eswaran, Parthasarathi Muthukkaruppan

### *REGIONS WITHIN INDIA AND OUTSIDE*

- Japan: June Gordon
- Kerala: Bindu Menon
- Maharashtra: Shailaja Paik
- North India: Laura Brueck
- Punjab: Charu Gupta
- Tamil Nadu: Parthasarathi Muthukkaruppan, Swarnavel Eswaran

### *GENRES AND THEMES*

- autobiography: Tapan Basu, Charu Gupta
- Brahmanical formulations: Mukul Sharma
- cinema: Bindu Menon, Swarnavel Eswaran
- education: June Gordon
- environmental studies: Mukul Sharma
- gender: Bindu Menon, Charu Gupta, Shailaja Paik
- law: Sumit Baudh
- literature: Laura Brueck, Parthasarathi Muthukaruppan, Tapan Basu
- performance, theater, and narration in folk forms: Shailaja Paik
- queer sexualities: Sumit Baudh
- reformist writings: Charu Gupta
- visual arts: Y. S. Alone

### *IDENTITIES AND PERSONAE*

- Dalit Tamasha performer Mangalatai Bansode: Shailaja Paik
- Burakumin of Japan: June Gordon
- Dalit Hindi writers like Ajay Navaria as well as Namishray and Bechain: Laura Brueck, Tapan Basu (respectively)
- Dalit Tamil writers and literary critics: Parthasarathi Muthukaruppan
- diasporic Dalit activists and movements: Shweta Adur and Anjana Narayanan
- an international NGO and its Brahmin founder Bindeswar Pathak: Mukul Sharma
- the anticaste icon Periyar: Swarnavel Eswaran
- Dalit actress P. K. Rosy: Bindu Menon
- anticaste Shudra reformer Santram BA: Charu Gupta

The selections have in common a committed exploration of the embodied nature of caste and how social practices of violence, intimacy, touch, and stigmatization organize caste's peculiar and pervasive imprint on our lives. Taken together, the essays—which go beyond the conventional life narrative forms of autobiography and biography to include oral histories, biopics, ethnographic interviews, legal testimonies, and visual arts—provide us with discrete points of connection, dialogue, and debate.

In bringing together these essays from different disciplines, we are interested in the broad issues associated with life narratives and how such narratives are important sites for the construction *and* dismantling of identities. At the same time, we wish to underline the distinctive ways lives are (re)told when seen through the lens of caste, and how caste politics in turn are intertwined with questions of embodiment and personhood. In other words, we deploy life narratives as a method for materializing and interrogating caste lives and histories. We attempt to offer a bridge between life narratives and caste.

This book, then, stands at the intersection where caste meets life narrative; neither term by itself is a motivating element for this edited volume—rather it is the conjunction of the two that gives the book impetus. Western paradigms have often provided much of our theoretical capital for conceptualizing life narratives. Implicitly, as well as overtly, this edited volume explores new paradigms by bringing "caste" and "life narrative" together. Here, the book might be seen as proceeding in the same vein as Gopal Guru and Sundar Sarukkai's trenchant critiques of the facile use of Western paradigms in theorizing "experience," a category certainly crucial to life narratives. Both what constitutes a life and what constitutes a proper narrative of a life vary across cultures. What constitutes a life is not regarded in the same way in India as in the United States or in Japan, nor are the proper generic conventions through which a life is to be narrated. It is in the interest of capturing the specificity of life narratives in India (that is, their difference from similar narratives elsewhere) that David Arnold and Stuart Blackburn have identified

> a formulation of self-in-society that is more complex and subtle than a mutually exclusive opposition between an all-subsuming collectivity on the one hand, and a rampant individuality on the other. . . . [N]early all of them [life narratives in India], in one way or another, demonstrate that Indians present individual lives within a network of other lives and that they define themselves in relation to larger frames of reference, especially those of family, kin, caste, religion, and gender. (19)

Bindu Menon's exploration in her essay of the multiple renderings of Dalit actress K. Rosy's life in print and cinema well illustrates the different ways in which the balance between individuality and society (thematically common enough to scholarly study of life narratives across the world) is weighted in India. Menon's essay also points to further specifications arising out of caste—the narration of an "upper caste" Nair life cannot be the same as the narration of a Dalit one, for the latter is inevitably contestatory with regard to mainstream Indian society in a way the former need not be. The many gaps in the way Rosy's life has been rendered, as searchingly revealed by Menon, provides evidence in this regard.

At a theoretical level, some of these questions and problems are not unique to Indian life narratives or to caste lives. The essays in this volume are wide ranging in their theoretical references, attending to whatever scholarship seems relevant and useful; at the same time, they take their points of orientation from theories and archives largely unknown outside of Dalit Studies or Critical Caste Studies (see, for example, Y. S. Alone's Ambedkarite Buddhist essay and Charu Gupta's recuperation of the lost voice of Santram BA). We suggest, therefore, that this collection might be regarded as a dialogue between life writing studies as constituted in the West and preoccupations coming out of caste life narratives. Our hope is to challenge canonical life writing studies from a postcolonial, Dalit, and Critical Caste Studies perspective, and at the same time, provoke new ways of entering into the burgeoning study of caste in India and elsewhere (as represented by June Gordon's essay on Japan and, in a different way, by Shweta Adur and Anjana Narayan's essay on Dalit activism in the South Asian diaspora in the US).

Taken together, the collection is interdisciplinary, interlinguistic, intercultural, international, and comparative. As should be easily evident, the comparative dimension is implicit throughout the collection. Though not represented here, a comparative study of caste can be extended to South Asian countries other than India such as Sri Lanka or Nepal; and, even beyond, for example to Africa or to Japan. Posing the comparative question along a different dimension, we might ask: how does caste compare to race or ethnicity as a system of social structuring? Dalits have often borrowed from the radical politics of African Americans—the most famous example being that of the Dalit Panthers. This form of comparison is also made evident in Adur and Narayan's essay. Less well known is the borrowing that has sometimes gone in the opposite direction. Scholars such as Gerald Berreman have argued that race in the US may sometimes be understood as a form of caste. Without denying either the particular salience or the ferocity of caste in India, the comparative study briefly sketched out here is meant to highlight the possibilities opened up for research into identity and difference when it comes to caste and similar social structures around the world.

Through this edited volume, then, we wish to present new research material along with novel "readings" and interpretations of figures and texts that challenge standard categories and concepts for exploring caste-worlds. The effort here is to go beyond simple binarisms in understanding life narratives of caste and to refuse reduction of the concept of life narrative to the mundane, the private, or the benign. The study of life narratives here emphasizes that stories of lives marked by caste tell us much about the private and the public, the self and the nation, the individual and the community, the intimate and the social, and the personal and political spheres.

Thematically, a number of concerns might be seen to anchor the collection. Through life narratives, we not only wish to recast caste, not only write/right caste histories, but also create a counter-archive of caste that may help us in reconstituting our theoretical, cultural, and historiographical perspectives. Recalcitrant histories of caste may be gleaned through life narratives. It is often argued that "upper caste" autobiographers celebrate their achievements with a sense of fulfillment and celebration, while Dalit narrations of the self are ambivalent and insecure, as they continue to search for an elusive freedom

(R. Kumar 208, 260). Yet it is life narratives that have given Dalits a sense of agency and creative freedom. Thus, autobiographies and even imaginary biographies have been significant attempts by Dalits to produce their own histories, which have been silenced, erased, and marginalized in official archives and mainstream scholarship. Carlo Ginzburg shows us how an early manifesto on history "from below" appeared in the form of an "imaginary biography," where the intention was to salvage through a symbolic character a multitude of lives crushed by poverty and oppression (111–14). Similarly, Dalits have not only produced autobiographies but have also written a large number of biographies of strong and brave Dalit women and men of the past. The revolt of 1857 against British rule of India particularly has invoked imaginative and mythical memorialization of biographies of Dalit women heroes and martyrs like Jhalkari Bai and Uda Devi. These biographies—studied for example in Badri Narayan's book *Women Heroes and Dalit Assertion in North India: Culture, Identity and Politics* and Gupta's essay "Dalit 'Viranganas' and Reinvention of 1857"—pick up selective fragments from archival, official, and academic historical records and blend them with oral traditions and local memories of the community, rivaling the biographical histories of a nationalist figure like Rani Lakshmi Bai. They enmesh history, memory, and life narratives with visuals, posters, *melas* (public festivals), and public meetings. A multitude of lives that have been destined to count for nothing find their symbolic redemption in the depiction of immortal characters. Further, Dalits and Dalitbahujans have written life narratives and hagiographies of their own gods and ancestors, for example, Raidas, Deena Bhadri, and Eklavya. Finally, there has been a valorization of radical caste reformers like Phule, Periyar, and Ambedkar through life narratives. To take another example, life narratives of Poyikayil Yohannan, a radical Dalit thinker in twentieth-century Kerala, have created mythical accounts around him, which ultimately lead to a project of salvation, as Sanal Mohan has shown in "'Searching for Old Histories': Social Movements and the Project of Writing History in Twentieth-Century Kerala." Taken together, such imaginative constructions from the past of Dalit lives have provided Dalits with a history, identity, and agency. The creation of this counter-archive is a major project among Dalits that allows them to emerge as socially significant actors. It also breaks down and rejects categories of nonfiction and fiction, underlined in the invented term "autobiofictionalography" by Lynda Barry.

Tied to this creation of a counter-archive is the role of print, education, and the vernacular in the relationship between caste and life narratives. Print and visual engagements with lived experiences are often couched in the vernacular. In this volume, we are thus attempting to discover vernacular inscriptions of caste through life narratives. The meanings of the vernacular have crossed disciplines, subjects, and themes, and are relevant for this book. Scholars of South Asia have particularly grappled with the vernacular, whereby distinctions between the vernacular as culturally specific, local, traditional, indigenous, popular, raw, low, and associated with the masses versus the official and the academic (often expressed in the English language) as universal, cultivated, modern, sophisticated, classical, high, and, for the few, have been reiterated and challenged. Shankar has argued that a vernacular sensibility suggests "an orientation toward rootedness and cultural autonomy and specific locality" and "a sense of local habitation based on genealogy . . . without becoming synonymous with it" (*Flesh* 22, 24). And Uday Kumar views the vernacular less as a linguistic indicator than as "a space of thinking, argumentation and truth production which differs from, even as it interacts with, more professional, technically self-conscious writing" (7). The potential of deploying the vernacular in the study of life narratives and caste cannot be overestimated. The language of caste lives often needs a corporeal presence and nearness of lived experience that the vernacular can offer (Chatterjee 18).

Connected to this are equally important questions about "distinguished" and "ordinary" lives; and about cataclysmic, big events and everyday life. For example, what is the role of caste in biographies of Indian nationalist leaders like Gandhi and Nehru? Is a life narrative significant only when it is about heroes and "important" people? In an autobiography of a Dalit, caste becomes a salient feature of self-representation, which sometimes makes the writing "marketable." Caste provides the lens by which the reading audience views the author, and the author's narrative subjectivity is predicated often upon a stereotypical Dalit identity (see Parthasarthi Muthukkaruppan's essay in this regard). At the same time, life narratives apparently not attentive to caste can also carry within them caste markers and prejudices. Even when effaced and erased, how does caste reappear in life narratives of "upper caste" people? And how does caste work in everyday lived experiences of ordinary people, where it is not the grand narratives but daily lived moments that are recorded? How is the mundane, the ordinary, the anecdotal, the fragmentary, and the everyday placed in life narratives of the oppressed, and how does one narrate a life that has been dismissed and is not seen as "worthy" of commemoration or remembrance?

The essays in this volume are interested collectively in how and why circuits of production and available repertoires of representations of individual lives informed by caste reveal and veil intersections with other social categories such as gender, sexuality, class, ethnicity, religion, and nation. For example, are women's life narratives different from men's, and what happens when they intersect with narrativizations of caste? Similarly, how does the narrativization of caste identities impact queer identities (as seen in Sumit Baudh's essay)? How are the politics of telling and not telling interwoven with gender, sexuality, and caste in life narratives? Some of the essays in this collection are also particularly keen to bring to the fore political deployments of the body through markers like touch, stigma, and performance (see, for example, the essays by Charu Gupta, Shailaja Paik, and Mukul Sharma). Life narratives, after all, can be seen as putting one's body on the page, the screen, and the stage, and thus evoking an aesthetic intimacy.

In general, the essays and indeed this project as a whole can be seen as continuing to struggle with notions of representation and representativeness. Through individual lives and their telling in various forms and genres, the collection explores how and why representation of caste in particular ways becomes a critical ground for identity formation and social positioning, both for "upper caste" individuals and for Dalits and Dalitbahujans or, in the context of Japan, Burakumin. These forms of representation of caste through life narratives not only reflect the hidden fears and desires of the individual and of the collective unconscious, not only make private feelings and images public, but also shape, image, and texture our lives in particular ways. Life narratives often represent dominant paradigms of caste, what Jacques Rancière calls "embodied allegories of inequality" (12). Caste can also be (mis)represented in different ways in biopics such as *Periyar*, *The Dirty Picture*, and *Bandit Queen*.1 Social media, websites, and blogs can enable and distort representation of lives marked by caste. At the same time, representations may challenge caste in profound ways. Dalit life narratives, for example, often frame events and represent caste in distinct ways, challenging ideas of the "unrepresentable" and investing in an ethics of testimony. Different practices of representing caste lives thus throw open for us possibilities of challenging dominant embodiments, where representation is not just about replication but also about innovation.

As both representation and representativeness, a life narrative might be thought of as that which mediates between the *varna-jati* complex as a social category on the one hand and the individual (real) experiences of a life on the other. In this sense, the recourse to life narratives in a critical mode may be understood in multiple ways: as an attention to the experiences narrated; as an inquiry into genre; and as a mode of reading that attends particularly to protocols of the real and the authentic in a wide variety of texts that narrate lives. The collection does not attempt to adjudicate among these different and sometimes competing ways of deploying life narratives methodologically, preferring rather to let a profusion of approaches prevail.

Some of these approaches might be brought to bear in reading Rohith Vemula's death note as a devastating form of life narrative. Rohith Vemula was a politically active Dalit PhD scholar who committed suicide in January 2016 after being suspended from Hyderabad Central University. Much controversy has surrounded his life, his identity, and the reasons for his death.[2] Many lessons regarding caste lives can be drawn from this tragic episode.

Vemula's note, with its unalloyed mix of idealism and despair, went viral on the Internet soon after his suicide and, in so doing, shook the national government for several weeks and brought unprecedented attention to the toxic mix of casteist prejudice and bureaucratic indifference that all too often greets vulnerable Dalit students like Vemula. Here is the note (reproduced verbatim, with repetitions, as reported in newspapers):

> Good morning,
>
> I would not be around when you read this letter. Don't get angry on me. I know some of you truly cared for me, loved me and treated me very well. I have no complaints on anyone. It was always with myself I had problems. I feel a growing gap between my soul and my body. And I have become a monster. I always wanted to be a writer. A writer of science, like Carl Sagan. At last, this is the only letter I am getting to write.
>
> I always wanted to be a writer. A writer of science, like Carl Sagan.
>
> I loved Science, Stars, Nature, but then I loved people without knowing that people have long since divorced from nature. Our feelings are second handed. Our love is constructed. Our beliefs colored. Our originality valid through artificial art. It has become truly difficult to love without getting hurt.
>
> The value of a man was reduced to his immediate identity and nearest possibility. To a vote. To a number. To a thing. Never was a man treated as a mind. As a glorious thing made up of star dust. In every field, in studies, in streets, in politics, and in dying and living.
>
> I am writing this kind of letter for the first time. My first time of a final letter. Forgive me if I fail to make sense.
>
> My birth is my fatal accident. I can never recover from my childhood loneliness. The unappreciated child from my past.
>
> May be I was wrong, all the while, in understanding world. In understanding love, pain, life, death. There was no urgency. But I always was rushing. Desperate to start a life. All the while, some people, for them, life itself is curse. My birth is my fatal accident. I can never recover from my childhood loneliness. The unappreciated child from my past.
>
> I am not hurt at this moment. I am not sad. I am just empty. Unconcerned about myself. That's pathetic. And that's why I am doing this.
>
> People may dub me as a coward. And selfish, or stupid once I am gone. I am not bothered about what I am called. I don't believe in after-death stories, ghosts, or spirits. If there is anything at all I believe, I believe that I can travel to the stars. And know about the other worlds.
>
> If you, who is reading this letter can do anything for me, I have to get 7 months of my fellowship, one lakh and seventy five thousand rupees. Please see to it that my family is paid that. I have to give some 40 thousand to Ramji. He never asked them back. But please pay that to him from that.
>
> Let my funeral be silent and smooth. Behave like I just appeared and gone. Do not shed tears for me. Know that I am happy dead than being alive.

"From shadows to the stars."

Uma anna, sorry for using your room for this thing.

To ASA family, sorry for disappointing all of you. You loved me very much. I wish all the very best for the future.

For one last time,

Jai Bheem

I forgot to write the formalities. No one is responsible for my this act of killing myself.

No one has instigated me, whether by their acts or by their words to this act.

This is my decision and I am the only one responsible for this.

Do not trouble my friends and enemies on this after I am gone.

Is this not a representation of a life, that is, a life narrative, which also has a defining relationship with death? How does one "read" a life narrative such as this when the very act of reading might seem like a desecration of a life marked by vulnerability? At the same time—how does one *not* read such a life narrative? Wasn't Vemula precisely trying to get us to attend seriously to the issues that brought him to his difficult decision? Not reading seems equally a dishonoring of Vemula's life, activist spirit, and anguished cry from the heart. Vemula's death note marks an existential moment that acknowledges and yet refuses narrativization of caste. Not all life narratives engaging caste take as fraught a textual form as Vemula's final message, but his text serves as a good illustration of the real stakes and unique challenges posed to academic criticism and scholarship in reading such narratives.

In the crucial section XX of "Annihilation of Caste," Ambedkar makes a distinction between rules and principles in relationship to caste (also referred to in Y. S. Alone's essay), averring that the practice of caste depended on rule-based approaches that externally ordained behavior. In contrast, principles simply offered guidelines to behavior that could be tested. "Rules seek to tell an agent just what course of action to pursue," he notes. "Principles do not prescribe a specific course of action" (298). He is clear that the terrible discriminations of caste are a result of the blind allegiances (superstitions) that rules fostered.

Life narratives about caste represent the myriad manifestations in the lives of individuals (agents in Ambedkar's language) of such blind allegiances to rules. They give flesh and blood to the point that Ambedkar makes more abstractly, more theoretically. They show how the rules of caste are experienced and acceded to not only by Dalits but all agents within the *varna-jati* complex, or within the hierarchical social order of Japan, and also how these rules are challenged, bent, resisted, and contested. As made evident by the essays in this collection, life narratives constitute a crucial archive for the study and critique of caste structures in all their diversity.

## NOTES

1. See Shankar's essay "Thugs and Bandits" on *Bandit Queen* in this regard.
2. For a recent newspaper article that tried to clear some of the controversy, see Mondal.

## WORKS CITED

Ambedkar, B. R. "Annihilation of Caste." *The Essential Writings of B. R. Ambedkar*, edited by Valerian Rodrigues, Oxford UP, 2002, pp. 263–305.

Arnold, David, and Stuart Blackburn. "Introduction: Life Histories in India." *Telling Lives in India: Biography, Autobiography, and Life History*, edited by David Arnold and Stuart Blackburn, Indiana UP, 2004, pp. 1–28.

Baker, Houson A., Jr. *Blues, Ideology, and Afro-American Literature: A Vernacular Theory*. U of Chicago P, 1984.

Banerjee-Dube, Ishita. "Introduction: Questions of Caste." *Caste in History*, edited by Ishita Banerjee-Dube, Oxford UP, 2010, pp. xv–lxiv.

Bayly, Susan. *Caste, Society and Politics in India from the Eighteenth Century to the Modern Age*.Cambridge UP, 1999.

Berreman, Gerald. "Caste in India and the United States." *American Journal of Sociology*, vol. 66, no. 2, 1960, pp. 120–27.

Chatterjee, Partha. "Introduction: History in the Vernacular." *History in the Vernacular*, edited by Raziuddin Aquil and Partha Chatterjee, Permanent Black, 2008, pp. 1–24.

Cox, Oliver Cromwell. *Caste, Class, and Race: A Study in Social Dynamics*. Monthly Review, 1959.

Dirks, Nicholas B. *Castes of Mind: Colonialism and the Making of Modern India*. Princeton UP, 2001.

Geetha, V., and S. V. Rajadurai. *Towards a Non-Brahmin Millennium: From Iyothee Thass to Periyar*. Samya, 1998.

Ginzburg, Carlo. *The Judge and the Historian: Marginal Notes on a Late-Twentieth-Century Miscarriage of Justice*. Translated by Antony Shugaar, Verso, 1999.

Gupta, Charu. "Dalit 'Viranganas' and Reinvention of 1857." *Economic and Political Weekly*, vol. 42, no. 19, 2007, pp. 1739–45.

———. *The Gender of Caste: Representing Dalits in Print*. U of Washington P, 2016.

Guru, Gopal, and Sundar Sarukkai. *The Cracked Mirror: An Indian Debate on Experience and Theory*. Oxford UP, 2012.

Human Rights Watch. *Caste Discrimination: A Global Concern*. United Nations World Conference Against Racism, Racial Discrimination, Xenophobia and Related Intolerance, Aug. 2001, https://www.hrw.org/reports/2001/globalcaste/caste0801.pdf. Accessed 18 Jan. 2017.

Kumar, Raj. *Dalit Personal Narratives: Reading Caste, Nation and Identity*. Orient Blackswan, 2010.

Kumar, Uday. *Dr. Palpu's Petition Writings and Kerala's Pasts.* Nehru Memorial Museum and Library, 2014, http://125.22.40.134:8082/jspui/bitstream/123456789/841/1/Udaya_Kumar_final_25_Aug.pdf. Accessed 23 June 2017.

Lejeune, Philippe. *On Autobiography.* Translated by Katherine M. Leary, U of Minneapolis P, 1989.

Mohan, Sanal. "'Searching for Old Histories': Social Movements and the Project of Writing History in Twentieth-Century Kerala." *History in the Vernacular*, edited by Raziuddin Aquil and Partha Chatterjee, Permanent Black, 2008, pp. 357–90.

Mondal, Sudipto. "Rohith Vemula: An Unfinished Portrait." *The Hindustan Times*, n. d. http://www.hindustantimes.com/static/rohith-vemula-an-unfinished-portrait/. Accessed 15 Jan. 2017.

"My Birth Is My Accident: Full Text of Dalit Student Rohith's Suicide Letter." *The Indian Express*, 16 Jan. 2016, http://indianexpress.com/article/india/india-news-india/dalit-student-suicide-full-text-of-suicide-letter-hyderabad/. Accessed 15 Jan. 2017.

Narayan, Badri. *Women Heroes and Dalit Assertion in North India: Culture, Identity and Politics.* Sage, 2006.

Pandian, M. S. S. *Brahmin and Non-Brahmin: Genealogies of the Tamil Political Present.* Permanent Black, 2007.

Rancière, Jacques. *The Emancipated Spectator.* Translated by Gregory Elliott, Verso, 2009.

Shankar, S. *Ghost in the Tamarind.* U of Hawai'i P, 2017.

———. *Flesh and Fish Blood: Postcolonialism, Translation, and the Vernacular.* U of California P, 2012.

———. "Thugs and Bandits: Life and Law in Colonial and Epicolonial India." *Biography*, vol. 26, no. 1, Winter 2013, pp. 97–123.

Literary Lives

# 2

# SPEAKING SELF, WRITING CASTE
## Recovering the Life of Santram BA

CHARU GUPTA

Figure 2.1: Santram BA (1887–1988), reproduced courtesy of Madhu Chadha, granddaughter of Santram BA.

Santram BA,[1] who lived for 101 years (d. 1988), was a veteran Hindi writer and a radical caste social reformer from Punjab. He published more than one hundred books and booklets, including his autobiography, *Mere Jeevan ke Anubhav* (Experiences of My Life). A member of the Arya Samaj, he founded the Jat-Pat Torak Mandal (Organization to Break Caste, henceforth JPTM) in 1922. In spite of his vast writing repertoire, Santram has been marginalized in academic scholarship. His claim to fame has largely been that he invited B. R. Ambedkar to deliver the keynote address at the May 15, 1936, annual conference of the JPTM. However, the invitation was canceled because of internal opposition, which was convinced that Ambedkar's views would be unacceptable and controversial. The text of Ambedkar's lecture became the classic *Annihilation of Caste*.[2]

The covers of Santram BA's autobiography require close scrutiny and need to be studied on their own terms for several reasons. Belonging to the Shudra caste, unlike other pioneering caste radicals like Ambedkar or Periyar, Santram, while he trenchantly critiqued caste, perceived caste reform within the paradigm of Hinduism, accounting both for his limitations and possibilities. Santram's life narrative is significant not only because caste suffering forms an axis of his life but also because there are other layers

Figure 2.2: Cover of *Mere Jeevan ke Anubhav*, 1974 edition.

discernible, as he hedges the middle ground between Gandhi and Ambedkar, bourgeois and subaltern, Arya Samaj and Ad Dharm, and love and hate for Hinduism. It is from this in-between space that Santram produced his anticaste rhetoric. Santram's allure lies in his *trishanku* (limbo, middle-ground) status. While studying his writings, one passes through crossroads and by-lanes littered with caste, reminding us of the routes traversed and those not taken, and our inability to "classify" or confine him in any definite slot. While he may appear dated amid other caste radicals, his quests are pertinent, leaving behind a legacy, a memory, something that stirs the oppressed while also baffling us by its constraints.

When Santram wrote his autobiography in the 1960s, he already had his life mapped out in distinct phases, which he painted in broad brushstrokes. Vivid and playful, *Mere Jeevan ke Anubhav* was also a piece of propaganda for challenging caste. Various episodes in the autobiography were slanted to fit larger scripts, as Santram's personal narrative was informed by such elements as his Shudra status, Arya Samaj, Ambedkar, and JPTM. Santram starts the text by underlining his ordinariness, while emphasizing caste as central to his identity:

> I thought that writing one's autobiography was like flaunting one's greatness. . . . I am no extraordinary person. . . . My whole life I have just struggled against caste and served the Hindi language. But my friends stated that caste is the biggest enemy of India. To remove it is the biggest service to the nation. Your autobiography in a way would be a history of fighting against caste in modern India and of diffusion of Hindi in Punjab. . . . Thus I decided to write this book. . . . When anyone engages in social reform to get rid of caste, then not only strangers, even his own family and relatives oppose him. His photos are not published in papers. No statue of his is made. He has to burn on the pyre all his life. (3–6)[3]

M. S. S. Pandian argues that many Dalit texts "accentuate and underscore the self-conscious ordinariness of the lives narrated" (35) and the French philosopher Jacques Rancière states that "ordinary life has to be recognized not only as a possible subject for a poem but as a poetic subject par excellence" (175). Santram's autobiography represents such a framing with caste as its focus.

Through Santram's life and writings, this essay attempts to illuminate and rethink a social history of caste in early twentieth-century North India. It examines the stories he told others about himself, his life, and his anticaste thought. Santram's responses to caste provide glimpses of Santram the individual, the anticaste reformer and the family man, and interplay his personal, literary, and social life. His autobiography underlines everyday caste taboos around *roti-beti* (food and marriage), the constraints of Gandhian and Arya Samaj politics, and critically attacks Sanatani Hindu orthodoxy. It defies any neat readings, embodying paradoxical constitutions of the caste self, social reform, Hinduism, and nation, and effortlessly moves between private and public, personal and political, self and nation, individual and community, and intimate and social. This essay argues that Santram's thought cannot be bound by rubrics of glorification or demolition; rather, his perspective symbolizes how reformers were entangled between contradictory currents in colonial India. Santram produced multiple meanings and mutable positions on caste, where on the one hand, he became a staunch advocate of intercaste marriages, and on the other enacted a language of caste reform and respectability with ambiguous implications. Equally, Santram's writings signify conflicting uses of modernity, where he relied on reason on the one hand and devotion on the other to attack caste. It is this dual straddling and mixed congregation of ideas that make his life narrative both a complex and politicized form of resistance and critique of caste, while simultaneously appearing as an account of accepted caste models and messages. His life thus suggests new socialities of caste, whereby caste was both enabled and transformed.

The essay further registers caste through intimacy by focusing on Santram's attempts to subvert endogamy and upend conformity by promoting intercaste marriages. Anthony Giddens observes how "the possibility of intimacy means the promise of democracy" (188). And according to Alex Lubin, "intimate matters" are inextricably related to "civil rights activism in the public sphere" (xi). Intimacy is experienced in love and pleasure, and also expressed through relationships and representations, associations and exclusions. Santram, too, called upon ideas of intimacy to get at the terribly material, embodied character of caste-gender dynamics and its divergent receptions in public life. By challenging endogamy and caste hierarchies, he folded caste into histories of intimacy, love, and marriage, and drew intricate and inextricable connections between caste and gender. This helped shape a counter-narrative of caste, symbolized in the JPTM.

## LIFE HISTORY AND CASTE: SELF AND COLLECTIVE IDENTITIES

Rancière underlines that an individual life narrative "is not a choice of method within an alternative that would set the particular against the general, the individual against the collective, the short-term against the long-term, the small-scale against the large-scale, or the cultural against the economic. . . . It is a way of putting the alternative. . . . Its principle is to bring out the general in the particular, the century in the moment, the world in a bedroom" (171, 176–77). In the Indian context, David Arnold and Stuart Blackburn stress that life histories in India reveal "a formation of self-in-society that is more complex and subtle than a mutually exclusive opposition between an all-subsuming collectivity on the one hand, and a rampant individuality on the other" (19). More recently, Udaya Kumar has stressed that self-narratives from nineteenth-century India "rarely speak of private interiorities" and the distinctiveness of individual life is not their focal point; instead, they become a pretext for revealing something larger (*Writing the First Person* 13–14). Similarly, Richard Eaton deploys the genre of life narratives to enumerate a social history of the Deccan over four centuries.[4] It is in this context that Santram's autobiography, too, might be seen to reflect his ethical-political involvement, as the self is in constant dialogue with social and public interventions on caste, providing an archive of individual caste memory and collective caste history. Other scholars have emphasized that self-reflexive writing in the autobiographical mode has long been a part of Indian literary tradition (Ramaswamy 1), and that "a normative use of the model of the modern biographical subject in the west might obscure the long and discontinuous history of this form" in India (U. Kumar, "Writing the Life" 56). Read through these critical lenses, Santram's autobiography reveals divergent connotations seeking multiple purposes.

Autobiographies or life narratives have been the historical tool of the downtrodden, subalterns, and Dalits (Pandey 131–32), in which pain, suffering, and quotidian caste violence, combined with a language of personhood and collective rights, have often appeared as cultural capital (Ganguli 429–42; Hunt 176–208; R. Kumar 157–256; Pandey 131–93; Rege, 9–92). More recently, Laura Brueck has argued that the Hindi Dalit literary sphere signifies a "counterpublic," and a distinct political and aesthetic movement (50), and Toral Jatin Gajarawala has emphasized that "Dalit literature is the space where realism now lives" (3). In his classic work, Paul Gilroy underscores that black autobiography is "an act or process of simultaneous self-creation and self-emancipation" (69). Reiterates Pandian in a similar vein:

> Not bound by the evidentiary rules of social science, the privileged notion of teleological time, and claims to objectivity and authorial neutrality, these [Dalit] narrative forms can produce enabling re-descriptions of life-worlds and facilitate the re-imagination of the political. (35)

Figure 2.3: Covers of *Humara Samaj*, 1949 and 2007 editions. The 2007 cover is reproduced courtesy of Samyak Prakashan, Delhi.

Similar to many Dalit life narratives, caste provides the overarching framework of Santram's autobiography, as he imagines, constructs, and scripts memories of his subalternity. His autobiography becomes the landscape where divergent readings of stigmatization, suffering, contestation, and self-liberation come to be staged. When read in conjunction with *Humara Samaj* (Our Society), his most important book, Santram's autobiography highlights the centrality of caste in his life, while also bringing out the ambiguities of the times.

Both books have gone into several editions and are being published to this date, not by Arya Samaj but by Dalit publishing houses. Many of Santram's other books and booklets on caste have also found a fertile ground in Dalit publishing. Significantly, Satnam Singh, a leading Hindi Dalit writer, and Samyak Prakashan, a prominent Dalit publishing house, interpreted and published parts of *Mere Jeevan ke Anubhav* in 2008, adding a subtitle that boldly proclaimed the book to be the "first autobiography of Dalit literature."

Satnam Singh states:

> It is sad that Dalit literature too does not include him [Santram]. . . . Taking into account the year of its publication, *Mere Jeevan ke Anubhav* is the first [Hindi] Dalit autobiography. Santram was also a fearless journalist of his times. He wrote in all prominent newspapers-magazines. In 1914 he took out the magazine *Usha*. His *Kranti* was a famous magazine of its times. . . . In this context, he may be hailed as the first Hindi Dalit journalist as well. (*Santram BA* 3)[5]

Figure 2.4: Cover of Satnam Singh's book, claiming Santram BA's *Mere Jeevan ke Anubhav* as the "First Autobiography of Dalit Literature." Reproduced courtesy of Samyak Prakashan, Delhi.

While Singh's claim may be disputed, it underscores the significance of Santram's autobiography, which operates on a register that overlaps with Dalit life testimonies. It is equally significant that Santram's name features in many Dalit anthologies and encyclopedia, underlining the profound heterogeneity of Dalit politics (Paswan and Jaideva 189–90; Kshirsagar 323–24). There has been a subversive drive among Dalits, as they have attempted to create genealogies of a long literary history of Dalit writing, which has sometimes encompassed a wider terrain of claiming the oppressed, pushing the boundaries of Dalit discourse. In his classic work, *Why I Am Not a Hindu*, Kancha Ilaiah shapes the word Dalitbahujan, whereby he articulates that in spite of contradictions "there are cultural and economic commonalities as well as commonalities of productive knowledge which mesh them [Other Backward Castes and Dalits] together like threads in a cloth" (ix). Similarly, Dalit Panthers cast their net wide and use the term Dalit in a generic, broad, and inclusive sense (Murugkar 237; Brueck 9; Shankar 67–74). This usage may account to an extent for the acceptance of Santram in Dalit anthologies.

## FAMILIAL AND SOCIAL ROOTS: CASTE DISCRIMINATION, ARYA SAMAJ, AND PROMOTION OF HINDI

Santram was born on February 14, 1887, in Purani Basi, a small village in the Hoshiarpur district of Punjab. His father, named Ramdas Gohil, was a central Asian trader with business interests in Yarkand and Ladakh. His mother was Malini Devi. Santram was fourth among seven sons and one daughter (Santram, *Mere Jeevan ke Anubhav* 5–6 and "Taunted" 2; Gopal 8). While economically his family had done well, Santram came from humble social roots, belonging to the Shilpkar *kumhar* (potter) caste, which came way below in the caste hierarchy, and had a Shudra status in Punjab. H. A. Rose draws on the work of Denzil Ibbetson, ethnographer par excellence of Punjab, to identify *kumhar* as

> the potter and brick-burner of the country. . . . He is a true village menial, receiving customary dues, in exchange for which he supplies all earthen vessels needed for household use. . . . He also, alone of all Punjab castes, keeps donkeys. . . . He is the petty carrier of the villages and towns. . . . His social standing is very low, far below that of the

> Lohar and not very much above that of the Chamar; for his hereditary association with that impure beast the donkey, the animal sacred to Sitala, the small-pox goddess, pollutes him; as also his readiness to carry manure and sweepings. (562)

It was also noted in the *Gazetteer of the Hoshiarpur District, 1883–4*, "Donkeys are kept by the potters (*kumhar*), who do a good deal of the carrying trade between Palampur and Hoshiarpur" (107). Many degrading caste sayings pertain to *kumhars*, marking their Shudra status. Goes one:

> *kumhar ki gadhi, ghar-ghar ladi*
> (The donkey of the potter is used by the whole village)
> (Singh, *Santram BA* 13)

Other sayings reveal the poverty of the *kumhar*:

> *kumhar ke ghar baasan ka kaal!*
> *kumhar ke ghar chukke ka dukh!*
> (A scarcity of pots in the potter's house!
> A want of saucers in the potter's house!) (Fallon 144)

And goes yet another:

> *dheel dhoti baniya, ulta munch subir,*
> *bainda pair kumhar, ke teenu ke pehchaan.*
> (A trader wears a loose dhoti, the brave keep their mustaches turned up,
> and a potter is bare footed—this is the identity of the three.) (Singh 14)

Amid this background, Santram realized the importance of education very early. It has been pointed out how in colonial India, while untouchability and caste hierarchies were reproduced through educational institutions, the first generation of Dalit intellectuals increasingly saw education, knowledge, language, and print as central to their assertion (Auxiliary Committee 217-28; Ciotti 900; Constable 385). It has also been argued that print journalism helped nurture a Hindi Dalit counterpublic, boundaries of which were "located squarely in the interpretive framework of caste" (Brueck 50). Santram deployed these tools effectively in his critique of caste, as through his education, pen, and writing he literally made himself. He, too, like many other Dalits, viewed print and publishing as critical tools for claiming upward mobility and dignity (Satyanarayana and Tharu, *No Alphabet* and *Steel*). Santram studied in Bajwara, Ambala, Jullundur, and Lahore, acquiring his BA degree in 1909, and started writing actively in 1912 (Santram, *Mere Jeevan ke Anubhav* 9; Singh 13). Since then, all his writings appeared without his caste nomenclature and Santram proudly displayed his educational qualification and degree as his surname, signature, and distinct identity—Santram BA—which became an integral part of his name (Gopal). Practices and politics of naming and renaming have been central to challenging stigmatized pasts (Paik 217–18; Pandey 207–10; Rao 205–13; U. Kumar, *Writing the First* 6). Santram gave his name distinct meanings by explicitly linking it to education.

It has been noted that Dalit autobiographies constantly recount experiences of humiliation, thereby making a "public claim regarding the norms that govern the treatment of each other in society" (U. Kumar, *Writing the First* 17). Santram's autobiographical memory, too, is infused with caste prejudices and attempts at carving out a life of dignity. He was harshly reminded of his Shudra status through some humiliating and bitter encounters in school and college, which form a vital part of how Santram represents himself in *Mere Jeevan ke Anubhav*. He narrates:

> When I was admitted in class four in Ambala, my caste was also mentioned in the register. . . . My co-students constantly harassed me, calling me by my caste name *kumhar*. And why would they have not done so when even a saint and poet like Tulsidas ridiculed *kumhara*. . . . I took the students' taunts quietly and painfully. (16)

At another place he writes about his experience in college:

> In my boarding house, the kitchen in which I had food was orthodox. . . One day a few fellow students . . . quarreled with me and kept a chit on my seat stating that since I belonged to a low-caste, I should have my food outside the kitchen, or else they would take the matter to the principal. . . . I angrily declared that forget the principal, even if they take the matter to the governor, I will have my food inside the kitchen only. (17–18)

Through such memories, Santram imaginatively weaves an "I" out of the contours of caste stigma. Santram's retelling encompasses everyday caste humiliation, myths of food and skin color, and a critique of caste intellectuals and scriptural Hindu texts, through which he shapes a multipronged critique of caste in private and public life.

Amid a contentious, casteist atmosphere, the teachings of Dayanand Saraswati and the spread of Arya Samaj in Punjab, which theoretically distanced itself from casteism (Jones 204), came to acquire a special attraction for Santram. Scholars have pointed out how many Dalits and "low castes" became followers of Arya Samaj, critically contributing to the creation of the first generation of Dalit intellectuals in Punjab (Juergensmeyer 72; Jones 309–10; Adcock, *Limits* 128). Many of the Ad Dharm activists, too, were initially associated with Arya Samaj (Juergensmeyer 27, 35–37; Ram 326). While in 1901 the Arya Samaj membership consisted overwhelmingly of Hindu "upper castes," by 1911 the Punjab membership had quadrupled through the entry of other castes. The census estimated that as many as two-thirds of the Arya Samajists of the region hailed from the "lowest castes"

(*Census of India, 1911* 123–24).[6] Hoshiarpur particularly proved a fertile ground as it boasted of a large number of "untouchables," approximately 23 percent of the population (Juergensmeyer 72). Significantly, both Santram and Mangoo Ram, the dynamic leader of the Ad Dharm movement, hailed from Hoshiarpur. Mark Juergensmeyer points out that Arya Samaj's ideology became particularly popular among the urban Hindus of mercantile castes (38). Santram covered this median ground by belonging socially to the Shudra caste while being economically associated with the urban mercantile class. His attraction for the relatively progressive ideology and egalitarian principles of Arya Samaj has to be understood in this educational, urban, and social context, which also ultimately proved to be his drawback. At the same time, like many other "low castes," Santram selectively appropriated or rejected the ideological underpinnings and teachings of Arya Samaj to suit his objectives of social status and equality (Rawat 136–44; Adcock, *Limits* 159). He was a supporter of vegetarianism, *shuddhi* (reconversion through purification), and *brahmacharya* (celibacy), the last of which he slowly came to reject totally. Arya Samaj's ambiguity regarding caste on the ground to an extent indicates the inconsistencies within Santram, even when he was in constant conflict with his Arya Samaj "upper caste" fellows and lamented the various hurdles in his way.

Santram's love for Hindi developed in conjunction with the headway that Arya Samaj was making in Punjab. He narrates in *Mere Jeevan ke Anubhav*:

> Hindi was taught in no school of Punjab. . . . I did not know any Nagari script till the third year of my college. In my adolescence I considered Persian to be the sweetest language, Iran to be the best paradise on earth, and Saadi, Omar Khayam and Firdausi the greatest poets. . . . However, Lahore and Arya Samaj changed my views dramatically. . . . Those days *Saddharma Pracharak*, the mouthpiece of Arya Samaj was published in Urdu. I used to read it with great enthusiasm. Its editor . . . Swami Shraddhanand announced a date from which the paper would switch over to Hindi. . . . To read the paper I started learning the Nagari script. . . . I left my love for Persian in favour of Hindi. (133–34)[7]

Santram was fluent in English and Urdu, and picked up Marathi and Gujarati from his second wife, Sunder Bai (*Mere Jeevan ke Anubhav* 109). His Hindi writings comprised a wide range of subjects and many translations, including of Alberuni and I-Tsing (142). Santram pitched himself as a promoter of Hindi language, creating a name for himself in the print-public life of the Hindi world, and was most influential via his books, pamphlets, and journals against caste.8 He edited two monthly magazines, one in Urdu called *Kranti* and the other in Hindi entitled *Yugantar* to spread the message of JPTM, both of which ceased publication after the partition of India. Post independence, he was associated with *Vishwajyoti*, published from Hoshiarpur (136).

Figure 2.5: Cover of JPTM's magazine, *Yugantar*, published for four years, beginning January 1932.

In Santram's hands, immersed in the world of Hindi, print became a significant, if ambivalent, site for the transformation and contestation of caste. On the personal front, a series of calamities—the death of his first wife, Ganga Devi, in June 1924, and of his son Ved Vratt in May 1928—profoundly affected Santram's transition into early adulthood, which he describes painfully in *Mere Jeevan ke Anubhav*.

After some years, his friend from JPTM, Bhumanand, persuaded Santram to enter into an intercaste marriage and with this marriage, Santram began a new phase of his life. Though Santram's extended family was well off, he constantly talked of his poverty and financial difficulties since he was uncompromising on his principles and never had a permanent job, nor was he ever satisfied with any jobs he did have (*Mere Jeevan ke Anubhav* 19, 32–33, 44–46).

In the rest of this essay, I take fragmentary examples from Santram's autobiography and other writings, parts of which are also a life narrative and history of JPTM, to underline how and why Santram attempted to create a hybrid liberal domain that traversed the middle ground between Gandhi and Ambedkar on the one hand and Arya Samaj and Ad Dharm on the other, the contradictory uses of modernity in Santram's critiques of caste, and his explorations of intimacy and intercaste marriages. These efforts highlight how Santram sometimes swam within the boundaries of Hinduism but more often went against its mainstream tide.

## SELF AND SOCIAL HISTORY OF JPTM

Deeply impressed by a fiery speech delivered by Parmanand in Lahore in November 1922, Santram and a group of his friends formed JPTM, which Santram named. Eighteen people were initially associated with the organization, including two women (*Mere Jeevan ke Anubhav* 184–85; *Jat-Pat* 1). Unlike other radical regional caste movements, JPTM was largely an urban-based movement among the literates.

Parmanand was JPTM's president in the beginning, but as its secretary, Santram was the driving force behind it. Articles were published on JPTM in newspapers, and the organization launched monthly journals like *Jat-Pat Torak*, *Kranti*, and *Yugantar*, with Santram as editor. JPTM also published many booklets against caste and distributed them free of cost. JPTM members also attended various Arya Samaj meetings and festivals, preaching against caste

Figure 2.6: Left: Ganga Devi, first wife of Santram BA, died June 1924. Right: Ved Vratt, son of Santram BA, died May 1928, fourteen years old. Reproduced courtesy of Madhu Chadha, granddaughter of Santram BA.

(*Mere Jeevan ke Anubhav* 185–87; *Jat-Pat* 2–3; Santram, *Caste Must Go* 1–2). JPTM's first priorities were to break the birth-based caste system and to promote intercaste marriages, focal points to which I will return later.

Scholars have highlighted that in colonial India, caste became a protean category for colonial capitalism, social reform, and Hindu nationalism, with the decennial census playing a central role in strengthening politicization of Hindu religion on the one hand and, on the other, "secularizing" and challenging configurations of caste (Banerjee-Dube xv–lxiv; Bayly 1–96, 144–86; Dirks 3–18; Cohn 224–54). In *Mere Jeevan ke Anubhav*, Santram entwines a part of his life narrative with JPTM's movement in 1931 to remove the caste-based column from the census and from forms at colleges and universities. This activism made JPTM famous and accelerated its mobilization, as people from all the big cities of India started joining it (*Mere Jeevan ke Anubhav* 187–88; *Jat-Pat* 4–5; Santram, *Caste Must Go* 2; "Anti-Caste" 44; *Census of India, 1931* 395–96). It was noted in the 1931 census of Punjab:

> At the same time a tendency was noticeable for persons of low castes, well placed in life, to return no caste, and there had been a propaganda in this connection, particularly by the *Jat Pat Torak Mandal*. . . . Instructions . . . issued . . . were that "no caste return" should be recorded in cases in which the person enumerated had a genuine objection to the caste entry, having ceased to observe caste in his marital and inter-dining relations. (*Census of India, 1931* 325; Maheshwari 106–09)

Interestingly, Juergensmeyer considers the 1931 census and the campaign of Ad Dharm around it as its "crowning moment" when "everything came together" because the movement was successful in listing Ad Dharmis as a religious community, separate from Sikhs, Muslims, and Hindus (72–80). Moreover, the movement exacerbated tensions between the Ad Dharm and the Arya Samaj. Santram's move in the 1931 census acquires significance amid this background.

JPTM and Santram, while close to the ideology of Arya Samaj, also had deep tensions with it and more so with the Ad Dharm movement. Santram lamented religious conversions, firmly supported *shuddhi*, and advocated vegetarianism. He framed his critique of caste by embracing the "lower castes" within a Hindu fold, and also attempted to "improve" some of the perceived characteristics and practices of the "lower castes." Yet, even in these arenas, he did not just replicate the teachings of Arya Samaj but often questioned and radically reinterpreted them, condemning and chastising their continued caste prejudices. For Santram, *shuddhi* did not so much symbolize a militant Hindu nationalism; rather, it was a way of assertion by the "lower castes" for radical caste reform (Adcock, "Brave" 261–86). As Lauren Berlant and Jay Prosser say: "Sometimes conventionality is a defense against norms too, a way to induce proximity without assimilation . . . and sometimes it's a way of creating another, counter conventional, space" (181). Some of the cartoons published in Santram's journal *Yugantar* transgressed normative discourses of caste. One 1933 cartoon in the journal shows a Brahmin male ogling a sweeper woman and, while desiring sex with her, categorically refusing to perform her *shuddhi*.

Figure 2.7: Cartoon published in *Yugantar* in October 1933: "You are sensuous, titillating and intoxicating, look at me with a smile! Even If I carnally embrace you, I will still always be a Brahmin! However, no purification of yours can be conducted; dear you will always remain a sweeper woman" ("Uncouth Brahmin" 26).

While Santram did express anxieties over religious conversions to Islam due to romance, love, and marriage, unlike many writings of Arya Samaj, there was no vociferous polemic in his writings against Muslims, *pirs*, or Islam. Santram appreciated the broadmindedness of Muslims in accepting such marriages within their fold and disparaged the narrowmindedness of Hindus in this regard (*Mere Jeevan ke Anubhav* 48–53). Even his attitude toward missionaries and Christianity appears soft. In fact, he drew selectively from Islam and Christianity to make his arguments. He dramatically wrote: "If I had been an untouchable, then to get rid of this slavery, I would have become a Muslim" (*Mere Jeevan ke Anubhav* 206). Critiquing Santram, a paper called *The Hindu* stated: "On reading Santram's articles, if his name is hidden, it appears that you are not reading a Hindu lover but a supporter of Miss [Katherine] Mayo" (qtd. in *Mere Jeevan ke Anubhav* 212). Santram thus seems to represent a somewhat "syncretic" culture, drawing from varied religious idioms to build a case against caste. And yet his overall framework remained that of a Hindu ethos. Thus he argued that the Chuhras (sweepers) had two different religious traditions. One, under Muslim influence, took Lal Beg as its icon of worship, and the other recognized Maharishi Valmiki as the teacher of the Balmikis. The former had to be forgotten actively, he argued, while the latter had to be championed (*Humara* 124; Prashad 98–99). This distinction underlines the paradoxes in his positions.

Even while functioning within the paradigm of Hinduism, Santram's Shudra background and his radical stances against the *varnavyavastha* (caste system) and intercaste marriages faced stiff opposition both from the Hindu orthodoxy and the Arya Samaj. Even the progressive and iconic Hindi writer Nirala revealed his Brahmanical leanings in opposing Santram. In a long article titled "Varnashram-Dharm ki Vartman Stithi" (The Present State of *varanashramdharm*), Nirala expressed his deep sadness at Santram's formation of JPTM and scathingly criticized both intercaste marriage and interdining (836–43). Santram's inherent contradictions with Arya Samaj are even more illuminating, as his views brought him in direct conflict with the leading ideologues of Arya Samaj, and he remained socially marginal to the organization, excluded from established hierarchies of power. Santram eloquently demonstrates these conflicts by narrating an incident from his life when he was working as an agriculturist in Patti in 1914–16:

> Something occurred that created a huge furore against me in society. I ordered many texts from agricultural departments of countries like Australia, America, France and England to improve my yield. My wife Ganga Devi did not believe in pollution taboos from before and got food cooked from a Muslim woman. It came to my mind to manure my fields with bones of dead cattle lying around. I collected a huge heap of it on my land when my friend, the famous story writer Sudershan, came to visit me. He was at that time the editor of *Arya Gazette*, and when he chanced on the heap of bones he was extremely angry with me, stating that in spite of being an Arya Samajist, I was indulging in this sin. I argued with him stating . . . that these bones were of dead animals . . . and a rich source of manure. . . . But he did not listen. . . . He wrote a stinging statement against me in *Arya Gazette*. . . . Hindu press condemned me in strong terms . . . threatening to drag me to the court. . . . A deputation of residents of Patti questioned me. . . . I argued that if they had no objection to keeping their match boxes, which were prepared from phosphorous, the essence of bones, inside their sacred kitchen, they should

> not oppose me providing manure to my lands. (*Mere Jeevan ke Anubhav* 38–40)[9]

Many such incidents occupy the pages of *Mere Jeevan ke Anubhav*, where Santram underlines that while JPTM was categorically against *varnavyavastha*, it was a sacred doctrine for the Arya Samaj (Santram, "Taunted" 2). The constant negotiations and tensions reached a breaking point, whereby Santram finally dissociated from Arya Samaj (Juergensmeyer 38–39), and was drawn to Buddhist ascetic traditions (Singh 3). His autobiography thus often invokes narratives associated with Dalit movements. And yet, unlike Mangoo Ram or Ambedkar, Santram could never bring himself to move away from a Hindu paradigm and often enacted a language of caste respectability with ambiguous implications.

His relationship with Dalit organizations and leaders appears equally troubling, and he did not fit into Dalit movements of the time. While repudiating caste in no uncertain terms and being a staunch advocate of intercaste marriages, he could not become a champion of the Dalit cause like Mangoo Ram. In fact, he never acknowledged the existence of the vibrant Ad Dharm movement though both he and Mangoo Ram hailed from Hoshiarpur and their periods considerably overlapped. Juergensmeyer states that the JPTM "was not a model for the Ad Dharm, since its urban, reform Hindu, intercaste composition was quite different from what the Ad Dharm would embrace" (39). It may also be argued that JPTM, like the Arya Samaj, was worried about the increasing assertiveness of the Ad Dharm movement and hoped to blunt its edge by absorbing Dalits within its fold and into a pan-Hindu identity. Significantly, Santram also led a strike of sweepers in Jullundar in 1938 (Kshirsagar 323). Both Mangoo Ram and Santram drew partial inspiration from Arya Samaj, but both found its ideology restricting, rebelling against it in different ways—Santram from within, and Mangoo Ram from without. The choices that Santram makes in his autobiography, where his tensions with Arya Samaj are repeatedly stressed while erasing and silencing Ad Dharm, underscores his median positionality.

Equally, Santram walked the line between Gandhi and Ambedkar, not fully opposing the "disturbing faults" of Gandhi, particularly his leanings toward Sanatani Hinduism, nor fully supporting the "superior merits"of Ambedkar, particularly regarding conversion. Santram's telling of his life not only contributes to the Gandhi-Ambedkar debate on caste but, by falling between their grids, signifies a third stance. He was uncomfortable with and for both of them, even though he appears closer to Ambedkar. Santram had some sharp exchanges with Gandhi. He narrates an interesting incident in an interview:

> I led a deputation of the JPTM to Gandhi at Lahore and requested him to help our movement. But the Mahatma said that caste was a good thing as it eliminated hard competition in the choice of profession. . . . At this I replied—"Mahatmaji, it is a good thing for a Brahman, or Kshatriya, or Vaishya boy to follow the profession of his father, but how can it be in the interest of a sweeper boy to continue to remove night soil and clean latrines for generations? Mahatmaji, you are a Bania by caste; your hereditary profession was to sell salt, oil and flour. Why don't you go and earn your living by selling those commodities? Why have you come here to preach politics and ethics?" At this there was laughter in which his wife and Seth Lal Bajaj also joined. (Manchanda 18–19)

Santram was in dialogue with both Periyar and Ambedkar, finding affinities with them. He published an article on Periyar in *Viduthalai*, the leading Tamil daily, in June 1953 (Santram, "Individual"; Manchanda 6). However, he appeared to be closer to Ambedkar, toward whom he often expressed great admiration rather than any overt criticism, and yet he was troubled by him, which is reflected in the cancellation of the JPTM Conference to which Ambedkar was invited. Many members of JPTM, on reading the text of Ambedkar's speech, found it too hot to handle, especially his direct, scathing attack on Hinduism and support of conversion. Though never directly stated, Santram seems to be in implicit agreement with some of the objections, though he continued to remain Ambedkar's personal friend (Santram, "Taunted" 7). In an exchange between Santram and Ambedkar, the latter wrote:

> I admire your efforts for breaking up the caste system. But allow me to say that I do not agree with the way you are attacking the problem. I do not see how you can break up caste without annihilating the religious notions on which the caste system is founded. I cannot develop the argument now. . . . In the meantime I must leave it to you to deal with the question in the way you like. (Ambedkar, "'Religious Notions'")

Significantly, Santram went on to translate *Annihilation of Caste* into Hindi and published it under the banner of JPTM (*Jatibhed*). He also published it in Urdu in his journal *Kranti* (Kshirsagar 323). The persistent problem with Santram remained his continuous reliance on Hindu idioms and on "upper castes" even in the realm of intercaste marriages. Yet, today, Santram's writings find greater acceptance from Dalits than among liberal Arya Samajis, even when his larger history is almost forgotten. Santram was no Mangoo Ram or Ambedkar; yet what he had to say about his life and his times tells us much about modern histories of caste. He signified a liberal premise and a middle ground and ethos, at times bound by his contexts and at others envisioning ahead of his time. His stances on intercaste marriages offer the most lasting legacy for anticaste politics, while also bringing forth his contradictory uses of sacred and secular, devotion and modernity, to which I finally turn.

## TRANSGRESSIVE INTIMACIES: INTERCASTE MARRIAGES, SANTRAM, AND JPTM

*prem na dekhe jat-kujat.*
*bhookh na dekhe jutha bhaat.*
(Love does not see any caste boundaries.
Hunger is indifferent to food taboos.) (Santram, *Antarjatiya* 31)

*Roti-beti* (food-marriage) taboos have been central to caste practices of spatial and bodily exclusions. Endogamy, a cornerstone of caste, also reveals the pervasive imprint of caste on women's bodies. Even while operating within heteronormative paradigms, intercaste marriages have produced daily policing and everyday violence, along the lines of what Foucault calls the alliance model of sexuality, where—through arrangement of marriages—relations and boundaries of caste and religion are policed (106–11). Increasing anxieties and fears around Dalit conversions forced Arya Samaj and the Hindu Mahasabha to support intercaste marriages at a rhetorical level,[10] but on the ground there were fraught debates and uneasiness on the question, as most reformers underwrote an exclusive grammar of difference in sexual regimes (Gupta 77–84). Significantly, Ambedkar argued that intercaste marriage was the hallmark of Dalit progress and the most important solution to annihilating caste, since it challenged the relationship between

Figure 2.8: Intercaste marriage performed by JPTM between Vijay Kumar MA (Vaishya) and Chand Rani BA (Brahmin). Santram on extreme right. Reproduced courtesy of Madhu Chadha, granddaughter of Santram BA.

maintenance of caste purity and control of women's sexuality (*Annihilation* 59–64; Rao 232–33).

Santram made a categorical intervention in this arena by bringing together caste, gender, sexuality, and desire in his discourse on intercaste marriages, making it a vehicle of his anticaste articulations. While hailing the arrival of JPTM under the leadership of Santram, the editor of *Indian Social Reformer* highlighted the limitations of reform movements like Brahmo Samaj and Arya Samaj:

> But very little has been done by the Arya Samaj and other bodies to break the citadel of caste system by the arrangement of inter-caste-dinners, inter-caste-marriages. . . . These movements, instead of coming forward boldly and frankly to champion the cause of social reforms, have become part and parcel of the orthodox retrogressive Hinduism. . . . It is with this object of infusing a new spirit that JPTM has been started recently. ("League" 320)

The first and foremost rule of JPTM was to break the birth-based caste system and to promote intercaste marriages. It was this central theme that propelled Santram's critique of caste and JPTM's activities. JPTM's rules stated that the only Hindus who could join the organization were those who pledged not to marry within their caste, and if married, promised the same for their children. There was a separate department of JPTM to promote intercaste marriages, which maintained "a register in which all eligible candidates for intercaste marriage" were entered (*Jat-Pat* 4; Santram, *Caste Must Go* 2). A list of such marriages was published in JPTM's booklet *Madhur Veena* and in the 1929 directory of JPTM (*Mere Jeevan ke Anubhav* 188; "Jat" 550). A review of the activities of the Mandal in 1939 stated that "at the least computation such marriages must be 500 in number" (*Jat-Pat* 4). JPTM had a limited, largely urban-based membership and following, but it cut across regions and functioned with intercaste marriages as its central paradigm. In his writings, including his autobiography, Santram gives many examples of intercaste marriages that he and the JPTM promoted and facilitated.

However, it appears that most of these intercaste marriages pertained to the top three *varnas*, the "twice-born" castes. Rather than vertical, it was horizontal alliances between the top three *varnas* that were more often encouraged in the name of intercaste marriages. For example, Santram describes an incident in 1914:

> I had two friends Parmanand and Bhumanand. Parmanand was Arora by caste and Bhumanand a Brahmin. . . . Parmanand requested me to persuade Bhumanand to marry his younger sister. . . . Bhumanand agreed. . . . His father, family and friends opposed it and no one came for the wedding. . . . It was a brave act to break caste taboos at that time. (*Mere Jeevan ke Anubhav* 36)[11]

Santram often faced threats for facilitating such marriages (*Mere Jeevan ke Anubhav* 56–59). Largely due to his efforts, intercaste marriages became a symbol of progressive urban modernity, operating through JPTM mainly among a small circle of elites. It was a sincere effort to break caste, but it often provided a view from top down, and a perspective from above, revealing both Santram's limitations and possibilities. Yet, it is to be noted that after the death of his first wife, Santram himself remarried a Maharashtrian Brahmin virgin widow Sunder Bai Pradhan in December 1929.

This was an interprovincial widow remarriage. It was also an intercaste *pratiloma* marriage—most attacked by the orthodoxy—between a Shudra man and a Brahmin widow, similar to Ambedkar's second marriage. In a sense, the central focus of intercaste marriages allowed Santram to underline how caste permeated our most intimate spaces, and to show that it was in such arenas that caste needed to be challenged the most.

Considering caste to be a disease, Santram said that it rested on the four taboos of touch, occupation, food, and marriage (*Humara* 3). Relentlessly questioning Manu12 and endorsing Ambedkar, he passionately promoted intercaste, interregional, and interreligious marriages as central to the eradication of caste. He offered multipronged arguments to disrupt the logic of endogamy, resorting to sacred, religious, devotional, and scriptural discourses on the one hand and relying on social, secular, modern, scientific, and rationalist arguments on the other. Selectively quoting from ancient texts, he constantly reiterated past examples of *anuloma* and *pratiloma* intercaste marriages. For example, Pramatta, a Brahmin woman, married a barber and

Figure 2.9: Santram BA (in center) with his second wife Sunder Bai. Reproduced courtesy of Madhu Chadha, granddaughter of Santram BA.

gave birth to Matang, the great *rishi*. Arundhati, a Kshatriya, was married to Vashishth Rishi, son of a prostitute. Their son Shakti married Adrishyanti, a Chandal girl. Shakti's son, Parashar, the great *rishi*, married Satyavati, a fisherman's daughter, and was father of Vyas, the writer of Mahabharat. Bhim married the demoness Hidamba, and Ghatotkatch was their child (*Humara* 11–14). Santram included in his list leading personalities like Gandhi, Paramanand, Nehru, Gokul Chand, and Raja Narendra Nath, who themselves had intercaste/interregional marriages, saying that none of them could be excommunicated from Hindu society ("Hindu Rishis" 6).

From here he easily moved to modern, scientific, and "secular" arguments, intermeshing them with equality and justice. Paul Gilroy talks of the African American autobiographer Frederick Douglass, who brought "the illumination of reason to the ethical darkness of slavery" (59). In India, the anticaste thinker Periyar passionately invoked radical empiricism and a verifiable view of science (Geetha and Rajadurai 514). In a similar vein, Santram used enlightened modern discourses and rationality to counter caste. Santram wondered, "Why such Hindu kings like Ramchandra, Harishchandra, Krishna, Shivaji and Pratap did not think of . . . providing education and full citizenship rights to untouchables and Shudras?" At another place he stated, "Attempting to take help of *shastras* in finding solutions to eradicate caste and untouchability is like washing dirt with more dirt" (*Mere Jeevan ke Anubhav* 222). Santram adapted a Western liberal model to a distinctly Indian register, which helped him in molding a new caste self. Santram often resorted to quoting from scholars like the German American anthropologist Franz Boas, a prominent opponent of ideologies of scientific racism, to support his arguments (*Humara* 124). Further, similar to many Dalit narratives, Santram selectively praised the British rule: "For many untouchables and Shudras, the British rule is an unmatched God's gift. . . . Untouchables will be very foolish to prefer a Hindu-dominated state over the British rule" (*Mere Jeevan ke Anubhav* 208).

Replete with discussions of "difference" and "sameness" and its varied connotations, Santram interrogated notions of homogeneity, oneness, self-sufficiency, self-knowledge, singular identity, and binarity, and stressed the advantages of what he called "crossbreeding," which, he argued, led to the birth of a stronger and more creative third. He stated,

> It is a universal principle of science that the mixing and coming together of two different products leads to a better and nicer third. Thus oxygen and hydrogen, when combined, produce the best and the purest product of water. . . . When horses and donkeys cross breed, the khachar is born, more powerful and stronger than the two. . . . Similarly inter-caste marriages lead to better relationships, more equitable society, and stronger nation. (*Antarjatiya* 1–2)

Santram argued that endogamy was an inferior form of marriage and even equated it with incest—a marriage between brothers and sisters. Simultaneously, he stressed that the coming together of the intellect and brain of the Brahmin and the physical strength of the Kshatriya would lead to a better progeny. Within Santram's arguments, however, also lay their limitations, domestications, and occlusions, as he sometimes recast stereotypical and essentialist perceptions pertaining to the "characteristics" of different *varnas*, as noted in the previous sentence. He appropriated ideas around national growth, development, progress, masculinity, and particularly eugenics to push for intercaste marriages, with dubious and double-edged implications. Lack of masculine power, weakness, lower levels of intelligence, constant defeats of Hindus in past wars, unhealthy progeny, weak nation—all were depicted as evils of endogamy. Inversely, he stressed, intercaste marriages ensured stronger, healthier, and brighter children; diversified occupational categories; increased masculine strength; and were central to Hindu progress (*Antarjatiya* 5–15). Visions of selfhood, equality, progress, freedom, modernity, and rationality were imparted in Santram's narrative in conjunction with Hindu religious, traditional, and ritualistic paradigms, revealing an argumentative pendulum swinging between the spiritual and the material.

Santram undercut caste power through his arguments, at times inadvertently reiterating stereotypes. Once at the annual conference of Arya Samaj, Lahore, there was a debate between Santram and Ramdev, a teacher at Gurukul Kangri, on *varnavyavastha*, with the latter supporting it and Santram vehemently opposing it. Santram stated in a light vein:

> You people say that people should be branded with their *varna* label, and men-women with same label should marry. . . . Now suppose the husband and wife are of the same *varna*, and have similar characteristics—both get easily angry, and tend to fight. Their qualities are the same. In such a home, there will be constant arguments and fights. As opposed to this, suppose one of them is calm and quiet, then there are much fewer chances of their family life breaking. . . . Similarly, marriage in same *varna* is not good. (*Mere Jeevan ke Anubhav* 199–201)

The language of disparaging binaries and boundaries could implicitly reinstate them. In an article published in the famous magazine *Sudha*, Santram replied to various objections leveled against intercaste marriages and contended that one Amritlal Rai had said that these would lead to clandestine sexual relations, romance, and elopement with women, domestic servants, or "low caste" men. Santram replied, albeit in a patronizing tone, that even the *dasi* could be beautiful, talented, and virtuous and that there were many fair and attractive Chamar women. He went on to disdain the argument that such alliances would greatly lower the ideal of women's purity and honor ("Antarjatiya" 596–608). At the same time, he challenged not only caste hierarchies but also patriarchal hegemonies through his accounts of intercaste marriages. He stressed that due to practices of endogamy, in *jatis* where women outnumbered men, there had been a phenomenal growth of dowry, whereas where it was the inverse, where men outnumbered women, the latter were sold as commodities and sex trade proliferated (*Antarjatiya* 17). He attacked the policing of women's desires whereby women laughing loudly or going out at night were viewed with suspicion, and he blamed the Ramayan for preaching false notions of women's purity (*Humara* 97–100). Questioning that exclusive endogamous marriage could in any way be regarded as more positive, stabler, or better than intercaste marriage, he underlined that intercaste marriages were more robust, rich, and meaningful.

On the side, it is to be noted that Santram also proved ahead of his times on questions of sex and gender. While initially believing in *brahmacharya*, he soon gave up the idea, arguing that it caused more harm than benefit (*Mere Jeevan ke Anubhav* 84–85). He became deeply influenced by Marie Stopes, exchanged letters with her, and translated some of her writings. For example, Santram translated her book *Married Love* as *Vivahit Prem* in 1925[13]—and penned a treatise on sex and sexual pleasure titled *Rativilas* (Tandon 307). In an article written in the magazine *Madhuri* in 1924, Santram argued that intricacies of sex and erotic life of the conjugal couple needed to be discussed explicitly. He went on to support the "true" publications on sexual science, which was also publicity material for sex manuals ("Rati" 601–05). Santram was also an advocate for birth control, a belief that Periyar may also have influenced.[14] For example, Santram translated the English book *Contraception* into Hindi in 1926, calling it *Dampati Mitra* (Friend of Married Couple). The book contained various methods of birth control and gave agency regarding reproductive rights largely to women (*Mere Jeevan ke Anubhav* 161). Santram wrote:

> Some people severely criticized the book, calling it obscene and threatened me with a court case. . . . But several thanked me for publishing it. . . . The publisher . . . told me that wives of many Arya Samajis, who had criticized the book, had secretly bought it and read it with great enthusiasm. (*Mere Jeevan ke Anubhav* 161–62)[15]

In these writings, too, Santram straddled multiple terrains, as on the one hand he drew from classical works on *kamshastra* (sexual science), referring to them as beneficial, and on the other relied on Western sexologists and eugenic arguments to underscore pleasure and desire as important facets of modern sexual life. Lauren Berlant argues:

> Central to the development of narratives that link personal life to larger histories, and to practices and institutions of intimacy, desire also measures fields of difference and distance. It both constructs and collapses distinctions between public and private: it reorganizes worlds. (13–14)

Santram's insights and narratives on marriage, sex, and pleasure not only conjoin the private and public, they open up an interesting ancillary terrain of textures of touch, sexuality, and intercaste registers of desire, intimacy, and transgressive sexual norms.

Santram thus seems to occupy paradoxical social sites—appropriating caste as a sign of privilege in some cases while disparaging it in others. He simultaneously moved on two registers to support intercaste marriages—the first one invoked a scriptural, theological, and ritualistic language, while the second was anchored in arguments of modernity, eugenics, nation, equality, and egalitarianism. This deft combination of hybrid means, whereby through various modes of articulation he described spaces and possibilities of intercaste marriages, had ambiguous implications. On the one hand, he opposed essentialized characteristics of different *varnas* and of women, and on the other his language of healthy progeny, of difference, of powerful nation had a potential to reinstate caste and patriarchy. But then, woven alongside was also the belief that children of intercaste unions not only inherited the qualities of both parents but also did not belong to one or another of the constructed caste categories and instead occupied a third, liminal space. While gendering intercaste marriages, he on the one hand upheld ideologies of productive and reproductive labor, and on the other, inherent in his arguments was also a plea to refigure relationships between women and men. Herein lay Santram's paradox: he used a version of the poison as its own remedy. At the same time, the disruption of endogamous marriages signified a challenge to caste difference and a transgressive space of intimate desires.

## CONCLUSION

Santram's autobiography and other writings are not merely literary ornaments; they are communicative acts through which he evolves his own anticaste idioms, codes, and practices. Infused with Santram's agency, *Mere Jeevan ke Anubhav* is not just about an individual but carries within it varied, uneasy, and aching caste attitudes of the era. Santram's life and writing act as an archive of anticaste thought in a particular context, becoming a site and repository of the social history of caste in modern India. His narrative offers a richly textured account of his private life and public commitments, whereby his anticaste tropes endeavor to reach a hybrid, liberal ground, jostling between Gandhi and Ambedkar, and between Arya Samaj and Ad Dharm, a process fraught with fissures. Individual, private life and collective, public histories coexist in his narrative, as both are caste marked. Santram's life and writings cannot be easily slotted as they ride on uncertainties with a deep hankering to get rid of caste without letting go of Hinduism. He navigated sacred and secular, devotional and modern discourses and brought the theological and the social together to refute caste, inescapably representing multiple and diverse subjectivities, which were often discordant with each other. In spite of his deep frustration with the Arya Samaj, he attempted to amalgamate Arya Samaji and anticaste ideas. Santram deployed social reform through largely urban, educated, "upper caste" characters, whereby terms of Hinduism were subtly reworked and reinstated. At the same time, Santram constantly negotiated with a contentious associational discourse around caste, which permeated his personal and social life, endeavoring to "unread" its dominant inscriptions.

Santram's writings also contribute to creating a counterarchive of caste, as he selectively took on the language of Arya Samaj, Ambedkar, and intercaste marriages. Recalcitrant histories of caste may be gleaned by studying Santram's life narrative. His vernacular articulations are often rooted in a cross-referential counterarchive, which is in dialogue with other hegemonic texts, and produces a history of anticasteism through a hybrid liberal paradigm. These enunciations open Santram's life to subversive appropriations and empancipatory practices of caste dissent. It is perhaps for this reason that Dalit writers and intellectuals have claimed Santram more than members of the Arya Samaj. His dual identification as a Shudra and a Dalit at one and the same time, as within and outside Arya Samaj, produces a radical edge to Santram's life. Similar to Phule, Periyar, and Ambedkar, his trenchant critique of endogamy provides the intersection between anticaste thought and gender, challenging connections between sexual regulation and caste reproduction. Santram's erudite enunciations in support of intercaste marriages call upon ideas of caste intimacy as a way to get at the terribly material, embodied character of caste and gender dynamics and as a way of breaking the shackles of the *varna-jati* complex. However, since it was annihilation of caste rather than sexual freedom per se that was Santram's focus, there was an instability in the otherwise radical connections he drew. It is important to resurrect the circumscribed life of this half-forgotten caste reformer, which is laden with radical possibilities.

## NOTES

1. Santram used his attainment of a baccalaureate degree as a kind of honorific.
2. See Ambedkar's preface for more information (i–viii).
3. All translations from Hindi are mine, unless otherwise stated.

4. See also Karlekar.
5. Reiterated also in personal interview with Satnam Singh.
6. The trend continued in 1921 (see *Census of India, 1921* 181).
7. Reiterated in his interview (Manchanda 1).
8. Many of these texts have been republished by Samyak Prakashan, Delhi.
9. *Arya Gazette* was an organ of the Arya Samaj.
10. For example, in its seventeenth session in Poona in 1935, the Hindu Mahasabha resolved "in favour of complete liberty of inter-marriage between all sections of the Hindu community," including with Harijans.
11. Also mentioned in Manchanda (4).
12. Once, while critiquing Manu, Santram was asked by a learned scholar if he was more knowledgeable than Manu. At this Santram replied, "Yes! Manu did not know what is meant by 'telepathy', what is a 'telescope', how did a rail run, while I know about all these things. If Manu was something, he may have been in his times. At present our knowledge is much greater." See Manchanda (8).
13. Also mentioned in a Catalogue of Books for the new year of a publisher, *Naye Varsh* (44).
14. For a discussion on the larger politics of birth control in colonial India, see Ahluwalia. On Periyar and birth control, see Hodges; Anandhi (39–66).
15. Santram also wrote another book on birth control called *Santan Sankhya ka Seema-Bandhan* (Control of Number of Children). I have not been able to locate the book, but it is mentioned in a Catalogue of Books, *Naye Varsh.*

## WORKS CITED

Adcock, C. S. "Brave Converts in the Arya Samaj: The Case of Dharm Pal." *Punjab Reconsidered: History, Culture, and Practice*, edited by Anshu Malhotra and Farina Mir, Oxford UP, 2012, pp. 261–86.

———. *The Limits of Tolerance: Indian Secularism and the Politics of Religious Freedom.* Oxford UP, 2014.

Ahluwalia, Sanjam. *Reproductive Restraints: Birth Control in India, 1877–1947.* U of Illinois P, 2008.

Ambedkar, B. R. *Annihilation of Caste: Speech Prepared for the Annual Conference of JPTM of Lahore but Not Delivered.* B. R. Kadrekar, 1936.

———. *Jatibhed ka Uchhed.* Translated by Santram BA, Jat-Pat Torak Mandal, 1937.

———. "'Religious Notions on Which Caste System Is Based Should be Destroyed': Dr. Ambedkar's Letter to Jat-Pat Torak Mandal." *Tribune*, 11 Dec. 1935, p. 5.

Anandhi, S. "Reproductive Bodies and Regulated Sexuality: Birth Control Debates in Early Twentieth Century Tamilnadu." *A Question of Silence?: The Sexual Economies of Modern India*, edited by Mary E. John and Janaki Nair, Kali for Women, 1998, pp. 139–66.

"Anti-Caste Census Campaign." *Indian Social Reformer*, vol. 61, no. 3, 20 Sept. 1930, p. 44.

Arnold, David, and Stuart Blackburn. "Introduction: Life Histories in India." *Telling Lives in India: Biography, Autobiography, and Life History*, edited by David Arnold and Stuart Blackburn, Indiana UP, 2004, pp. 1–28.

Auxiliary Committee of the Indian Statutory Commission. *Review of the Growth of Education in British India*. Government of India P, 1930.

Banerjee-Dube, Ishita. "Introduction: Questions of Caste." *Caste in History*, edited by Ishita Banerjee-Dube, Oxford UP, 2010, pp. xv–lxiv.

Bayly, Susan. *Caste, Society, and Politics in India: From the Eighteenth Century to the Modern Age*, Cambridge UP, 1999.

Berlant, Lauren. *Desire/Love*. Punctum Books, 2012.

Berlant, Lauren, and Jay Prosser. "Life Writing and Intimate Publics: A Conversation with Lauren Berlant." *Life Writing and Intimate Publics*, special issue of *Biography*, vol. 34, no. 1, Winter 2011, pp. 180–87.

Brueck, Laura. *Writing Resistance: The Rhetorical Imagination of Hindi Dalit Literature*. Columbia UP, 2014.

"Caste and the Census." *Indian Social Reformer*, vol. 61, no. 25, 21 Feb. 1931, pp. 395–96.

*Census of India, 1911*. Vol. I, part I, Superintendent Government Printing, 1912.

*Census of India, 1921*. Vol. XV, part I, Superintendent Government Printing, 1922.

*Census of India, 1931*. Vol. XVII, part I, Khan Ahmad Hasan Khan, Civil and Military Gazette Press, 1933.

Chadha, Madhu. Personal interview. 25 Jan. 2016.

Ciotti, Manuela. "'In the past we were a bit of a "Chamar"': Education as a Self and Community Engineering Process in Northern India." *Journal of the Royal Anthropological Institute*, vol. 12, no. 1, Dec. 2006, pp. 899–916.

Cohn, Bernard S. *An Anthropologist among the Historians and Other Essays*. Oxford UP, 1987.

Constable, Philip. "Sitting on the Verandah: The Ideology and Practice of 'Untouchable' Educational Protest in Late Nineteenth-Century Western India." *The Indian Economic and Social History Review*, vol. 37, no. 4, 2000, pp. 383–422.

Dirks, Nicholas B. *Castes of Mind: Colonialism and the Making of Modern India*. Princeton UP, 2001.

Eaton, Richard M. *A Social History of the Deccan, 1300–1761: Eight Indian Lives*. Cambridge UP, 2005.

Fallon, S. W., editor. *Hindustani-English Dictionary of Idioms and Proverbs*. 1886. Star Publications, 1991.

Foucault, Michel. *The History of Sexuality: An Introduction*. Translated by Robert Hurley, vol. 1, Vintage, 1978.

Gajarawala, Toral Jatin. *Untouchable Fictions: Literary Realism and the Crisis of Caste*. Fordham UP, 2012.

Ganguli, Debjani. "Pain, Personhood, and the Collective: Dalit Life Narratives." *Asian Studies Review*, vol. 33, no. 4, Dec. 2009, pp. 429–42.

*Gazetteer of the Hoshiarpur District, 1883–4*. Civil and Military Gazette Press, 1885.

Geetha, V., and S. V. Rajadurai. *Towards a Non-Brahmin Millennium: From Iyothee Thass to Periyar*. Samya, 1998.

Giddens, Anthony. *The Transformation of Intimacy: Sexuality, Love, and Eroticism in Modern Societies*. Stanford UP, 1992.

Gilroy, Paul. *The Black Atlantic: Modernity and Double Consciousness*. Verso, 1993.

Gopal, Madan. "A Hundred Years of Writing." *Times of India*, 16 Feb. 1987, p. 8.

Gupta, Charu. *The Gender of Caste: Representing Dalits in Print*. U of Washington P, 2016.

Hindi Mahasabha. Seventeenth session in Poona, 1935. Hindi Mahasabha Papers, M-3, Nehru Memorial Museum and Library, Delhi, India.

Hodges, Sarah. *Contraception, Colonialism and Commerce: Birth Control in South India, 1920–1940*. Ashgate, 2008.

Hunt, Sarah Beth. *Hindi Dalit Literature and the Politics of Representation*. Routledge, 2014.

Ilaiah, Kancha. *Why I Am Not a Hindu: A Sudra Critique of Hindutva Philosophy, Culture, and Political Economy*. Samya, 2002.

"Jat Pat Torak Mandal, Lahore." *Indian Social Reformer*, vol. 36, no. 35, 1 May 1926, p. 550.

*The Jat-Pat Torak Mandal*. General Review, 1939.

Jones, Kenneth. *Arya Dharm: Hindu Consciousness in 19th-Century Punjab*. 1976. Manohar, 2006.

Juergensmeyer, Mark. *Religious Rebels in the Punjab: The Ad Dharm Challenge to Caste*. 1982. Navayana, 2009.

Karlekar, Malavika. *Voices from Within: Early Personal Narratives of Bengali Women*. Oxford UP, 1991.

Kshirsagar, R. K. *Dalit Movement in India and Its Leaders (1857–1956)*. M. D. Publications, 1994.

Kumar, Raj. *Dalit Personal Narratives: Reading Caste, Nation, and Identity*. Orient Blackswan, 2011.

Kumar, Udaya. *Writing the First Person: Literature, History, and Autobiography in Modern Kerala*. Permanent Black, 2016.

———. "Writing the Life of the Guru: Chattampi Swamikai, Sree Narayana Guru, and Modes of Biographical Construction." *Biography as History: Indian Perspectives*, edited by Vijaya Ramaswamy and Yogesh Sharma, Orient Blackswan, 2009, pp. 53–87.

"League to Abolish Caste System." *Indian Social Reformer*, vol. 33, no. 20, 13 Jan. 1923, p. 320.

Lubin, Alex. *Romance and Rights: The Politics of Interracial Intimacy, 1945–1954*. UP of Mississippi, 2005.

Manchanda, Shyam Lal. Interview with Santram BA, oral history transcript. 15 May 1971, accession No. 238, Nehru Memorial Museum and Library, Delhi, India.

Maheshwari, Shriram. *The Census Administration Under the Raj and After*. Concept Publishing Company, 1996.

Murugkar, Lata. *Dalit Panther Movement in Maharashtra: A Sociological Appraisal*. Popular Prakashan, 1991.

*Naye Varsh ka Suchipatra*. Rajpal & Sons, n.d.

Nirala, Suryakant Tripathi. "Varnashram-Dharm ki Vartman Stithi." *Madhuri*, vol. 8, no. 1, Mar. 1932, pp. 836–43.

Paik, Shailaja. "Mahar-Dalit-Buddhist: The History and Politics of Naming in Maharashtra." *Contributions to Indian Sociology*, vol. 45, no. 2, 2011, pp. 217–41.

Pandey, Gyanendra. *A History of Prejudice: Race, Caste, and Difference in India and the United States*. Cambridge UP, 2013.

Pandian, M. S. S. "Writing Ordinary Lives." *Economic and Political Weekly*, vol. 43, no. 38, Sept. 2008, pp. 34–40.

Paswan, Sanjay, and Paramanshi Jaideva, editors. *Leaders*: *Encyclopaedia of Dalits in India*, vol. 4, Kalpaz Publications, 2004.

Prashad, Vijay. *Untouchable Freedom: A Social History of a Dalit Community*. Oxford UP, 2000.

Ram, Ronki. "Untouchability, Dalit Consciousness, and the Ad Dharm Movement in Punjab." *Contributions to Indian Sociology*, vol. 38, no. 3, 2004, pp. 323–49.

Ramaswamy, Vijaya. Introduction. *Biography as History: Indian Perspectives*, edited by Vijaya Ramaswamy and Yogesh Sharma, Orient Blackswan, 2009, pp. 1–15.

Rancière, Jacques. *The Politics of Literature*. Translated by Julie Rose, Polity, 2011.

Rao, Anupama. *The Caste Question: Dalits and the Politics of Modern India*. Permanent Black, 2009.

Rawat, Ramnarayan. *Reconsidering Untouchability: Chamars and Dalit History in North India*. Permanent Black, 2012.

Rege, Sharmila. *Against the Madness of Manu: B. R. Ambedkar's Writings on Brahmanical Patriarchy*. Navayana, 2013.

———. *Writing Caste/Writing Gender: Reading Dalit Women's Testimonios*. Zubaan, 2006.

Rose, H. A., editor. *A Glossary of the Tribes and Castes of the Punjab and North-West Frontier Province*. Vol. II, Civil and Military Gazette P, 1911.

Santram BA. "Antarjatiya Vivah." *Sudha*, July 1929, pp. 596–608.

———. *Antarjatiya Vivah hi Kyun?* Jat-Pat Torak Mandal, 1959.

———. *Caste Must Go: A Word About the Jat-Pat Torak Mandal, Lahore*. Jat-Pat Torak Mandal, 1938.

———. "Hindu Rishis and the Caste." *Tribune*, 28 Feb. 1936, p. 6.

———. *Humara Samaj*. 1st ed., Nalanda Prakashan, 1949.

———. "Individual Collections: Papers of Santram BA." List 430, Nehru Memorial Museum and Library, Delhi, India.

———. Letter to Marie Stopes. 16 Mar. 1930, MSS no. ADD 58578, Stopes Papers, Department of Manuscripts, British Library, London, England.

———. *Mere Jeevan ke Anubhav*. Hindi Pracharak Pustakalya, 1963.

———. "Rati Rahasya." *Madhuri*, vol. 3, no. 1, December 1924, pp. 601–05.

———. "Taunted and Scoffed by Orthodoxy: Anti-Caste Movement in the Punjab: Experiences of a Social Reform Leader." *The Sunday Observer*, 13 July 1952, pp. 2, 7.

Satyanarayana, K., and Susie Tharu, editors. *No Alphabet in Sight: New Dalit Writing from South India, Tamil and Malayalam*. Penguin, 2011.

———. *Steel Nibs Are Sprouting: New Dalit Writing from South India, Kannada and Telegu*. Harper Collins, 2013.

Shankar, S. *Flesh and Fish Blood: Postcolonialism, Translation, and the Vernacular*. U of California P, 2012.

Singh, Satnam. Personal interview. 9 Feb. 2016.

———. *Santram BA krit Mere Jeevan ke Anubhav: Dalit Sahitya ki Pehli Sva-Jeevni*. Samyak Prakashan, 2008.

Stopes, Marie. *Married Love*. Translated by Santram BA, Saraswati Ashram, 1925.

Tandon, Ramnarayan, editor. *Hindi Sevi Sansar*. Vol. 1, 2nd ed., Lucknow, 1951.

"Uncouth Brahmin." *Yugantar*, Oct. 1933, p. 26.

# 3

# THE DALIT PERSONAL NARRATIVE IN HINDI
## Reflections on a Long Literary Lineage

TAPAN BASU

*Day in and day out, this Manusmriti is burning us, burning us,*
*Not letting us climb up, it is degrading us, degrading us,*
*While Brahmins and Kshatriyas are allowed to rise and rise,*
*"Wear your old clothes," for us is the advice.*
*No wealth can we earn, what we save is not secure,*
*Sheer depression is our lot, since we are always dubbed impure.*
*Lower in stature than dogs or cats or flies,*
*Provided no habitation under the village skies,*
*We labour like bullocks, with no returns to await,*
*Just abuses and thrashings are our fate.*
*Our toils are enforced, not even food as recompense,*
*Our children wail with hunger, their torture makes no sense.*
*O listen, o Hindus, on you only misfortunes will descend*
*For shedding the tears of innocents, and for their suffering without end!*

—Swami Achhutanand Harihar, "Manusmriti Is Burning Us"[1]

Swami Achhutanand Harihar's poem, "Manusmriti Is Burning Us," which was written sometime between the late nineteenth and early twentieth centuries, is no doubt one of the earliest statements, in Hindi, made by a member of the so-called "untouchable" castes of Hinduism against Hinduism's *varna*-based social order. But what is remarkable about the composition is that, apart from its sharp critique of the exploitation and the oppressiveness inherent in the birth-determined caste system, it is also an articulation of a radical self-consciousness on the part of a caste subject who belongs to the most downtrodden ranks of India's Hindu population. In fact Achhutanand deployed the term "Dalit" as a signifier of the outcaste communities' politicized and oppositional self-awareness long before it became current in other regions of India like Maharashtra, where it was popularized, decades later, by anticaste organizations such as the Dalit Panthers. Thus, in one of his better-known verses, "How Long Will the Dalit Lie Dormant?" Achhutanand writes,

> Manusmriti's inhuman laws will cease to affright
> Once the Dalit, the deprived, the outcaste arise and unite. (qtd. in Singh 73)

Achhutanand's writings, in verse as well as in prose, habitually refer to the "undercastes" as a collective entity whose sorry plight he attempts to record through stirring narratives of resistance. Although he is often credited with being the first published Dalit writer from the Hindi belt, it is now acknowledged that he was by no means the only one of his times to print accounts of the sufferings of the "untouchables."

What could be designated as a Dalit print culture was indeed rather vibrant in North India in the early decades of the twentieth century and was the vehicle for members of the "untouchable" castes to reach out to a growing number of literate caste fellows in this region. As Badri Narayan and A. R. Misra have pointed out, this was not quite a negligible constituency—"the number of untouchables successful in obtaining education in the United Provinces alone was 46,000 in the year 1917" (16).

The earliest known example of a text authored by an "untouchable" to appear in print was a poem that Hira Dom composed in 1914. It was entitled "Achut Ki Shikayat" and repudiates the servitude traditionally expected from "untouchables" by members of the "upper castes"—the Brahmins, the Thakurs, the Banias, the Ahirs, or the Bhats. The poem is a staunch assertion of "lower caste" self-reliance and solidarity, and includes the following lines:

> We shall earn by the labour of our sweat,
> And eat with the members of our family
> distributing whatever there is.
> [. . .]
> They fear to even touch us as we are doms. (Narayan and Misra 16)

As the title—translated in English as "The Complaint of an Untouchable"—attests, the poem is a personal narrative in verse, as is Swami Achhutanand Harihar's poem, "Manusmriti Is Burning Us." But more important is the fact that both poems are narratives about the self—couched all along in the first-person plural voice. The predicaments referred to are as much shared as they are individual. The "we" in either poem claims representational capacity and also an implied addressee of fellow sufferers, all victims of stringent caste laws. Sharmila Rege's theorization of Dalit personal narratives as "testimonios," writings "which forge a right to speak both for and beyond the individual, and contest, explicitly or implicitly, the 'official forgetting' of histories of caste oppression, struggles and resistance," applies as much to these narratives as to the contemporary Dalit women's narratives which she has translated (11–13).[2] The testimonial element in some of the earliest Dalit poems in Hindi by Dalits, cited above, is indicative of the existence of a reading public, however small, whose constituents possess a common experience of being with the writers on the receiving end of the precepts and practices of untouchability. My focus in this essay will be on the emergent genre of the Dalit personal narrative in Hindi, which began to make itself more and more visible in North India during the last two decades of the twentieth century. These narratives are legatees of the Achhutanand tradition of anticaste writing that took shape as early as the earliest decades of the twentieth century.

Swami Achhutanand was a prolific writer. But there is no doubt that it was the assurance of an empathetic reading public that prompted him to take to the pen and initiate the publication of the newspaper *Achhut* in 1917. Born Hiralal on May 6, 1879, in the Mainpuri district of the United Provinces, Achhutanand, like B. R. Ambedkar, was the son of a father with a job in the British army and was thus able to attend school, unlike many children of his caste of leather workers, the Chamars. Achhutanand's performance at school was exceedingly creditable, and by the age of fourteen he had mastered four languages: Hindi, Urdu, Gurmukhi, and English. During his teens, he came into contact with some peripatetic sannyasis and with them toured several pilgrimage spots across India. Thus he became close to the Arya Samaj, which, in those days, was purposefully wooing members of the "lower castes" so as to prevent them from falling prey to the seductions of conversion to other religions. But Achhutanand's involvement with the Arya Samaj, despite his attainment of key positions within its administrative structure, was short lived. His interrogative mind saw through its complicity with traditional Hindu beliefs. He declared the Arya Samaj to be a

> trickery of the Vedic religion weaved to save the Brahmanical religion from attacks by the Christians and Muslims. Its philosophy is hypocritical and principles lop-sided. Its purification programme is mere deception and the talk of varna system based on action and quality is a mere jugglery of words. It is an enemy of history, murderer of truth and adept in useless and alluring gossips. Its perception is faulty, speech illogical, establishment empty and discourses on Vedas purely manipulated. What it says it does not do. Its aim is to declare enmity with Muslims and Christians, enslave the Hindus and put them under the control of Vedas and Brahmins. (105–06)

By 1917 he had opted out of Arya Samaj's fold and commenced engaging with philosophies that were more attuned to the needs of Hinduism's "undercastes." In 1922, he founded the Adi Dharma, a religion more suitable, in his opinion, for the "untouchables" because it divested them of their Hindu belonging and projected them as India's primal dwellers who had been subdued by Aryan invaders in a distant pre-Hindu epoch. It must be noted that while Swami Achhutanand's racial hypothesis about the beginnings of caste had a definite affinity to Jotirao Phule's theorization in this context, in his critique of the Arya Samaj, Achhutanand more or less anticipated the views Ambedkar expressed in *Annihilation of Caste*.[3]

Swami Achhutanand's numerous writings did not find forums for publication in mainstream Hindi presses of the era. Instead certain niche presses, which had been opened to enable access to publication to the totally marginalized minority of niche writers, offered him the opportunity to print and circulate these writings. The most prominent of these presses was Bahujan Kalyan Prakashan, formerly christened Hindu Samaj Sudhar Karyalaya, which Chandrika Prasad Jigyasu founded as an educated person born in 1899 to a relatively prosperous "lower caste" family of Lucknow. As per his own account, Jigyasu first came into contact with Swami Achhutanand in 1926 and, following that, he was inspired to write and publish through his press, founded in 1959, his chronicle of the outcaste communities in ancient India based on Adi Dharma ideology entitled *Bharat Ke Adi-Nivasiyon*. In this treatise, Jigyasu argues that the original inhabitants of India had been degraded and made into its modern-day "untouchables." Swami Achhutanand's own press in Kanpur, a 1925 initiative, was also the source of many books, periodicals, and newspapers: *Achhut*, the monthly newspaper that later became a daily called *Adi Hindu* and was in publication until 1932, and *Usha*, a monthly journal published from 1928. Not surprisingly, Swami Achhutanand, as one of the prominent Dalit leaders whose lives attained legendary status in the annals of the North Indian Dalit movement, became the subject of Dalit writing, specifically life writing, the most elaborate of which was a text that Jigyasu published in 1960. Another biography of Achhutanand, Guru Prasad Madan's text titled *Swami Achhutanand Harihar: Jivan Aur Krititva*, was published in 1969.

Indeed, life writing about eminent Dalit leaders gained currency in the period immediately following Achhutanand's death in 1933 and the rapid decline of the Adi Hindu mobilization, and several biographies of exemplary public figures among Dalits were brought out by presses sympathetic to the cause of the "undercastes." Of these, the notable were the booklet-form biographies of the mediaval-era poet-saint Ravidas (including Badloo Ram Sonkar's *Mahaprabhu Ravidas Ka Chamatkar* and Maharishi Ramdasjee Shastrapati's *Sri Ravidas Bhagwan Ki Prabhuta*), and of the modern-day messiah, Babasaheb Ambedkar (Chandrika Prasad Jigyasu's *Bhagwan Baba Saheb Ka Jeevan Sangharsh* and Ram Sajivan's *Bhagwan Baba Bheemrao Ambedkar*). Clearly, the production of these biographies, almost all of them more or less written in the tradition of hagiographies, was part of a project to inculcate a sense of self-esteem among ordinary Dalits by offering them worthy Dalit role models.

Supplementing the production of biographies of Dalit heroes was an enterprise of translating into Hindi the published works of front-ranking "undercaste" thinkers who had authored tracts in other languages. After the 1950s, Bahujan Kalyan Prakashan, Lucknow, Ashok Pustakalya, Kanpur, and other publication centers in Uttar Pradesh released the works of Jotirao Phule, E. V. Ramaswami "Periyar," and Babasaheb Ambedkar, among others.[4]

The 1960s also witnessed a trend of narrativizing the history of India from perspectives alternative to those of mainstream nationalist historians who, from the turn of the nineteenth century, started to frame counter-histories in response to the British imperial point of view in consonance with the rise of the nationalist temper. As scholars such as Badri Narayan and Charu Gupta have shown, Dalit historians endeavored to recover the lost memories of Dalit protagonists who were stellar participants in India's fight for independence from foreign rule starting with the 1857 Revolt. The case of Jhalkari Bai, a close associate of Rani Laxmibai of Jhansi, is crucial in this respect. The point that Dalit historians make through the invocation of Dalit nationalists, particularly in the context of the First War of Independence, is that it was actually "undercastes" who fought for the freedom of the country, while the "upper caste" aristocracy only fought the foreign conquerors to restore their own deprived sovereignty.[5]

Dalit stories about the past, as Sarah Beth Hunt has pointed out in her book *Hindi Dalit Literature and the Politics of Representation*, were in circulation for a long time through printed material that Dalit presses produced (25–82). The rise of the Dalit pamphlet was particularly symptomatic of the growth of a new literary culture, or rather, a new literary counterculture, in North India by the middle decades of the twentieth century. This counterculture was obviously evidence of the presence of a subaltern counterpublic, another Dalit public similar to, but ahead in time, of the Dalit public that Ambedkar was instrumental in forging in the Maharashtra region from the 1940s through the 1950s. What is puzzling is why, in contrast to the Dalit counterpublic in Maharashtra, the Dalit counterpublic in North India, specifically in the United Provinces, has attracted such scarce attention from Dalit Studies academics and activists, especially given that more and more Dalit literary production started to be made available in the post-Indian independence years.[6] The neglect of these texts has made the contemporary proliferation of Hindi Dalit writings (including life writing) seem to be an unprecedented phenomenon.

Toral Jatin Gajarawala has cited a comment that Badri Narayan and A. R. Misra made to explain the tentativeness with which the Dalit counterpublic built itself up in the Hindi belt:

> [Dalits] were forced to stay away from the historical mainstream, peripheral as they were, deprived of access to education and surrounded by terror.

> They were not only forced to stay away from history but any kind of leisure, which is such a critical source in the creation of the culture of a community. The very nature of their jobs, and social functions that they were coerced to perform, prohibited them from owning and developing any cultural compartment for themselves or their community. They were not allowed to carry or own any weapon. Thus doomed to serve and comply, they were never in a position to be either donors or recipients of the contents of the existing civilization and culture. Orality was their only possession, or medium of communication of their anxieties, tribulations, of deprivations and anguish. They did not even have their religion to console themselves and in such an alienated state, they feared even to entertain the idea of expression of their woes in the world after death, for it was their evil actions in their previous life that has placed them in such a precarious social position and any questions pertaining to their existence would be considered to be violative of the divine design. (30)

From this extended comment on "an absent historical and cultural archive that is only now being recognized," Gajarawala deduces that there is an "unfortunate burden" on Dalit literature, meaning contemporary Dalit literature, to supplement what is missing (30).

It is indeed difficult to subscribe to the view of an archival lack in the face of ample proof that indicates otherwise. Misra and Narayan themselves send signals contrary to those emanated by the passage Gajarawala quoted from their edited volume:

> Contestations between various types of ideologies are evident in the literature published from the 1930s in India. Dalits challenged the Brahminical hegemonic order by utilizing the print medium; they further used it to counter the value framework erected by the dominant power group. In other words, the print medium was being utilized by the Dalits to subvert the ideological and cultural structure persisting since ancient times. It was commonly assumed that devoid of literacy and publications, Dalits were essentially a part of just the oral tradition. Their representation was considered to be confined to orality alone and the memories contained in it were expected to become fossilized and static when confronted with an ever-flowing cultural stream. Therefore, for injecting a new confidence and enthusiasm with greater mobilization power, the print medium was found to be highly effective by the Dalits . . . the print medium gives cultural self-expression to such groups through the efforts of organic intellectuals of the community. This was understood by a visionary like Achhutanand in North India, and the Dalits in future followed rigorously the tradition laid down by him. (19)

Hence, it is not that there were no Dalits in print in North India in the early twentieth century—rather, printed texts by Dalits, as Mohandas Naimishray has pointed out, "remained ignored or unrecognized by the elite or upper castes" (qtd. in R. Gupta 33). The same point, broadly, has been made by Francesca Orisini, who notes that as far as the Hindi public sphere's engagements went, topics that were perceived by the male-dominated, "upper caste" middle classes, who were its custodians, to be not of "general" interest or of interest of a "parochial" kind alone (for instance, caste and gender-centered topics), were to be strictly kept beyond the pale of public debate. Public debate, it was felt, could not or should not address the agendas of discrete, "vested interest" sections within society. These sections had no claim to participate in debates in the public sphere; instead, "authorized" participants would "represent" the agendas of these sections. According to Orsini, this was the vantage point that granted more legitimacy to Munshi Premchand's narratives about society's "victims" than the narratives of the "victims" themselves (Hunt 19).

At a moment of ascendant anticolonial sentiment, the favored forms of public debate would, of course, be the issues that nationalism generated. But over time, the Ambedkarite discourse did find its resonance in the debates because of its head-on, high-profile collision with Gandhi's ideas, which framed India's national liberation enterprise. Perhaps this is the reason the Ambedkar movement's offshoot of the Dalit counterpublic has attained a hegemonic status and all too often subsumes other Dalit counterpublics that took shape simultaneously, or even earlier, in the rest of the country. For example, tracking the history of Dalit literature, Pradeep K. Sharma writes:

> The guiding force of Dalit literature becomes the Ambedkarite philosophy which represents a comprehensive worldview different from the upper caste hegemonic philosophy and incorporates Buddhism, Bhaktism and other protest traditions prevalent in the Indian society, like the verses of Shankaranand and Achhutanand (prevalent in Uttar Pradesh).
>
> Kanwal Bharti conclusively writes that the guiding ideology of Dalit authors cannot be centrist, leftist or rightist, not even Dalitist, but can only be the Ambedkarist vision. (79)

But more recently, Ramnarayan Rawat, who has done extensive and valuable work on the Chamars in Uttar Pradesh, has interrogated this position. After an acknowledgement of the fact that "most Dalit histories have focused on Maharashtra, particularly on movements for access to temple and wells in the 1920s and on Dr. Ambedkar's interventions in constitutional politics," and further that "these events are generally viewed as marking the beginning of Dalit struggles in India" (Rawat 156), Rawat prepares to pit himself against the reductionist theorizations, such as that of Sudha Pai, about the "delayed development of Dalit consciousness" (Pai 38) in Uttar Pradesh. Is it true, he asks, that Uttar Pradesh, unlike Maharashtra, witnessed no Dalit awakening during the colonial period? His effort to answer the question alerts him to the scantiness of research undertaken in this field:

> There is not a single monograph that discusses the Adi-Hindu movement or its agenda in colonial Uttar Pradesh. Most of the studies that we have focus on urban Dalits, like Owen Lynch's study of the Jatavs in Agra and, more recently, Nandini Gooptu's chapter on "untouchable" assertion in the urban centres of Uttar Pradesh. There are few anthropological studies of Chamars except Brigg's in 1920 and some articles by Bernard Cohn in the 1960s. In fact the only historical accounts of the Adi-Hindu movement we have are by Dalit academics and activists. . . . So far, non-Dalit historians have shown no interest in these accounts and practically no effort has been made to engage with them, leaving the development of Dalit struggles nicely veiled. (156)

The issue, then, is not one of archival paucity versus plenitude, but one of unequal investigative energy invested in the examination of Dalit movements across the country. As a consequence of this, some Dalit movements, such as the ones in the Hindi belt, remain insufficiently scrutinized. This failure to study the movements by Dalits of different regions in their entirety has often prevented an appreciation of the cross-fertilization and supportive encouragement lent by these movements to one another. After all, how many remember the momentous signature campaign that Swami Achhutanand and his disciples mobilized to endorse Babasaheb Ambedkar's plea for separate electorates to be awarded to the "Depressed Classes" at the Round Table Conferences held in London between 1930 and 1932?

The most obvious reason for the oblivion to which Dalit self-expression of all kinds was relegated was the absence of the "three main platforms—books, journals and Kavi sammelans" that Orsini identified as being instrumental in the development of the Hindi public sphere (52). Because the Dalit print medium did not expand through similar platforms, especially the notable platform of journals in which many mainstream Hindi writers invested for the purpose of "serving Hindi," the presence of Dalit writers in Hindi remained obscure and often totally unacknowledged (Orsini 224).

Contemporary Dalit writing in Hindi, especially the autobiographies that several writers since the 1990s have penned, are evidence of the accumulated force of Dalit Chetna (Dalit identity politics) in North India prior to the post-Mandal-Mandir era, and indeed for over a span of almost a century. Although my focus in the rest of this essay will be on two autobiographies only—namely *Apne Apne Pinjre* and *Mera Bachpan Mere Kandhon Par*, written by Mohandas Namishray and Sheoraj Singh Bechain respectively, both members of the Chamar caste—at this moment there are already a host of Dalit personal narratives in Hindi available in the marketplace. The transition decades between the two centuries have proven to be as fertile for Dalit's personal narratives in Hindi as the 1970s and the 1980s were for Dalit personal narratives in Marathi.[7] The most prominent among the other personal narratives are Omprakash Valmiki's *Joothan* and Surajpal Chauhan's

*Tiraskrit*, narratives of members of the Bhangi (sweeper) caste. However, I have chosen to look at Chamar narratives in particular because of an interest in the examination of the literary lineage of Achhutanand, himself a Chamar as mentioned earlier, as well as the vanguard status of the Chamars among the "untouchable" castes of North India, somewhat akin to that of the Mahars in Maharashtra. Like the Mahars, the Chamars availed of the advantage of early absorption within the colonial administrative apparatus, albeit at subordinate strata, to educate their offspring who, in turn, developed from within their own ranks the nucleus of a nascent Dalit intelligentsia. The two life writing texts that I discuss below testify to the agency and autonomy of thought that present-day Chamars have inherited.

Arjun Dangle, in his introduction to the iconic volume *Poisoned Bread: Translations from Modern Marathi Dalit Literature*, has called the period between 1978 and 1986 as the "golden" period of Dalit autobiographies in Marathi. He mentions, in particular, Daya Pawar's *Baluta*, P. E. Sonkamble's *Arthvaninche Pakshi*, and Laxman Mane's *Upara* in this connection, and also praises the personal narratives of women writers such as Shantabai Kamble, Kumud Pawde, and others. For Dangle, the most notable phenomenon was the Ford Foundation's conferment of awards on *Bahuta* and *Upara*, an indication, in his opinion, of the responsibility shown by Dalit literature to raise Marathi literature to an international status, "since *Baluta* and *Upara* were the first Marathi books to win these awards" (xlii). None of the first-generation Dalit autobiographers in Hindi—Mohandas Naimishray, Omprakash Valmiki, Surajpal Chauhan, or Sheoraj Singh Bechain—forceful though their writings are, have yet earned even a national award at the level of the Sahitya Akadami awards, proof of the exclusivist character of the still-mainstream Hindi literary domain.

Since all of the above writers were born and brought up in a social milieu in which caste markers were etched deep into their identities, "concealment of caste," a trope made famous by the title of Dalit writer Baburao Bagul's short story collection, *Jevha Mi Jaat Chorali Hoti* (When I Concealed My Caste), is not an option that any of them can exercise. Therefore, in their retrospective life stories, they invariably proclaim their caste affiliations frankly and without embarrassment. Mohandas Naimishray, who grew up as a boy in a slum in Meerut, is nonchalant in his declaration:

> Our basti was like other bastis in the town. The basti was called Chamar Gate to begin with, and later came to be known as Chamar Darwaza. People mostly referred to it as Chamar Darwaza. At the entrance to the basti, there was a huge gate. To begin with our basti was within the town, in one corner of it. As soon as it was evening, the gate would be shut. This is why the basti was called Chamar Gate. As the residents of the slum gathered awareness, they started to call it Jatav Gate. As such, in the municipal registers it was

> recorded as Karam Ali. In the election papers too, the same name was used. Some people, however, insisted on referring to it as the Chamar neighbourhood. Even today, rickshaw and tonga-drivers hail their clients by calling the destination Chamar Gate.
>
> About eighty families of our caste stayed in the basti. They were all wage-earning families. Some were shoe makers, some made slippers and some were coolies. (*Apne* 16–17)[8]

Naimishray—and Bechain—make the inextricable link between ancestral calling and caste abundantly clear. Before his father's premature death, Bechain, his elder brother, and father tried to earn a livelihood by collecting the carcasses of lifeless animals, skinning them and preparing them for tanning.

> At the time of my birth . . . Babba, Tau my father, would collect the dead animals from the village, skin them and take them to the hut on the outskirts. The entire process was an arduous one. The animal would be turned on its back and its four feet would be tied. A couple of bamboo rods would be passed through the tied limbs and four men would be required to lift the dead animal on their shoulder. . . . On account of the monopoly the Chamars enjoyed over the resources of production, the Banias, the Telis and the Yadavs would denigrate their profession. Muslims are now running a lucrative trade in dead animals. However the basic work is still done by Chamars. At Zarifnagar and Pali, several of my maternal relations . . . are working as contractual labourers at a minimal wage for lifting and skinning dead animals. It is for this reason that there has been no change or improvement in the quality of their lives. Even today, none of them is literate. Ignorant of the letter, they do not even vote according to choice and therefore their judgement has no role to play in the making of governments. (78–79)[9]

The "persistence of caste," as Anand Teltumbde has designated it, as a system of cultural, political, social and economic discrimination, and the key cause for the degradation of the untouchables, troubles both Bechain and Naimishray. It is this anxiety that is articulated by Naimishray through his aphorism, "The geography of the town [Meerut] was changing, but its history has remained unchanged" (*Mera* 11).

The paradox of a timeless history is, of course, a staple attribute of the civilizational paradigm against which India's survival as an apparently seamless community of people from antiquity to the current moment is often explained. Both of the autobiographers I discuss below highlight the disastrous implications of this idea of transtemporality, especially for the downtrodden sections of India's society. To paraphrase Naimishray's remark, history seems to be a state of eternal stasis for the downtrodden, yet the disruption of this illusion is imperative and can be achieved only if and when the downtrodden struggle to alter their circumstances. Thus, Bechain's effort to track his genealogy back to Jawahar, the helpless, landless peasant from Bhojpur village in Bulandshahar District who was a direct ancestor, proceeds out of an anxiety for self-validation.

> There is no historical record that testifies to the lives of these five or six generations that spanned a period of two to four hundred years. It is in recognition of the necessity to belong to a context and the need to be rooted to one's past, that I have brought this record into the public domain. I may have got a few names or time sequences mixed up but nothing has been added on. The generations descending from Jawahar shared his fate—deprived of any means of livelihood, they were forced into working for others—on fields, in homes and other places. No one can comprehend the import of my struggle for existence without knowing this generational pattern. (*Apne* 11)

In recalling the unvariegated pattern of the lives of his forefathers, Bechain is proud of the distance he has traveled to become the person he is. Similarly, Naimishray attests to the crucial function of "undercaste" agency in helping to break fatalism, albeit with a certain amount of reluctance.

> The sun of Independence was beginning to shine more brightly. Its light and its shadows played around us, but we had more of the share of shadows than of light. However we were always prepared to struggle for more light. We did not want to beg for it, but nor did we want to linger on in the shadows. The conflict was within us and outside us too. (*Apne* 25–26)

At the same time there is an air of self-assurance and self-confidence in both writers as they narrate the past, because the past is a place they no longer inhabit. While they have been witnesses to it, they are today, as Hunt has put it, "securely part of the middle classes":

> Through much struggle and against many obstacles, these individuals availed of the reservation facilities provided by the Indian Constitution, acquired high levels of education and government jobs, and joined the Delhi middle classes. This period of the 1970s and the early 1980s was also a time of increasing politicization of Dalit identity within the Hindi public sphere, which led to the establishment of the Dalit labour organization BAMCEF in Delhi in 1976, the political mobilisations of the BSP across North India from 1984 and the controversy over the implementation of the Mandal Commission Report in 1990. Entering the urban middle classes opened up a new range of possibilities for these writers, including middle-class habitus, or cultural practices and values, as well as the ability to consume and to produce middle-class cultural commodities, particularly literature circulating in the mainstream Hindi public sphere. (134)

While these writers, therefore, in their private lives may be said to straddle two worlds, as writers they are firmly located in the metropolis.

Vani Prakashan, a renowned mainstream publishing house in Delhi, has published both Naimishray's and Bechain's autobiographies, which have been reviewed in the mainstream Hindi media. And, without a doubt, their intended and implied readership is a middle-class reading public. Gradually, too, autobiographies such as these have been engaging the attention of professional academics and finding space in university syllabi and curricula. The study of Dalit autobiographies in Hindi is more and more becoming a focus of master's of philosophy and PhD dissertations not just in Hindi departments but in departments of comparative literature, English, and sociology as well. Translation projects of major English-language publishing houses have further enhanced their readership as well, giving them a global reach.

All this is not to suggest that access to the Hindi literary mainstream has been easy for Dalit autobiographers who write in Hindi. Very often their autobiographies have been isolated from their other sometimes superior literary productions and published because of a popular misconception, on the part of publishers, that autobiographical writings are the most popular form of Dalit self-expression and therefore will attract the maximum number of buyers. This certainly holds true in the case of both Bechain and Naimishray. Correspondingly, other forms of "creative" writing are not only neglected, as mentioned earlier, but these writers are also not considered to be thinkers who hold their own opinions on matters of general interest. Thus all these writers, notwithstanding how thought-provoking their pronouncements might be on issues apart from caste, have been perceived as Dalit thinkers at best and not thinkers at large. Why is it that not one of the Dalit autobiographers from the Hindi belt, or Dalit writers in Hindi for that matter, has ever been ascribed the designation of a public intellectual?

The answer to this question is to be found in the straitjacketed definition of the literary as far as the Hindi literary mainstream is concerned and its inability to accommodate within its sphere more than a very limited range of Dalit self-expression. To quote Badri Narayan and A. R. Misra:

> Although abundant in literature containing self-expression of the Dalits, North India lacks in producing an established mode of Dalit literature acceptable to the educated and professionally well-placed population. . . .
>
> Further, in the oral tradition, Dalit expressions have assumed many forms, for example, songs, drama, caste-oriented history but their acceptance too has been discouraging. These kinds of literature have been constantly knocking at the door but have always been refused entry even into the amphitheatre of the established and recognised arena of articulation. The terrain of Hindi literature is so well tailored and designed that unless a writing corresponds successfully to its demands, it has no chances of inclusion; iconoclastic forms are hardly encouraged. (35–36)

The noted Dalit writer Kanwal Bharti further reinforces this point:

> From the point of view of the Dalit intelligentsia, Hindi literary history and Hindi criticism are both casteist. Within the context of either, a Brahmin writer who has written as few as three stories will find mention, but not so a Dalit writer who has a dozen or more books to his name. I am not here referring to Hira Dom . . . I am speaking about Swami Achhutanand who was a poet, and a playwright and the editor of a monthly journal as well. But there is no discussion of him in Hindi literary history . . . Because in the view of [the literary historians], he was casteist, he talked about Dalits and wrote about them.

It is for the benefit of the mainstream Hindi reading public that both Naimishray and Bechain cast an ironic glance at elite representations of their respective home turfs. On the one hand, Bechain takes on the Gandhian idealization of Nadrauli, his native village, rendered in verse by the freedom fighter, Raghunath Shastri:

> Shastriji had a long poem about our village, entitled "Nandnandini Nadrauli," and presented it to me. The poem highlighted the village's scenic beauty and was from an aesthetic perspective, no doubt, praiseworthy, but it had a subtext of self-advertisement that one finds in the compositions of courtier poets. . . . The seamy side of village life—the curse of untouchability, the pitiable existence of its subaltern groups such as Dalits and women, group rivalries born out of unenlightened attitudes—did not find any mention in his text. Since Shastriji himself belonged to the dominant Yadav caste within the village, he was not anchored within the dynamic of oppression which operated within village society. (*Mera* 31–32)

On the other hand, Naimishray soaks with satire his preliminary panegyric on the town of Meerut:

> The town was not very big. But it was grand in its history, its culture and its traditions. From time to time people would commemorate its illustrious past. In their speeches, leaders would dwell on its greatness. At school, children would be taught to be proud of their town. The teachers themselves felt their chests swell up as they celebrated their town's name and fame. (*Apne* 9)

The "glorious heritage" of the town, as Naimishray outlines it, however, includes a fair amount of Chamar-baiting, an everyday phenomenon that has been elevated to the status of a fine art and has often become a popular mode of entertainment for "upper castes" (11–12, 35).

The subversive edge in these narratives obviously derives from the readerly consciousness that informs them. Both Naimishray and Bechain are, in their own time, drawn toward books and become avid readers. To a great extent their politicization grows out of their perusal of radical, especially

Marxist literature (Hunt 137). But their acquaintance with left movements in the country alerts each of them to the limitations of Marxist praxis in dealing with the dynamics of caste oppression.

Not surprisingly the description of the complexities and the contradictions in Chamars' day-to-day lives in these autobiographies is unprecedented in non-Dalit literature about caste, even in Munshi Premchand's emotive fiction.[10] There is no attempt made in these texts to shy away from the blotches and blemishes of Dalit society and of the conflicts within it—the animosity of the Chamars toward the Bhangis for instance, or the pervasiveness of patriarchy in Dalit communities. These are constitutive elements of the experience that have molded Chamars and Bhangis into Dalit subjects and have prevented them from being reduced to paradigms of the predicament of untouchability.

What is at stake here, as Gajarawala has pointed out, is an aesthetics of solidarity rather than an aesthetics of sympathy:

> Dalit texts may be labelled as such not only on the basis of identity but through a different narrative structure, one that aspires to a solidarity rather than to a sympathy.
>
> The radical shift in worldview is the preeminent mode by which this occurs. It isn't enough to say that Dalit literature seems to be about Dalit peoples, in Dalit spaces, doing "Dalit things." Replacing a hegemonic space and time with a Dalit one, or Dalit ones, re-anchors ideologically every Dalit moment, plot turn, dialogue, action. Following a tradition set by realist writers in many places and times, Dalit writing creates new literary spaces (a Valmiki home, for example) and new literary actions (the prototypical animal skinning), as narrative forms of compensation, and demands that they be read. Dalit characters do not simply happen upon a predetermined hegemonic stage but rather are legitimate actors in spaces no longer contrived elsewhere. The ideological spaces that ensue are in fact born from that space rather than pre-fabricated. (53)

Within these spaces, which might be called Dalit-determined spaces, the shortcomings of relationships among Dalits may be acknowledged and enlarged upon without fear or favor. "Truth telling" has a different register for Dalit autobiographers than for realist non-Dalit writers who look upon Dalits only as objects of commiseration. Both Naimishray as well as Bechain are candid about the sexism of Dalit men in their individual conduct as well as in their collective functioning. Educating girls was not the norm in the *basti* in which Naimishray was born and brought up. Almost all girls were confined to the home and hearth, and most of them were married off at a tender age:

> The idea of girls venturing out of their homes before marriage was frowned upon. Not only that, girls who were unmarried were submitted to a strict code of behavior. In any case, such girls and women were fewer in number

> than men and boys in our slum. Among the female population, there was a predominant number of grandmothers, mothers, aunts and wives of brothers. There were a relatively small number of unmarried females. The father of a new-born girl child would clasp his head in his hands in despair. And the mother would turn grim. The girl child was associated with sorrow, deprivation, contention and conflict. (*Apne* 37)

Bechain's mother, married and widowed at an early age and remarried twice after that, at her father's behest, to men of her father's choice, is the embodiment of the travails of an average Dalit housewife. Burdened with several children and systematically maltreated by her husband, she is a much-battered person who grows old before her time and eventually succumbs to her many ailments. The discriminatory treatment that Dalit women and girls have to put up with is highlighted through the example a choric song women sing on the occasion of Bechain's sister's marriage:

> O dear father, you gave my brother
> A palatial home to live in style
> And I have been sent into exile.
> O dear father! I am the garbage pile
> In your courtyard, disposed of the very next day.
> O dear father! I am the bird of this house
> That will fly abroad one day. (*Mera* 107)

The subordination and silencing of Dalit women and girls that Dalit autobiographers (who are usually men) evokes exposes the hierarchical nature of the Dalit counterpublic in North India, a feature that Narayan does not stress in his book *The Making of the Dalit Public in North India: Uttar Pradesh 1950–Present*.

Nor does Narayan's book offer due consideration to the fragmentary nature of the counterpublic that reveals itself in Naimishray's and Bechain's autobiographies. Ruminating upon the contempt with which Chamars held Bhangis, Bechain wonders "why the Chamars considered themselves superior to the Bhangis":

> Whenever people gathered under the neem tree to relate long stories, caste distinctions would be immediately visible in the manner in which the Chamars would occupy the higher parts of the hill and the Bhangis the lower. If a Yadav or a Muslim turned up, then both bhangis and chamars would vacate their places and sit on the ground. Before joining the Arya Samaj even I was deluded into believing that Chamars were superior to Bhangis, whereas economically we were weaker than them. (*Mera* 82)

Naimishray concurs with Bechain on the issue and is even more sharp in his criticism of intra-Dalit rivalries:

> Even among the Dalits there are innumerable networks of castes and subcastes which sometimes scatter and splinter Dalit identity and unity. There were far too many incompatabilities between the caste groups—and always plenty of people to aggravate them and few to resolve the knots. (*Apne* xxiv)

These incidents of glaring inequities within Dalit communities of North India raise questions about the real and potential exclusions from the emergent Dalit counterpublic in the region. Narayan, who has researched extensively on this topic, concedes, in line with Fraser's theorization of the subaltern counterpublic, that "the Dalit public, as a counter-public, may not be seen as a homogenous alternative public but as heterogeneous and varied and full of various kinds of tensions that are present within the Dalits as a group" (*Apne* 63). However, he stops short of the admission that Dalits, because of the very architecture of the system that condemns them to being downtrodden, are sometimes as complicit with the system's governing ideology of marking distinctions by birth as are the "upper castes," and that this possibility often compromises the desired subaltern militancy with their numerous, top-to-bottom arranged ranks. It is therefore difficult for Dalits to develop, in the short run, an autonomous and authentic counterconsciousness to the caste-consciousness within which they are imbricated from the moment of their socialization. As the autobiographies studied have shown us, a coordinated and consolidated Dalit opposition, beyond all internal schisms, may still be a long time in the making, at least in North India. In this period of the movement's gestation, therefore, different shades of resistant Dalit public opinion from individual as well as collective quarters have made themselves heard and have been circulated in print, and these currently form the nucleus of a steadily expanding Dalit counterpublic that is likely to crystallize in the future.

What is the heritage of the counterconsciousness of present-day Dalit writers in Hindi, such as Naimishray and Bechain? Ambedkar is a presence in both of these personal narratives, but he is definitely not the central presence in either. In Naimishray's narrative, he is a distant, almost mythic figure. The news of his demise envelops all the Chamar households in gloom. Bechain reports in his narrative that he learned about Ambedkar at an advanced phase of his young adulthood. Neither of the authors expresses an indebtedness to Ambedkar as a literary mentor. On the contrary, in their discursive prose, both of them have paid glowing tributes to Achhutanand as a man of letters. For Bechain,

> an exploration of the foundations [of Dalit literature in Hindi] that emerged after the attainment of our independence in 1947 would . . . require the researcher to investigate the period immediately preceding that of Ambedkar during which Swami Achhutanand, the founder of the Adi Hindu Mahasabha

> and of the journal *Adi Hindu*, and poet, dramatist, historian and propagandist of a distinct religious faith, articulated through his literary productions a community consciousness of the Dalit people. ("Voices")

Naimishray goes a step further with his remark:

> If there were to be a fact based re-writing of Dalit history, then maybe Swami Achhutanand's role in the context of North India would not be seen as less than Ambedkar's. Also, the extremely important role of accumulated local consciousness on small stages in the colonial period transforms Dalits into an united community with the power of writing. (*Hindi* 52)

Rather than a utopian vision of the annihilation of caste, Acchutanand provided the successive generations of Dalit writers who were under his influence with an ideological apparatus to combat caste, the foundational tool of which was the print medium. Badri Narayan and A. R. Misra attest to Acchutanand's importance: "Through [his publications] Achhutanand not only conveyed the philosophy of liberation from social castigation, but also established the significance of the print media in Dalit mobilization and identity-formations" (18). Namishray and Bechain, and other contemporary Dalit writers of North India, continue to make avid use of the print medium and sustain the Dalit counterpublic in their region while, to quote Gail Omvedt, "the early promise of Dalit literature in Marathi [in this direction] has withered" (xvi). The "silent revolution," an epithet which Christophe Jaffrelot coined to describe "the rise of the lower castes in North India"[11] has no doubt been accomplished by factors such as the steady efflorescence of an "undercaste" literary culture.

## NOTES

1. All translations from the works of Swami Achhutanand Harihar, Mohandas Naimishray, and Sheoraj Singh Bechain that feature in this essay are my own.
2. See Amardeep.
3. There is surprisingly very little material available on Swami Achhutanand. The sole full-length publication in English on him, as far as I am aware, is Gooptu's brief monograph. The book, *Multiple Marginalities*, is, however, also very useful in this connection. There are, of course, a few more books in Hindi available on this key anticaste intellectual of North India.
4. For more information about Dalit print culture in North India in the early decades see Amardeep and Rawat.
5. See Dinkar.
6. See Amardeep.
7. The last two decades of the twentieth century was a period of extreme political ferment, especially in North India, as a result of both "upper" and "lower caste" mobilization around the issue of "reservations" for members of the so-called

"backward" castes in the sectors of education and employment, and a reactionary Hindu communal mobilization on the issue of construction of a Ram Temple on a spot at Ayodhya in Uttar Pradesh, which was claimed to be the birthplace of Lord Ram.

8. Because the English translation of this text is not yet available, I am providing page numbers for the original text, written in Hindi, here and in all subsequent quotations.
9. Deeba Zafir and I have prepared these quotations from an unpublished translation of the text. Page numbers are for the original Hindi text, here and in all subsequent quotations.
10. "The Problem of Premchand," as Brueck calls it, has engaged more or less all students of Dalit writing in Hindi. It is almost as though Premchand casts a shadow over Dalit writing in Hindi, and the steering clear of his shadow is necessary for Hindi Dalit writing to be seen in a proper light. For more on this, see Gajarawala.
11. This phrase is taken from the title of the book.

## WORKS CITED


Achhutanand Harihar, Swami. "Manusmriti Is Burning Us." *Hans*, vol. 19, no. 1, Aug. 2004, p. 188.

Amardeep. "The Making of Dalit Print Culture in Uttar Pradesh 1913–1978." PhD dissertation, Jawaharlal Nehru University, 2012.

Bagul, Baburao. *Jevha Mi Jaat Chorali Hoti*. Akshar Prakashan, 1963.

Bechain, Sheoraj Singh. *Mera Bachpan Mere Kandhon Par*. Vani Prakashan, 2009.

———. "Voices of Awakening." *The Hindu*, 8 Mar. 2008, http://www.thehindu.com/todays-paper/tp-features/tp-literaryreview/Voices-of-awakening/article15402505.ece. Accessed 4 Aug. 2008.

Bharti, Kanwal. "They Call Us Casteist." Facebook, 17 Nov. 2014. Accessed 5 Apr. 2016.

Brueck, Laura. *Writing Resistance: The Rhetorical Imagination of Hindi Dalit Literature*. Columbia UP, 2014.

Dangle, Arjun. "Introduction: Dalit Literature, Past, Present and Future." *Poisoned Bread: Translations from Modern Marathi Dalit Literature*, edited by Arjun Dangle, Advent Books Division, 1992.

Dinkar, D. C. *Swatantrata Sangram Mein Achhuton ka Yogdaan*. Gautam Book Store, 2007.

Gajarawala, Toral Jatin. *Untouchable Fictions: Literary Realism and the Crisis of Caste*. Fordham UP, 2013.

Gooptu, Nandini. *Swami Achhutanand and the Adi Hindi Movement*. Critical Quest, 2009.

Gupta, Charu. "Dalit 'Viranganas' and the Re-invention of 1857." *Economic and Political Weekly*, vol. 42, no. 19, 2007, pp. 1739–45.

Gupta, Ramanika, editor. *Dalit Chetna: Soch*. Navlakhan Prakashan, 1998.

Hunt, Sarah Beth. *Hindi Dalit Literature and the Politics of Representation*. Routledge, 2014.

Jaffrelot, Christophe. *India's Silent Revolution: The Rise of the Lower Castes in North India*. Columbia UP, 2003.

Jigyasu, Chandrika Prasad. "The Founder of Adi: Hindu Movement, Shree 108 Swami Achhutanandji 'Harihar.'" *Multiple Marginalities: An Anthology of Identified Dalit Writings*, edited by Badri Narayana and A. R. Misra, Manohar, 2004, pp. 101–29.

Naimishray, Mohandas. *Apne Apne Pinjre*. Vani Prakashan, 1995.

———. *Hindi Dalit Sahitya*. Sahitya Akademi, 2011.

Narayan, Badri. *Documenting Dissent: Contesting Fables, Contested Memories and Dalit Political Discourse*. Indian Institute of Advanced Study, 2001.

———. *The Making of the Dalit Public in North India, Uttar Pradesh, 1950–Present*. Oxford UP, 2011.

Narayan, Badri, and A. R. Misra, editors and translators. *Multiple Marginalities: An Anthology of Identified Dalit Writings*. Manohar, 2004.

Omvedt, Gail. "Preface: Literature of Revolt." *Poisoned Bread: Translations from Modern Marathi Dalit Literature*, edited by Arjun Dangle, Orient Blackswan, 2009, pp. x–xviii.

Orsini, Francesca. *The Hindi Public Sphere 1920–1940*. Oxford UP, 2002.

Pai, Sudha. *Dalit Assertion and the Unfinished Democratic Revolution*. Sage Publications, 2002.

Rawat, Ramnarayan. *Reconsidering Untouchability: Chamars and Dalit History in North India*. Permanent Black, 2012.

Rege, Sharmila. "Debating the Consumption of Dalit 'Autobiographies': The Significance of Dalit 'Testimonios.'" *Writing Caste/Writing Gender: Reading Dalit Women's Testimonios*. Zubaan, 2006, pp. 9–92.

Sharma, Pradeep K. *Dalit Politics and Literature*. Shipra Publications, 2006.

Singh, Rajpal. *Swami Achhutanand Harihar, Byaktitva and Krititiva*. Siddharth Books, 2009.

Teltumbde, Anand. *The Persistence of Caste: The Khairlanji Murders and India's Hidden Apartheid*. Navayana, 2016.

# 4

# TAMIL DALIT LITERATURE
## Aesthetics, Politics, and Life Narratives

PARTHASARATHI MUTHUKKARUPPAN

The emergence of Dalit literature in Tamil in the forms of poetry, short stories, plays, novels, and life narratives, along with subsequent Dalit criticism, has enriched Tamil literature in unprecedented ways, demanding that the literary canon shift while redefining the field of aesthetics. Life narratives have a special significance in the field of Dalit literature across India. Though life narratives were not a prominent mode of Dalit literary experiments in Tamil, the sensibilities that are generated around life narratives in general, I suggest, do play a significant role in constituting what Tamil Dalit literature is. That is to say, life narratives are not merely part of Dalit literature but in many ways these narratives determine and constitute Dalit literature.

In this essay, I address some fundamental questions: what is Dalit literature? What do we mean when we say Tamil Dalit literature? What are the aesthetics that mark Tamil Dalit literature as singular, distinguishing it from other critical developments in modern Tamil literature such as Dravidian and Marxist literatures? My interest here is not to *define* Dalit literature but to show how these questions continue to have a ghostly presence in discussions of Dalit literature and in the criteria that enable and are constitutive of categories like Dalit literature or Dalit aesthetics. I suggest that these questions are historical in nature and warrant historical explanations rather than abstract normative ones. That is to say, these questions warrant certain attention to the historical contexts from which they have been posed and from which explanations have been sought. They cannot be viewed as questions of an abstract nature devoid of any historicity. The emergence of life narratives and their roles in constituting the gamut of Dalit literature assumes enormous significance in this regard.

Ideologically, to name something is to assign it a place in the horizon of social and historical order. Thus, it is worthwhile to explore what the term

"Tamil Dalit literature" entails. Discussing Dalit literature in the context of Maharashtra, Aniket Jaaware has pointed out that there is a contradiction in the very constitution of the name. On the one hand, Dalit literature, like any other literature, entails universal protocols of reading and interpreting, and on the other hand, it also seeks a particular treatment by underscoring difference (Jaaware 6). Jaaware detects a parallel contradiction in the history of Indian polity in the way Ambedkar configured the relationship between Dalits and citizens, insofar as Dalits are citizens like anybody else but are also in need of special constitutional protection. Significantly, Jaaware's analogy rightly locates the historically emergent problematic of Dalit literature as it is often determined by the identity of the writer. Jaaware's analogy also brings to view another problem: the disjuncture between the field of welfare policy that claims to ameliorate the conditions of the needy and the domain of art and literature that "works at the level of fundamental attitudes," as Theodor Adorno would put it (78). If these are the contradictions historically posed by the very constitution of the term "Dalit literature" to the realm of literary theory, the adjective "Tamil" adds yet another level of complexity within the field of literary history. In what follows, I signpost some of the experimental moves that Tamil Dalit writers make through their negotiation of existing forms of literary expression and underscore their aesthetic and political significance.

Bama's life narrative, *Karukku*, published in 1992, is often considered the first work of Dalit literature in Tamil. It is significant that the text was written as a life narrative. *Karukku*'s publication designated Bama as a Dalit writer. In the world of letters, the emergence of "Dalit," and in this case "woman" as well, was significant particularly because of how Bama has often been identified as both "Dalit" and "writer." It is precisely because of certain aesthetic connotations of a life narrative that Bama's subjectivity gained such importance. However, writers' social backgrounds have continued to wield importance even when authors produce texts that are not life narratives. While there were writers from "untouchable" backgrounds writing long before Bama, it was not until years after the initial publication of their works and the movements for Dalit liberation that critics, in some cases writers themselves, assigned the terms "Dalit" and "writer" to those early writers. While the designation "writer" has been understood as a universal category of creativity, the insertion of the category "Dalit" into the literary world challenged the universality of "writer" and revealed how the writer position had been occupied primarily by "upper castes."

Untouchable communities and those within the world of literary production have had at least three responses to the crisis of the supposed universality of the term "writer." First, a set of people, most of whom have already established themselves as writers, do not want to claim that they are

Dalit writers—they want their writings to be evaluated *not* on the basis of what caste they belong to but on the basis of the aesthetic significance of their work. Imayam, Poomani, Cho Dharman, and others firmly hold this position. Dharman's statement is exemplary here: "I am a Dalit by birth; not by writing" (24).[1] They have insisted on the aesthetics of writing—including craft, nuanced understanding about social relationships, and command over narrative language—and have argued that the labels "Dalit literature" and "Dalit writer" stigmatize on the basis of writers' identity. They claim that similar works by "upper caste" writers are hailed as literature without any qualification. A second set of writers has noted a certain kind of transformation after they designated themselves as Dalit writers, claiming that there has been a perspective change in their writing. For instance, Abhimani notes, "Initially, I was absorbed in the philosophy of Marx, Periyar, Ambedkar—in that order—but soon changed the order of importance to Ambedkar, Periyar, Marx" (Satyanarayana and Tharu 73). And a third set of writers who have emerged as both "Dalit" and "writer" reveal that they have primarily identified themselves as Dalit writers since they first started writing. They are a new generation of writers who largely belong to the lower-middle-class strata in which Bama, too, could be located. It is important to note that the writers' Dalit identity and authorial status have been constituted simultaneously. They have objected to the first set of writers and their emphasis on how aesthetics are seemingly assigned a sacred space beyond the bounds of the ideology of writing and literary production itself. They have argued for Dalit literature on the basis of identity and foregrounded politics rather than aesthetics. By and large, the problems of aesthetics and politics are placed in opposition to each other.

While there are variations in identifying and not identifying as Dalit writers, a larger conceptual problem has emerged through debates around Dalit writing that has often posed the categories of aesthetics and politics as two poles. I suggest that ideas about Dalit literature often bear a certain subjective determinism whereby the writer's identity largely determines what is and what is not Dalit literature. It seems to me that one of the specific aesthetic features of life narratives—for example, the centrality of the writing subject and her social position—continues to determine overall perspectives on Dalit literature. While this particular aesthetic of life narratives and their extension onto the field of Dalit writing made possible the emergence of many writers from Dalit background as not just consumers but also producers, the same has also stigmatized writers from "untouchable" communities in such a way that they will forever remain incapable of transcending their identities as "Dalit writers."

Since the aesthetics of life narratives help determine the field of literary production, a social phenomenon external to the fabric of the text, let us look at *Karukku* and its textual operation to locate the ways in which this life narrative forges community relationships within the text and negotiates with the dominant forms of realism. This analysis helps us in understanding the ways in which the Dalit authorial subject, the one who transformed her place in the social world from a mere consumer of literature to a producer, claims to locate herself within the community. While the community still occupies the side of physical labor within the ideological grids of the division of physical and mental labor, through remembering the past, the author re-members herself in the community.

*Karukku* recounts the life experience of the author in nine short chapters. The experience recounted spans the village life and years in school, college, and a Roman Catholic nunnery, from which Bama eventually walks out. In all these spaces, both modern institutions (like the church, the college, and the hostel) and traditional village settings, her experience of caste and "untouchability" is central. The book speaks of the communal life of Christian Parayars filled with humor, hardships, helplessness, and courage. *Karukku* opens the windows to readers of Parayars' lives and their joys and sufferings. Until *Karukku*'s publication, emergent literary texts did not provide firsthand access to and familiarity with Parayars' lives. In addition, unlike most of the Dalit literary works that foreground Hindu caste practices, *Karukku* discusses caste practices within Christianity.

When *Karukku* was published, initial responses focused on the language Bama used. Much of the public discussion missed the significance of the book, and many evaluated the book on the basis of standard yardsticks of literature such as artistry and diction. One of the bases on which the book received criticism was the use of "vulgar" Tamil that Bama subsequently claimed as a Dalit language (Suryachandran). Bama claims, however, that *ketta varthai* (abusive language) is a weapon for Dalit women who are otherwise bereft of any power and authority. It was not uncommon in Tamil literature—at least after the arrival of Karisal literature (a set of literary works emerging from "the black soil regions" of Tamil Nadu and largely written in a regional dialect)—that "vulgar" terms were used in literary texts. Unlike the young feminist poets (largely belonging to "middle class/intermediate castes") who emerged a decade later and deployed explicit political language to speak about sexuality, the female body, and the perversity of male chauvinism, Bama's concerns focused on everyday communal and caste relationships and used the language of common people without sanitization. In certain ways, Bama's language prefigured the social significance of sexual economies, their intimate connections with casteism, and the ways of translating them into literary artifacts. Sexuality, however, assumes a minimal importance in *Karukku*, and it is caste that runs through the text as the prominent problem that subjugates Dalit men and women.

If autobiography is putting one's "self" out and being exposed to the public, *Karukku* brings a new dimension of such exposure to the fore. Writing on the strategies that Bama deploys in *Karukku*, M. S. S. Pandian notes that the text produces a certain anonymity by not disclosing the names of the village, individuals, and places ("Writing" 36). However, community members from Bama's village perceived the opposite of what has been suggested by Pandian's reading. Even more so than the author of the narrative, Bama's community demonstrated their concern over their lives being displayed for public consumption. Indeed, after her text's publication, Bama was not allowed to enter her village for some time, and there were instances of villagers quarreling with her family members (Suryachandran). It would be wrong to read community members' responses as a result of the collapse of the distinction between the narrating subject and the subjects within the narrative. The important point to note here is that the villagers were not identifying Bama as one among them, but were in fact able to grasp the gap between themselves and Bama. In other words, it is not a sense of a collectivity that prompted the villagers to oppose Bama but the absence of such a collective self. It is evident from these instances that the villagers felt that their pathetic life conditions were exposed and they felt humiliated. More importantly, they also criticized how Bama's account revealed the nicknames of many Dalits from her village but not the nicknames of her family members.[2] This critique brings into stark relief notions about the form of Dalit autobiography and the suggestion that the Dalit autobiography is not about an individual self but rather about the collective self of the Dalit community.[3] On the contrary, what is important is to recognize the presence of the narrating subject, narrativized subjects, and the relationship between both.

Like any other Dalit life narrative, *Karukku* appears to present itself as a life narrative of a community or a collective self. This presentation manifests at the formal structure of the language that Bama's life narrative inhabits. However, the kind of relationship between the community and the self that is forged in *Karukku*'s substratum in an ideological register is quite different. Unlike many writings that preceded Bama's, the narrator's language in *Karukku* and the characters' language, appearing within inverted commas, are not presented in a hierarchical relationship. Following modern Tamil literature, Dalit literature has mostly deployed a narrative language in which a hierarchy is maintained between the language of the narrator and the subject's language within the narrative. Even in the works of most canonical Dalit writers, the narrative language is largely in standardized Tamil, while the characters within the narrative speak in colloquial dialect, which is always in quotes. As observed by Colin MacCabe, this hierarchical aesthetics of writing belongs to nineteenth-century bourgeois English realist novels:

> While those sections in the text which are contained in inverted commas may cause a certain difficulty for the reader—a certain confusion vis-a-vis what really is the case—this difficulty is abolished by the unspoken (or more accurately the unwritten) prose that surrounds them. (8)

The transgression of this specific feature of the nineteenth-century English realist novel—that is, of a particular style of hierarchy within the language—is something new that is strikingly visible in Bama's writings. The significance of such enunciation is that the gap between the narrative language and the language of the subjects who speak within the narrative is erased at the level of the formal structure of language. Does this mean that, since Bama maintains this language treatment in all her works, Bama's works transgress a realist aesthetic? It may sound irrelevant to ask whether Bama's life narrative is realist or not, since any life narrative is "realist" in an obvious but trivial sense insofar as it is about real lives. However, it is Bama's reworking of the form, bearing the narrative conventions of both life narratives and the novel, that allows for a discussion of realism. And it is the question of realism that poses the need to comprehend the relationship between the narrative language and the language of the subjects who speak.

If one steps back from an examination of Bama's formal language structure, one might identify the gap between the narrative language and the language of the subjects who speak within the narrative working in *Karukku* at a deeper level. In other words, this gap exists between the enunciation and what has been enunciated. The narrating subject presents herself as a representative of the community while simultaneously distancing herself from it by marking out a singular space for herself. She does this by narrating a political awareness, a concern for the unity of the subjugated castes, heroic adventures, and a Dalit consciousness of the self. These same qualities are not present in her community members who appear in the narrative. The narrator is a rational political being unlike the subjects who appear within the narrative. For instance, within the Christian nunnery, Bama gets frustrated by the obedience and obsequious behavior of the subservient Dalit workers who tolerate the abusive language of "upper caste" nuns (27). She laments that Dalits internalize the perceptions of "upper castes" about Dalits and believe that they are ugly and "untouchables" and also transfer that knowledge of inferiority to their next generations (28). Bama continues to preach that Dalits should dare to break caste and transform caste society. The novelty of this narrative is that though it is presented in the same dialect the subjects speak, it marks the narrator as a politically aware and conscious individual.[4] The obedient subjects in the narrative remain like the slave whose consciousness is nothing but the consciousness for the master in the classical Hegelian dialectic and they are presented as if progress in the dialectic has ceased forever. This is the way in which the individual self is asserted and *Karukku* falls in line with the realist narrative.[5] What is also interesting is that in the abolition of the gap in the formal language between the narrating self and the subjects within the narrative, what has also been abolished (not in a real sense but as a strategic deployment of language) is the class distinction between the community and the narrating self.

While the autobiographical form was easily accepted by the general readership, other forms, such as poetry and fiction, were resisted by general readers on various grounds. It is worth recalling that Dalit autobiography as a form was much appreciated among the middle-class/"upper caste" readers as long as the autobiographical narrative did not bring to a crisis the way they had been making sense of the social world and the institution of literature. If life narratives are to be understood as exposing the intricate economy of caste and its transactions in a communal context, the real paradox emerges in a subsequent conjuncture where the larger society welcomes life narratives as literary artifacts, even as the persistence of caste continues to demonstrate its vulgarity on an everyday basis.[6] This conjuncture leads us to cast our suspicion at the risk of sounding politically incorrect: do life narratives normalize the practice of caste by the processes of repeatedly narrating the barbarity of caste as such in the text? It also has to be mentioned here that life narratives have a special place among educated middle-class readers and are welcomed more enthusiastically than other fictive narratives. While it appears self-explanatory in the case of life narratives that it is not possible for one to write somebody else's life experiences, this problem of subjective determination occupies a centrality even in Dalit fictive narratives on caste.

*Nokkadu: Tamil Dalit Sirukathaikal* (Disease: Tamil Dalit Short Stories) was one of the earliest literary works to carry the term "Dalit" in the title. Abhimani, himself an associate of the Indian People's Front, a Marxist-Leninist outfit, wrote in the preface that his stories were based on the conflict between the "dominant backward castes" and the subjugated Dalits. He believes that his work could serve as a spark to the ongoing struggle for social liberation that Dalits are undertaking. Further, he notes that his stories "would shake the barbaric roots of the feudal culture" (Abhimani n.p.).[7] He also warns that his stories would bring revolt and quotes Maxim Gorky as stating that literature is meant to bring revolts. He concludes the preface by declaring that literature is about truth and "truth is meant to be red hot. Let the dead-leaves-like-rubbish culture turn to ashes in truth" (n.p.). Abhimani's stories are not so much oriented toward offering political resolutions to the problem of caste than to disclosing the complexities of caste relationships, oppression, and the economy of humiliation.

A story in the collection entitled "Nokkadu" needs special mention. The story discloses the plight of Karuthayi, an Arunthathiyar woman, who cleans the dry toilets in a small town. Left with no other source of income, she depends on the people of the town for her sustenance. In a torrential rainy season, Karuthayi falls sick from dysentery and is not able to work for a few days. Eventually, a landlady forces a sickened Karuthayi to clean the lavatories and when Karuthayi does, she cannot resist using a lavatory due to her dysentery. Abhimani's narrative brings to the fore how, because of deep-rooted casteism, the Hindu world is horrified by the very idea of Karuthayi using this lavatory. In a way, Abhimani plays on the term *nokkadu* (disease) to expose the sickness of caste society and the need for a cure.

In 1994, Devakanthan, a Sri Lankan writer then living in Tamil Nadu, reviewed Abhimani's short story collection in his quarterly magazine, *Elakku*. Devakanthan posed a few questions concerning the distinct nature of Dalit literature. Devakanthan's questions were critical of the very term "Dalit literature." The following are his questions:

> Are the stories called Dalit literature due to the stench of feces and urine? . . . Is Dalit literature called so because it is written by Dalits? . . . Can a non-Dalit with a Dalit consciousness write Dalit literature? If not, how is it possible for Dalits who are not engaged in menial occupations? . . . Does Dalit literature refuse to be confined in the category of realist literature? Why does not Dalit literature evolve into a broader category such as workers' literature? (qtd. in Sivasankaran 49, 51, 51–52, 53)

In a subsequent issue, T. K. Sivasankaran, a prominent Marxist critic, responded to these questions. Sivasankaran noted that the stench of feces and urine is not new to Tamil and, indeed, works of K. Daniel (a Sri Lankan Tamil writer from an "untouchable" washerman community) introduced them after the 1960s in the notable works *Panchamar* and *Panchakonankal*. Sivasankaran states that experiments with language can be appreciated as long as they strengthen a particular work of art, but at the same time, it is the freedom of the readers to reject those works that violate the boundaries of civility. He also traces the legacy of Dalit literature to Subramania Bharathi (1882–1921), an Indian nationalist writer from Tamil Nadu, and views Dalit literature as part of progressive literature since the 1930s. According to Sivasankaran, Dalit literature is not necessarily written only by Dalits, and even works by non-Dalits that carry a Dalit consciousness could be called Dalit literature. He adds that it is a narrow view to consider only Dalits as Dalit writers, and asserts that the view that only Dalits engaged in traditional, demeaning occupations could produce Dalit literature is not productive. Overall, Sivasankaran suggests that there has been a tradition of Dalit literature in Tamil Nadu and that the new Dalit writings need to be located within the legacy of such progressive literature and viewed as part of its tradition.

While Sivasankaran places the history of Dalit literature parallel to the history of modern literature in Tamil and suggests a diachronic explanation,

Raj Gowthaman arrives at a synchronic explanation to suggest a rupture in the way Dalits are represented in modern Tamil literature, a rupture occasioned by the emergence of Dalit writers in the early 1990s. In *Poi + Abatham = Unmai* (Lie + Nonsense = Truth), Gowthaman ruthlessly critiques both the way the question of caste was given resolution and the way the Dalit subject is represented in the literary imaginations of modern Tamil literature. He points out that the entire field of literature is overwhelmingly male, with writers belonging particularly to Brahmin and vellala castes (a cluster of castes who own large tracts of fertile land and continue to dominate the sphere of literature as well). He identifies certain patterns of representation by which Dalit characters are portrayed in modern Tamil literature, particularly ones that reinforce the hegemony of Brahmins and vellalas: redeeming the wretched "untouchable"; highlighting the lowliness of "untouchables" and the generosity of "upper castes"; establishing the rebellious and progressive nature of "upper castes" by showing them eating at "untouchable" locations; associating "untouchables" with lowliness, evil, and sin; expressing anxieties about "untouchables" converting to Islam and Christianity; evoking a certain jouissance among the readers by graphic descriptions of violence that "untouchables" endure; representing "untouchables" as cheap laborers and slaves; and resolving the liberation of "untouchables" necessarily within the Hindu religion. In the interest of carving out a niche within Tamil literary history and underscoring the rupture occasioned by the emergence of Dalit literature, Gowthaman also launches an ideological critique of what has been understood as Marxist and Dravidian literature in Tamil. In his view, in Marxist works that writers largely functioning within the folds of Communist parties produce, "untouchables" appear as agricultural classes and the politics of class is centralized. Economy is given primacy over culture in the call for industrial and agricultural laborers to unite to undermine caste. Much of leftist literature has been aesthetically structured within the style of social realism. According to Gowthaman, the Dalit question dissolves into the Marxist question in the literary experiments of leftist writers whose stories were structured around labor unions, red flags, and wage increases. Unlike Marxist literature, Dravidian literature has a better understanding about caste and culture. In certain ways Gowthaman also suggests that Dalit literature is a move away from the realist writing that emerges in modern Tamil literature and toward postmodern aesthetics (*Poi* 60).

The questions and answers that appear in *Elakku* as detailed above are significant in two ways. First, they point out that "What is Tamil Dalit literature?" and "What are the aesthetics of Tamil Dalit literature?" are not purely abstract questions, nor can they be resolved within the domain of literary theory. Rather, they show that the issue is more historical and inseparable from both the emergence of the Dalit writer as well as the conditions for that possibility. Second, those questions continue to recur even now and have been met with several differing explanations from Dalit critics. Most of the subsequent concerns regarding Dalit criticism have been indirect responses to those questions and answers that *Elakku* poses. Broadly speaking, Sivasankaran and Gowthaman contest the historical trajectories of Tamil Dalit literature. The contestation in certain ways is also about what Dalit literature is, what it constitutes, and what the conditions are for its emergence.

While Gowthaman's synchronic account rightly recognizes Dalit literature as a rupture in Tamil literary history, it fails to account for the presence of Dalit writers who existed before the 1990s and presents Dalit literature as an outcome of the state's policy measures and subsequent consciousness among Dalits. In addition, it is difficult to demonstrate that the rise of Dalit writers within the Tamil literary world has completely transformed the ways in which Dalit characters have been portrayed. Indeed, Dharman's critique builds up to this provocative statement about Dalit characters in Dalit literature: "The Dalit images/portrayals that have been shown so far remain one dimensional—men in stinking dirty cloths, women who easily fall, illiterates, violence maniacs, submissive coolies, ones who protest only for food and wages, etc." (25). That is to say, the characterization of Dalits by Dalits is not wholesale transformation, as Gowthaman wishes; rather, similar portrayals continue to exist even within the narratives Dalit writers produce. On the other hand, Sivasankaran misrecognizes the new developments as if Dalit literature is very much inscribed in the old order.7 In many ways this misrecognition also reveals certain "upper caste" anxieties about the emergence of Dalit writers into the literary world and the way established writers cope with these new developments.

In the final analysis, it is clear in the discussions around Tamil Dalit literature that most often every opposition posed between aesthetics and politics, synchronicity and diachronicity in literary history, and the Dalit writer as an ontological and epistemological subject in literary theory, seems to be false in a way that the characteristics of one pole are inherently present in the other pole of the opposition. That is to say, aesthetics cannot be separated from politics, neither can synchronicity from the diachronic, nor can Dalit subjectivity be fully defined in terms of epistemology or ontology. While these are the theoretical problems that emerge in discussing "Tamil Dalit literature," historically speaking, "Dalit" in Dalit literature has largely been understood in ontological terms and stated explicitly.

The idea that the writing subject determines the peculiarity of literature posits the definitional problem (what is literature?) in terms of ontology. This question seems only to complicate the issue in new ways. The first reason for this is that the category "Dalit" does not quite fit with the logic of ontology since it is a political and historical category, not an ontological one. Ontologies, in a way, negate both historical and political formulations and formations. Ontology assumes the subject is always already there. The second reason there cannot be any such thing as Dalit literature in ontological terms is a corollary to the first. One has to consider what has been inadequately formulated as "subcaste issues" within Dalit discourse. It is precisely the ontological determination that has produced a crisis within the field of Tamil Dalit literature.[8]

It is also worthwhile to look at how Dalit studies as a discipline or an area of critical enquiry is largely understood as different from Dalit literature. It seems that an association with a life narrative and the emphasis on the place of the experiencing subject tends to give a different meaning to the category of Dalit literature. Dalit studies, on the other hand, is received largely as a field of inquiry, and what has been expected is a scholarly intervention on not only caste experienced by "untouchables" but on general issues of all kinds. Thus, Dalit life narratives seem to have been central in Dalit literature. This is perhaps why life narratives such as Bama's have played such an important role in the constitution of the category "Dalit literature." However, Dalit life narratives are only one among many contingencies that have constituted Dalit literature. Life narratives can neither be an exemplary case for Dalit literature nor can they be considered as exhausting the aesthetics and politics of Dalit literature, despite the historical role they played in constituting the field.

## NOTES

1. All the translations from Tamil are mine unless otherwise noted.
2. In another context, a similar problem has been identified by Mathivannan in his review of Perumal Murugan's *Koolamadari*, published in 2001. Mathivannan notes that Murugan's narrative uses names that are not socially respectful for the Arunthathiar characters, while largely the names of landowning Goundar caste children were given respectable names. Unlike Bama's work, here the difference is between names of people who belong to two different castes.
3. M. S. S. Pandian, for instance, has suggested that *Karukku* displaces the autobiographical "I" with the collectivity of a Dalit community ("On" 130). Kumar extends Pandian's idea and asserts that the invocation of a collective self is a strategy that almost all Dalit autobiographies adopted (232).
4. A few subjects within the narrative show a knowledge of Ambedkar and equality but still lack the full consciousness of the narrator.
5. While Bama's narrative in *Karukku* distances itself from the community members and presents her as a rational political subject, on occasion, the entry of the other "untouchable" castes into the narrative shows a certain shift in Bama's strategy, whereby her narrative erases the gap between herself and her community by relocating the irrational outside her community and placing it on the other community of "untouchables."

6. Laxman Mane, author of the Marathi autobiography *Upara* (Outsider), asks this question: "Can the enlightened people of our society who have appreciated *Upara* and its author come out in the open, breaking social barriers and joining hands with the hundreds of 'Uparas' who have no houses, no shelter and who live like animals?" (12).
7. There are also attempts by scholars to trace the presence of Dalits from the sixth century in epics (Swaminathan). While it is true that the names (here "Dalit literature") have a retroactive effect, it is historically inaccurate to locate certain mythologies and epics as Dalit literature. This diachronicity conceals certain conservative ideological interests to disavow anything that is new and to impose a seamless continuity across history.
8. Dalit, a non-Tamil term, found difficulty in gaining easy acceptance in the Tamil vernacular publics. Gowthaman suggests in one of his papers published by IDEAS in 1991 that "instead of Dalit, the term from an alien language, the derogative term 'Parayan' that is pervasive in Tamil usage to refer to untouchables, could be used" ("Thamilaga" 27n2). It is common knowledge that "Parayan" is a term used to refer to a particular caste rather than a term that could fairly represent the oppressed groups in Tamil Nadu. Though his suggestion is to remedy the usage of an "alien term," it unmistakably opens up a new problem regarding how a particular caste name could replace a term that is essentially anticaste. The term "Dalit" in its initial manifestations in Marathi and in the secondary appropriations in many non-Marathi languages never connoted a reference to caste and was popularized to emphasize the existential possibilities of the anticaste subject and the rejection of the caste order. However, Gowthaman's suggestion would get actualized not in terms of "Parayan/Paraya" formally gaining currency over "Dalit" but in a much more substantial way by which "Dalit," at least in the cultural and literary domain, largely came to denote the Paraya caste. Dalit activities of writing, performing arts, and politics in the 1990s resulted in rendering the two terms "Parayan" and "Dalit" as synonyms, and it resulted in non-Parayan "scheduled castes" disclaiming the name Dalit.

## WORKS CITED


Adorno, Theodor. "Commitment." *New Left Review*, vol. 1, nos. 87–88, 1974, pp. 75–89.

Abhimani. *Nokkadu: Tamil Dalit Sirukathaikal.* Thamarai Selvi, 1993.

Bama. *Karukku.* Bharathi Puthakalayam, 2010.

Dharman, Cho. *Cho Dharman Kathaikal.* Marutha, 2001.

Gowthaman, Raj. *Poi + Abatham = Unmai.* Vidiyal, 2010.

———. "Thamilaga Thalithum Thalith Ilakkiyamum." *Thalithiya Vimarsana Katturaikal.* Kalachuvadu, 2003, pp. 11–28.

Jaaware, Aniket. *Destitute Literature.* U of Mumbai, 2012.

Kumar, Raj. *Dalit Personal Narratives: Reading Caste, Nation and Identity.* Orient Blackswan, 2011.

MacCabe, Colin. "Realism and the Cinema: Notes on Some Brechtian Theses." *Screen*, vol. 15, no. 2, Summer 1974, pp. 7–27.

Mane, Laxman. *Upara*. Sahitya Akademi, 1997.

Mathivannan, M. *Velicchangalai Puthaitha Kuzhigal*. Karuppu Pirathikal, 2005.

Pandian, M. S. S. "On a Dalit Woman's Testimonio." *Gender and Caste*, edited by Anupama Rao, Kali for Women, 2003, pp. 129–35.

———. "Writing the Ordinary Lives." *Economic and Political Weekly*, vol. 43, no. 38, 2008, pp. 34–40.

Satyanarayana, K., and Susie Tharu. *No Alphabet in Sight: New Dalit Writing from South India*. Penguin, 2011.

Sivasankaran, T. K. "Dalit Ilakkiyam: Sila Kelvikalum Pathilkalum." *Elakku*, 1994, pp. 49–55.

Suryachandran. "Dalith Penkalukku Ketta Vaarthaikale Ayutham." *Puthagam Pesuthu*, Mar. 2004, www.azhiyasudargal.wordpress.com. Accessed 22 May 2017.

Swaminathan, Venkat. "The Dalit in Tamil Literature: Past and Present." *Indian Literature*, vol. xliii, no. 5, 1999, pp. 15–30.

# 5

## BENDING BIOGRAPHY
## The Creative Intrusions of "Real Lives" in Dalit Fiction

LAURA R. BRUECK

This essay interrogates two contemporary literary negotiations of the twentieth-century biographies of M. K. Gandhi, B. R. Ambedkar, and Dhanpat Rai Srivastava, better known as the towering icon of modern Hindi literature, "Munshi" Premchand, as well as the broader politics of their twenty-first-century resurrection and reevaluation. I focus on the writings of Uday Prakash and Ajay Navaria, both contemporary Delhi-based Hindi-language authors who write about the dynamics of caste in contemporary India,[1] to consider each author's innovative usages of metafictional narrative techniques to blur the boundaries between "real" and fictional life narratives. I argue that reading these texts through the critical lens of postrealism allows us to understand them as signaling new opportunities for Dalit writers to "challenge conventional forms of fiction and history through . . . an acknowledgment of their inescapable textuality" by reconstituting, *with a difference*, biographical narratives from "real life," as well as history and literature (Hutcheon 129). I suggest that a postrealist turn in Dalit literature provides some relief for the seemingly intractable debates over identity politics that continually inhibit the free movement of Dalit knowledge production, both literary and historical.[2] Ultimately, this paper probes the apparently arbitrary generic distinctions between auto/biography and fiction in Dalit narratives with a careful analysis of the strategically interventionist employment of real lives and biographical details in Dalit fiction.

I explore the narrative strategy of reemplotment in the following discussion as a key component of the critical stance of postrealism in two short stories—both of which variously seek to reconstitute new meanings for the historically embodied signifiers of Gandhi, Ambedkar, and Premchand. I argue that such an analysis of literary strategies, rather than the politics of authorial biographies, allows us to set aside for a moment the strained identity politics peculiar to the Dalit literary movement, about which I say more below using a contemporary example, and consider the innovative narratives of Navaria and Prakash together for the fact of their mutual preoccupation with caste and Dalitness, irrespective of their own individual claims to Dalit or non-Dalit caste status.

In recent years, scholarship on Dalit literature (simplistically but perhaps most commonly defined as anticaste literature produced by authors who belong to—or for some, stand in solidarity with—India's former "untouchable" castes) has eschewed the more traditional celebration of the intervention of the "authentic" voice of experience associated with autobiographical—or testimonial—writing, focusing instead on the narrative strategies of Dalit fiction (Gajarawala; Brueck). In these works, both realism and modernism have rightly emerged as the defining critical frameworks for understanding Dalit literature in the context of the Ambedkarite social movement in which it is embedded, as well as in its ties to a more diverse modern Indian literary heritage. This paper seeks to extend these frameworks to contend with a newer, more postmodern Dalit literary trend exemplified by two recent works in Hindi by contemporary Delhi-based authors Ajay Navaria ("Uttar Katha," a story I have translated elsewhere as "Hello Premchand!") and Uday Prakash ("Mohandas"). Using the critical lens of "historiographic metafiction" that Linda Hutcheon developed in her seminal book *A Poetics of Postmodernism: History, Theory, Fiction*, I argue that the reconstitution in these stories, beyond the temporal limits of their own historical context, of such iconic figures as Gandhi, Ambedkar, and the Hindi literary giant Premchand establishes an important literary shift toward postrealism. I advocate here for the productive possibilities in a turn to postrealism in Dalit literature *as* literary criticism and historical revisionism. Such a turn allows for a framework in which we can recognize the intersecting demands that Dalit literary aesthetics and certain meta-historically constituted Dalit subjectivities place upon dominant understandings of caste society.

As Toral Gajarawala has succinctly pointed out, "in Hindi especially, the central question in Dalit literature revolves around issues of realism, the real, and the cult of authenticity" (2). I have written extensively elsewhere about the ways in which Dalit *chetna*, or a Dalit consciousness, which we might define as a kind of politicized awareness and anticasteism in the Ambedkarite mode, has emerged in Hindi-language Dalit literary critical discourse as the benchmark qualification for the critical embrace of a Dalit literary work. The concept of Dalit *chetna* in Dalit literary critical discourse developed in the margins of Hindi literary realism, which was inaugurated, as many have pointed out, with Premchand. It was none other than Premchand, a leading figure of the progressive Hindi-Urdu literary movement of the 1920s and 1930s that wedded literary narrative to the ideology of the nationalist movement, who introduced the subject of the peasant, "the basis of a literary trope that would endure throughout the twentieth-century literary canon" (Gajarawala 33). But as Gajarawala points out, Premchand and the realist literary movement he inspired animated through their stories a social discourse of *sympathy*, and it is this affective result of literary realism that contemporary Dalit writers resist. Gajarawala writes:

> Why, says the Dalit critic, weren't Dalits represented by Premchand not only as they are but also as they might be? . . . Sympathy, as a narrative channel helped to produce the literary Dalit, but more importantly a literary type with limited potentiality. Types have socio-cultural longevity as well as political implications that are more clearly real than realism. The radical gesture of the Dalit literary movement is its refusal of a sympathetic discourse that has been central to a progressive realism—and, in fact, to unearth sympathy as the faulty affective architecture via which the old mode of realism was deemed progressive at all. (67)

The "affective architecture" of sympathy that realist literature in Hindi has traditionally constructed might also be understood as an aesthetic of detachment. Readerly sympathy is enabled by this detachment, such that a reader can feel *sorry* for an exploited Dalit protagonist rather than feel personally implicated in the social system of exploitation itself. Said another way, a reader can engage emotionally but not politically with the literary object of sympathy.[3] It is the detachment enabled by the sympathetic narratives of progressivist realism that angers Dalit critics and inspires them to construct a new politics of writing and reading: the politics of Dalit *chetna*.[4] Central to this new politics of Dalit *chetna* are the lives—as they were lived, as they are written, and as they circulate—of prominent historical figures in the politics of caste in India. In the following section, I consider for a moment a recent debate over the literary and political "lives" of Gandhi, Ambedkar, and Ambedkar's most notorious critique of caste society: *Annihilation of Caste*, written as a speech for the Jat-Pat Todak Mandal in 1936.[5] Though Ambedkar was not allowed to deliver it, the speech has circulated widely in numerous print publications ever since and become one of the most important texts of the Dalit movement in India. This twenty-first-century debate exemplifies the fraught negotiations over the lives and life writing of prominent twentieth-century Indian politicians, intellectuals, and artists and provides an important context to the detached aesthetic of sympathy that Dalit writers claim realism enables and into which Navaria and Prakash intervene with innovative experimentations in postrealism.

## READING AND WRITING LIVES: THE POLITICS OF *ANNIHILATION OF CASTE*

"When I first read it I felt as though somebody had walked into a dim room and opened the windows. Reading Dr. Bhimrao Ramji Ambedkar bridges the gap between what most Indians are schooled to believe in and the reality we experience every day of our lives" (Roy 17). So writes Arundhati Roy in "The Doctor and the Saint," her lengthy introduction to *Annihilation of Caste*, one of the most famous works by B. R. Ambedkar, perhaps India's most significant social and political reformer of the twentieth century. Originally written as a speech in 1936 but never delivered to its intended audience of Hindu reformists who caught wind of its radical message, Ambedkar's vigorous critique of caste in *Annihilation of Caste* has gone on to become one of the most widely printed and circulated books in India and now includes dozens of editions available freely on the Internet. At the Delhi launch of the new volume in the spring of 2014, S. Anand, the text's editor and publisher, said that the book had the "curious distinction of being one of the most obscure as well as one of the most widely-read books in India." This is because while the book is virtually sacred (however they might eschew such a religiously loaded term) for many in India's vast Dalit demographic, the privileged castes have exercised and protected their privilege by not reading it and willfully not taking into account its careful deconstruction of the very philosophical and political frameworks that consolidate their privilege.

The republication of *Annihilation of Caste* by the anticaste publishing house Navayana, and the strategic choice of the internationally recognizable author and activist Arundhati Roy to write its introduction was meant to resurrect the historical figure of Ambedkar for a new audience: elites in India and beyond for whom Gandhi's legacy nearly swallows Ambedkar's whole. In her introduction, Roy admits that before the publisher's invitation she, too, like so many other members of the "privileged castes," had never read the book. According to Roy,

> History has been kind to Gandhi. He was deified by millions of people in his own lifetime. Gandhi's godliness has become a universal and, so it seems, an eternal phenomenon. It's not just that the metaphor has outstripped the man. It has entirely reinvented him. (Which is why a critique of Gandhi need not automatically be taken to be a criticism of all Gandhians.) Gandhi has become all things to all people. . . . History has been unkind to Ambedkar. First it contained him, then it glorified him. It has made him India's Leader of the Untouchables, the King of the Ghetto. It has hidden away his writings. It has stripped away the radical intellect and the searing insolence. (40, 43)

The irrefutable centrality of an idealized Gandhian biography in India's contemporary self-assessment is evident: take for example the poll by *Outlook India* in 2012 calling for votes for "The Greatest Indian *after Gandhi*" (the winner was none other than Ambedkar) or historian Ramachandra Guha's mammoth history of postcolonial India titled *India after Gandhi: The History of the World's Largest Democracy*. Nonetheless, Anand's and Roy's much publicized resurrection of Ambedkar, couched as it is in Roy's lengthy and deeply critical revision of Gandhi's popularly vaunted biography, was one that many among the text's "old" audience, its Dalit audience, has vociferously criticized in social and mainstream media sources. Their critique has to do with Roy's principal attention to deconstructing the global icon of Gandhi as "Mahatma" (great soul) with a specific critique of his attitudes on race during his time in South Africa and his conservative approach to caste when he returned to India in lieu of any deep engagement with Ambedkar's text. On December 16, 2014, Murali Shanmugavelan wrote in London's *The Independent* about Roy's lecture at a promotional event for the book at Columbia University:

> Her introduction, in fact, barely references the original text and mainly focuses on comparing Gandhi with Ambedkar, which seems to be the real purpose of the book. Roy, by her own admission, said at the launch at Columbia University that she had chosen not to publish her text as a stand-alone book, because she is . . . "pretty sure it would have been banned or disappeared in some ways. So it was a bit of a Trojan horse operation."

In other words, by her own admission it seems Roy yoked a *new* biography of Gandhi to an *old* iconic text by his political rival in order to provide her own work legitimacy and publishability. Implicit in Shanmugavelan's critique is a weariness in the face of yet another instance wherein Gandhi overshadows Ambedkar and a member of the "upper castes" (Roy, and also Anand, who annotated Ambedkar's text) overshadows an unnamed Dalit who might have been chosen to introduce the version of the text meant to bring Ambedkar and his writings to the world but is present only in his conspicuous absence and the angry cries of Dalit critics after the publication of the volume.

A particularly vocal critic in the debate that followed the book's publication was Anoop Kumar, founder of the Delhi-based Insight Foundation and regular contributor to *Round Table India*, a prominent online media platform for raising consciousness about Dalit issues. Comments from his Facebook page, later compiled on *Round Table India* in an essay called "Resisting a Messiah," included: "You need Omprakash [V]almiki's *Joothan's* English version to know the caste horror. Need *Fandry* to get shocked. You require 60–70 years to discover Ambedkar. You also need your own high priestess to now interpret Ambedkar for you. To tell you what was right and wrong with Ambedkar. To force you to even start reading him. How long will this go on man, just how long!"[6] Kumar here excoriates a non-Dalit audience who engages with Dalit voices and politics through "mediated" forms such as translations and films and who ostensibly don't or won't read Ambedkar until a member of their own ranks—here, Roy—urges them to. Later, in an address to a conference at the University of Mumbai called "The Collective Dilemma of Left, Right, and Centre: What to Do with Ambedkar?" also published on *Round Table India*, Kumar continues,

> My question was about this whole narrative that was being built around this book; "Ambedkar needs an introduction. Ambedkar needs to go west. The upper caste people need to engage with Ambedkar and that is why Arundhati Roy has to write this." That was the narrative being sold to us and that is what we are challenging. What I need to know first is what stopped Ambedkar from getting introduced until now? Dalits have been fighting for Ambedkar, carrying him all their lives. Why isn't he *already* a part of your academic or media discourses?

For Dalit thinkers like Kumar, the supposed "elevation" of Dalit literature to the status of world literature is not only irrelevant, it's an affront. This is because, as David Damrosch has explained, world literature is not a set canon of texts but what he calls instead "a mode of reading: a form of detached engagement with worlds beyond our own (read: Euro-American) place and time" (281). It is this detachment that is so troubling for many Dalit writers and thinkers, for Dalit literature demands anything *but* detachment; it is a call instead for political engagement and social revolution. What Dalit literature teaches us is that it is not only an impossibility but an *unethical* reading practice to engage merely in a "detached" way because this detached reading is an affront and a usurpation of both Dalit pain—from which their literature is born, according to their own critical frameworks—and, in the case of Ambedkar, the very specific labor of producing and disseminating *Annihilation of Caste*, for the masses, yes, but not for the world. In the discussion that follows I explore the ways in which both Prakash and Navaria critique the sympathetic aesthetic of detachment in their fiction by cannily manipulating and reemploting the "real life" biographies of Gandhi, Ambedkar, and Premchand, illustrating the critical possibilities of Dalit literature to represent not only in a realist way the lives of Dalits in India, but also to renegotiate the contemporary understanding of historical, political, and literary giants.

## THE POLITICS OF "REAL LIVES" IN DALIT FICTION

Hutcheon seeks to define postmodern narrative practice, considering "issues such as those of narrative form, of intertextuality, of strategies of representation, of the role of language, of the relation between historical fact and experiential event, and, in general, of the epistemological and ontological consequences of the act of rendering problematic what was once taken for granted by historiography—and literature" (xii). She seeks the places where literature and history overlap, and the explicit engagement with the constructed nature of both, to develop her understanding of "historiographic metafiction," which she argues manifests both thematically and formally for an ultimately ethical reevaluation of historical truth. She writes, "Postmodern fiction suggests that to re-write or to re-present the past in fiction and in history is, in both cases, to open it up to the present, to prevent it from being conclusive and teleological" (110). And further, "Postmodern intertextuality is a formal manifestation of both a desire to close the gap between past and present of the reader and a desire to rewrite the past in a new context" (118). In the cases of Prakash and Navaria and the ethical imperatives of their Dalit narratives, the desire is also to develop a new (or we might also say, Ambedkarite) perspective that questions the certainties of popular historical understanding—the hitherto unquestioned greatness of Gandhi, for example.

According to Eileen Williams-Wanquet, a scholar of British literature who has built on Hutcheon's conception of historiographic metafiction to understand postrealism as a particular narrative approach within a broader postmodern ideological context, if realist literature aims for the truthful representation of an external reality and if a postmodern text eschews realism to create its own reality, untethered to the truth of experience, then the postrealist text—situated between the others—"re-emplots facts that have been severed from the world, only to send them back to the world with new meaning" (393). She writes:

> As it attempts to find a new way of conveying the world, the "postrealist" novel of postmodernity incorporates historical characters and events (Hutcheon's "historiographic metafiction"), as well as characters and events from earlier fiction (Hutcheon's "modern parody"). . . . Postrealist texts tend to privilege intertextual parody, reproducing various texts with a difference. (392)

The following discussions of Uday Prakash's "Mohandas" and Ajay Navaria's "Hello, Premchand!" will illuminate the ways that both employ various postrealist and metafictional narrative strategies, creatively manipulating the intertexts of the biographical traces of three of the most significant interlocutors of the modern experience and politics of caste in India: M. K. Gandhi, B. R. Ambedkar, and "Munshi" Premchand.

## "MOHANDAS"

In 2005, the prolific Hindi novelist and short story writer Uday Prakash published a short novella called "Mohandas" in the monthly magazine *Hans*, the premier Hindi literary magazine in India and the world.[7] The issue in which he published the story was dedicated to the literary legacy of Munshi Premchand, the founding editor of *Hans* in 1930, and an icon of Indian letters in the twentieth century who wrote primarily in Hindi (but also sometimes in Urdu) and ushered in a new realist aesthetic into Hindi-Urdu prose with special attention to the material conditions of life as a rural, poor, and sometimes also "low caste" Indian.[8] Prakash's story does indeed echo Premchand strongly in its theme of an educationally and spiritually rich but economically poor "low caste" protagonist, outwitted and undone by the malevolent forces of casteist hierarchies and bureaucratic corruption. The narrator of Prakash's story is self-conscious about the specter of Premchand, whose thematic and stylistic traces color this new story and addresses the reader mid-story in the following metafictional aside:

> Let's stop here for a minute. I bet you're thinking that I'm taking advantage of the one hundred and twenty fifth anniversary of the birth of Premchand, the King of Hindi Fiction, to spin you some hundred-and-twenty-five-year-old story dressed up as a tale of today. But the truth is that the account I am putting before you, in its old and backward style, manner, and language, is a tale of a time right after 9/11, in the aftermath of the collapse of the World Trade Center in New York; a time when two sovereign Asian nations were reduced to ash and rubble. (68–69)[9]

The contemporary story of "a time right after 9/11" (and yet easily mistaken for a tale from another era) is of a man named Mohandas, poor and Dalit from a village in Chattisgarh but educated and hopeful and eligible for a public-sector job reserved for "Untouchables" like him. Yet he struggles to find a job as each new opportunity falls to nepotism, bribery, and other forms of corruption. When he finally secures a job at a mining company, a scheming Brahmin steals Mohandas's name, caste, and educational certificates and takes the job for himself, leaving Mohandas in a downward spiral of poverty and hopelessness without even the security of his identity. The struggle to reclaim his identity is tortuous and ultimately unsuccessful despite the support of a precious few: lawyers and judges and well-wishers, all of whom Prakash names after other important authors of twentieth-century Hindi fiction.

In addition to Premchand's animating traces—evident in the venue of the story's publication (the Premchand anniversary issue), the themes and literary style of the story, and the narrator's aside—the ghost of Mohandas Karamchand Gandhi also haunts the story, evident in the name of the protagonist and members of his family. Once again, the narrator simultaneously acknowledges and denies the story's resurrection of Gandhi in the author's second parenthetical "aside"—its status as marginalia to the story belied by its length at nearly a page and a half:

> (Please stop for a moment and tell the truth: did you begin to get the feeling that I'd gone and started telling you some kind of encoded, symbol-laden tale? The main character of the story is called Mohandas, the wife is Kasturibai, the mother is Putlibai and the son's name is Devdas . . . ?
>
> Kasturibai reminds you of Kasturba—and, well, Mohandas couldn't be more clear. If you read Mahatma Gandhi's autobiography, also known as *The Story of My Experiments with Truth*, you'll discover that his father, Karamchand, was also called Kaba. And his mother was Putlibai . . . and who

> doesn't know the tale of his son, Devdas? Look at Mohandas, his build, and the state he's in: he shares the same history as the Mahatma. The difference is that Mohandas looks the way he does not because of Porbandar—the place where Gandhi was born—or Kathiawar, Rajkot, England, South Africa, or Birla House, but as a result of the hunger and heat, sweat and sickness, insult and injustice in the fields and pastures, caverns and caves, jungles and marshes, of Chhattisgarh and Vindhya Pradesh. Otherwise, the rest is all the same. . . .
>
> You'll have to take my word, and don't read too much into it. It isn't some symbolic story or allegory or coded fable. It's totally on the level. Though, truth be told, it's not really a story. As I'm wont to do, I wind up detailing the real life of a real person—someone alive now, living among us in our society—concealing it behind the veil of a story. Mohandas is a living, breathing human being . . . Mohandas is real. If you'd like to verify this, you can do so by asking any inhabitant of our village, or any other village in this country.) (50–51)

This passage is emblematic of the self-conscious metafictional engagement of the narrator with his audience throughout Prakash's story, as well as a sustained play on narrative genre such that Prakash challenges our expectations of realism, metaphor, and allegory. He underscores the "reality" of his *kahaani* (story), a modern genre, and scoffs at our implied assumption that this belongs to the "older" forms of *prateek kathaa* (symbolic narrative), *rupak* (allegory), or *kootakhyaan* (symbolic fable). Instead, Prakash writes in the original Hindi version, "*Yeh to ek bilkul sapaat-sa kissa hai*" (this is a plain and simple story). And in the next breath, "*Balki sach to yeh hai ki yeh kissa bhi nahin hain*" (but the truth is this isn't really a story at all) (12).[10] Because, he writes, "*Mohandas ek asliyat hai*" (Mohandas is a reality) (12).[11] He is a "real" man whose neighbor stole his identity and ruined his life. But again, a beat later, Prakash challenges us to ask "*hamaare gaon ki nahi, is desh ke kisi bhi gaon ke kisi bhi vashinde se*" (any inhabitant of our village, or any other village in this country), forcing us right back into the terrain of the *kootakhyaan*, the *pratheek katha*, or the *rupak*—symbolic, metaphorical modes of narration all (12).

Such a playful destabilization of generic expectations and the sudden shifting of the narrative ground beneath the reader's feet by an overtly controlling narrator who problematizes the subjectivities of both the Gandhi of history (marked by the intertextual evocation of Gandhi's autobiography, *My Experiments with Truth*) and the Mohandas of the story suggests but refuses to confirm parallels between the two, which is consistent with postmodernism's critique of reality. Yet, unlike many postmodernist practitioners, Prakash is not interested in challenging the foundations of "reality" in his story but rather demands that we take a closer look at the artifice of socially determinative categories such as caste and class to recognize the reality of marginalization and exploitation in "any village" in India. But to convey this reality in its starkest terms Prakash relies not only on "realistic" description and detail but makes effective use of metaphor, symbol, and allegory. He skewers Premchand's realism even as he pays it homage, and simultaneously resurrects—as did Roy in her introduction to *Annihilation of Caste*—the historical figure of Mahatma Gandhi, reemplotting Gandhi's biography in a story that excoriates the very foundation of Gandhi's moralistic authority: his assertion that the soul of India resides in its villages. According to Alessandra Consolaro's analysis of "Mohandas," "This Dalit avatar of Gandhi finds himself again and again in a helpless situation, yet not even a single Gandhian activist or organization is made available in the story to help him . . . the text makes no allowance for any sympathetic argument about whatever is left of the Gandhian project in the contemporary world" (10).

Hutcheon has pointed to "a formal marking of historicity—both literary and worldly" as constitutive of what she terms historiographic metafiction, a kind of writing that at once grounds itself in the world while simultaneously "querying the very basis of the authority of that grounding" (5). She writes, "The intertextual parody of historiographic metafiction . . . offers a sense of the presence of the past, but this is a past that can only be known from its texts, its traces—be they literary or historical" (4). Both Roy and Prakash—in different ways in their respective texts—resurrect from historical traces the figure of Gandhi and the significant symbolic weight that his memory wields in India to destabilize the meanings of equality and independence and an ethical nationalism that have coalesced around him as a historical figure by offering two "real" alternatives to Gandhi himself: Ambedkar as a man with a more radical message of social equality and the character Mohandas as Gandhi's doppelgänger, brought to ruin by the failure of Gandhian idealism. As I have noted, Williams-Wanquet has described this practice of grounding a contemporary text in both an empirical past and a literary one as postrealist narrative: one that is neither fully mimetic (aiming to recreate "reality") nor postmodern (creating its own autonomous reality) but rather a narrative practice that "re-emplots facts that have been severed from the world, only to send them back into the world with new meaning" (393). The next thing we must ask is if a past can only be known from its texts, and if contemporary texts can intervene to rewrite or reemplot those texts from the past, can we in fact rewrite the past—if not empirical, then at least literary—itself? Williams-Wanquet continues, "Historiographic metafiction shows fiction to be historically conditioned and history to be discursively structured, and in the process manages to broaden the debate about the ideological implications of the Foucauldian conjunction of power and knowledge—for readers and for history itself as a discipline" (392). In the case of Prakash's story and also in empirical reality, as the metatextual attestations to the "reality" of Mohandas make clear, Mohandas might have otherwise been "lost to history" by way of his stolen identity and caste, class, and geographically based marginalization. It is only through narrative/fictionalized resurrection as *Gandhi* that Mohandas's story is recorded as history, and that Gandhi's legacy is rewritten, and reduced, in the present.

## "HELLO, PREMCHAND!"

The possibility of the postrealist rewriting of reality through historiographic metatextual play is addressed even more unabashedly in the 2009 story "Uttar Katha," by Ajay Navaria. *Uttar katha* literally means the story that serves as an answer or a response, but in order to avoid the inelegance of this phrase in English as well as to recognize the historical figure to whom Navaria is in fact responding, I translated the story with the title, "Hello, Premchand!" in *Unclaimed Terrain.* Navaria here creates a frame story in which the ghosts or specters or unnamed people who at first only "look like" Premchand and Ambedkar emerge out of historical sync and appear to a young typist, asking him to type up their new manuscripts. Inside this frame, in the story that the man who "looks like Premchand" asks the typist to type, Navaria principally retells the story of Mangal—engaging in a parodic retelling of the tale of the pitiable protagonist in one of Premchand's more famous short stories, "Dudh ka Dam" (The Price of Milk, first published in 1910) while also referencing and rewriting the fates of several of Premchand's Dalit characters from his other stories. In this savvy and literarily reflective story-within-a-story, a typist meets the specters of both Premchand and Ambedkar and types a story the Premchand look-alike presents to him that is meant as a "responding story" (*uttar katha*) to Premchand's "Dudh ka Dam." In Navaria's story, the Premchand look-alike "responds" to a single line quoted from "Dudh ka Dam": "whatever else may change in this world, Bhangis [sweepers] will always remain Bhangis" (125). But in this rewritten version of the famous Premchand story, written in a sympathetically realist style about a Dalit boy who shares with a stray dog table scraps from an "upper caste" house for his dinner, a Bhangi does not in fact remain so; instead, he is educated, leaves his village, becomes a government official, and returns to his village having succeeded in spite of his caste. This is a story enriched by its insight into the power of Dalit writers to change the literary landscape Dalit characters have typically inhabited. It is the point of view of the literary critic, fictionalized.

In Navaria's rewriting of Premchand's story, the orphan boy Mangal is buoyed by both his mother's dream that he should transcend his supposed fate as a Bhangi and only do work that brings him respect, as well as a community of relatives and teachers and well-wishers who encourage his education. A host of characters from Premchand's other famous "untouchable" stories published in the 1930s—including Ghisu and Madhav from "Kafan" (The Shroud), Halku from "Pus ki Raat" (January Night), Gangi and Jokhu from "Thakur ka Kuaan" (The Thakur's Well), and Ghasiram from "Sadgati" (Deliverance)—make telling cameo appearances as well. All of these characters are treated completely differently in Navaria's story than in Premchand's stories: unsympathetic "upper caste" characters in Premchand's stories become champions of Dalits in Navaria's narrative. Dalit characters consigned to death or a hopeless existence in Premchand's stories are resurrected, educated, and politicized in "Hello, Premchand!"

At the end of Navaria's story, Mangal travels back to his village, returning as a respected government official to the place where his mother once shoveled shit. The story is set in its peculiar postrealist frame (set off by the action of "typing") in which a young typist meets the specters of both Premchand and Ambedkar, who give him rejoinders to the narratives of pity and condescension and fetishization that have dominated literary representations of Dalits from Premchand to Roy. Premchand, in the postrealist reality that Navaria's narrative strategies of resurrection and reemplotment envision, replaces Gandhi with Ambedkar as his ideological inspiration and consequently rewrites his most famously Gandhian stories on the subject of caste from an Ambedkarite perspective, while Ambedkar's writing is also influenced by Premchand's stories. Navaria's story rewrites literary history and thus effectively recasts the supposed inevitability of caste identities in modern India:

> It was a strange coincidence that as I finished typing, I met the gentleman [who looked like Premchand] again that same evening. This time he wasn't alone. There was another gentleman with him who looked just like Dr. Ambedkar. . . .
>
> "This great man is Dr. Ambedkar. Surely, you must recognize him?" The gentleman said, introducing the man next to him.
>
> "Babasaheb!" I lurched forward and grabbed his hand.
>
> "Here, read this! . . . After reading several of Premchandji's stories, I drew some conclusions. In 1941, I gave this speech at the annual meeting of the Bombay Municipal Worker's Union."
>
> "You have to read this with the story . . . this is the placenta and the umbilical cord. These come out at birth with the child." The gentleman who looked like Premchand patted my shoulders. "Come, let's sing together the national anthem of Independent India." He took my hand and walked ahead. (153–54)

In this extraordinary rewriting of history in the present, Navaria imagines a dialogue between Premchand and Ambedkar, and the kind of social and literary politics of political engagement and Dalit *chetna* that Premchand *might have had* had he been able to read Ambedkar (*Annhilation of Caste* was written in 1936, the same year that Premchand died). Navaria here not only rewrites Premchand's stories from the early decades of the twentieth century but actually resurrects the ghost of Premchand himself to do it, newly awake as he is (in Navaria's imagination) in Ambedkarite anticaste ideology. In other words, Navaria reimagines the historical exchange of ideas between the real-life figures of Gandhi, Premchand, and Ambedkar, and reemplots this exchange in the present, enabling a complete rewriting of literary history in light of a more radical and contemporary political understanding of caste and the power of fiction to produce new wrinkles in the fabric of the real. As Williams-Wanquet explains, "History is critically re-evaluated in the light of the present, by fictionally revisiting its textualized remains" (267). In the postrealist fiction of *both* Navaria and Prakash, the history that is being reevaluated is the literary history of Dalit representation itself, as well as the previously unassailable political legacy of Gandhian attitudes toward caste.

## CONCLUSION

Various processes of reinvention have been at the heart of the contemporary Dalit movement from its inception. A case in point is wresting the very term "Dalit" from its context as a hateful epithet and investing in this term a new set of meanings to include a person with a politicized consciousness who rejects the narrative of inferiority on which he or she was raised and seeks a new, universal equality. According to Badri Narayan, a historian of the Dalit movement,

> To fulfill the need for a past to suit their purpose, the social and historical meaning of the Dalit past is being re-created and reinvented. In this process, the past is intrinsically built into the present; it becomes the subject of present reflection and re-construction as a primary mechanism for changing the marginalized social position of Dalits. Thus, their past is one that helps in their ongoing struggle of carving out their future against an oppressive present, constructing an identity that grants them the self-respect to elevate themselves above their present, still largely socially degraded status. (171)

Such temporal shifting—and the uncanny renarration of historical lives from the past (Gandhi, Ambedkar, and Premchand in these stories, and in Roy's book, too, though to somewhat different effect due to the political exigencies of the present), who are then reemplotted in the "oppressive present" to point toward a more ideal future—proves a critical intervention in these recent examples of Hindi fiction about Dalits[12] that pushes Dalit literature out of its established realist and modernist frameworks, and their attendant modes of sympathetically detached reading, and toward new postmodern, postrealist possibilities.

## NOTES

1. This focus is present in nearly everything Navaria has written, and for Uday Prakash in particular his novella *Pīli Chhatari Walī Laḍkī* and the stories collected in *The Walls of Delhi: Three Novellas*.
2. Ajay Navaria is a Dalit and a leading voice in the contemporary Hindi Dalit literary sphere. Uday Prakash, by contrast, is not a Dalit but engages nonetheless in a political critique of caste in the story I will analyze here as well as others. In conversation, he has explained to me his sense of isolation from the Dalit literary sphere since he does not share the same caste identity. Similarly, and also in conversation, Ajay Navaria is quick to name Uday Prakash as a major influence on his own writing.
3. For a more detailed discussion of the limitations of the language of sympathy in the context of representations of Dalits, see Gupta, *Gender.*
4. For examples see Valmiki's *Dalit* and Limbale.
5. For a more thorough discussion of the constitutive role of the Jat-Pat Todak Mandal in the twentieth-century discourse of caste, see Gupta, "Speaking Self," published in this same volume.
6. He refers here to the English translation, by Arun Prabha Mukherjee, of Valmiki's Hindi autobiography titled *Joothan*. *Fandry* is a 2013 Marathi-language film about young love reaching across caste divisions, directed by Nagraj Manjule.

   Another essay of the same name by Anoop Kumar appears in the 2015 publication *Hatred in the Belly* that does not include these comments, which can still be accessed at the *Round Table India* website.
7. In this paper I quote from Jason Grunebaum's excellent translation of Prakash's collection of stories titled *The Walls of Delhi*, with additional references to the original Hindi.
8. Premchand's best-known "untouchable" stories include "Kafan" (The Shroud), "Dudh ka Daam" (The Price of Milk), "Sadgati" (Deliverance), and "Thakur ka Kuaan" (The Thakhur's Well).
9. This nod toward twenty-first-century American imperialism as a marker of modernity is emulated in a different story by Ajay Navaria (who has often commented on Prakash's influence on his own writing). In the story "New Custom" in the collection *Unclaimed Terrain*, Navaria writes, "On the television set, an international channel was now showing pictures of Saddam Hussein. . . America was making him an example to the world, issuing a warning" (74). In these metafictional details that nod toward contemporary events, both Prakash and Navaria point out the irony of the existence of feudalistic caste oppression in a modern, globalized world, while also making a parallel commentary on power and its abuses by the powerful.
10. Here I provide a more literal translation of the Hindi than Grunebaum's literary one quoted previously. I am analyzing the sudden shift of narrative ground between what is "real" and what is "fiction," and I want to make the narrative mechanics of that clear.

11. Mohandas's status as "real" is also underscored in the paratext of this translation by Grunebaum's own afterword, in which he describes his trip with Prakash to his home state of Chhattisgarh: "I suppose I shouldn't have been surprised that as we were leaving town, Prakash, seeing a man on the road walking toward us, said, 'Oh, there's Mohandas.' And so it was: the man who he had based his character on, looking just as haggard and resilient as described in the story. We stopped, spoke at length, took some photos, and went on" (223–24).
12. I say this instead of "Hindi Dalit Literature" again to acknowledge the fact that Uday Prakash is not a Dalit. However I hope by now, after this examination of the interplay of stylistics and narrative strategies in Navaria's and Prakash's works, that it is clear how "Dalit Literature," if defined by the caste identities of its authors, is an unsatisfying and restrictive category that in fact hinders us from engaging with the ways in which authors can creatively articulate a critique of caste. Without disavowing the political import of the intervention of Dalit voices in the literary sphere, this article may be read also as a case for a more expansive understanding of the category of Dalit literature.

## WORKS CITED


Anand, S. "Book Launch: *Annihilation of Caste* 15th March 2014." *YouTube*, uploaded by India Habitat Centre Lodhi Road, 3 Apr. 2014, www.youtube.com/watch?v=GzHRvS1DVPs. Accessed 17 May 2017.

Brueck, Laura. *Writing Resistance: The Rhetorical Imagination of Hindi Dalit Literature*. Columbia UP, 2014.

Consolaro, Alessandra. "Resistance in the Postcolonial Hindi Literary Field: *Mohan Dās* by Uday Prakāś." *Orientalia Suecana*, vol. LX, 2011, pp. 9–19.

Damrosch, David. *What Is World Literature?*. Princeton UP, 2003.

Gajarawala, Toral. *Untouchable Fictions: Literary Realism and the Crisis of Caste*. Fordham UP, 2012.

"The Greatest Indian after Gandhi." *Outlook*, 11 June 2012, www.outlookindia.com/magazine/story/the-greatest-indian-after-gandhi/281103. Accessed 17 May 2017.

Gupta, Charu. *The Gender of Caste: Representing Dalits in Print*. U of Washington P, 2016.

———. "Speaking Self, Writing Caste: Recovering the Life of Santram BA." *Caste and Life Narratives*, ed. S. Shankar and Charu Gupta, Primus Books, 2019, pp. 19–46.

Guha, Ramachandra. *India after Gandhi: The History of the World's Largest Democracy*. HarperCollins, 2007.

Hutcheon, Linda. *A Poetics of Postmodernism: History, Theory, Fiction*. Routledge, 1988.

Kumar, Anoop. "The Collective Dilemma of Left, Right, and Centre: What to Do with Ambedkar?" *Round Table India*, 15 June 2015, http://roundtableindia.co.in/index.php?option=com_content&view=article&id=8199:how-can-they-say-they-are-above-caste&catid=119&Itemid=132. Accessed 11 May 2017.

———. "Resisting a Messiah." *Hatred in the Belly: Politics Behind the Appropriation of*

*Dr. Ambedkar's Writings*, by the Ambedkar Age Collective, The Shared Mirror, 2015, pp. 112–14.

———. "Resisting a Messiah." *Round Table India*, 4 Mar. 2014, www.roundtableindia.co.in/index.php?option=com_content&view=article&id=7263:you-are-already-a-messiah-ms-roy&catid=119:feature&Itemid=132. Accessed 17 May 2017.

Limbale, Sharankumar. *Towards an Aesthetics of Dalit Literature: History, Controversies, and Considerations*. Translated by Alok Mukherjee, Orient Longman, 2004.

Narayan, Badri. "De-Marginalisation and History: Dalit Re-invention of the Past." *South Asia Research*, vol. 28, no. 2, 2008, pp. 169–84.

Navaria, Ajay. *Unclaimed Terrain*. Translated by Laura Brueck, Navayana Publications, 2013.

Prakash, Uday. "Mohandas." *The Walls of Delhi*. Translated by Jason Grunebaum, UWA Publishing, 2012, pp. 43–132.

———. *Mohandas*. Vani Prakashan, 2006.

Roy, Arundhati. "The Doctor and the Saint." *Annihilation of Caste: The Annotated Critical Edition*, edited by S. Anand, Navayana, 2014, pp. 15–180.

Shanmugavelan, Murali. "Arundhati Roy's Book on Caste Rejected by Some Anti-Caste Activists." *The Independent*, 16 Dec. 2014, www.independent.co.uk/arts-entertainment/books/features/arundhati-roy-s-book-on-caste-rejected-by-some-anti-caste-activists-9929233.html. Accessed 26 June 2016.

Valmiki, Omprakash Prakash. *Dalit Sāhitya kā Saundaryashāstra*, Radhakrishna Prakashan, 2001.

———. *Joothan: An Untouchable's Life*. Translated by Arun Prabha Mukherjee, Columbia UP, 2003.

Williams-Wanquet, Eileen. "Towards Defining 'Postrealism' in British Literature." *Journal of Narrative Theory*, vol. 36, no. 3, Fall 2006, pp. 389–419.

# Lives in Visual and Performance Cultures

# 6

## *PERIYAR* AS A BIOPIC
## Star Persona, Historical Events, and Politics

SWARNAVEL ESWARAN

What do we expect when we go to watch a biopic? In most cases, "a slice of history" would be the immediate response, which then leads to questions regarding the challenges of representing history through a (sometimes larger than life) protagonist and the balancing of the personal and the political or the domestic and the public. The biopic of Periyar E. V. Ramasami, the radical leader from South India, offers an ideal space for an interesting and absorbing narrative, as his life, both in the private and the public spheres, was consistently marked by provocative and subversive acts aimed at challenging the status quo of a highly conservative, religious, and casteist society through his championing the cause of *suyamariyathai*—"self-respect" for historically discriminated castes or *jathigal*. The challenges inherent in reducing sociopolitical complexities to a catalogue of dramatic events in the life of a radical leader are understandable. Nonetheless, and ironically, the biopic on Periyar's eventful life is dull and tedious. The lackluster quality of the film sheds light on the problems of depicting a leader of the masses through a star persona. A star persona has a different kind of mass appeal generated through a corpus of films that rely on the star as a commodity and as cultural capital. The status quo of the star himself, therefore, is at odds with the impulse toward anarchy that underlies the radicalism of a leader like Periyar. The dichotomy identified here begs a detailed interrogation of the manner in which key events are reenacted through the figure of the star.

This essay, therefore, engages with the biopic *Periyar* to analyze how history is represented through the life of one of the most significant revolutionary figures in Indian politics of the last century. It focuses on the representation of the key events in the life of Periyar, a honorific (meaning "great") conferred on E. V. Ramasami by Dalit women. Periyar E. V. Ramasami was a member of the Justice Party and the Congress Party before starting his own party,

Dravidar Kazhagam (Federation of the Dravidians, hereafter referred to as DK), and the biopic retells his vibrant story through the persona of a leading star of Tamil cinema—Sathyaraj. Periyar was an unparalleled social reformer who fought relentlessly against caste and religion and for the equality of women and the downtrodden.[1] A detailed analysis of the narrativization of the life and times of such an iconic figure would shed light on sociopolitical history and also enhance our understanding of the way a biopic engages with the reenactments of historically significant moments. Periyar was a radical leader who tried to dismantle the rigid structures of caste hierarchy among the Hindus by challenging oppression in the name of religion and foregrounding the voices of the people in the peripheries and the fringes.

The biopic as a genre has often been criticized, particularly when it adopts the historical drama structure, because it simplifies the complexity of life into a narrative with a neat beginning, middle, and end (Rosenstone 123). As a genre, the biopic has also garnered critical attention relatively late—George Custen's book *Bio/Pics: How Hollywood Constructed Public History* was published only in 1992. Almost two decades later, Dennis Bingham's 2010 book, *Whose Lives Are They Anyway: The Biopic as Contemporary Film Genre*, as the title suggests, astutely argues that the biopic has come a long way through films like *Citizen Kane*, *The Karen Carpenter Story*, and *The Notorious Bettie Page.* From the days of the classical Hollywood idiom-driven biopics *The Story of Louis Pasteur* and *The Life of Emile Zola*, to the contemporary times of the postmodern biopic, such as *I'm Not There* with its self-reflexivity and parody, the genre has broken new ground. It experiments with form and relates to an informed audience that gets more than its quota of linear, classical biopics from television (even as television also undermines the aura surrounding the celebrity through gossip, rumor, and talk and reality shows, and distances its viewers from unconditionally accepting naive hagiography as it might have in the past).

In the Indian context, too, the biopic has come a long way from *Dr. Kotnis Ki Amar Kahani* to films like *Bandit Queen*, *Bose: The Forgotten Hero*, *Gandhi: My Father*, *The Dirty Picture*, *Paan Singh Tomaar*, *Bhaag Milkha Bhaag*, and *Mary Kom.* The recent interest of Indian audiences seems to be veering toward narratives of sports celebrities, as exemplified by the huge box-office success of the last three films listed. However, it is in the realm of the biographies of politicians (and their families), as in the case of *Gandhi: My Father*, that personas are deconstructed and stereotypical hagiography is challenged. In the context of *Periyar*, Shekar Kapoor's biopic on Phoolan Devi, *Bandit Queen* is a significant film, as Phoolan's revenge against the "upper caste" Rajputs is spurred by the unjust and violent oppression she has to endure as a woman belonging to a "lower caste." *Bandit Queen*'s narrative thus resonates with Periyar's simultaneous preoccupation with women's empowerment and the abolition of caste. Nevertheless, as a film, *Bandit Queen* substantially differs from *Periyar* in its realism-driven aesthetics, particularly in its disavowal of the typical song and action sequence of the popular *dakoo*/dacoit genre film. This is perhaps because it was produced by Britain's Channel 4 and, therefore, was made for a transnational audience, unlike *Periyar*, which primarily targeted the local audience in Tamilnadu. Seema Biswas, who was a relative newcomer with a background in theater, became a celebrity as she won the national award for her performance in/as *Bandit Queen*.[2] Usually, however, as we can see from the list of films above, the already established star or the actor who plays the protagonist in a classical biopic, as in the case of *Periyar*, becomes arguably as important as the director. This essay will, therefore, engage in detail with the Tamil star Sathyaraj's performance as the protagonist in *Periyar*.

As far as biopics in Tamil are concerned, the most popular ones have been films like *Veerpandiya Kattabomman* (Kattabomman, the Brave Warrior), which mainly drew from the legends surrounding a chieftain who challenged and fought against the British, and *Kappalottiya Thamizhan* (The Tamizhan Who Steered a Ship), which was again a narrative about a patriot who rebelled against the British. *Kappalottiya Thamizhan* was based on the biography of V. O. Chidamabram Pillai, written by Ma. Po. Sivagnanam, who was involved in politics as well as literature. The film was more of a melodrama, though it meticulously restaged some of the significant events during the British rule of India. There were also films like *Sivagangai Seemai* (The Border of Sivaganga), which focused on the lives of the Marudu brothers, who challenged British rule. Unlike *Veerapandiya Kattabomman*, *Sivagangai Seemai* was less spectacular; it pursued realism within its own fictive universe.

We must view *Periyar* through this Tamil cinematic context. The director of *Periyar*, Gnana Rajasekaran, had directed a biopic on the Tamil poet Bharathiyar, *Bharathi*, which was also episodic but focused mainly on Bharathiyar's politics as a rebel. For instance, Bharathiyar's investment in projects of translation and his spirituality as a poet were omitted to delineate issues surrounding caste and oppression. Unlike in *Periyar*, Rajasekaran elides certain key events and personalities in Bharathiyar's short life of thirty-eight years even if the narrative, through a flashback, covers his life from childhood onward. In *Periyar*, however, Rajasekaran is not able to make clear choices regarding the time periods he focuses on since he wants to engage with all the key moments in Periyar's life that were instrumental in changing the course of history in Tamilnadu. He strives to offer an insight into the radical politics of his humane protagonist by juxtaposing him with the casteism, religious beliefs, conservatism, and prejudices of Hindu majoritarian society. As a result, *Periyar* is a catalog of vignettes from Periyar's eventful life.

Rajasekaran comes from an unusual background: he is a retired Indian Administrative Service (IAS) officer. The film, too, has an unusual history: it was mainly funded by the ruling government in Tamilnadu. Given this structure of funding, my essay also explores how financial support from the state has affected the film both in its narrative (in terms of the choice of sequences) and reception. Toward this end, my essay will consider the beginning—the first fifteen minutes of the film to be precise—wherein Sathyaraj plays the young Periyar, and the concluding scene where Karunanidhi is foregrounded as the chief minister. Then I will delve into the body of the film to discuss the representation of Periyar's interventions in the public sphere to spread his radical messages about social reform. The final segment of the essay will engage with Periyar's unconventional and provocative acts of radicalism and their representation in the film.

## EPISODIC BIOPIC

*Periyar* narrates its subject's life from his youth until his death at the age of ninety-four in 1973. Because of this chronology, perhaps, the narrative is episodic in structure and struggles with a compilation model wherein every key event is showcased as a two- to four-minute scene. The first fifteen minutes give us an idea of the film's long and contrived structure: the film begins with an elderly man waking up the sleeping Ramasami (Sathyaraj) because his mother, Chinna Thayamma (Manorama), has been searching for him. As Ramasami reluctantly gets up and puts on his silk clothes and head gear and joins his mother, we see that she is busy in a puja. She interrogates the priest regarding the prospects of her son's marriage. When the priest says that the auspicious time has arrived, Ramasami, sitting near his mother, seeks her attention. He touches her on her shoulder, leading her to ask him if he has taken a bath. When he replies in the negative, she rushes off upset to remove the "impurity" by taking a bath again. Subsequently, a nonchalant Ramasami learns that the people standing around him and participating in the puja are all involved with astrology or palmistry; he plays a prank on the priest, who advises him regarding the rigid hands of destiny, by pulling down the cord that holds the wooden venetian blind. The heavy blind comes down on the head of the priest as Ramasami smiles. As Tamilinian points out in his blog, according to Periyar's biographer Sami Chidambaranar, this event occurred when Ramasami was twelve years old. The star Sathyaraj is manifestly too old for this prank scene. This opening scene, thus, sets the tone of the film: *Periyar* will take liberties with history in combining the personal—in this case, his background as hailing from an orthodox conservative Naicker family—and juxtaposing it with the political, his rebellion and challenging of the traditions predicated on superstition, religion, and most importantly caste/casteism.

In the next scene, an apparently bored Ramasami walks through the drawing room, where guests are busy in a feast, and moves toward priests chanting

Sanskrit mantras, such as Vishnu Sahasranamam (the one thousand names of Lord Vishnu). This time it is his father, Venkata Naicker (Sathyanarayana), who is seated on a long chair in front of the chanting priests with closed eyes. The mischievous Ramasami pats the backs of the priests, who stop their chanting, and starts chanting his own (concocted) mantras. When his absorbed father opens his eyes and beamingly asks his apparently religious son, "Rama, how do you know these mantras?" Ramasami, making fun of his father's credulity, says, "Father, I've been listening to these from my childhood. . . . Besides, there are only ten or fifteen sentences, and one can easily concoct a version. . . . As you don't know the language, I get away with my fakery."[3] The angry father asks him to get out. This scene continues to portray Ramasami's humor before he gradually transforms into a more serious rebel and radical thinker. Periyar's subversive politics were characterized by always being in the public sphere and, therefore, humor was a useful tool to him in making people reflect on their own naivety and prejudices. While scenes like this help to gradually set up Periyar's skeptical character, as expressed through his laziness, bored reactions, and nonchalance, which is juxtaposed with humor, it also underscores Rajasekaran's objective of making a popular film on Periyar rather than an artistic or alternative film. The body language and mannerisms of popular actor Sathyaraj are retooled to reinvent a Periyar persona that could appeal to the regular Tamil filmgoer.

The song "Idai Thaluvi Kolla" (To Fondle My Waist) that follows not only appeals to a mass audience but also undermines our expectations of biopics insofar as it engages seriously with Periyar's radical views and provokes discussions among younger audiences. In fact, the lyrics, music, and choreography remind us of the songs of an earlier studio era where a seductive song by a courtesan was a highlight meant to draw in the audience both through the song and the dance and also by showcasing the studio interiors, production design, and lighting. Later in film history, the courtesan appearing in this typically fleeting scene evolved into a staple of Tamil cinema: the vamp or femme fatale. In *Periyar*, the narrative tries to validate the song situation by portraying a Ramasami disinterested in the dance and the women, and by underscoring his pragmatic sense in the way he calculates the income received by the musicians and the dancers to conclude that dancing for the feudal clientele is an unprofitable venture.

This dance, performed by actress Ragasya, to the lyrics "*Idai thaluvi kolla / Jadai thadavi kolla / Zameen ezuthikkodu seemane*" (To fondle my waist / To stroke my braids / Grant me your land, O gentleman/landlord), recalls the popular song "O! Rasikkum Seemane" (Oh! Gentleman Spectator) from *Parasakthi* by invoking the *seeman* (gentleman). Here it is worth noting that *Parasakthi*'s dialogue was written by M. Karunanidhi, whom the film thanks in the initial credit titles. However, in *Parasakthi*, the artifice of the song is validated, as it is part of a sequence that reveals how the protagonist Gunasekaran is relieved of his money when he arrives in an independent India to participate in his younger sister Kalyani's marriage. R. Sudarsanam's music, M. S. Rajeswari's melodious voice, and Kumari Kamala's dance have made "O! Rasikkum Seemane" an iconic song of seduction in Tamil cinema's history, whereas the song in *Periyar* is unexceptional in its rendering on the screen. This song seems out of place in the narrative due to its lackluster quality. If the intention was to showcase Ramasami as a practical young man from a wealthy business family who, unlike his peers in the song, is not a philanderer, the notion does not come through effectively. The stereotypical song, then, illustrates that *Periyar* is an episodic biopic targeted at mainstream Tamil cinema audiences who expect customary features like item numbers. The song also prefigures the difficulty of navigating between the trenchant radical politics of a revolutionary figure and the box-office demands to keep the audience entertained through humor, song, and dance.

The first three sequences reveal the difficulty inherent in biopics of prioritizing and representing through anecdotes some of the key events in the protagonist's life. One could argue that *Periyar* is a tapestry of vignettes presenting dramatic moments in Periyar's life. On the one hand, it aspires to a smooth narration where one event seamlessly follows the other and, on the other hand, it wants to capture Periyar's interventions, which were ruptures in this apparent seamlessness and superficial coherence. For instance, in the above song-and-dance sequence where we see women soliciting men and the dancer seducing her wealthy clients, Ramasami's inquiry about the cost of the fruit and the fees paid to the women and the accompanying musicians for their services is uncomfortable for the viewer, mainly because of the banality surrounding the stereotypical song and its picturization. The sequence reminds us of M. Madhava Prasad's notion of assemblage in the context of popular Hindi cinema's "heterogeneous mode of production," wherein disparate parts that are produced in relative isolation are put together, and as exemplified by the song picturization—lyrics, music, choreography, and dance—in this sequence (42–45).

The fourth sequence begins with the (child) marriage of Venkata Naicker's sister's daughter, Ammayi. When Ramasami affectionately invites his foster mother, sitting alone in the corner of an adjacent room, to participate in the wedding, she declines: "I should not participate in an auspicious event [like this]. You go [inside]." Ramasami's silent and poignant reaction indicates his disapproval at this exclusion of a poor widow. As an extension of such awareness of discrimination, Ramasami is also portrayed as reacting to his mother's scolding him when he engages in a conversation with his cousin Nagammai (Jyothirmayi), who expresses her love for him and promises to be his Nalayini—the mythological character from the Mahabharatha who served her husband, the leprosy-afflicted sage Maudgalya, with devotion. Ramasami retorts by questioning the hypocrisy of his now-affluent mother disclaiming a past when his father was an ordinary mason linked to Nagammai's family who had helped them. This sequence represents a shift in the tone of the film. The humor in the earlier scenes gives way to seriousness on Ramasami's part as he shouts at his mother (and father) in front of his relatives and the guests, and showcases his anger at the discrimination against his foster mother/widow and his uncle's less affluent family. In contrast to Ramasami's justified anger, the background music, ripe with melodramatic pathos during the sequence with the foster mother, segues into the Tamil cinema staple of the chanted marriage mantra: "*Mangalyam tantunanene mama jeevitham hetuna / Kanthe badhnami subhage tvam jiva saradam satam*" (This is a sacred thread that is essential for my longevity / I tie this around your neck so that, O maiden of many auspicious features, we may live happily for a hundred years). The chanting of such a mantra for the longevity of a husband is immediately undermined, as the succeeding sequence reveals the sorry plight of the widowed child Ammayi. Nevertheless, as Ramasami had made clear through his ridicule earlier, the paradox would be lost on most audiences due to their unfamiliarity with the Sanskrit language.

Thereafter, to the wailing of the women on the soundtrack, Ramasami enters to discover Ammayi surrounded by lamenting older women, his parents, and other relatives uncontrollably weeping at the predicament of the widowed Ammayi. One of the women breaks the ice: "*Enna than irundhalum shastira samparathayappadi seyya vendiyathai senchuthane aaganu*" (Whatever it may be, we have to follow the tradition and the customary rituals). The women surrounding Ammayi break her colorful bangles by forcefully banging her wrists together. Ramasami expresses his shock and dismay at the way they aggressively wipe away the bindi on her forehead and remove the *thali* (marriage) necklace from around her neck. As the women try to remove the flowers in her hair, Ammayi runs toward Ramasami, who consoles her and warns the other women to leave the flowers as they are. He also tells them, "*Ammayikku nadanthathu kalayaname illai. Ava vasukku vanthathukkapuram unmayana kalayanatha naane panni vaikkiraen. Athu en poruppu*" (What happened in Ammayi's case was not a marriage. When she comes of age, I will organize her real marriage. That's my responsibility). This sequence depicts Ramasami's profound understanding of the oppression of women and also foretells his profound investment in their welfare.

In the next sequence, we see Venkata Naicker walking into his *mandi* (a wholesale shop), where his employees bow to him with respect. Next, a municipal officer with a folder in his hand arrives, questions Venkata Naicker about his new *choultry* (a resting place for visitors where often free food is provided as part of charity, a common custom that successful businessmen observe) near the railway station, and expresses his intention to visit the site to calculate the tax. Ramasami observes his anxious father getting up from his seat and offering it to the officer, and asking an employee "to pack a little of everything" in his shop and deliver it as a gift to the officer's house. Ramasami is perplexed at his father's subservience, as his father is the municipal counselor and the officer is only a bill collector in the municipal office. The experienced accountant explains his father's strange behavior: "We may have the [financial] status, but upper caste is upper caste and lower caste is lower caste." Again we see a brooding and dismayed Ramasami in a mid-close shot at the end of the sequence. Although this scene engages with caste hierarchy and prefigures his lifelong struggle against the oppression and evil of the caste system, Ramasami is too old for such a revelation in the Indian context. As Kuzhali points out in his blog, Ramasami would have been exposed to such behavior from childhood.

The six sequences discussed above run for approximately fifteen minutes and give us an idea of the structure and length of *Periyar*. Each scene in the episodic biopic on average runs between two and four minutes. The narrative thereafter is an expansion and a variation on the themes of Periyar's crusades against superstitions, conservative traditions, religion, oppression of women, and casteism through vignettes of key events from his life. The classical format of generally establishing or setting up a scene with a long or mid-long shot, then covering the bulk of the drama through mid-shots, and finally closing with a close or mid-close shot remains generally unchanged and predictable through many of the sequences until the end. One reason for such a predictable technique could be the difficulty of making a period film that traverses substantially back in time. Since Periyar was born in 1879, *Periyar* has to travel back more than a century to stage events that occurred during his youth. Accordingly, a minimal style of sequencing events would offer fewer problems in terms of authentically recreating the past through production design for a film with a modest budget like *Periyar*.

## STAR PERSONA

The opening sequences of *Periyar* inform us that Rajasekaran's biography of Periyar is neither a reinterpretation nor an attempt to retool his ideas for contemporary times but a chronicling of events in a classical format with songs to cater to a large audience. The collaboration of stars is not unusual in historical-event-driven biopics. For instance, the protagonist of *Dr. Babasaheb Ambedkar* is Malayalam star Mammooty; similarly, *Sardar* featured the popular character actor Paresh Raval; *Elizabeth* had the versatile Cate Blanchett; and *Lincoln* had Academy Award–winner Daniel Day-Lewis, to mention a few. However, Sathyaraj's donning of Periyar's role marks this particular biopic's difference, too. In the scenes discussed above, Sathyaraj plays a young man by wearing a wig, an act that recalls the trope of old heroes, well beyond their fifties, playing college students in many Tamil films. College campuses usually provide the backdrop for romance in these films; in *Periyar*, however, the real education for Ramasami takes place on the stage of life. The fictive realism of the film gets diluted due to the star text of Sathyaraj—a popular villain turned hero who gradually transformed himself into a character actor by the late 1990s. Just before the release of *Periyar* in 2007, Sathyaraj had played the on-screen father to real-life son and young hero Sibiraj in films like *Jore* and *Vetrivel Shakthivel*. To see Sathyaraj, who has often appeared bald on screen, playing a young Periyar in his twenties calls for our willing suspension of disbelief. Such a suspension becomes possible because of Tamil cinema's habitual portrayal of toupee-wearing older stars performing as young men.

At the same time, such casting also means imagining youth in the garb of the persona of the star. Often the costume, body language, gestures, voice, and dialogue of the star subsume the freshness and energy of young people. In other words, the explicit artifice of the star obstructs the audience's ability to be absorbed into the fictive world of the protagonist. In the case of *Periyar*, Sathyaraj as a star remains outside, despite his deep investment as an actor in the film and his belief in and adherence to Periyar's ideology in real life. He—as much as the audience—is a witness to the happenings within Periyar's family. This witnessing helps the narrative by having Ramasami observe events that shape the Periyar persona, but it also interferes with our identifying with the protagonist and becoming a part of his journey—the persistent struggle against the deeply entrenched caste system that many Tamilians across the board agree to be a part of. While Sathyaraj's Kongu Tamil Kovai dialect (Coimbatore style delivery of Tamil) suits the film, as Periyar was from Erode near Coimbatore, this dialogue shifts our attention from the lived reality of the young Ramasami to the star charisma because of our familiarity as a Tamil audience with Sathyaraj's dialogue delivery. Sathyaraj's persona interferes and creates other kinds of expectations in a manner reminiscent of Oliver Stone's biopic *W*, as discussed by Edward Luce:

> But, much like *Nixon*, Stone's previous presidential biopic—where you cannot help wondering whether Anthony Hopkins is about to turn into Hannibal Lecter and eat Henry Kissinger's liver for breakfast—Stone's *W* teeters on the brink of *Animal House*. . . . Played semi-convincingly by Josh Brolin, Stone's W is a tragic-comic fool. . . . With the exception of Richard Dreyfuss's Dick Cheney, who captures the vice-president's militantly laconic mien, Stone's characters never slough off their cardboard cut-outs.

Bernard Weinraub in the *New York Times* says that even a veteran like Anthony Hopkins found his role in the biopic on Nixon "the hardest of his 35-year career":

> Seated in his trailer during a lunch break, the actor said he was concentrating on the Nixon voice and accent. Even off camera, Mr. Hopkins tries to walk and talk and gesture like the former President. Yet the role seems to torment Mr. Hopkins, who wears only a fake hair piece and false teeth to hint at a physical resemblance to Nixon. (Mr. Stone said, "I didn't want makeup to get in the way of his ability to allow people to look into him.")

The two passages above inform us of a star's commitment to the biopic as an opportunity to get into the shoes of a larger-than-life personality; they also draw attention to how the star persona, predicated primarily on the significant roles the star has played thus far, subsumes any such role and creates expectations/imaginings even if the director is careful, unlike Rajasekaran, of the makeup not getting in the way of our identification with the protagonist. Additionally, historical dramas come under rigorous scrutiny for the dialects and accents of the actors, as the style of the written as well as spoken language becomes a marker of time/history. For instance, Sathyaraj's Kovai dialect, popularized by the seminal screen writer K. Bhagyaraj and versatile actresses like Kovai Sarala, is embedded in the Tamil cinema imaginary as privileging humor and fluidity through its conspicuous extravagance, unlike the more rural-oriented and hierarchy-driven Tirunelveli dialect. *Periyar* is unorganized in terms of its dialogue delivery: when compared to Ramasami, his mother Chinna Thayamma's dialect lacks the Kovai slant, and his father Venkata Naicker's, with its dominant nasal base tone, sounds professionally dubbed from Telugu.

This problem is not limited to *Periyar.* For instance, Peter Bradshaw's review in *The Guardian* of Stone's *Alexander* emphasizes this crucial aspect:

> Alexander grows to be a sensitive, but fiercely ambitious, visionary youth; Colin Farrell plays him with his natural Irish accent rather than all-American or Bardspeak Brit. Very oddly, however, to cover any anomaly, Stone gets Val Kilmer playing his father King Philip to speak with an Irish accent as well, and Jared Leto has to do the same thing playing Alexander's friend Hephaistion. Interestingly, his formidable mother Olympia, played by Angelina Jolie, speaks as if she runs an Italian restaurant. This is one of the most scary performances currently to be seen in the cinema: she is like Anthony Perkins' mom in *Psycho*. With a mommie dearest like Angie, you too would rather hazard everything in battle rather than come in for your tea.

While the disparateness of the voices reflexively draws our attention to the difficulty of staging history for the screen on a modest budget, Stone as quoted in *The Guardian* points to the real problems of dramatizing such unwieldy characters as Alexander:

> According to Screendaily.com he told an audience at the Moroccan event: The script was just too ambiguous, too questioning about an action-hero

> who was masculine/feminine. . . . These are tough qualities in Hollywood. . . . It's just too big a life. It doesn't fit in into [*sic*] the Hollywood formula.

Periyar's "just too big" a life also poses a substantial challenge for anybody venturing into his biography.

By adopting an episodic format that is monotonous and repetitive, without any differentiation in its rhythm according to the depth of the events (for instance, by attending to his crusade against caste and religion), *Periyar* impedes its audience from seeing beyond the image of Sathyaraj: the image of the actor collides with the image he tries to embody or project. Think of Spike Lee's *Malcolm X*: Denzel Washington, too, was popular, having acted in films like *Mo' Better Blues* and *Mississippi Masala* just prior to *Malcolm X*. In terms of radical politics and charisma, Malcolm X's life could make for the best comparison with Periyar's. In *Malcolm X*, the narrative singularly focuses on race and the mobilization of his community by the black nationalist leader and human rights activist. In *Gandhi*, too, Attenborough never loses sight of Gandhi's mobilization of the Indian masses and his fight against the British. Both biopics made the difficult choice of excluding certain events and personalities in favor of a particular goal. For instance, in *Gandhi*, iconic South Indian leaders like Rajaji and Kamaraj were not given their due. In *Malcolm X*, key events in Malcolm's childhood, like his father's death or his mother's mental illness, are narrated through flashbacks. As a result, Malcolm X's rebellion against racism resonates with similar struggles in the present, whereas Periyar's struggles to transform society seem to be frozen in the past. The relatively diligent *Gandhi* and *Malcolm X* are successful in making the audience identify with their protagonists and root for them. However, *Periyar* is not similarly successful in reinventing Periyar for contemporary times, wherein the divide across caste is as entrenched as it was anytime in the past, mainly because of its rudimentary approach to storytelling.

## EVENTS, CHARACTERS, AND REPRESENTATION

Periyar's life was "too big" and does not easily fit into the Tamil film formula of reducing complex struggles into easy binaries. Either the film papers over ruptures, such as how the party Dravida Munnetra Kazhagam (DMK) departed from Periyar and his ideology, or disavows them, as in the case of Periyar's demonstration against religion through a call for breaking the statues of Hindu idols in public spaces. This is not to minimize Rajasekaran's monumental task in compiling landmark events. Research and choices regarding reenactments, particularly in the case of recent history, is not easy. Steven J. Revele, who along with his coauthor Christopher Wilkinson has written for such biopics as *Nixon*, *Ali*, and *Copying Beethoven*, shares his experience of research and dramatization in biopics in an interview by Don Coppola:

> We do a lot of research before we start. We don't start writing before we have a clear understanding of the nature of the character and the events that we want to portray. So when we get to those lacunae of research, where there is no hard evidence about what was actually said, or how situations were resolved, we make it up. That's what we do as dramatists. . . . If we can write a really compelling, entertaining drama that will bring people to the character, then we've achieved a great deal. If they want to then learn more and find out whether or not we were shading the facts for the sake of drama, they can read about it. If they do that then we have also succeeded. So our goal is to bring these characters to life for an audience and we do that the best way we can, consistent with our research. (Coppola and Revele 16–17)

Rajasekaran's goal as the writer and director of *Periyar*, too, seems to be the same. Given Periyar's prominence in Tamilnadu today, Rajasekaran has carefully chosen from the huge corpus of popular anecdotes and documented events and efficiently woven them together. Nonetheless, as Revele informs us, one of the major challenges in a biopic is the dramatization of events where there is no "hard evidence" or there are many different versions of the same event. One example is Periyar's sojourn in Kasi and his interactions with the (womanizing) Hindu monks or swamijis. Such dramatizations underscore the very purpose of the biopic as they shed light on the particular way the writer/director chooses to interpret the character. It is one thing for Periyar to have a profound conversation on "upper caste" hypocrisy, which would later force him to leave the Justice Party and start his own DK, and another for him to be a witness to the clandestine activities of the monks that only entrench mainstream stereotypes of the salacious swami and his sensuous female devotees, particularly in the way these stereotypes have been portrayed in films. This scene would have benefitted from focusing on Periyar's interiority, as it is his experience in Kasi, where he is a witness to deceit and hypocrisy, that reinforces his disbelief in religion. Though biopics could be argued to be as plot-driven as they are character-centered, characterization is key, as the historical drama that drives the plot attains its significance due to the singularity of the main character who offers possibilities for reinterpreting history and questioning the official or popular historiography. In the absence of such a unique and differential representation of the protagonist, the focus shifts to the scale of the spectacle, or to the generic criticism surrounding the faithfulness of the adaptation to the historical events depicted, or to the depth of the characters showcased and to the looks and performances of the artists.

It is in the blogs that we get to see detailed and provocative analyses of the film, whereas popular magazines are generally uncritical and effusive in their praise due to the political and social import of the subject. In *Periyar*'s case, many of the reviews praised the film but criticized the makeup and acting: "Anna [Annadurai] and Kalaignar's [Karunanidhi] makeup should have been done more carefully. The respective actors could have performed better. . . . In one or two places Sathyaraj has merged into the Periyar persona," writes Navam in his insightful response to Agathiyan's review of the film. The popular Tamil weekly *Ananda Vikatan* praises Sathyaraj's acting and says, "Sathyaraj is visible only during [Periyar's] youth since his gait, dress, and gesture become that of Periyar later" ("Cinema Vimarsanam") whereas Pazha Athiyaman's review in the literary magazine *Kalachuvadu* is highly critical of it, stating that Periyar aspired for an egalitarian society in which the masses were not oppressed by "mythology, history, ritual, Brahmin, man, caste, foreign language [and] economy. . . . His life till 1925 is showcased as in popular films. Thereafter, the film suffers because of the insertion of [too many] scenes. Then it ends abruptly." Athiyaman also points to the superficiality surrounding the scenes of Karunanidhi, M. G. R., and others who "seem to be thrust into the narrative while Periyar's politics has been pushed to the background." Athiyaman, too, agrees that Sathyaraj is more convincing in the second half of the film and is "amazing" when he is "not speaking" on screen. Wondering how *Periyar* would have affected novices, he expresses his concern as to whether Periyar would have "registered as an extension of Sathyaraj's garrulous persona" in their minds.

The reviews in a blog post, a popular magazine, and a serious literary journal demonstrate the varied responses to the film, while also reaffirming the difficulty of casting a star as the protagonist and of negotiating which life events to include in the biopic. As Athiyaman notes, some of the problems in *Periyar* could be related to the difficulty of the ninety-four-year-long life, for as Periyar himself acknowledged, it was "twice that of an average human lifespan." Periyar's life has been documented through books and it is well entrenched in the Tamil psyche from different perspectives; therefore, there is difficulty "retrieving it from the view-point of those that were connected and close to him" and one must account for the "impossibility of offering a unique perspective on it due to the unavoidability of such a baggage." Revele reminisces about a similar problem in his interview:

> The big challenge in *Ali* was reducing his enormous life to a manageable size. That means selecting the events that we wanted to dramatize and creating a structure in which we could portray those events. It was a huge task of selecting the specific events we wanted to focus on in order to create a portrait of the man that would speak to an audience today. (Coppola and Revele 18)

The reviews on *Periyar* also highlight the problems involved in addressing a contemporary audience through a narrative driven by historical events that have contemporary relevance. Revele further adds:

> We basically covered Ali's life from 1960 to the present time. Michael [Mann, the director] chose to focus on a ten-year period, from 1964 to 1974, and that's because what interested Michael was not so much Ali's spiritual journey as his sociological significance. He selected that twelve-year period and focused on the relationship between Ali's career and his religious transformation and the social context in which that occurred. (Coppola and Revele 18)

Mann's choice of that particular period is understandable as Ali's religious conversion to Islam could be expected to provide topical interest for today's audiences. *Periyar*, however, did not allow such a luxury to Rajasekaran.

## POLITICS, NARRATIVE, AND RECEPTION

Rajasekaran did not have the freedom that Mann had in privileging a particular period of his subject's life. The primary reason why Rajasekaran sought to be more comprehensive could have been that despite the Dravidian parties ruling the state for almost five decades, this is the first biopic on Periyar; hence, the undeniable desire to include all the major events and leaders who came in contact with or were inspired by Periyar while narrating a story that would cover his entire lifespan. The other reason could have been the role of the ruling DMK government in supporting the production of the film. DMK gave 99 lakh rupees (approximately $150,000) toward the production of the film, and the film acknowledges its debt to the then Chief Minister Kalaignar (Karunanidhi) in the very first title card that appears on screen when the film begins.[4]

This card mirrors the concluding scene wherein Kalaignar as the Chief Minister (in 1973) is asking the chief secretary Sabanayagam to follow up on his official orders of state honor to Periyar. This scene, during the final procession with Periyar's cortege, projects Karunanidhi as challenging the central government in his heated conversation with the secretary, who reminds him of the protocols. Karunanidhi replies with an argument regarding Mahatma Gandhi's receiving a similar state honor when he, too, was not a part of the government. He also expresses his willingness to accept the (extreme) consequence of his government's dismissal by the central government for transgressing the rule. He claims that Periyar was to Tamilnadu what Gandhi was for the nation. As noted by Athiyaman, this scene might have helped showcase Karunanidhi's courage but does not help the film, which has failed to elevate Periyar to the level of Gandhi through its narrative. In the discourses surrounding *Periyar*, the comparison with Richard Attenborough's *Gandhi* becomes inevitable, though the scale of production and the markets they targeted were vastly different. For instance, Suguna Diwakar in his detailed review says, "it is funny to watch Gandhi and Ambedkar talk in Tamil" and claims, "*Periyar* is not emotionally as compelling as *Gandhi*." Though *Periyar* ran for one hundred days in Chennai, it was not as impactful as *Gandhi* in terms of reaching every nook and corner of Tamilnadu and provoking discussions.[5] One of the main reasons for this limited reach, it could be argued, is the casting of the main character: Ben Kingsley was a fresh face who could engage the audience without bias or preconceived notions regarding the Gandhi persona whereas Sathyaraj's star status, at least in the early segments of the film, was obtrusive.

Even more important to note is how the DMK's involvement in the film colored reviews and the reception of the film. For instance, the popular daily *Dinakaran*, which likely supports the DMK since it is owned by the family of Karunanidhi's nephew, the late Murasoli Maaran, claims in its review, "the scene in which we see Periyar blushing when Anna meets him after 18 years" is excellent ("Oru Sagapthathin"). But earlier the same review highlights the factual inaccuracy of the delayed meeting between Periyar and Annadurai since Anna met Periyar much earlier at the Tiruchi jail after a year of their separation. Scholars like M. S. S. Pandian have detailed how the young DMK ideologues split from DK (Dravidar Kazhagam) because of their investment in consensual politics (759–70). Periyar, however, could prefigure what electoral politics would mean for his social reform movement and was not invested in convincing or keeping his young followers with him. It was, therefore, logical to think of Anna as a disciple making amends and feeling embarrassed, as exemplified by the concluding part of the same scene. When Anna asks Maniyammai (Periyar's much younger second wife, played by Kushboo, whom the DMK relentlessly targeted through print media as one of the main reasons for their separation from Periyar), to forget the past, the moment is as unconvincing as when Maniyammai, in a stereotypical Tamil cinema response, alludes to the cup of coffee on the plate in her hands and says: "Please have coffee."

As noted above, key historical moments that have significantly affected Tamilnadu are stereotypically dramatized in film, in this case to subsume Periyar's radical reformist agenda within the objectives of DMK's consensual politics. The parties claiming lineage to Periyar's DK, both the DMK and Anna Dravidian Progress Federation (ADMK), have opportunistically aligned with both the Congress and the Hindu right-wing Bharatiya Janata Party (BJP, also known as Indian People's Party). These strategic coalitions are some of the main reasons for *Periyar*'s unsatisfying closure, as Thudippu's blog post points out: "The final scene related to Karunanidhi seems to be thrust in." The Chief Minister Karunanidhi's challenging of the central (Congress) government in 1973, in a film made in 2007, is emblematic of the more than three-decade-old empty rhetoric of the Dravidian ideologues whose opportunistic trajectory Periyar's action of allowing the breakaway faction under Annadurai to split from DK could forebode in 1949. Moviebuzz's review exemplifies this popular sentiment and underscores the chasm between Periyar and the DMK politicians:

> The film traces the life and times of Periyar from his youth to his death. There is a lot of heroism in the character of Periyar, a crusader and reformer who stood for his ideals, at the same time was the messiah of the poor and downtrodden. A man, who was in touching distance of power, but never hankered after the spoils of office. Which modern day politician will shun power and all its heady comforts to be with the man on the streets?

Opposed to DMK's appropriation of *Periyar* are the voices on (and politics of) the other side, wherein the present DK party (under K. Veeramani) and DMK are held responsible for *Periyar*'s limited theatrical run in Tamilnadu. Selventhiran in his blog says that *Periyar* failed at the box office because of political interference as it was "colored" as a film driven by Dravidian ideology. While appreciating Rajasekaran for his research and as a director who has reinvented iconic characters like the great poet Bharathi on screen through his informed and ambivalent approach in *Bharathi*, Selvendran focuses on distribution and reception in his analysis of *Periyar*'s failure: "Initially they asked those who belonged to the DK and DMK to watch the film. Then they asked the government employees to sell the tickets. Now they have announced that school children must watch the film and write essays." Of course, he attributes such compulsions to how the DMK government funded the film. Consequently, the posters of the film carried the Dravidian party stamp. Nonetheless, he says *Periyar* revealed Periyar's complexities beyond his anti-Brahminism. Periyar scholars and bloggers have detailed some of the factual mistakes in the film, like Karunanidhi's presence when the DMK was initially formed, or V. V. S. Iyer's presence in the 1924 Cheranmahadevi meeting when Periyar questions the segregation of non-Brahmin students in the dining hall. They have also criticized the omission of some significant characters like Periyar's brother, or key events like the social reformer and activist Moovalur Ramamirtham's split from Periyar's DK, or Periyar's Sri Lankan visit, or the protest against Salt Satyagraha. The film has also been critiqued for its overemphasis on Periyar's friendship with Rajaji at the cost of his proximity to people like V. Anaimuthu, as well as important events like Periyar's protest against Katherine Mayo's book *Mother India*. A *Dinakaran* reviewer notes in his blog the omission of Chinnakkuthusi, who was very close to Periyar ("Oru Sagapthathin"). What is more important than these criticisms, which are unavoidable when it comes to biopics, is the dramatization of the specific events in the life of the iconic protagonist that had a profound and lasting impact on the Tamil populace due to their highly rebellious nature. Such events, like provocative announcements repeated in the media and Periyar's extensive campaign to break religious idols in public spaces, are absent in the film. Consequently, Periyar's persona as an aggressive and ideologically driven activist/reformer is undermined.

## RADICALISM, DRAMA, AND THE PUBIC SPHERE

The hallmark of Periyar's subversive politics was how he educated and transformed people, provoking the masses by destabilizing norms. Take, for instance, his investment in intercaste marriages. One could argue that enabling/performing a marriage between people of different castes might not have the same shock value for a contemporary audience, but the repercussions it has on casteist Tamil society to this day cannot be denied. The film has two scenes that look contrived despite being based on well-known events, wherein we see Periyar directly involved in intercaste marriage. Of equally great import is Periyar's call to break the statues of highly revered Hindu gods like Ganesha or Rama in public. The film does not foreground such shocking events. It would be productive, therefore, to look briefly at other key scenes in *Periyar* to interrogate the dramatization surrounding Periyar's radicalism and effectiveness. How does the film engage with the "making of Periyar" or the transition from E. V. Ramasami to Periyar? An answer to such a question would shed light on the very purpose of the film. The film's structure informs us of its intent to remind an audience familiar with Periyar's history about the chronology and the significant events in his life and to educate an audience not familiar with his continuing relevance to and singularity in Tamil society. The structure also reveals the (in)effectiveness of Rajasekaran's approach to the biopic on Periyar. Most reviewers and bloggers are in agreement that Sathyaraj's acting is more convincing when he plays the older Periyar in the later half of the film, but they also point to the many events and personalities that have been thrust into the narrative. In a way, the episodic format becomes increasingly monotonous and abbreviated, and at times events are combined.

The key events in the film, as in the initial segment reviewed in detail above, include both the personal and the political. The young Periyar marries Nagammai when she tries to commit suicide to avoid getting married to another man, but is upset when his father slaps him in his shop for having challenged a Brahmin monk for not allowing non-Brahmins to eat in his choultry and settling scores with the monk for cheating their employee by forcing him to accept the warrant for fraud. Ramasami feels particularly insulted, as he expected his father to honor his status as a married man, which leads him to embark on a journey to Kasi/Benaras, but his experience there further reinforces his distaste for swamijis, as he is a witness to their promiscuity and indulgence in the name of religion. When Ramasami returns from Benaras, where he shaved his head, we see his gradual transformation, particularly after his father retires, to a more responsible businessman who is equally invested in "serving the society." Sathyaraj appears more comfortable with playing a relatively older Periyar, the smart entrepreneur and social reformer. The arguable rite of passage represented by the Kasi episode (from the moment Periyar is slapped by his father and journeys to Kasi) is punctuated by two seminal moments.

The first is the song Periyar sings with two of his fellow travelers in Hyderabad to collect funds for their continued travel to Kasi. "*Kadavul ulagatha padachaan, irukkattum kaduvula yaaruvoi padachaan*?" (God created the world, okay! But who created that god?) is cinematic in terms of recalling the songs from the golden age of Tamil cinema set to classical ragas. This song also underscores Periyar's interest in music and singing, which is well documented, and prefigures his investment in addressing the masses directly about the need to challenge and reflect on irrational beliefs, particularly the myth surrounding the three lines on squirrels' backs.[6] Periyar retools this popular myth for his discourse on rationality: "if it were because of Rama's tender touch, what about Sita's bare back? Did he not touch her?" he asks.

The second important moment is Periyar's discovery of caste hierarchy, even among non-Brahmins, at the choultry for Chettiars where he is denied entry and food, whereas his two Brahmin friends are able to get in and dine easily. This barring prefigures Ramasami's later dissatisfaction with the "higher caste" Vellalas and Mudaliyars in the Justice Party, which makes him break away from them and form his own DK. This episode also resonates with contemporary discourses surrounding the hierarchy and domination of non-Brahmin "upper castes" and their oppression of Dalits. Presently, prominent Dalit public figures, like ex-member of the Legislative Assembly Ravi Kumar and scholars like Stalin Rajangam, have been critical of Periyar's stance toward Dalits. Rajasekaran's film does not address the contemporary discourse surrounding Periyar in Tamilnadu, where he is portrayed not as part of the historical trajectory of Dalit icons in the struggle against caste oppression, but as part of the binary opposite to Dalits where all non-Brahmin "higher castes" are collapsed together as the epitome of caste-based oppression. Scholars therefore address Periyar, from the Naicker community, as a leader of the "other backward castes" (OBCs)—other than the Dalits. *Periyar*, however, does not engage with this debate as it focuses on a straightforward critique of Brahminism/casteism.

If the purpose of the film was to portray the radical life and times of Periyar, it fails. During the last five decades of Dravidian Party rule, statues of Periyar were installed in many cities in Tamilnadu. Below the statues, Periyar's advocacy of rationality, mainly in the form of his provocative statements against religious beliefs, feature prominently—for instance, through a statement such as "*Kadavulai nambugiravan muttal*" (One who believes in god is an idiot). In contrast, right from the outset, DMK's founder Annadurai treaded a path of compromise, as necessitated by the dictates of electoral politics. Annadurai's manifesto changed drastically from Periyar's atheistic philosophy: "*Ondre kulam; oruvane devan*" (One clan; one god). Starting with Annadurai and leading to Karunanidhi, DMK's hypocrisy surrounding atheism has become fodder for cartoonists.

For Periyar, Hindu religion was at the core of the provenance and propagation of caste and had to be uprooted if caste was to be erased and eradicated. In the film, Periyar's radical acts of provoking and insulting believers through print media and in highly visible public areas near bus and railway stations is reduced to a scene in an enclosed alley wherein we see a *chappal* (sandal) flung over an adjacent compound wall as Periyar is traveling by bullock cart. Catching hold of the *seruppu*, Periyar loudly asks, "*Kadavulai karpithavan ayokiyan. Kadavulai vanagubavan muttal*?" (One who teaches about god is a rascal. One who worships god is an idiot). We see the other *seruppu* come flying, and Periyar happily catches it—having both *seruppugal* now makes a pair that he can use. This sequence, again, reduces Periyar's political polemics to witty humor. His strident radicalism aimed at waking up sleeping Tamilians is contained as much by the narrow, bounded alley as it is by the foregrounding of his frugal nature. Lost in this scene is his provocative call to challenge the status quo. Similarly, the film totally disavows Periyar's investment in the rights and freedom of women.

*Periyar*'s aesthetic revolves around a mise-en-scène economy; shots are mainly staged indoors or in controlled outdoor situations wherein characters enter and exit the frame mouthing key lines selected from Periyar's documented history, often mechanically. Such an approach, though understandable for a film with a modest budget, undermines Periyar's spirit. Apart from print media, drama in the public sphere was one of the major means by which Periyar mobilized the public for his subversive activities against religion and caste. By denying itself the public sphere for the reenactments of Periyar's iconoclastic acts, the film contains his throbbing radical spirit and paints him as another leader with a difference. As Jennifer Jihye Chun has pointed out in her well-researched essay on the struggles of the union of janitors in these contemporary times of globalization, "public drama . . . [t]hrough colorful protests and mass demonstrations" are effective in publically shaming "corporations for profiting off the working poor." This view echoes Periyar's belief in the possibilities that "public drama" can shame religious and caste-based institutions that he perceived to be the root of all evils in his society. By denying Periyar the freedom to perform his acts of anarchy in the public sphere, the film contains his rebellious character and sanitizes his subversive politics. Thus, Rajasekaran's *Periyar* is a retroactive construction of a sanitized version of Periyar—sans his radicalism—where Karunanidhi, who bookends the film, seems to carry on his legacy. The key moments in Periyar's life, like the struggle for temple entry for Dalits in Vaikkom, marriage of devadasis, intercaste marriage, and denouncements of religion and caste, are touched upon but not engaged with any depth to make them relevant or provocative for the contemporary viewer.

In her essay "E. V. Ramasami as Dissenter and Provocateur," Paula Richman details Periyar's investment in public dramas:

> In order to focus public attention on the need for social change, he designed "dramas of dissent," performances in public places that spotlighted the flaws of Brahminical Hinduism's power in an allegedly secular state. "Dramas of dissent" made audible in public plays dissenting voices of those who opposed the dominant ideology of his day. . . . One drama of dissent, centered on Ganesha, unfolded as a conflict between Ramasami and C. Rajagopalachari, who soon wrested away control over the event. (23)

As Richman informs us, Periyar's call to break the Ganesha idols in the public sphere did not meet with as much success as his protest in Vaikkom for temple entry or the picketing of liquor shops. Nonetheless, such dramatic events were key to his subversive, radical politics. Richman also notes, "After assessing the results of Ganesha-smashing, Ramasami choreographed his next drama of dissent in a more tamper-proof way. He focused on pre-event pedagogy in order to incorporate opportunities for teachable moments *before* his public civil disobedience took place" (28). Here it is important to note that Periyar not only treated his protest tactics as public dramas, but also used public dramas as a protest arena where he could address the audience before and after the play, often infusing them with the spirit to challenge accepted norms. For instance, one of Periyar's steadfast followers was the iconic actor M. R. Radha, whose plays—particularly the *Keemayanam*, a subversion of the Ramayana—Periyar effectively used as a space for pedagogy and preparation for protest. Periyar's protégé Annadurai has also praised the effectiveness of M. R. Radha's play as equaling that of their hundred *manadu*/big rallies.[7]

Periyar's preoccupation with public expression of dissent was not restricted to popular plays, as he used even his cadres' regular parades at the village level to showcase the significance of rationality and expose the superstitious belief underlying religious rituals. For instance, he would deconstruct the mysterious aura surrounding "fire walking" during religious festivals by having a trained cadre smoke a cigarette and walk over the fire. Until his last breath, Periyar was committed to public dramas and speeches, as signified in the film by his willing participation despite his poor health, and the advice of Maniyammai, in a final speech during which he collapsed on stage and soon died. Despite this depiction, Rajasekaran's film denies the radicalism of Periyar's politics by disavowing the centrality of the dramas in the public sphere in his life. The film's reenactments, therefore, are not infused with Periyar's rebellious spirit and seem like a necessary ritual; rather, they offer portrayals in a biopic aesthetic that goes against Periyar's very spirit. Rajasekaran's painstaking efforts in *Periyar* are, ultimately, unfulfilling, and also unfulfilled when viewed in the context of what might have been possible if the task of narrating the life of an anticaste reformer had been approached differently.

## NOTES

ACKNOWLEDGMENTS: I am grateful to S. Shankar and Ram Mahalingam for their advice on this essay.

1. See Geetha and Rajadurai for a detailed account of the Dravidian movement and Periyar's centrality to the imperatives of women's empowerment, rationality, the abolition of caste, and protests against religious/casteist prejudices and oppression.
2. See Fernandes for a detailed critique of the representation of Phoolan Devi as a subaltern woman in *Bandit Queen*.
3. Unless otherwise noted, all translations are mine.
4. Viswanathan in *The Hindu* informs us that "Tamil Nadu's Information and Publicity Minister Parithi Ilamvazhuthi told the State Assembly on May 7, 2007, that the State Government had granted Rs. 10 lakh to dub the Ambedkar film in Tamil. He also recalled that the State Government provided a grant of Rs. 99 lakh to make a film on the champion of the social justice, Periyar E. V. Ramasamy, and ordered tax exemption for screening the film."
5. For details on the critical acclaim and box office success of *Periyar*, see Dhananjayan (459).
6. The folkloric myth about the lines on squirrels' backs is that the squirrels wanted to help Rama in his efforts to build a bridge to Sri Lanka to retrieve his beloved Sita, who Ravana had abducted. Rama was moved by the squirrels' gesture and gently caressed them on their backs, resulting in the three distinct vertical lines they have today.
7. This information also comes from my interview with Olichango, who was closely associated with Periyar for more than four decades, for the documentary *Periyon* (2017), a work in progress. See also Manaa (202–03), for Periyar's appreciation, despite his reservations about popular cinema and theater, of M. R. Radha's efforts at disseminating his progressive ideas through his plays. See Vindhan (88) for details.

## WORKS CITED

Athiyaman, Pazha. "Thirai: Periyar-Pothu Buddhi Charntha Pathivu/Screen: Periyar—A Commonsensical Documentation." *Kalachuvadu*, no. 90, June 2007, http://www.kalachuvadu.com/archives. Accessed 15 June 2016.

Bingham, Dennis. *Whose Lives Are They Anyway?: The Biopic As Contemporary Film Genre*. Rutgers UP, 2010.

Bradshaw, Peter. "Alexander: Review." *The Guardian*, 31 Dec. 2004, https://www.theguardian.com/film/2004/dec/31/1. Accessed 15 June 2016.

Chun, Jennifer Jihye. "Public Dramas and the Politics of Justice: Comparison of Janitors' Union Struggles in South Korea and the United States." *Work and Occupations*, vol. 32, no. 4, 2005, pp. 486–503.

"Cinema Vimarsanam/Cinema Review: Periyar." *Vikatan*, 16 May 2007, http://www.vikatan.com/anandavikatan/2007-may-16. Accessed 16 June 2016. Coppola, Don, and Stephen J. Revele. "Bringing Historical Characters to Screen: An Interview with Stephen J. Revele." *Cinéaste*, vol. 27, no. 2, Spring 2002, pp. 16–19.

Custen, George F. *Bio/Pics: How Hollywood Constructed Public History*. Rutgers UP, 1992.

Dhananjayan, G. "Periyar (2007)." *Pride of Tamil Cinema: 1931 to 2013, Tamil Films That Have Earned National and International Recognition*, edited by G. Dhananjayan, Blue Ocean Publishers, 2014, pp. 457–59.

Diwakar, Suguna. "Mithakkum Veli: Periyar Padam-Kallukkadaiyoda Nindru Pona Mariyal/Floating Space: Periyar Film—The Protest That Stopped at the Liquor Shop." *Sugunadiwakar*, 8 May 2007, http://sugunadiwakar.blogspot.com/2007/05/blog-post.html. Accessed 15 June 2016.

Fernandes, Leela. "Reading 'India's Bandit Queen': A Trans/national Feminist Perspective on the Discrepancies of Representation." *Signs*, vol. 25, no. 1, pp. 123–52.

Geetha, V., and S. V. Rajadurai. *Towards a Non-Brahmin Millennium: From Iyothee Thass to Periyar*. Samya, 1998.

Kuzhali. "Periyar Oru Unarchi Kaviyam/Periyar, an Emotional Epic." *Kuzhali*, 6 May 2007, http://kuzhali.blogspot.com/2007/05/blog-post.html. Accessed 15 June 2016.

Luce, Edward. "Bush Biopic Veers Toward Frathouse Comedy." *Financial Times*, 20 Oct. 2008, https://next.ft.com/content/03e2cd04-9e43-11dd-bdde-000077b07658. Accessed 15 June 2016.

Prasad, M. Madhava. *Ideology of the Hindi Film: A Historical Construction*. Oxford UP, 2001.

Manaa. M. R. *Radha: Kalaththin Kalaignan/M.R. Radha: Artist of (Our) Times*. Uyirmmai Pathippagam, 2012.

Moviebuzz. "Periyar." *Sify Movies*, 5 May 2007, http://www.sify.com/movies/periyar-review-tamil-pclwoTifajdei.html. Accessed 15 June 2016.

Navam. "Periyar Thiraippadam/Periyar Film." *Yarl*, 13 May 2007, http://www.yarl.com/forum3/topic/23618. Accessed 15 June 2015.

Olichango. Personal interview. July 2014.

"Oru Sagapthathin Varalaru: Periyar Thiraippada Vimarsanam/The History of a Legend—Periyar Film Review." *Sivabalanblog*, 2 May 2007, http://sivabalanblog.blogspot.com/2007/05/blog-post.html. Accessed 15 June 2016.

Pandian, M. S. S. "Parasakthi: Life and Times of a DMK Film." *Economic and Political Weekly*, vol. 26, no. 11/12, Mar. 1991, pp. 759–70.

*Periyar*. Directed by Gnana Rajasekaran, Liberty Creations Limited, 2007.

Richman, Paula. "E. V. Ramasami as Dissenter and Provocateur." Forthcoming 2017.

Rosenstone, Robert A. *Visions of the Past: The Challenge of Film to Our Idea of History*. Harvard UP, 1995.

Selventhiran. "*Periyar* Tholvikku Yaar Karanam?/Who Is Responsible for *Periyar*'s Failure." *Selventhiran*, 26 June 2007, http://selventhiran.blogspot.com/2007/06/blog-post_26.html. Accessed 15 June 2016.

"Stone Says Alexander is Too Complex for 'Conventional Minds.'" *The Guardian*, 10 Dec. 2004, https://www.theguardian.com/film/2004/dec/10/news. Accessed 15 June 2016.

Tamilinian. "Kuraintha Oli: Periyar Padam-Sila Thirubugalum Purattugalum/The Lesser Light: Periyar Film—Some Twists and Lies." *Ini2006*, 10 May 2007, http://ini2006.blogspot.com/2007/05/blog-post_10.html. Accessed 15 June 2016.

Thudippu. "Periyar: Oru Thirappadam/Periyar—A Film." *Thudippu*, 3 May 2007, http://thudippu.blogspot.com/2007/05/blog-post_03.html. Accessed 15 June 2016.

Viswanathan, S. "Ambedkar Film: Better Late Than Never." *The Hindu*, 24 May 2010, http://www.thehindu.com/opinion/Readers-Editor/Ambedkar-film-better-late-than-never/article16302923.ece. Accessed 15 June 2016.

Vindhan, M. R. *Radhavin Siraichalai Sindanaigal/M.R. Radha's Prison Diary*. Bharathi Puthagalayam, 2008.

Weinraub, Bernard. "Stone's Nixon Is a Blend of Demonic and Tragic." *New York Times*, 30 May 1995, http://www.nytimes.com/1995/05/30/movies/stone-s-nixon-is-a-blend-of-demonic-and-tragic.html. Accessed 15 June 2016.

# 7

# AFFECTIVE RETURNS

## Biopics as Life Narratives

BINDU MENON

*Not on screen*
*Not in dream*
*She runs into the heart of darkness*
*P. K. Rosy*
*Sprouted in the sesame fields*
*Onto the thorns and rose petals, she fell.*
[. . .]
*The night closes in the Tamil land*
*Where palm leaves and sunshine*
*Write cinema in a play of light and shadow*
*Rootless, nameless ends Rosy*
*Star witness of the madhouse!*

—Kureeppuzha Sreekumar, "Nadiyude Raatri" (Actress's Night)[1]

P. K. Rosy, known as both Rosamma and Rajamma, the heroine of the first-ever local film production in Kerala, has made appearances in Kerala's contemporary history in numerous ways. "The Actress's Night," a poem that Malayalam poet Kureeppuzha Sreekumar wrote in 2003 is one such visitation. My attempt in this essay is to take a fragment of P. K. Rosy's life and weave a textured fabric from the uneven warp and weft of her life narratives, cinema, and political history. Rosy (P. K. Rosy's screen name) was the heroine of the first ever local film production, *Vigatakumaran* (The Lost Child) in Thiruvithamkoor, also known as Travancore. Belonging to a Dalit Christian family, Rosy was a laborer in the paddy fields of Thiruvananthapuram town, at times acting in the folk theater of Kakkarissi Nadakam.[2] The first screening of *Vigatakumaran* was held at Capitol Theatre in Thiruvananthapuram town on October 23, 1930. *Vigatakumaran* was announced all over the town by way of notices in both Malayalam and English pasted on bullock carts and street walls. The news of the screening was publicized in the local newspapers and also through public announcements using loudspeakers (Vijayakrishnan 23). Malloor S. Govinda Pillai, lawyer and member of *Sreemoolam Prajasabha*, the Travancore Legislative Assembly, inaugurated the screening.

Accounts of the screening narrate the presence of hundreds of people jostling with each other to get into the temporary theater. Twenty minutes into the film, the screen was pelted with stones accompanied by loud jeering and booing. The audience started destroying the chairs and benches and tore the screen (Mani, "Vigatakumarano"). Whenever Rosy appeared on screen, the audience pelted it with stones. The producer-director, J. C. Daniel, and some of the guests present had to take refuge behind the projector and leave the hall. On order from the palace, the screening was stopped and the hall was sealed the next day. The violence did not stop at the screening, however. It was redirected at Rosy.[3] From the few accounts of the period from varying sources over the last seventy or more years, it can be safely assumed that Rosy, as a consequence of this violence, fled the town, never to return to screen or stage.[4] It is interesting to note that *Vigatakumaran* had uneventful screenings in other towns like Alappuzha, Kollam, and Thrissur (Gopalakrishnan, *Cinemayude* 24).

The poem that I quote at the beginning of this article, published in 2003, speaks of the terrifying disappearance of a woman into the darkness of the night who reappears in a different land to live a rootless life severed from her family and community. Some of these lines speak of the violent disappearance in metaphorical ways, and others are literal descriptions of the violence. The poem constitutes a moment of silence not by rendering evidence and spelling out the event but through an act of unsaying. It constitutes an act of mourning for the dreadful fact that histories that disappear are lost forever. It produces an affect, stirring up visceral energies underneath or beside conscious ways of knowing, an affect that propels toward thought and movement, as we will see in the many narratives and voices that emerge out of this disappearance.

In addition to the poem, Rosy's memory inspired the formation of a Rosy Memorial Arts and Sports Club in Thiruvananthapuram city in 2005. The specter of the "disappeared actress" also haunts the contemporary in fictional registers, as in Vinu Abraham's novella *Nashtanayika* (The Lost Heroine). This haunting also partially provides the context for the 2013 award-winning biopic *Celluloid* on J. C. Daniel, the director of the film *Vigatakumaran*. Revisiting Rosy's memory today in each of these narratives requires negotiating political and moral stakes for a range of constituencies. Undertaking an analysis of Rosy's disappearance and the life narratives that have emerged around her disappearance enables us to engage with a contemporary history of cinema publics, caste relations, life narratives as a genre, and affective politics.

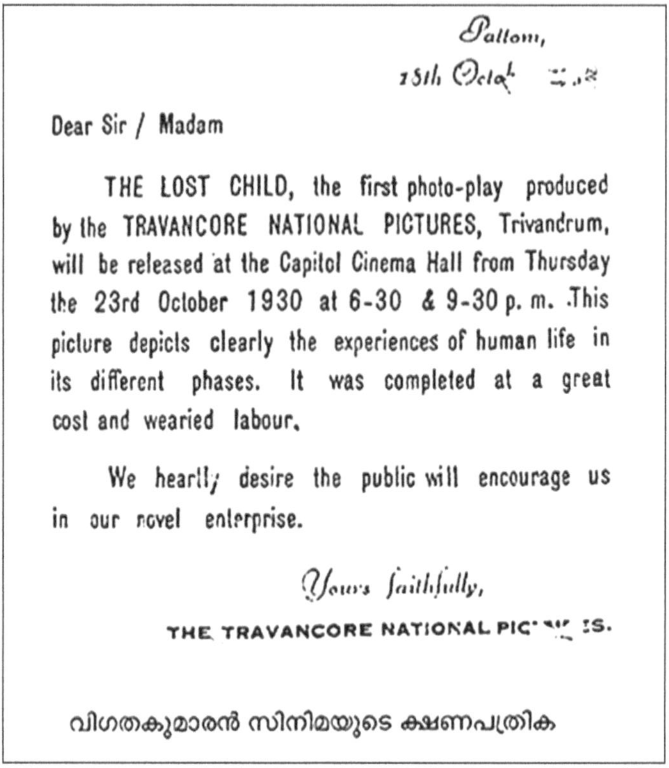

Pattom,
15th Octr ...

Dear Sir / Madam

THE LOST CHILD, the first photo-play produced by the TRAVANCORE NATIONAL PICTURES, Trivandrum, will be released at the Capitol Cinema Hall from Thursday the 23rd October 1930 at 6-30 & 9-30 p. m. This picture depicts clearly the experiences of human life in its different phases. It was completed at a great cost and wearied labour.

We heartily desire the public will encourage us in our novel enterprise.

Yours faithfully,
THE TRAVANCORE NATIONAL PIC[illegible]ES.

വിഗതകുമാരൻ സിനിമയുടെ ക്ഷണപത്രിക

Figure 7.1: Invitation letter for *Vigatakumaran* (1930).

The principal burden, then, is to locate Rosy's fragmentary life narrative in the context of caste relations in the early twentieth century and the history of subaltern caste movements in Kerala. When placed within a comparative framework, Rosy's various life narratives reveal digressions, divergences, and stopgaps. I treat the caste violence that Rosy endured and the narratives that have emerged around it as an important nodal point in the highly diffused history of caste relations in Indian and particularly Malayalam cinema.

## P. K. ROSY: CHRONICLES OF A DISAPPEARANCE

The violent event in the cinema hall is a vortex that has thrown various fragments and narratives about Rosy into the present. Fragments of the event have been activated in the present, illuminating relationships among the past, present, and perhaps the future, as well as different orders of the past. I attempt to enter a discussion of this event through different narrative forms: biopic, novella, poetry, popular film history in Malayalam language, the historian Kunnukuzhi Mani's biographical essay on Rosy, and a few essays on prominent Dalit Bahujanweb platforms, blogs, and social media.

In June 2004, Mani wrote his biographical essay on Rosy when, for the first time, we are provided a glimpse into her life after her disappearance.[5] In "Charithram Thedi Durantha Nayika," Mani states that when Rosy fled to the highway, she was rescued by Kesava Pillai, a truck driver of the Pioneer Motor Company. Rosy left with him for his town, Nagercoil, married him, and had children. She spent the rest of her life in Nagercoil working in a textile manufacturing unit. An outcast from her family and community, she did not visit them for years to follow. Rosy paid only one visit to her relatives after her father's death (5). Vijayakrishnan, on the other hand, states that it became increasingly difficult for Rosy to live in Thiruvananthapuram town and her house was attacked many times by "upper caste" men who pursued her for sexual favors (26).[6]

The making of *Vigatakumaran* met with many difficulties in its production stage and when Lana, an Anglo Indian actress from Bombay, who was commissioned for the film and withdrew from the project demanding a hefty payment, Daniel was forced to look for a local actress. Johnson, one of the actors in the film, suggested Rosy, by then a well-known Kakkarissi performer, for the role. Rosy and two other women from her neighborhood went to the studio at Pattom every day carrying their lunch, as they worked as laborers in the paddy fields of Thiruvananthapuram. The film was shot on a roofless studio in daylight and Rosy, according to Daniel, was about twenty-five years old when she started acting in *Vigatakumaran* (Gopalakrishnan, *Malayala* 22). Like many other families of her caste in the town, Rosy's family converted to Christianity by joining either the London Missionary Society or the Salvation Army (Mani, "Charithram" 16). Rosy, according to her biographer, had started performing in the Dalit folk theater, Kakkarissi Nadakam, at age sixteen and was a very popular actress. Two competing theater troupes in Rosy's town came to clashes on the issue of hiring her for their productions, creating social tension in the locality that forced the family eventually to shift to Thycaud, another part of town. Rosy continued performing in seasonal Kakkarissi theater and worked in the fields until she acted in *Vigatakumaran* and eventually disappeared (Mani, "Charithram).

Historians faced with the challenge of a lack of textual evidence and crippled by the lack of reliable procedures for verification set out to compensate through conjecture. Historical inquiry thus involves what Carlo Ginzburg describes as something similar to a hunter's search for clues and evidence. Like the hunter crouched in mud, searching for the trace of some invisible game, the historian has to deduce behavior from minute and subtle indicators (96–125).

Within the corpus of stories presented to us, silences are produced both by the absence of facts and the circulation of competing interpretations. The traces I distinguish here overlap in real time. Following Michel-Rolph

Figure 7.2: Photograph of Capitol Cinema Thiruvananthapuram (photographer and year unknown). Source: private collection of B. Vijaya Kumar, Cochin.

Trouillot, I treat these traces as heuristic devices that distill aspects of historical production, which aid in and expose not just the entry and exit of power in the story but are constitutive of the story. The violence at the cinema hall causes a kind of turbulence, and the materiality of this event creates an array of bodies and artifacts. This inquiry is made possible by working through traces of traces—an absent film text, sparse newspaper reports, missing police records, the first film notice, still photographs from the film, and the pamphlet for the film.

Historical research on silent cinema in general and within the Indian context in particular stands at odds with Michel de Certeau's injunction that "'going to the archives' is the statement of a tacit law of history" (77). With more than 90 percent of silent films lost and in some cases only fragments preserved (Chabria and Usai 8), the silent film archive itself is an assemblage of traces, gaps, silences, and absences, rendering extant-centric film history an irrational and unviable project. The material property of the film archives makes the film historian turn toward the processes through which archives make meanings. A call to treat the object of archives itself as a trace is present in Arondekar's words when she argues "both within and beyond the Derridean spectrality model, to consider, as it were, both the forensics and metaphorics of the trace. That is, one must work with the empirical status of the materials, even as that very status is rendered fictive" (3). There is, in short, no ready dialogic relationship between the trace objects and historical analysis, since trace objects are not ready bearers of any transparent historical meanings. Astonishingly enough, the photographs and notices in this case do not ensure the "truth effect" but form only one part of a network of such trace objects and the discursive world of rumors and scandal (Mukherjee 31). In a brilliant discussion of relics and trace objects that travel into the contemporary and the problems in reading them, Bhatnagar provides a rare insight into the nature of the trace object. On the linguistic trace object in Braj language, she states, "It evokes the early modern in its persistence into the 20th century modern by a flash of illumination in which characters, bodily gesture, the perceiving eye combine with the trace object to compose a visual ekphrasis of language as a set of moving pictures" (77). Much in the same way, Rosy's print and visual traces illuminate the present with early twentieth-century print characters, unfamiliar bodies, and visual iconography to quite literally form a visual ekphrasis in conjunction with the perceptions of the contemporary. I intend to offer a few remarks towards recalibrating the transactions between the event, life narratives, and the work of caste in structuring them by reading these trace objects. When working with the early twentieth-century film archives, recognizing this analytical remove and the ephemerality of the visual objects is imperative while also relinquishing the practice of writing history based on evidence.

## SITUATING THE EVENT IN CASTE STRUCTURE

*Vigatakumaran* was made during a period of urban development in Thiruvananthapuram town, the capital of the princely state of Travancore. Societal modernization and cultural modernity were initiated in Travancore as early as the first half of the nineteenth century. The emergence of a commercial economy in Travancore and its integration into a world capitalist order through agrarian expansion with the development of plantations and the importation of foreign capital was the starting point of this modernization (Mahadevan). Subaltern caste movements that emerged in this context thus sought to lay claims over social spaces as part of their social transformation project. The role of Protestant missionary work in the process of Dalit social transformation is well documented, as they recorded the intertwined relationship between caste and slavery in Travancore and made the issue international. The missionary activities among the erstwhile "untouchable" communities since the nineteenth century and their conversion to Christianity made them a distinct community by the end of the 1890s (Mohan, "Religion" 37).

The missionary work, however, framed in patronizing terms, introduced concepts of equality along with a pursuit of salvation, which brought in both a sense of millennial transformation and a search for equality. P. Sanal Mohan argues that the missionary discourse, literacy, and schooling encouraged more engagement with emergent discourses on citizenship, rights, judiciary, and political powers, enabling the oppressed castes to lay claims over public spaces as well as administrative and natural resources, and subsequently to force open the legislative space ("Religion" 35).

Various works on Travancore history show that development and progress worked differently among various caste communities and have a history ridden with conflicts.[7] An example of this would be the breast cloth struggle by the Channar women.[8] Enabled by ideas of progress since the first half of the nineteenth century and inspired by reform movements such as the Vaikunda swamy cult and interventions by the Protestant missionaries, the Channars demanded the right to cover their breasts in public (Yesudas 69–70). In a perceptive essay on individual Dalit women's conversion to Christianity and Islam during the colonial period, Charu Gupta reads these acts by Dalit women as embodying a language of intimate rights and finds in these narratives accounts of resistant materialities. She argues, "The recalcitrance of desire threw up emancipatory possibilities of intimate rights where highly ritualized acts of conversion, clothing, and marriage could at times become a metaphor for a new vocabulary of body, of interiority, of subjectivity" ("Intimate" 681). In Rosy's traces, which travel to us from the early twentieth century, how do we read the figure of a converted Christian from one of the most oppressed castes, a popular actress in folk theater by night, a laborer by day, the first actress of the Malayalam silver screen, and later a forgotten figure? What social relations and aesthetic modes enabled Rosy to enter the silver screen and what expelled her from her life and community?

Until the early decades of the twentieth century, entertainment forums were clearly demarcated by gender, caste, and class boundaries in almost all parts of Travancore. The cumulative effect of reordering public spaces was a "democratic" subversion of this old social order.[9] New spaces were created that were secular in their access and modern in organizing the bodies that inhabited them, yet remained resolutely exclusivist and ordered through the existing caste structure. Drawing from contemporary journals and secondary works on early theater as well as reports on cinema halls, one can discern the emergence of social spaces organized in a hierarchy of bodies. Locating the configuration of space and the ordering of bodies in theater in Travancore in the early twentieth century might help us understand the existing mode of visuality and its relationship to the body.

In the Malayalam region, the first recorded performances of women actresses in song and dance or amateur productions emerged in the early 1930s (Madathil 23). Traveling Tamil song and dance drama companies occasionally featured actresses. Thus, Rosy and other women who were part of folk theater forms were some of the first women to perform in public. Furthermore, while the presence of Dalit communities in the context of traditional arts in the subcontinent is well documented, performances like folk and local forms of theater and dance were particularly related to Dalit women's bodies, which were often positioned as objects of arousal (Rege, "The Hegemonic" 24).

Whatever the extent of the publicness of these forms, Rosy's passage from theater to the new visual register of cinema is a shift that demands our critical attention. The acceptance of Rosy as a folk theater performer and her banishment from the modern space of cinema, a yet-to-be-formed public space, is more than a sporadic or singular event of violence. While bodies in folk theater were located within sanctioned social relations and were thus shorn of the power to represent anything other than themselves as caste bodies (Groesbeck 93), the cinematic image was a commodity untethered to its conditions of production and set loose within a domain where it takes on a life of its own. In this sense, the fear of the Dalit woman entering the new public space in the 1930s through a new technology of representation resonated with the larger fear about Dalit communities gaining rights over public spaces.[10]

In Travancore, the reorganization of public spaces also meant that the body, with its particular, gendered characteristics (ideal "manliness" and "womanliness"), was subjected to disciplinary mechanisms and seen as the site where reforms had to be performed (Devika). This structure also embraced representational practices such as portraiture, photography, theater, and cinema. The discursive effect of this embrace was the pervasiveness of the female image in modernity and the emergence of a female image as an index of modernity. I would like to draw on a premise familiar to feminist theory: that the modern mechanism of looking is predicated on gender asymmetry such that women are defined by their visibility. Many historically inflected versions of this thesis concur with the view of the emergence of woman as object, but they ground their argument on the changing perceptual field of modernity rather than on the psychoanalysis of male sexuality (Conor 14). Martin Jay, in his seminal work on vision, titled *Downcast Eyes*, proposes the emergence of the "hegemony of vision" as the most important sensory perception and as a corollary of Western modernity (267). These conditions in modernity resulted in barring women from the modern subject position of the spectator because of their existence as embodied, spectacular objects. In the context of early photography in the region, Parayil argues that the visual iconography of photography emerges within a semiotics of the caste body defined in conjunction with colonial anthropometrics and labor. His work maps the photographic representations of female body within an aesthetic regime and an exacting matrix of caste and gender relations.

The upshot of reform strategies among "upper castes," Devika argues, is the centralization of a certain nonreciprocal relationship of visibility in the complementary sexual exchange between "domestic woman" and "public man." On this point of the "aestheticization" of women, Conor's work on spectacular modernity and how women's bodies become part of a spectacle, deeply implicated in modern forms of subjectivity, functions as an invaluable corollary text. In his work on autobiographies and Kerala's colonial modernity, Udaya Kumar elucidates the moves through which the body was invested with a new regime of disciplinary technologies (290). How do we understand these broad processes in modernity that seek to define gender and caste as visible economies and continue to confer a central position of visuality in subsequent articulation up until the present?

In this context we can approach the variously gendered discourses of Dalit social struggle in the early twentieth century, where Dalit reform discourse on Dalit femininity had focused differently from Savarna femininity. Dress reforms, conjugal relations, women's education, and motherhood all became the sites of these conceptual refashionings of women's selves in all communities. Dalit and other "lower caste" women who have a longer history of being in public spaces as laboring bodies and participating in public activities further problematize the categories of "domestic woman" and "public man." Subaltern social reform discourses in the 1930s, for instance, turned repeatedly to the historical legacy of caste and gender to articulate a violated Dalit femininity, one that worked specifically to expose and challenge the cultural and corporeal effect of the dominant caste patriarchy. Sanal Mohan's work on Prathyaksha Raksha Daiva Sabha (PRDS), a new Christian religious sect established by the legendary and charismatic Dalit leader Poykayil Appachan, provides an important account of how the new bodily practices of Dalit communities were considered significant for claiming social equality in the larger society and argues that this claiming formed a central part of the colonial modernity of the Dalit community ("Religion" 165). The PRDS reform project put equal emphasis on spiritual and bodily cleanliness as an essential endowment of a new Dalit self.

Rekha Raj, analyzing the Dalit movements of the early twentieth century, argues that Dalit Movements cannot be seen as derivative of other "lower caste" reform movements like the Ezhava reform movement, since communities enter the space of modernity with differing cultural capabilities (71). She argues, "as far as the historically marginalized 'lower castes' were concerned, they had to be recognized as humans first so as to claim citizenship rights. It points to a structural disparity; a crisis of representation and inclusion endemic to the then existing social system" (71). Through an examination of Dalit women's struggles such as the Kallayum Malayum Samaram, a movement to abandon ornaments that were markers of caste, and the struggles of women who were part of the PRDS, she shows how each of these struggles was woven into the complex relationship of community and rights (83).

Feminist theory's lengthy and crucial exploration of the visible economy that governs sexual difference has most often been limited to the figure of woman. The spectacular female body can be read along with another significant figure in the turn of the century—the figure of the "modern girl." As a sign of social, economic, sexual, and political empowerment as well as a site of anxiety, the modern girl was constituted through advertising, cinema, and photography as an essential aspect of commodity culture. The modern girl has been seen as the work of a range of modernist aesthetic processes, and her surface image and representation have been viewed as an outcome of this work (Weinbaum 16). Visuality was seen as important in the self-representation of women who considered themselves "modern," and women used photography, paintings, portraiture, and literary representations to stage spectacle and the self (Conor 6). Analyzing the modern girl in the Indian context, Priti Ramamurthy argues that in 1920s India, the figure of the modern girl inhabited a "charged space" where colonial, international, and national categories of inclusion and exclusion were articulated, fortified, contested, and disordered (165). The visual iconography of the modern girl in Indian cinema of the 1920s, she argues, was a creation of such global aesthetics and transnational cultural exchanges. The contested, unstable, and subversive relationship of the modern girl to institutions of marriage and heterosexuality, and her transgressions of racial and other boundaries infuses the figure with a critical charge.

Figure 7.3: Rosy, photograph found in 2011. Reproduced by permission of Matrubhumi.com.

Let us now return to Rosy. How do we view her as the first woman to access the status of a "modern girl" in a caste society where women, particularly Dalit women, hardly exercised any control over their bodies? The relationships among caste, performance, and gender extend the consideration of questions of the visible by focusing on the sexual economy that underlies spectacular violence as a disciplinary practice for patriarchal and dominant caste control at the turn of the century. Here, the commodification of the Dalit woman's body that accompanied the transformation from theater to cinema, which opens up challenging and contradictory possibilities, is mediated through a complicated process of sexualization and gendering. We can see from the sparse descriptions of what ensued at the screening that, besides moral anxiety, the violence Rosy endured also gestures toward an anxiety about her independence, enhanced cultural status, and appeal as a new figure of urban modernity.

## REVERBERATIONS: CASTE, GENDER, AND LIFE NARRATIVES

Enfolded within the diffuse tides of the social relations discussed above, Rosy's life narratives in different forms and genres are larger than her life itself. Out of the debris of this apparently seamless historiography, there seems to emerge new political and historiographical possibilities. The performativity of the self and its account in autobiography and the representation of the self in a variety of forms in biographies, life writing, and its various forms like biopics give us important traction in the study of life narratives "that can produce enabling re-descriptions of life-worlds and facilitate the re-imagination of the political" (Kapoor 39).

The resurrection of Rosy from the debris of history and the density of narratives around the violence at the cinema hall together limn a new and different genre of political consciousness and purpose regarding her previous absence. The narratives that have been spawned out of the event and Rosy's life have not just been represented in various forms but also have differing and complex relationships to that event and that life. Whereas the poem and popular history writing better testify to the importance of the violence Rosy endured, *Celluloid*, the recent biopic on J. C. Daniel that I discuss below, makes Rosy's life a footnote to the life of the male artist, a life haunted by the specter of caste violence. The poem recalls the abject subject back into history through allegorical devices, and popular history writing mobilizes a counterhistorical representation through a range of referential evidence like newspapers, biographies, and oral history of the community. Rosy's disappearance is reiterated and made more palpable by a special kind of representation that replaces the "original" in a way that produces affect.

Despite her absence in contemporary periodicals and newspapers, Rosy is mentioned a decade later in print. In 1939, a few years after the release of the film, K. P. Raman Pillai wrote about Malayalam film history thus: "The silent film *Vigatakumaran* put together by one Daniel from Pattom and 'Padakkara Hollywood harijan' women happens to be the first Malayalam film." Pillai's mocking tone in regard to Dalit labor in general and Rosy in particular is unmistakable. Chelangad Gopalakrishnan, a veteran Malayalam film journalist writing since the 1940s, offers in his search for J. C. Daniel a sympathetic reference to Rosy by identifying the sexual harassment she faced and how she had to endure a life away from her community and family. However, while Daniel emerges as a tragic figure in Gopalakrishnan's text, an artist crushed under the juggernaut of capitalist industry, Rosy has, at best, remained a footnote to this history. These cases of minimal reporting or absence of reporting in early twentieth-century Malayalam print culture forecloses the possibility of finding dissenting voices that truly took up Rosy's cause and critiqued the violence she experienced. Further, it lays bare the limitations of contemporary print culture when confronted with new developments in vernacular modernity—new visual technologies, "lower caste" entrepreneurship, and the entry of "lower caste" bodies into new public spaces governed by structures of modernity. As noted, Dalit women's bodies have always been regarded with extreme moral ambivalence and repeatedly brought into focus through questions of sexual promiscuity (Gupta, *Gender* 15).

We can see from a description of the violence at the cinema hall that the presence of a Dalit woman on screen challenged the political and ontological assumptions of even the most radical thinkers of early twentieth-century Travancore. This presence, in other words, was an unthinkable fact in the framework of political thought.11 In this sense, the first Malayalam film, its form of investment, and its use of performing bodies was unthinkable for its time; it challenged the very framework within which proponents and opponents examined caste, gender, and reform in vernacular modernity. Only cinema as a specific assemblage of technology and representation revealed with severity the rigidity of this framework in the early twentieth century.

In 2013, Kamal, a prominent filmmaker in Malayalam commercial cinema, made the film *Celluloid* as a tribute to the father of Malayalam cinema, J. C. Daniel. The film won several awards, including the Kerala state award for the best film and the national award for the best feature film in Malayalam. The film has become controversial since then and has been at the center of debates that propelled Rosy's tragic personal story into the nucleus of a larger sociological discussion on the relationships of caste, gender, and cinema. The film foregrounds the life of Daniel, his struggles, and his melancholic existence after his unsuccessful attempts at filmmaking and the many assaults on his career by various forces. Though Rosy's stage and film career and the violence against her is depicted empathetically, Rosy disappears from *Celluloid* soon after the filmmaking is over. The controversies involved questions about the actual sequence of events, historical details, the liberty to fictionalize history, and the politics of Dalit representation and commercialization. The debate assumed significance in Dalit writings on prominent Dalit websites like *Round Table India*, and in social media and print (Ramachandran and Cheruvally).

*Celluloid* is narrated from the point of view of the film journalist Chelangad Gopalakrishnan and moves between the present and past as if on a journey through the archives of memory. The film participates in a retro mode of filmmaking that makes the past visible in the cinematic narrative through an interspersion of fact and fiction, memory and loss (Sreedharan and Abraham). *Celluloid* strives against a deafening silence in the archive and tries to recover lost voices from the past. It uses a film-within-a-film format to produce an ensemble encompassing both the filmmaking process of the original *Vigatakumaran* and the process of writing film history.

This recovery project itself is complex, involving questions of exclusion and inclusion and of the voices that get foregrounded. For Kamal, the project was to rewrite film history by foregrounding the pioneer J. C. Daniel's story as a biopic.[12] Kamal's belief in history takes him very close to other projects in cinema that display the faith that a biopic can redeem the past and rescue the real from myriad versions of the past.[13] While this faith concurs with the speaking position the film assumes on behalf of the failed filmmaker, for many others such faith involves questions of exclusion. Ajith Kumar points out that the film features Rosy for more than half of its screen time and yet refuses to foreground Rosy's voice. The treatment of Rosy as a tragic and mute figure has come under attack for misrepresenting Dalit and working-class life. Says Rupesh Kumar, "Considering the physical environment, the geographical environment and the working class atmosphere in which this Dalit woman lived, there is no way she would be this submissive" (Sebastian 6).

Figure 7.4: Rosy, as imagined by illustrator Pradeep Kumar. Reproduced by permission of *Chitrabhumi Weekly*.

Kamal's representation of Rosy reflects the ambiguities related to caste bodies in the context of cinema in the 1930s. A popular song from the film, "Enithonnum Arinjatheyilley" (I

Am Unaware of This), calibrates all the ambiguities in a succinct fashion. The song, set in a style reminiscent of a reinvented folk tradition of the Malayalam theater of the 1950s, expresses Rosy's fears and anxieties about entering the new space of cinema. At the beginning of the song sequence, Rosy gazes at her reflection in a sliver of a mirror that reflects sunlight on her, prefiguring her entry into a regime of reflections and gazes through the cinema. The mirror here is more than a metaphor for cinema and certainly plays with the idea of reflection in the song, reminding us of the reflections and gaze of the audience, the camera, and the lights that will make her visible in the public in the future. In the song, she doubts her beauty and the appropriateness of her body for an emerging visual iconography of cinema. Further, Rosy is elaborately dressed like a Nair woman by Janet Daniel, J. C. Daniel's wife, in preparation for the role of the "upper caste" woman. This sequence prepares Rosy for her role and in the process erases her caste markers, making her available to the audience as a desirable body; an easy passage into a casteless/"upper caste" visual iconography, an act of passing that has contradictory meanings. What modes of corporeal investments did she have to make in order to perform a body socially different from hers?

K. K. Kochu argues that, in the film, Rosy is not shown to have experienced difficulties in this passage because of the mediation of her femininity through Janet. The political context of *Celluloid* also draws attention to questions of representability of experience, as voiced in the concerns raised in the subsequent public debates. Jenny Rowena, in a perceptive analysis of continuing structures of caste, writes, "Those who write on Rosy, describe it as an atrocity which happened when a rigid caste system existed." Rowena's point about the continuing structures of violence calls upon us to reflect on the status and singularity of violence. The violence at the screening is one point, although an outstanding point, in a larger series of caste violence before and after this event. Many argued that, however critical of the caste system, the film treats caste hierarchy as one that existed only in Malayalam cinema's past (Rowena; A. Kumar). Though overtly sympathetic, the argument goes, *Celluloid* is not capable of opening up the space of "otherness" and reconciling memory with hope. K. K. Kochu views this unrepresentability of caste experience through the prism of the very nature of commercialized cinema (Kochu).

What possible affective constellations can open up this space of "otherness" in cinema? *Celluloid*, instead of settling the questions about the origins of Malayalam cinema, seems to open out a new set of questions around the very idea of representability. The Dalit explorations through writings on Rosy and *Celluloid* are two different kinds of historical inquiries. While the film tries to mourn a lost film history, Dalit mourning is for the figure of the actress. In differing ways, these inquiries try to interrogate the archives and find gaps in them from which to speak out. The Dalit Bahujan critique is more than a debate on misrepresentation and demands an assessment of the interpretative framework that the biopic thrusts upon the event. The figure of the "film historian" in *Celluloid* helps in recrafting personal memories and individual recollections into an alternative archive. Cinema does not have to stand the test of "authenticity" and "factuality"—it brings forth the contradictory impulses of the archives. In the Dalit historical inquiry, the structural and visible architecture of caste ideology is a recurring theme. The belief in creating an alternative archive of Dalit knowledge has inspired Dalit intellectuals to announce a new film on Rosy, the work on which is underway (Sebastian 6). This archive, Kochu argues, lies in its ability to call upon an affective Dalit cultural memory and can be most effectively redeemed in cinema. What emerges in this discourse is not a deterministic or diagnostic category of Dalit cinema, but the radical vision of how Dalit identity in cinema can be enacted in a confluence of politics, history, culture, and aesthetics.

## AFFECTIVE RETURNS: EVENT, STRUCTURE, NARRATIVES

All these narratives, including the biopic, through their disparate techniques have attempted to create a legible object of history. The scene of the violent event at the cinema hall in 1930 and the lingering violence on Rosy that has been described in narratives, poetry, cinema, and popular history so far, is one of passion, transgression, invasion, and exhilaration. These heterogeneous narratives also speak of power, violation, purity, and strict, rigid, and obsessive fascination with boundaries between different caste groups. The description and memory of the violence terrifies, enrages, entraps, or shields us according to the bodies and subjectivities we inhabit within this cultural symbolic. For Dalit and "lower caste" women, narratives of the violence Rosy endured are reminders of Brahmanical patriarchy's techniques of controlling and governing their bodies and social lives. For "upper caste" women, the narrative about the moral anxiety surrounding Rosy's story is a reminder of caste borders and control over women's bodies. In a variety of ways, the memory of the violent event stirs anxieties linked to the most turbulent history of caste in Kerala. The description of this particular violent event resonates with existing nightmares about caste violence that are still in circulation. Rarely discussed but omnipresent, the narratives boil and bubble just below the surface of the silver screen, mutely, perpetually, without ever surfacing but nevertheless shaping the surface. This latent nightmare and fear of caste boundaries sets the scene for playing out of some of the worst cultural anxieties—desire, fear, and violence—about gender, sexuality, and caste, and about history and bodies at the site of cinema.[14]

The coding of this scene of violence and the way it is rendered through contemporary periodicals and in film history is not explicit. This scene of a "lower caste" female body on the screen and the accompanying unruly violent audience response has led to competing interpretations. Until Dalit historian Mani wrote about Rosy, this scene had been rendered as one with no caste signifiers. Divided against positions of aggression and defense, cinema became the site where all female bodies were delivered to an unruly male audience. It is through the work of memory and history that Dalit historians, poets, and filmmakers make the coding of this scene explicit. Through this history of representational practices in poetry, popular history, and cinema, we can see how caste society comes to be pitted against a Dalit woman's body at the site of cinema. This scene marked by violence, marked her body and her specular exposure to pain, as a spectacle, the visible economy of which is its claim to truth.

Set in continually changing caste relationships from colonial past to the present and in political imaginations of annihilating caste in the future, we need to attend to the relationship between the violence Rosy experienced and the genre of life narratives. Assessing this relationship is not just an attempt to understand a singular event of violence but an act of encountering the logic of violence vital to the unfolding of modernity. Historical knowledge plays a pivotal role in the process of identity formation and the consciousness that emerges from it. It has been observed that "lower caste" communities in the context of social change imagine history as a resource to affirm their social rootedness (Mohan, "Creation"; de Heering). Recent works on Dalit history in Travancore foreground a historical project that attempts to retrieve the experiences of suffering and pain, which the ancestors of "lower caste" communities endured in Travancore, and which is unthinkable outside of colonial modernity.15 These discourses made the "lower castes" realize the erasure they experienced as a collectivity because of the complete absence of any "valid history" of their own. For the "lower castes," historical knowledge tends to acquire a liberatory function as it attempts to challenge the dominance of the "upper castes."

This notion of the past and the lack of resources to write history frames Kunnukuzhy Mani's 2004 biographical essay on Rosy titled "Tragic Heroine in Search of History." In this case, retrospective significance is created by the political actors themselves as a past within their past and also as a future projected onto the present. Life writing has provided a language which speaks to memories and experiences on the one hand, and engages with disciplinary knowledge production on the other. This language does not follow the protocols and grammar of the fields of art, creativity, history, or fiction. It expresses itself in an impressionistic mode and hence is visible only as traces or through the effects it produces. In the domain of historical knowledge, the new registers of life writing have given the experiences of the present and memories of the past a new status of genuine "evidence" or at times bare the problem of evidentiality, altering not only the past but the very process of knowledge production. This has enabled not just a sifting through the debris of normative history, but also the creation of another archive based on memory.16 Life writings reactivate the affect of the event that has been silenced through routinization.

As the title of Mani's biographical essay indicates, Rosy enters the archive as a tragic figure who bears the marks of violence inflicted upon her community. Is there a historical method that would enable her to speak? At the site of film history, we are forced to ask the question whether subaltern subjects like Dalit women can speak for themselves. In her seminal work on the place of fantasy in feminist historiography, Joan Scott recognizes that the feminist historian's daunting task is to translate, interpret, and represent. Scott—much like Steedman (83)—argues that archives can be the source and space for historical imagination (Scott 147). Imagining the archive in its most expansive manner, as memory's potential space, helps us to understand archives of all kinds as repositories of both passion and information. The emphasis, it follows, should be on a historiography that nurtures "imaginative capabilities," from the "circulating critical passions" from women's struggles (Scott 72).

While Rosy enters the space of cinema in the early twentieth century as an agential folk theater actress, she leaves the space of cinema mutely. As we saw while reviewing the debates on this, this disappearance has prompted questions about the very nature of the cinematic apparatus, as structured by caste relations. In revisiting this singular act of violence, tensions that were earlier read primarily in gendered terms have been particularly reopened to questions of gender as mediated by caste. This excursion through various forms of life narratives, has also reinterpreted memory, oral sources, and archives. The affect of the event, silenced and routinized in history so far, is reactivated in these life narratives.

In the spirit of Walter Benjamin's approach, it can be argued that when images from the past are brought into constellation with the present, "the lightning flash" generates an illumination of history (121). The discarded and outdated image emerges from the past and becomes legible in the present so that we may gain critical knowledge of the present. In this case, the lightning flash produced between the past and the present illuminates the Dalit female actress from the recesses of history and renders visible the mutable identities of Dalit womanhood: folk performer, actress, laborer, modern girl, all at once. In these divergent life narratives, Rosy emerges as a critical metaphor that offers possibilities of progressive and different readings.[17] As the introduction to this volume eloquently states,

> Dalit life narratives . . . often frame events and represent caste in distinct ways, challenging ideas of the "unrepresentable" and investing in an ethics of testimony. Different practices of representing caste lives thus throw open for us possibilities of challenging dominant embodiments, where representation is not just about replication but also about innovation. (Shankar and Gupta 11)

I now return to the question of the singular event and the various life narratives that correspond to it. What if we were to read the event as not a singular event in the past, but as a continuing relationship with different orders of time? The event has left traces and constituted memories. This is a call to restore cinema's disavowal of caste histories to an ethics of memory and to mobilize the affective veracity. I have already suggested a quasi-Benjaminian form to these traces and their relationship to the event. Biopics as a genre, we see, are affective returns that are spread across many kinds of genres, acts, and performances. Cinema and life narratives, both of which in a sense are specific kinds of exercises in memory keeping and making, offer the possibility of perpetual return, of immortality. When Kochu makes an insightful argument for creating an archive that has the ability to call upon an affective Dalit cultural memory that can crystallize it in cultural forms and probe contagious sites of counter power, he is making an invaluable countertext to official history's relationship to the event. The many illuminations of the past that these life narratives offer can perhaps be fully appreciated as affective returns. In Brian Massumi's reckoning, the event "can't be restricted to one occurrence. Its quality of experience is bound to return" (104). In Rosy's life narratives, we see the reactivation of the past in the passage toward an already altered future, through the past and future of caste and gender relations, but also between different orders of the past in relation to gender and caste.

## NOTES

Acknowledgments: I am grateful to the editors of this volume S. Shankar and Charu Gupta for their detailed comments. I have greatly benefitted from the comments and suggestions by the participants of the workshop on "Caste and Life Narratives" at the University of Hawai'i at Mānoa in September 2016. The gestation and subsequent reworking of this paper, which is part of my unpublished doctoral dissertation, has been significantly shaped by critical comments from Ranjani Mazumdar and conversations with Devika J., T. T. Sreekumar, Ajith Kumar A. S., Aarti Sethi, and K. N. Sunandan. I am particularly grateful to Sudhir Mahadevan, Shivani Kapoor, and Ajit Chittambalam for comments on an earlier draft.

1. Unless otherwise noted, all translations are mine.
2. Rosy was born into the Pulaya caste, an erstwhile agricultural slave caste in Kerala. The Pulayas were technically freed from agricultural slavery after the Travancore

abolition of slavery act in 1855. Political mobilization, education, and economic independence led to their upward social and economic mobility to a limited extent (see Saradamoni; Basu). Caste names like "Pulaya" and "Paraya" widely used in colonial scholarship and in the later period are derogatory in nature, and hence I use these terms in this footnote, keeping in mind their historical context and complexities. I have mostly used the term Dalit, which literally means "broken" or "shattered," to refer to an agential identity and political gesture of self-recognition. The other terms currently used to refer to relationship among castes are "oppressed caste" and "dominant caste." In the essay, I use the terms "upper caste" and "lower caste" to refer to their existing usage in academic scholarshipwhile problematizing them.

3. Chelangad Gopalakrishnan, the first journalist to write about the film and its fate, states that a large angry mob attacked and set fire to Rosy's house, which was nothing more than a shack, the third night after the screening. Two police men on guard were forced to flee, the family escaped, and Rosy ran as far as to the highway, seeking help (*Cinemayude* 22).
4. The narratives about Rosy's disappearance order the events differently. In the descriptions by Gopalakrishnan and by Mani ("Charithram"; "Vigatakumaran"), Rosy fled the town on the third night of the first screening, following the violence against her. In my interview with him, Kavil Krishnan—Rosy's cousin, Indian National Congress activist, and the only relative who maintained ties with Rosy—claims that attacks against Rosy, pressure for sexual favors, and attempts to molest her continued for almost a year after the screening. He also claims that she fled once when she was attacked while returning home after a Kakkarissi performance.
5. As we will see soon, while Gopalakrishnan mentions Rosy's story and the violence against her, Mani centralizes Rosy's life and analyzes it within the complex history of Dalit labor and Dalit history in Malayalam cinema (see Gopalakrishnan, *Cinemayude*).
6. My interview with Kavil Krishnan provides a different version of this story. According to Krishnan, after the violence and attacks against her house, Rosy continued her work for the Kakkarissi plays. Almost a year after *Vigatakumaran*'s screening, Rosy was attacked by dominant caste men on her way back from a Kakkarissi performance near the Karamana bridge, when she was rescued by Kesava Pillai.
7. Various contemporary histories and state manuals record and describe these transformations in Travancore missionary narratives. Often written as memoirs of missionary work in Travancore, these texts focus on the despotic situation in the country due to the caste system and the missionary attempt to fight against "spiritual poverty." They also give detailed accounts of material life and its transitions (Mohan, *Modernity*). Robin Jeffrey's pioneering study of the powerful Nair caste and its decline brings forth questions of caste and power relations.
8. Channar is a community who belong mostly to the Thiruvananthapuram district of Southern Kerala. What used to be referred as the Channar Breast Cloth controversy in colonial scholarship has been recognised as Channar Revolt

in recent scholarship (Yesudas 4). Subsequent critical assessment of the historiography of the Channar Revolt argues for recovering the idea of Channars as social agents and as sensory and perceptive beings (Sheeju 313).

9. Secondary literature on theater testifies to these new spaces of Tamil, Sanskrit, and Malayalam theater. They map the formation of a new public in urban centers in the early twentieth century. See Sreekumar, *Malayala Sangeeta Nataka Charithram*.
10. In this volume, Shailaja Paik's essay, "Mangala Bansode and the Social Life of Tamasha," argues how women performers of the art form negotiated the sexual economy for their own survival and benefits.
11. Pierre Bourdieu defines the unthinkable as that for which one has no adequate instruments to conceptualize: "In the unthinkable of an epoch, there is all that one cannot think for want of ethical or political inclination; at the same time, the unthinkable may also be for want of instruments of thought such as problematics, concepts, methods, and techniques" (224).
12. In an interview that preceded the release of the film, Kamal said, "My curiosity was piqued by Vinu Abraham's book, *Nashta Nayika*, on Rosy, the heroine of *Vigatakumaran*. But I felt that the focus should be on Daniel, now acknowledged as the father of Malayalam cinema. I thought this is one film that ought to be made to remind us of our history" (Kamal qtd. in Nagarajan 11).
13. Swarnavel Eswaran's essay in this volume on the recent Tamil language biopic *Periyar*, on the founder of the Tamil self-respect movement and the Dravidar Kazhagam party, points to the inadequacies of the biopic aesthetic and stardom in enacting Periyar's radical politics.
14. Cinema halls have had a long and checkered history of being a contentious site of various conflicts in colonial Andhra Pradesh and in post-partition Delhi as pointed out by S. V. Srinivas and Aarti Sethi, respectively. Discussing a series of hostile caste encounters in Chunduru, Andhra Pradesh, Tharu and Niranjana map the space of the cinema hall as one of caste tensions and, in this particular case, involve a framed case of sexual violence brought by "upper caste" women against Dalit men.
15. For a detailed discussion of these differing notions of the past in Dalit history writing, see Mohan, "Religion" and "Creation."
16. Contemporary practices in world cinema gesture toward the reconstitution of history through cinema often through fiction, myth, or ritual. A vast body of work by the Black Audio Film Collective, intercultural cinema/hybrid cinema, and experimental cinema undertake this archaeological exercise of excavation, falsification, and the making of myths. See Marks.
17. Charu Gupta, in her reading of the persuasive and compelling popular Dalit narratives of Dalit Viranganas of 1857, shows how a symbolic redemption takes place in these narratives (*Gender* 86–109).

## WORKS CITED

Abraham, Vinu. *Nashtanayika*. DC Books, 2009.

Arondekar, Anjali. *For the Record: On Sexuality and the Colonial Archive in India*. Duke UP, 2009.

Basu, Rajsekhar. "A Page from Dalit History in Kerala: The Pulaya Movement in Travancore–Cochin in the Pre-Communist Phase." *Studies in People's History*, vol. 3, no. 1, 2016, pp. 45–58.

Bhatnagar, Dube Rashmi. "Feminine Ecriture, Trace Objects and the Death of Braj." *Unarchived Histories: The "Mad" and the "Trifling" in the Colonial and Postcolonial World*, edited by Gyanendra Pandey, Routledge, 2013.

Benjamin, Walter. *On the Concept of History*. Classic Books America, 2009.

Bourdieu, Pierre. *Distinction: A Social Critique of the Judgement of Taste*, translated by Richard Nice, Routledge, 1984.

De Certeau, Michel. "The Historiographical Operation." *The Writing of History*, translated by Tom Conley, Columbia UP, 1992, pp. 56–113.

Conor, Liz. *The Spectacular Modern Woman: Feminine Visibility in the 1920s*. Indiana UP, 2004.

Chabria, Suresh, and Paolo Cherchi Usai, editors. *Light of Asia: Indian Silent Cinema, 1912–1934*. Wiley Eastern, 1994.

De Heering, Alexandra. "Oral History and Dalit Testimonies: From the Ordeal to Speak to the Necessity to Testify." *South Asia Research*, vol. 33, no. 1, 2013, pp. 39–55.

Devika, J. "The Aesthetic Woman: Re-forming Female Bodies and Minds in Early Twentieth-Century Keralam." *Modern Asian Studies*, vol. 39, no. 2, 2005, pp. 461–87.

Eswaran, Swarnavel. "*Periyar* as a Biopic: Star Persona, Historical Events, and Politics." *Caste and Life Narratives*, ed. S. Shankar and Charu Gupta, Primus Books, 2019, pp. 97–119.

Gaines, Jane. "Film History and the Two Presents of Feminist Film Theory." *Cinema Journal*, vol. 44, no. 1, Fall 2004, pp. 113–19.

Ginzburg, Carlo. *Clues, Myths, and the Historical Method*, translated by John Tedeschi and Anne C. Tedeschi, Johns Hopkins UP, 1989.

Gopalakrishnan, Chelangattu. *Cinemayude Charithram*. Prathap Publications, 1972.

———. *Malayala Cinemayile Vanavarum Veenavarum*. DC Books, 2012.

Groesbeck, Rolf. "Classical Music, Folk Music, and the Brahmanical Temple in Kerala, India." *Asian Music*, vol. 30, no. 2, Spring–Summer 1999, pp. 87–112.

Gupta, Charu. "Intimate Desires: Dalit Women and Religious Conversions in Colonial India." *The Journal of Asian Studies*, vol. 73, no. 3, Aug. 2014, pp. 661–87.

———. *The Gender of Caste: Representing Dalits in Print*. U of Washington P, 2016.

Hansen, Kathryn. "Theatrical Transvestism in the Parsi, Gujarati and Marathi Theatres (1850–1940)." *South Asia: Journal of South Asian Studies*, vol. 24, no. 1, 2001, pp. 59–73.

Jay, Martin. *Downcast Eyes: The Denigration of Vision in Twentieth-Century French Thought.* U of California P, 1993.

Jeffrey, Robin. *The Decline of Nair Dominance: Society and Politics in Travancore 1847–1908.* Oxford UP, 1976.

Kapoor, Shivani. "Reading Untouchability: Hindi Autobiographical Narratives among Two Untouchable Castes in Uttarpradesh." MPhil diss, Centre for Political Studies, Jawaharlal Nehru U, 2011.

Kochu, K. K. "Celluloid: Charitrathinte Varthamanam." *Utharakalam*, 2 Dec. 2013, www.utharakalam.com/?p=7806. Accessed 20 Sept. 2013.

Kosambi, Meera. *Gender, Culture, and Performance: Marathi Theatre and Cinema Before Independence.* Routledge, 2015.

Krishnan, Kavil. Personal interview. 17 July 2006.

Kumar, Ajith. "Caste in Cinema and Music: The Kerala Experience." *Round Table India*, 22 June 2013, http://roundtableindia.co.in/index.php?option=com_content&view=article&id=6677:caste-in-cinema-and-music-the-kerala-experience&catid=119:feature&Itemid=132. Accessed 23 July 2013.

Kumar, Udaya. *Writing the First Person: Literature, History and Autobiography in Modern Kerala.* Permanent Black, 2016.

Madathil, Sajitha. *Malayala Nadaka Sthree Charithram.* Matrubhumi Books, 2013.

Mahadevan, Raman. "Industrial Entrepreneurship in Princely Travancore: 1930–47." *South Indian Economy: Agrarian Change, Industrial Structure and State Policy*, edited by Sabyasachi Bhattacharya, et al., Oxford UP, 1991, pp. 159–207.

Mani, Kunnukuzhy. "Charithram Thedi Durantha Nayika." *Chithrabhumi Film Weekly*, 24 June 2004, pp. 14–19.

———. "Vigatakumarano Balano Adya Malayala Cinema." *Film Rama*, July 2005, pp. 32–36.

Marks, Laura U. *The Skin of the Film: Intercultural Cinema, Embodiment, and the Senses.* Duke UP, 2000.

Massumi, Brian. *The Power at the End of the Economy.* Duke UP, 2014.

Mohan, P. Sanal. "Religion, Social Space and Identity: The Prathyaksha Raksha Daiva Sabha and the Making of Cultural Boundaries in Twentieth Century Kerala." *South Asia: Journal of South Asian Studies*, vol. 28, no. 1, 2005, pp. 35–63.

———. *Modernity of Slavery: Struggles Against Caste Inequality in Colonial Kerala.* Oxford UP, 2015.

———. "Creation of Social Space through Prayers among Dalits in Kerala, India." *Journal of Religious and Political Practice*, vol. 2, no. 1, 2016, pp. 40–57.

Mukherjee, Debashree. "Scandalous Evidence: Looking for the Bombay Film Actress in the Absent Film Archives (1930s–1940s)." *Doing Women's Film History: Reframing Cinemas, Past and Future*, edited by Christine Gledhill and Julia Knight, U of Illinois P, 2015, pp. 29–42.

Nagarajan, Saraswathy. "Flashback in Tinsel Town." *The Hindu*, 11 Oct. 2012, http://www.thehindu.com/features/cinema/Flashback-in-tinsel-town/article12553583.ece. Accessed 6 July 2017.

Paik, Shailaja. "Mangala Bansode and the Social Life of Tamasha: Caste, Sexuality, and Discrimination in Modern Maharashtra." *Caste and Life Narratives*, ed. S. Shankar and Charu Gupta, Primus Books, 2019, pp. 173–201.

Parayil, Sujith Kumar. "Photography(s) in 20th Century Kerala." PhD diss, Manipal U, 2007.

Pillai, Raman K. P. "Balan: Malayalathile Adya Shabda Chitram." *Malayala Manorama*, 6 Dec. 1939.

Raj, Rekha. "Politics of Gender and Dalit Identity: Representation of Dalit Women in Contemporary Dalit Discourses in Kerala." PhD diss, Mahatma Gandhi U, 2015.

Ramachandran, G. P., and Radhakrishnan Cheruvally, editors. *Celluloid: Charitrathilillatha Jeevithavum Cinemayum*. Chintha Publishers, 2013.

Ramamurthy, Priti. "The Indian Modern Girl in the 1920s and 1930s." *The Modern Girl Around the World: Consumption, Modernity, and Globalization*, edited by Alys Eve Weinbaum, Lynn M. Thomas, Priti Ramamurthy, Uta G. Poiger, Madeleine Yue Dong, and Tani E. Barlow, Duke UP, 2008, pp. 147–74.

Rege, Sharmila. "The Hegemonic Appropriation of Sexuality: The Case of the Lavani Performers of Maharashtra." *Contributions to Indian Sociology*, vol. 29, no. 1–2, 1995, pp. 23–38.

———. *Writing Caste/Writing Gender: Narrating Dalit Women's Testimonios*. U of Chicago P, 1999.

Rowena, Jenny P. "Celluloyidile Dalit Yuvathiyum Malayalikalum." *Utharakalam*, 3 Dec. 2013, http://utharakalam.com/?p=7128. Accessed 12 May 2013.

Saradamoni, K. *Emergence of a Slave Caste: Pulayas of Kerala*. People's Publishing House, 1980.

Sreedharan, Darshana, and Vinu Abraham. "When Ghosts Come Calling: Re-'Projecting' the Disappeared Muses of Malayalam Cinema." *SARAI Reader*, Sept. 2013, pp. 336–45.

Pandian, M. S. S. "Writing Ordinary Lives." *Economic and Political Weekly*, vol. 43, no. 38, 20–26 Sept. 2008, pp. 34–40.

Scott, Joan Wallach. *The Fantasy of Feminist History*. Duke UP, 2011.

Sebastian, Meryl Mary. "The Name of the Rose." *TBIP*, June 2013, http://thebigindianpicture.com/2013/06/the-name-of-the-rose/. Accessed 23 Dec. 2013.

Sethi, Aarti. "Cinematic Sites: Encountering Film Exhibition in Delhi." MPhil diss, Jawaharlal Nehru U, 2009.

Shankar, S., and Charu Gupta. "'My Birth Is My Fatal Accident': Introduction to Caste and Life Narratives." *Caste and Life Narratives*, ed. S. Shankar and Charu Gupta, Primus Books, 2019, pp. 1–15.

Sreekumar, Kureeppuzha. "Nadiyude Raatri." *Samakaleena Malayalam Varika*, 6 June 2003, n. p.

———. *Malayala Sangeeta Nataka Charithram*. Current Books, 2002.

Srinivas, S. V. "Is There a Public in the Cinema Hall?" *Framework: The Journal of Cinema and Media*, vol. 42, 2000, pp. 1–25.

Shankar, S. "Thugs and Bandits: Life and Law in Colonial and Epicolonial India." *Baleful Postcoloniality*, special issue of *Biography*, vol. 36, no. 1, Winter 2013, pp. 97–123.

Sheeju, N. V. "The Shanar Revolts, 1822–99: Towards a Figural Cartography of the Pretender." *South Asia Research*, vol. 35, no. 3, 2015, pp. 298–317.

Tharu, Susie, and Tejaswini Niranjana. "Problems for a Contemporary Theory of Gender." *Subaltern Studies: Writings on South Asian History and Society*, vol. 9, edited by Shahid Amin and Dipesh Chakrabarty, Oxford UP, 1996, pp. 232–60.

Trouillot, Michel-Rolph. *Silencing the Past: Power and the Production of History*. Beacon Press, 2012.

Vijayakrishnan, N. *Malayala Cinemayude Katha*. DC Books, 2007.

Weinbaum, Alys Eve, Lynn M. Thomas, Priti Ramamurthy, Uta G. Poiger, Madeleine Yue Dong, and Tani E. Barlow, editors. *The Modern Girl Around the World: Consumption, Modernity, and Globalization*. Duke UP, 2008.

Yesudas, R. N. *A People's Revolt in Travancore: A Backward Class Movement for Social Freedom*. Kerala Historical Society, 1975.

# 8

# CASTE LIFE NARRATIVES, VISUAL REPRESENTATION, AND PROTECTED IGNORANCE

Y. S. ALONE

This essay is an attempt to interrogate certain visual manifestations as a perceptual means of understanding and to approach caste and life narratives from the conceptual framework of "protected ignorance." Caste life narratives are typically regarded as literary works, but they have also become subjects of visual language, wherein experiences of caste life become a means to create visual metaphors as potential critiques of the hegemonic and the normative in dominant Indian society. This essay is concerned with the experiences of caste life and attempts to move away from narratives of "protected ignorance."

Colonial India saw the production of four dominant modes of discourse in understanding Indian history and culture: (1) an imperial discourse in which race and Western superiority were assumed; (2) a Brahmanical discourse mainly rooted in the idea of divinity, an outright trust in textual traditions, and a politics opposed to imperial interpretations; (3) a Marxist/socialist discourse mainly associated with economic interpretations; and (4) a non-Brahmanical discourse displacing the above three. Many of the Indian discursive processes under the colonial conditions were distinctly marked by a Brahmanical dominance located in a political context of nation and nationalism. Brahmanical hegemony produced metanarratives of a nationalist imagination rooted in an intellectual politics of homogenized precolonial, colonial, and postcolonial Indian traditions. Such a process produced the two subjective categories of the political and the moral, rooted in conscious imaginations. As I have discussed elsewhere, B. R. Ambedkar was the first person to offer systematically a critique of the first three dominant discourses listed above from a non-Brahmanical perspective by adhering to the theory of dependent/interdependent origination, or the *pratitya samvutpada* of Buddha.[1]

The imperial discourse gave prominence to a racial theory of superiority and produced a distinctive meaning of power. Even today, the power of the West dominates perceptual understandings and worldviews, while the West's authoritarianism allows it to ignore its own beliefs in stereotypes. Perhaps because of its inherent nature, the West has produced white supremacy and "white ignorance," as Charles Mills observes. In her critique of the authoritarian nature of mainstream Western academic knowledge production, Gayatri Chakravorty Spivak analyzes the three philosophical traditions of Kant, Hegel, and Marx—along with the psychoanalytical categories that Freud and Lacan proposed—by relying on deconstruction as the main discursive practice of reading. She offers a constructive critique of what she calls "sanctioned ignorance" (*Critique* 2). While stimulating, Spivak's critique does not investigate the inherent nature of "ignorance," which is both embedded in dominant cultural practices and thinking and is produced by a native local hegemony in a country like India. It is imperative to understand knowledge-formation processes and their conceptual frameworks and objectives more deeply. Furthermore, it is critical to understand rationally the intricate connection between societal practices and their governing ideas, such as the sacredness of religious textual traditions and belief systems. One may argue that rationality is relative, but its relativity depends on its objectives. If the objective of rationality is to kill ignorance, then it becomes a righteous rationality, and if it is the opposite, it signifies an unrighteous rationality and, consequently, a "protected ignorance." A critique of "protected ignorance" is a conceptual means to interrogate knowledge formation-processes and their objectives. It is equally aimed at demystifying metanarratives of the claimed theoretical groundings of "sanctioned ignorance."

"Protected ignorance" is a day-to-day phenomenon that is seen in every sphere, including in the creative realms of visuality. Perceptual understandings of visual signifiers, being socially and politically located, are gauges of "protected ignorance." Expressive urges are manifested through language, where language need not mean only an accepted notion of language, but may encompass all possible expressive means and capacities. In this context, "subaltern" as it is understood and applied as a category in India becomes problematic, particularly when it is read against Ambedkar's understandings of caste. Ambedkar defines caste as not only a division of labor but also of laborers. The experience of division of laborers cannot be understood by the nomenclature of "subaltern." "Subaltern," being a generic rubric and more class oriented, does not empower us to understand caste differences and conflicts. Caste entails graded hierarchy, whereby levels of discrimination and exclusion are different in each case.

"Caste life narratives" are often associated with life experiences produced in relation to the social category of caste and are never homogenous experiences. Essentially, caste life narrative connotes a literary movement. However, this movement has touched upon all spheres of creative expressions and has also become a part of visual representations. This essay attempts to show how caste life narratives become an agential means to understand visual representations that are markedly different from and also challenge the hegemonic Brahmanical narrative.

## I.

While colonial modernity entered Indian conditions as a superior power, art patronage became increasingly popular and gallery space became the new arena of art activity, even as access to such space was restricted based on caste stratification. However, colonials were not challenged by the modernist agenda of "high caste" Indian society. The imperial government established art educational institutes, which sought to break the shackles of Indian society. Ironically, the biggest beneficiary of this endeavor ended up being the caste-Hindu society, which claimed that tradition was sacred and a marker of purity.

Caste-Hindu society used the textual tradition of the past as a tool to reinvent a discursive process that was exclusive and culturally hegemonic. Because of the mobility that colonial modernity offered in artists' traditional occupations, pictorial conventions became hybridized to cater to the colonial administration's interest in getting Indian subjects to accept the cultural superiority of Western tradition. Political power empowered colonial modernity. However, at the level of cultural relics of the past, social norms persisted. Despite education being a decisive tool of initiating rationality, religious ritualistic tradition could never become an object of critique. Due to the objective formulations of knowledge production on the basis of tradition, the institution of *varna* and caste has become an integral part of the sacredness of tradition that cannot be questioned.[2] At the same time, people like Chhatrapati Shahuji Maharaj of Kolhapur, who financed the education of "untouchables" and "backwards," including art education, envisioned inclusive development.

When religious dogmas entered as pictorial subjects in colonial modernity, there was an exoticization of and belief in the greatness of tradition. Violence is an embedded aspect of caste consciousness, which becomes normative for caste-Hindus (that is, Hindus above the "untouchable" castes). Meanwhile, the notion of spirituality becomes an intervening tool of opposition to the Western critic, as exemplified in defending dogmas of tradition. Philosopher S. Radhakrishnan takes refuge in the chronology of tradition and talks about the continuity of tradition as a great achievement. Radhakrishnan maintains, "The Vedic tradition became surrounded with sanctity, and so helped to transmit culture and ensure the continuity of civilization" (18). The likes of Radhakrishnan seek to understand continuity and multiplicity of tradition as a part of an absorption process of the Hindu civilizational state. It is equally important to understand the defense of caste as an institution in his view of Indian society. For caste-Hindus, caste is normative and beyond interrogation. Caste life narratives and their visual manifestations contradict such hegemonic thinking and positions.

Ananda Kentish Coomaraswamy's writings have been dominant in the field of art history in India and are still taught reverently abroad as the representative perspective of an Eastern-Oriental icon and accepted as the most legitimate source on Indian art. While narrating the historical nature of Indian art, Coomaraswamy successfully advocates the idea of spirituality in *Transformation of Nature in Indian Art* and even defends the tradition of sati (widow burning) as a union of Shiva and Shakti in his essay "Sati: Defense of Eastern Women." Equally crucial in reinforcing hegemony is textual language, which propels a desire to see the cultural object as "spiritual sacred," devoid of any social objectives, conflicts, tensions, and politics. The material cultural object thus became evidence to support the religious textual tradition of Brahmanical superiority. The claimed continuity of tradition has neither been critiqued nor has there been any effort to make the discursive process rational or aimed at killing ignorance. The body of material evidence in the form of sculptures and architectural monuments becomes the preferred modes of disseminating an art tradition in which text is a guiding tool to contextualize the content of art.

Caste life narratives and their representation in visual art have emerged as antithetical to such a homogenized Brahmanical understanding of Indian art. Cultural difference displaces the discursive process of homogeneity of tradition. Attempts to reconstruct the past as well as its cultural residues from a non-colonial as well as a non-Brahmanical perspective can become intervening tools of investigation and understanding, and directly challenge the political project of homogeneity of tradition. When the oppressed challenge homogenizing discourses through caste life narratives in text and in art, they enable a shift of focus from the textual tradition of a Brahmanical past. The oppressed formulate a language of caste narratives distinct from conventional understandings of the hegemonic group. Given that language has already been rendered hegemonic in every sphere of life, it is the task of the oppressed to carve out a different language, written and pictorial, that is rational and aimed at killing ignorance.

Mahatma Jyotiba Phule (1827–1890) and B. R. Ambedkar (1891–1956) were instrumental in enacting a paradigmatic shift from a mere acknowledgment of the dogmatisms of tradition to the ineffectiveness of ritual practices as legitimized in religious texts. For Ambedkar, the political project of fighting untouchability meant not only to question the exclusive nature of caste practices and traditions, but also to underline their self-centered proclamations and political designs that religious texts sanctioned. Additionally, he brought out the ways in which cultural behaviors were reflected through a series of behaviors dictated by caste. While presenting a critique of *varna* and caste, Ambedkar also states that "caste is a perversion of *varna*," which explains the embedded connection between *varna* and caste as a hierarchical, unequal system that cannot be deemed as an ideal social system (3: 146).[3] Ambedkar critiques caste as hierarchy and further observes the distinction between rules and principles: "Rules are practical; they are habitual ways of doing things according to prescription. But principles are intellectual; they are useful methods of judging things. Rules seek to tell an agent just what course of action to pursue. Principles do not prescribe a specific course of action" (1: 75). Through religion, as a set of rules and principles of command, Ambedkar analyzes the idea of caste as power: "What is called Religion by the Hindus is nothing but a multitude of commands and prohibitions" (1: 75).

Ambedkar's engagements with the modernity project question the rationale of behavioral practices of caste-Hindus. He systematically dissects the corpus of Brahmanical textual tradition and, consequently, completely rejects the conventional idea of the "Gupta period" as a "golden age."[4] He rejects Brahmanical cultural nationalism as a basis of understanding, regarding it as a methodological tool to maintain intellectual dominance. Brahmanical cultural nationalism failed to create any fraternity and address the social injustices that were inflicted on "lower caste" communities in India, such as being labeled "untouchable," falling at the bottom of the caste hierarchy itself, being subordinate in the nation's government, and being excluded from nation building. Thus, Ambedkar's task was to offer a discursive process of displacing Brahmanical hegemony and to provide an alternative framework based on rationality, pragmatism, and political morality. This idea of Ambedkar's discursive process later generated numerous caste life narratives that became stumbling blocks for the dominant discourse of nationalism.

## II.

Ambedkar also understood the limitations of Marxism in addressing cultural practices, as he discusses in the essay "Buddha or Karl Marx." He observes that socialists in India followed a European economic interpretation of history. In "Annihilation of Caste," he writes:

> They propound that man is an economic creature, that his activities and aspirations are bound by economic facts, that property is the only source

> of power. They, therefore, preach that political and social reforms are but gigantic illusions and that economic reform by equalization of property must have precedence over every other kind of reform. (1: 44)

Ambedkar further drew attention to the power of religion and how Indian caste society was consciously following caste rules as religious duties. Caste life narratives, as literary products and pictorial representations, produce a critique of the power of religion.

The concept of divinity, attached to the origin and existence of caste, has a meaningful social implication in advocating a Brahmanical perception of the present and the past. The artisan community of Prajapati is designated as belonging to that divine architect, but in reality the *varna-jati* division never allows such artisan social groups to have the same power in the realm of social behavior as that of the divine being, or for that matter, the same status as that of a Brahmin or a Kshatriya. Even during the postcolonial period, such irony hardly gets discussed in the intellectual domain. As Shete Vaijayanti demonstrates in "Expressive Theory of Caturvarnya and the *Shilpa* Texts: References to Caste and Gender," all the Shilpa texts, for example treatises on art and architecture, have profoundly categorized differences in various media on the basis of *varna* formulations, including the advocacy of image worship as per the *varnas*. Their theoretical conception is based on the four-fold division of *varna* society, which has gone into the making of their aesthetic perception.

Modernity had multiple strands and manifestations in the colonial period. At the political level, it was a struggle to advocate democracy as a modern means to espouse nation and nationality, as it went hand in hand with cosmetic adaptations of caste-based society without bringing any social change. A mere adoption of formalism in pictorial language denied the very principle of modernity, as modernity is associated with a rejection of hierarchical values and adherence to equality. Indian painters formulated a modernity that did not create space for an interrogation of cultural caste practices. Consequently, modernity needs to be reinvestigated as a systemic tool for maintaining power relationships that operate within caste hierarchy. While tradition, as put forth by the Brahmanical reconstruction of the cultural past, negates the ideas of critical modernity, Sanskritization, under the banner of modernity, generates a debate regarding cultural modernity that is confined to an urban-centric idea of tradition's greatness. Urban and non-urban have become a subject of discussion in the pictorial language.

Dominant Brahmanical understandings underscore life narratives and representations of M. K. Gandhi (Mahatma Gandhi) in the realm of art. The idea of village society, as Gandhi advocated, remains one of romantic realism and does not address caste perceptions. Village India as a social category has been subject to Orientalism and thus reduced to highly exoticized representations. Given how influential Gandhi remains and the pervasiveness of such reductive representations, it becomes clear how difficult it would be for an artist to think from a non-Gandhian perspective and, consequently, how caste narrative could not become and is not a subject of dominant pictorial language. It is in this context that the Gandhi-Ambedkar debates are revealing. While both men are located in a colonial modernity, Gandhi adheres to *varnashramadharma* (caste society), whereas Ambedkar is committed to the destruction of the caste-*varna* model.

Intellectual and creative realms are directly and indirectly connected with caste-Hindu perceptions. Even so-called progressives, including socialists and liberals in the fields of creative writing and art practice, have endorsed the idea of superiority based on caste. As I have discussed elsewhere, the general intellectual sphere of "high caste" dominates artists and intellectual caste-Hindus' worldviews, wherein the self-centered, normative, and unchanged representation of the new nation is not questioned. This static caste perception dominates both the intellectual and creative realms to the extent that it becomes difficult, perhaps even impossible, for one to differentiate between the modernist project of Gandhi-Jawaharlal Nehru and that of Phule-Ambedkar. Ambedkar vehemently opposed Gandhian perceptions of morality, which were based on following caste duties as a supreme way of living. The caste-Hindu modernist uncritically absorbed Gandhi's cultural nationalism. Such hegemonic conceptions percolated in the minds of many because of the deep roots in Brahmanical reconstructions, and many people had no problem accepting Gandhi as the sole representative of freedom struggle. Radhakrishnan finds in Gandhi a persona that represents the tradition of honesty and duty, stating, "From ṛṣis is of the Upaniṣads down to Tagore and Gandhi, the Hindu has acknowledged that truth wears vestures of many colors and speaks in strange tongues" (36). Further, G. Alyosius explains:

> The political process in colonial India was dichotomous in an ideal-typical sense: the traditionally dominant communities of Brahmins and allied upper-castes brought together in terms of newly created economic and political interests, raised the slogan of nationalism when the British attempted to withdraw their exclusive patronage. (216)

The nationalist class, predominantly caste-Hindus, failed to see caste as a problem and closed their minds against any anti-caste sensibilities, including caste life narratives.

The discursive process of interpretation/understanding was narrativized in the projection of Gandhi as the Father of the Nation. There is no difference and no oppositional logic between the modernist and the postcolonialist;

both of their desires have often been to eulogize Gandhi. Because images of Gandhi appear as a part of the nationalist metanarrative of struggling for freedom, all images of Gandhi in the public domain can position him as a figure of struggles for freedom. Even today, quite a number of artists have painted Gandhi in a celebratory mode. A contemporary painter, Sudhanshu Sutar, paints Gandhi walking on a pointed saw, whereas in another painting, he uses the gardener's watering can to signal his dedication to community. According to Sutar, "When Gandhi was shot dead, the first person who held Gandhi was the gardener whose name was Raghu Nayak and he was from my village. Raghu Nayak happened to be the first witness in the Gandhi murder case, and yet nobody talks about him. The story of Raghu Nayak is told among our community with lot of reverence." Though Sutar could easily relate to Gandhi's image, the same could not be said for Mahatma Phule, who was also from the gardener caste and was radical in his thinking and functioning. When asked about Phule, Sutar says, "I do not know about Mahatma Phule but I shall study him." Sutar's lack of knowledge about Phule may indicate how dominant Brahmanical discourse has not allowed Indians to know people like Phule and Ambedkar who also stand socially and culturally for social transformation.

Intellectuals involved in knowledge production often create a discourse of "protected ignorance," and the dominant narrative and representation of Gandhi in colonial and postcolonial writings and in art symbolizes this "protected ignorance." Akeel Bilgrami and many others have showered considerable love on Gandhian ethics. While situating Gandhi, Bilgrami says, "I repeat that on his lips and pen, the question and the anxiety about the transformation of the concept of nature into the concept of natural resources was an essentially religious person's question and anxiety." Bilgrami further states, "With this aim of generality in place, let me, then, turn to saying something to situate the very issues that Gandhi was raising in a more secular idiom and philosophy than his, stressing more the notion of *value* in nature than the notion of *sacred* or the spiritual in nature" (27, emphasis in original). Bilgrami did not see any contradiction or problem in analyzing Gandhi's ethics. For example, in the 1921 October issue of *Young India*, Gandhi declared himself to be a Sanatani (orthodox) Hindu and voiced his firm belief in the *shastras* (sacred religious texts) and in the institution of caste and *varna*. Caste positions have often assumed considerable importance in hermeneutic understandings. However, caste narratives empower readers to rethink the whole idea of human value and question the ethicality of caste-Hindus.

Ramkinker Baiz and Dalit artists, through their own lived experiences and caste life narratives, have challenged dominant representations of Gandhi. Baiz, a sculptor from Bengal, showed courage to be different and did not

Figure 8.1: Top: Ramkinker Baiz, *Gandhi after Pune Karar*, cement, 1953–55, size with pedestal approximately 13.6 feet. Bottom: detail. Photo by Professor Snjoy Mallik, Kalabhavan, Shantiniketan.

allow his consciousness to accept the normative understanding of Gandhi. Between 1953 and 1955, he created a huge sculpture of Gandhi in the premises of Shantiniketan University (Fig. 8.1). He created a number of key models as a precursor to this sculpture. Baiz's large rendering of Gandhi—which literally depicts Gandhi on a pedestal and with a human skull under his foot—remains the sole example from a modernist who refuses to accept Gandhi's persona as that of an extraordinary person. According to Baiz, "Gandhi became Mahatma by crushing people." Baiz made this statement when Ritwik Ghatak made a documentary showing Baiz before the colossal image of Gandhi, explaining the importance of the human skull.[5] Baiz decodes Gandhian achievements by placing the skull under the feet of a tall, towering Gandhi. The sculptor's deliberate intervention is rooted in pragmatic understandings and not in romanticizing this icon of the freedom struggle. Baiz therefore harshly critiques the idea of Gandhi as a figure of "nonviolence." Baiz's image of Gandhi is conceptualized through a formalistic engagement and offers a different reading of Gandhi that challenges Brahmanical representations.

## III.

As delineated above through the example of Gandhi, modern art practices in India remained Brahmanical in their thinking and practice, thereby adhering to the ideas associated with "protected ignorance." Modern Indian art practices have engaged more with formalism, and very few have shown an inclination toward political themes and subjects. The "Place for People" exhibition has been pivotal in representing Indian modernity as a return to narrative figurative expressions. Those involved in the exhibition claimed to be painting and representing the life of the working class, but they failed to adequately question their own self or positionality, and thus, caste was not a category of intervention in their pictorial thinking. The modernity that was being taught and practiced by these artists continued to be a "Brahmanical modernity," which would always be legitimized when the dominant hegemonic group dictated the nature of aesthetic canons. As I argue above, "protected ignorance" has been a part of Brahmanical meta-narrative, and consequently, neither a caste narrative nor a critique of hegemony could emerge as part of an alternative thinking.

Caste life narratives, however, reveal structures of power as well as subjugations, and also empower us to interrogate the "rules" and "principles" as Ambedkar proposed. Ambedkar's followers began to think differently and attacked the very canons of language in art communities. For example, caste life narratives emerged as a powerful medium of expression in the Marathi literary circle that shook the consciousness of readers. However, a similar caste life narrative in modern and contemporary art practices had to wait until the emergence of Savi Sawarkar, who painted caste life narratives. Later, a few more came forward who also challenged the way caste was conceived of in visual art, and they started seriously questioning the ongoing aesthetic canons. These included artists like J. Nandakumar, Jaya Daronde, Pavan Kumar, Prakash Gaikwad, Sudharak Owle, Prajapati, Lokesh Khodke, Malvika, Rajaneesh, Navneet, Vinu, and Baiju.

Among writings on Dalit art, Gary Michael Tartakov's edited book *Dalit Art and Visual Imagery* is a pioneering attempt to discuss imagery in visual art that Dalits have produced. In spite of its various strengths, the book is devoid of alternative representations of Dalits, discussions of differences, or even experiences of conflicts. The book's limitations are disappointing because caste life narratives, as reflected in Dalit art, not only challenge modernity in India, but also interrogate the nomenclature of "subaltern" and the idea of "postcolonial." In the rest of the essay, I take examples from the works of various Dalit and non-Dalit artists who, through their personal experiences of caste, repudiate, ridicule, and critique Brahmanical hegemony in their art.

J. Nandakumar's works exemplify how the personal experience of oppression can become a fundamental tool in working against "protected ignorance." Nandakumar belongs to an Ambedkarite family and received a BFA in drawing and painting from the Government School of Arts, Aurangabad, Maharashtra. Nandakumar studied modernist ways of painting

Figure 8.2: J. Nandakumar, *Gandhi after Pune Karar*, acrylic on canvas, 54 inches x 66 inches, 2010.


and turned out to be a fabulous abstract painter. Despite his poor conditions, he pursued his education and interest in art and confronts the dominant caste groups throughout his education. Because of the discrimination he endured, Nandakumar rethought his painting practices and ended up connecting with Sawarkar, who emerged as an important figure in Indian contemporary art. Nandakumar's constant engagements with his own society and many literary youngsters made him rethink societal values. His disagreements with Gandhi's ideals, which the Ambedkarite community in the state of Maharashtra also shared, became his artistic point of departure.[6]

Dalits' everyday caste narratives generate a sense of disgust within caste-Hindu society. Nandakumar paints *Gandhi after Pune Karar* (Fig. 8.2) to express this disgust. Interestingly, only one photograph is in circulation among the Ambedkarite community on the Poona Pact, showing Ambedkar and others standing beside Ambedkar's car in front of the Yervada prison in Pune. There was one popular oleograph in circulation nearly three decades ago showing Ambedkar and others signing the Poona Pact. It is painted in a realist style, imagining what it may have looked like when the pact was signed. However, Nandakumar is the first gallery artist to paint this theme. Recalling the historical pact between Gandhi and Ambedkar, Nandakumar paints Gandhi not as a crusader of nationalist narratives but as a destroyer of political rights for the scheduled castes. Gandhi and the Congress opposed the demand that Ambedkar put forth for the political rights of the depressed communities in the form of separate electorates. A fundamental question would be the following—is the subject (in this case the scheduled caste of India) so blind that it would not speak against the politically charged morality of suppression? The history of the Round Table Conference tells us that the Indian National Congress had agreed to the communal award for Muslims and others, but refused the same for the scheduled castes. Nandakumar creates a pictorial representation of Gandhi as a lean and thin person, the way he was, posing in the foreground. In the background, he paints a flat reclining traumatized image of a Dalit whose distress is evident by his posture (Fig. 8.2). Gandhi has trampled upon the other body of a Dalit painted in the foreground, and Gandhi's walking stick is converted into a trident and a lance piercing into the body of the Dalit, signifying a systemic, traumatic death of the oppressed. Gandhi has multiple heads shown in a horizontal tier. This representation of multiple heads is drawn from mythic figural representations (like the multiheaded Rudra or Shiva and the ten-headed Ravana of the Ramayana), and Gandhi is portrayed as a caricature of tradition. The trauma that Dalit artists experience inform a field of pictorial signifiers, and in this case also allow the artist and the viewer to revisit the historical event of the Poona Pact. Nandakumar claims that the painting represents his reaction after reading the Poona Pact between Ambedkar and Gandhi. Remembering is an attempt to revisit trauma, and in this case remembering is a continued process of expressing displeasure toward Gandhi and others. Nandakumar's image of Gandhi gave rise to a storm in the Mumbai art world. His exhibition was shut down. Neither critics nor custodians of opposition to censorial cultural policing in India came forward to discuss his work or even bothered to acknowledge it.

In a recently painted second version (Fig. 8.3), Nandakumar reads Gandhi differently, painting him like the Hindu god Shiva though Gandhi was a devout Vaishnavite. A snake coming out of his neck and frightening a Dalit marks a striking representation of oppression, fear, and the might of caste-Hindus, whose hate for "lower castes" is deeply embedded and operates as an invisible reality. This painting is a powerful representation of Gandhi in the minds of Ambedkarites, who reject being a part of Gandhism. It also signifies events in the political sphere of post-independence India where Gandhi's Harijan ideology condemns Dalits to supplicate to the Congress Party (with which Gandhi was associated) with a begging bowl forever.

As discussed earlier, modernist painters have not addressed caste in their pictorial representations, as their artistic pedagogies and political understandings would prevent them from doing so. Sawarkar happened to be the first gallery artist who challenged the very discourse of Brahmanical

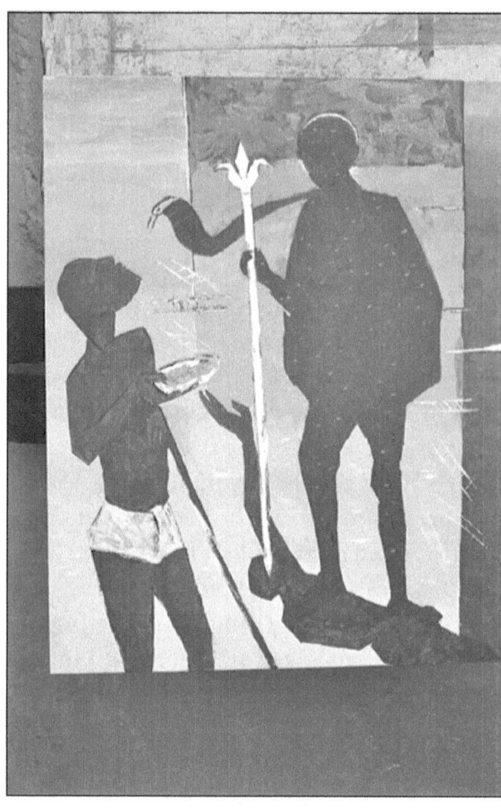

Figure 8.3: J. Nandakumar, *Gandhi after Pune Karar II*, acrylic on canvas, 3 feet x 4 feet, 2011.


cosmetic modernity and its aesthetic canons. Sawarkar is from Nagpur and studied drawing and painting at the Government Chitrakala Mahavidhyalaya, Nagpur, for his bachelor's degree. Part of the Ambedkarite movement, Sawarkar finely observes the naked realities of caste life. His own life narrative became a repository of events; he visualized his own caste narratives as a point of departure from what was expected of him. Sawarkar assigns his own iconographic symbols to the social identity of the "untouchable" community. By aiming to challenge viewers with his volatile images that disrupt perceptions of caste-Hindus, Sawarkar's art becomes inherently political in the way it upsets social and aesthetic norms, especially given that his personal intervention had its genesis in how he portrayed his community. By the time Sawarkar started painting, Dalit life narratives had emerged as a powerful means to explore the world of caste realities.

*Untouchables under the Black Sun* is a telling work that makes a profound statement on the abject poverty of "untouchable" communities and their miserable condition of living i166n open spaces (Fig. 8.4). The black sun is a symbolic representation of the darkness in daylight that forbids "untouchables" any freedom, though the sun is usually a general symbol

Figure 8.4: Savi Sawarkar, *Untouchables under the Black Sun*, oil on canvas, 11 feet x 5 feet 6 inches, 1990. © Copyright and reproduced courtesy of the artist.

of hope because its emanation of light and energy is crucial to everyone's survival. But in the life of the "untouchable," no such luxury exists. Though it operates at an imaginary level, the image equally aims to remind caste-Hindus of a glaring physical and material fact of life of an untouchable, where freedom is completely absent from their life. It is interesting to see a parallel in the caste life narrative from Laxman Mane, the author of *Upara*. Mane's narrative shows the startling condition of his community living on the outskirts of society and on the garbage of both the village and the city. In a similar manner, Sawarkar's painting shows a narrative of caste life and the ways in which a particular caste has to survive even in a postcolonial situation.

Many elements contributed to Sawarkar's evolution as an artist. Sawarkar listened to a song by Tulsiram, a professor in Jawaharlal Nehru University in New Delhi: *manu mahā thagvā ham janire aur kaisā kaisā rās rasāiye* (Manu was a great cheater, we have realized how he played tricks). On listening to this song, Sawarkar realized how Manu was a villain to Dalits and others.[7] Around 1990, there was a large-scale attack on Dalits near Agra. When Sawarkar visited the location, he was filled with anger and hate regarding caste and its legitimacy. He discovered how heinous Manu and his ideas about caste were, and how these ideas of hierarchy, in human's treatment of socially lowered communities, generating hate and violence, are present in the everyday narratives of caste-Hindus. Sawarkar's series on Manu offers a visual representation of the past and the present. For him, Ambedkar becomes a cardinal figure of inspiration

Figure 8.5. Savi Sawarkar, *Dalit Pissing on Manu*, oil on canvas, 10 feet x 6 feet, 1991. © Copyright and reproduced courtesy of the artist.

who critiqued Manu in the strongest possible manner. *Dalit Pissing on Manu* is indicative of how the Ambedkarite society rejected Manu (Fig. 8.5). An image is inherently symbolic; at the same time it is equally real. There is a desire to create an imagery that will not be transcendental but more physical and real. Symbolism, in this case, denotes the caste-Hindu who is absent in the pictorial space but is part and parcel of the violence that is imposed, codified, and practiced as a societal norm.

Ambedkar's and other Dalits' conversion to Buddhism in 1956 at Nagpur was pivotal, forcing Dalit Buddhists to distinguish their own cultural symbols and signifiers from Brahmanical conventions. Sawarkar's ability to draw rapidly with minimal details and bold lines, which he acquired as an art student, is a hallmark of his skilled labor. Sawarkar attempted to create an image that would signify the historic 1956 event, while pictorializing the *varna* hierarchy of Indian society. Through a process of continual reflection and by deploying a creative vocabulary, Sawarkar painted *Foundation of India* (Fig. 8.6), a work that represents the residues of the past and the transformational, structural change that he desires for society. The four-fold division of the *varna* system is represented through conventional symbols. The image of the male is conceptualized, as has been advocated in the *purushsutta* of the Rigveda. The top head signifies a Brahman, the arms as weapons denote the Kshatriyas, whereas the potbelly represents wealthy trading. The feet represent the Shudras. Sawarkar does not stop here. He shows bells hooked to the garland tied at the bottom, denoting "untouchables." The last block is

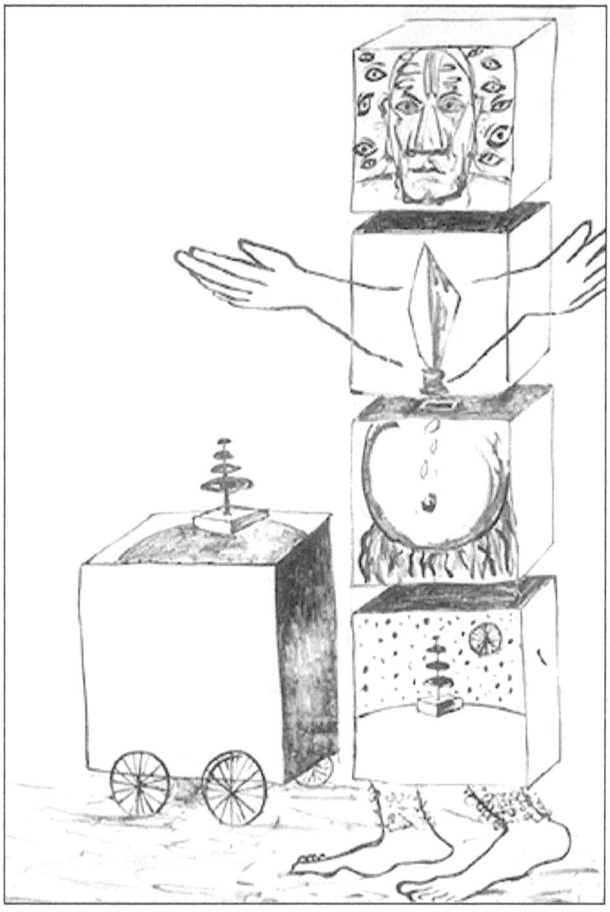

Figure 8.6: Savi Sawarkar, *Foundation of India*, oil on canvas, 5 feet x 6 feet, 1986. © Copyright and reproduced courtesy of the artist.

also broken and moving on wheels toward Buddhism, showing the *ati-shudra*, the term that Mahatma Phule advocated for instead of "untouchable." Being witness to the ongoing celebration and conversion at Dikshbhoomi Nagpur had a deep impact on Sawarkar's worldview. He systematically observed his surroundings and how caste life was key to the violence and pain of life. His self-narrative, touching on caste, is reflected through the series of paintings he made on these issues.

The other important theme Sawarkar painted is related to devadasis (a tradition whereby an adolescent girl from a scheduled caste, such as a Dalit or "lower caste" community, is married to the temple in the village and consequently the Brahmin priest and the caste-Hindu patron sexually exploit the girl under the religious custom). Sawarkar visited Soundati in Karnataka in 1985, after completing his postgraduate studies from the Faculty of Fine Arts, Baroda. He first visited Narayan Surve in Mumbai and discovered many devadasis in the red-light district in Grant Road, Mumbai. The devadasis had largely come from Soundati, an area that Sawarkar visited. He initially saw a festival of giving away green saris and bangles to the adolescent girls from the scheduled caste community. He listened to all their ritualistic songs. He witnessed that one devadasi could not even walk properly. It bewildered him and he later discovered that this was due to inflammation around the genitals. Sawarkar lived in disguise with a long beard and initially slept in an open tea stall and later rented a house near the temple. He was a regular visitor to the temple and witnessed the initiation ceremony of the devadasis and how they were sexually exploited. It was a mental trauma for Sawarkar to witness such practices. He saw how an old Brahmin priest would have sex with a fourteen- or fifteen-year-old girl as a part of the devadasi tradition and later how the girl would be used constantly by a caste-Hindu patron. It angered Sawarkar and he realized that all the devadasis were from scheduled caste communities. He recorded the life narratives of devadasis quietly. When temple authorities realized that Sawarkar did not belong to their fraternity, Sawarkar left the place and later met Uttam Kamble, who wrote on devadasis in Marathi, producing a source book and a firsthand account of the devadasi tradition, *Devadasi Ani Nagṇapujā*. The same devadasi paid visits to Dikshaboomi at Nagpur, where they became Buddhists. Sawarkar witnessed these events. This traumatization of Dalit women and girls in the name of religious practices, rituals, and belief systems angered Sawarkar, who foregrounded these women and girls as the subjects of his paintings as an act of resistance to voice their pain. As an Ambedkarite, Sawarkar chose to represent this trauma to critique caste-Hindu consciousness.

Sawarkar's earlier works on devadasis had a different narrative quality, showing cardinal events, emphasizing the caste-narrative ordeal through tormenting sexual exploitations. Many viewers found his works extremely hard hitting. In his later works, elements of caste violence take a different turn. Without compromising his quality of expression, Sawarkar's endeavor to critique caste explores the language of minimalism, loaded with a background of caste narratives. A devadasi is shown escaping from the body of a Brahmin (Fig. 8.7). Here embracement has a dual meaning. One is the control of Brahmins over other social orders. The second meaning is connected with the lust of a Brahmin who would not like a devadasi to be free from his control. Perversion is a fundamental aspect of sexuality when it comes to the heinous practice of devadasi. The Brahmin's embrace of the devadasi is indicative of the Brahmanical control over her body, and at the same time, the devadasi extending her hand out of the Brahmin body and holding to the *dhammachakra* (wheel of law shown as spokes of a wheel) shows the possibility of her freedom. It is important to understand how the complex nature of sexuality operates through a religious institution and the way it is nurtured as a part of male dominance over pleasure, whereby an adolescent

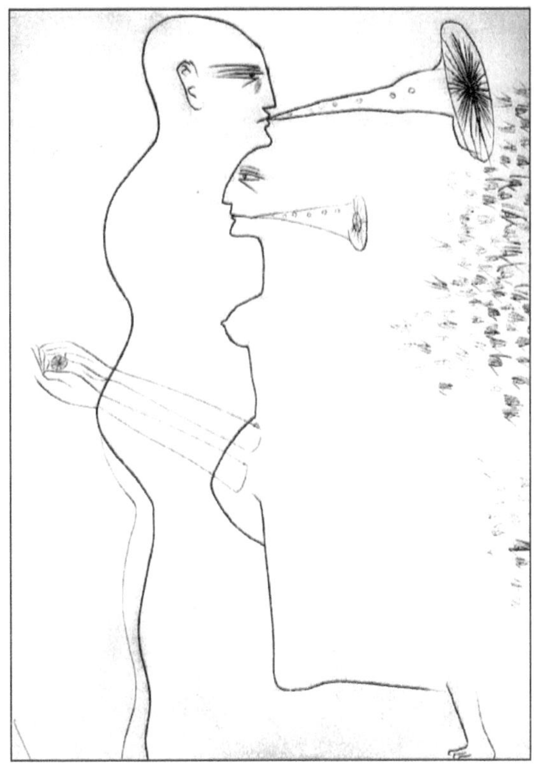

Figure 8.7: Savi Sawarkar, *Freedom to Devadasi*, dry point, 54.5 cm x 37 cm, 2001. © Copyright and reproduced courtesy of the artist.

girl is initiated as a devadasi who is first enjoyed by the priest and later by the chief patron, usually the landlord.

One may recall the ways in which psychoanalyst Sudhir Kakkar analyzes the nature of upbringing in Indian society in *The Inner World.* For Kakkar, the ideal of a Hindu household involves following the Rama-Sita model. However, the tradition and practice of devadasi completely undoes the Rama-Sita ideal in Indian society. The mythic becomes an ideal that does not get critiqued under protected ignorance. The moral self becomes embedded in a caste-ridden perception and the ideals of caste living. In fact, the Puranic tradition and larger Hindu traditions do not allow followers to be enlightened beings, as there is a fear that there would be a collapse of "agency," which would lead to the egoist male not being able to exercise sexual perversions. The life of a devadasi is traumatic. Sawarkar depicts their trauma through the physicality of the body—a desired and yet mutilated body. Devadasis go through a series of abortions. Sawarkar captures a graphic representation of this by showing the static body with a surgical cut mark on the stomach (Fig. 8.8).

Jaya Daronde paints the lived relationship between a Brahmin male and an "untouchable" girl (Fig. 8.9). Though it is not directly related to Jaya's life

Figure 8.8: Savi Sawarkar, *Devadasi with Crow*, etching, 40 cm x 28 cm, 1987. © Copyright and reproduced courtesy of the artist.

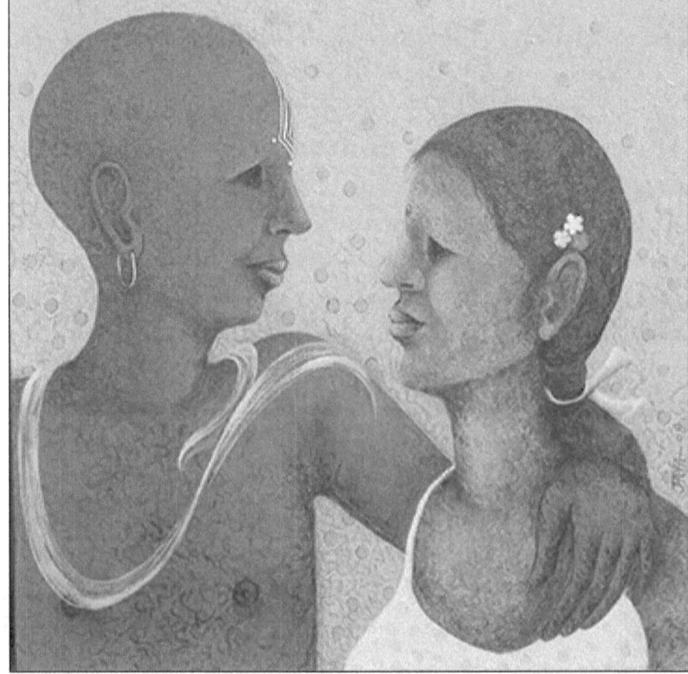

Figure 8.9: Jaya Daronde, *Relationship*, oil on canvas, 18 inches x 18 inches, 2009. © Copyright and reproduced courtesy of the artist.

experiences, her work invokes caste life narratives of observed realities that go into a perceptual understanding of creating an image that is loaded with caste narrative itself. She attempts to show a kind of psychological unrest between two human beings, despite their being emotionally and physically in love with each other. Daronde's large body of work explores various dimensions of this relationship and the ways in which the Dalit female is structured in the patriarchal world. Daronde's figures are simple and have no sexual overtones. There is a deliberate attempt on her part to go away from the usual sensual representations of the Dalit female body. In her work, caste life tensions are observed as part of social realities. Textures in the pictorial surface of Daronde's paintings are decorative in nature and reflect everyday existence. Some of her work shows groups of women involved in themselves in a manner that declares their independent existence away from the collective caste-Hindus.

Intervention on issues of caste is not just confined to one section of the community. When others venture into such a thematic expression, viewers are offered another side of caste practices. Lokesh Khodke produced a few paintings after his engagement with an Ambedkarite NGO. When Khodke was exposed to the writings of Phule and Ambedkar, he found his own Brahmanical tradition extremely problematic and draconian in nature. His painting on Trivikrama is an apt example of the brutality with which the imagery of Trivikrama is guarded by the Brahmin household (Figs. 8.10 and 8.11).[8] This work of art exhibits how the Brahmin family reveres the myth of Trivikrama and how, despite understanding its violent nature, they are taught not to critique it because of the supposed sacredness of Brahmanical traditions.

Pavan's engagement with caste narrative took a long time to evolve. As a part of graphic design practices, he preferred to draw decorative figures with certain caste affiliations. A priest's head upon legs and a broom is a graphic representation of the caste divide in Haryana society (Fig. 8.12). In another work, a cow with a priest's head is shown as a political critique of the Hindu fondness for cow protection, a mainstay in the politics of India. Vishnu, another artist, paints a Dalit carrying a saffron trident on a scooter, which represents Kerala's modernity and the ways in which specific caste groups are used to carry out menial work in caste-Hindu society. Political overtones in this work reflect how Dalits are used as foot soldiers of caste-Hindu society. Thus, an everyday caste life narrative enters the political sphere. In a recent exhibition titled "Tear, Cut, Rip," curated by Kanika Gupta and Rohit Ukey in east Delhi from September 25 to October 1, 2016, Prakash Gaikwad from Nagpur showed his work, based on caste life narratives of "untouchability." His installation is noteworthy (Fig. 8.13).

Figure 8.10: Lokesh Khodke, *The Theater of a Painter*, oil on canvas, 48 inches x 72 inches, 2008. © Copyright and reproduced courtesy of the artist.

Figure 8.11: Lokesh Khodke, *The Legacy*, oil on canvas, 48 inches x 72 inches, 2007. © Copyright and reproduced courtesy of the artist.

Knowing well the fact that "untouchability" exists in Indian society and that societal practices still adhere to caste "untouchability," he placed two earthen pots in the installation. The bigger earthen pot had the words "drinking water" and the small earthen pot had written on it "spit here." These signs represent the continued cultural practices of "untouchability" in independent India, undermining societal claims of civility and liberty. The installation was also a reminder of a well-known incident from Ambedkar's life when he was working in Baroda Maharaja Sayajirao Gaikwad's office. Ambedkar was given a separate earthen pot to drink water from in the office. Evoking caste life narrative becomes a necessary means to express the realities of Indian psychotic perversions like this episode from Ambedkar's life.

Prajapati is another artist who referred to his own life narrative when he critiqued caste-Hindu cultural practices, this time of cremations at the banks of the river Ganga at Varanasi (Fig. 8.14). He used the motif of the cremation bed with a currency note painted on it to refer to the practice that goes in the making of the *bhataji-shethaji* (priest and trading community) nexus. Prajapati, being from a "backward caste" community and sensitized to Ambedkarite consciousness, dared to present a pictorial critique of the

Figure 8.12: Pawan Kumar, *untitled*, acrylic on canvas, 24 inches x 36 inches, 2015.

Figure 8.13: Prakash Gaikwad, *Nostalgia* (installation), mixed media, 2016.
© Copyright and reproduced courtesy of the artist.

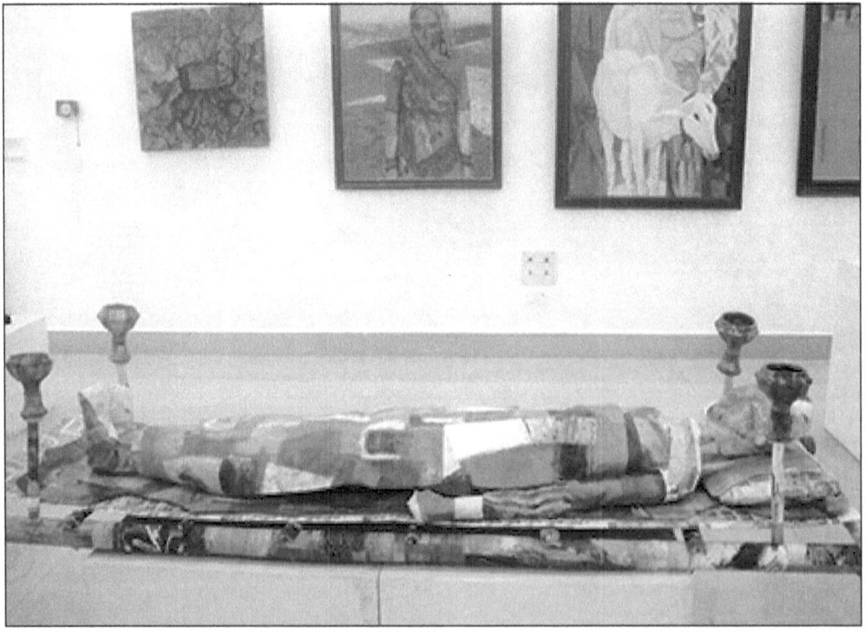

Figure 8.14: Prajapati, *Installation,* mixed media, 80 inches x 33 inches x 28 inches, 2012.
© Copyright and reproduced courtesy of the artist.

Figure 8.15: Malvika, *Dr. Ambedkar*, monochrome, 30 inches x 40 inches, 2016. © Copyright and reproduced courtesy of the artist.

caste-Hindu belief system. He depicts generic objects used at the time of cremation for covering dead bodies such as four flame lamps attached with sticks and the bier (bamboo bed to carry the dead body).

Malvika, a painter from Bihar who studied fashion design, uses the Madhubani tradition to paint Ambedkar's life narrative (Fig. 8.15). The lower left corner of her painting is dominated by a big portrait of Ambedkar holding the constitution, and his other life events are depicted in the surrounding area. She preferred to choose known events, mainly the caste humiliations that Ambedkar faced, his education at Columbia University, his marriage, the Mahad tank agitation, the Nasik temple entry agitation, the Baroda event, his constitution drafting, and his conversion to Buddhism. All the events are woven together in an unusual arrangement of time and space. Malvika's Ambedkarite consciousness helped her critique the draconian caste-Hindu system and she paints Ambedkar's experiences of humiliations to underscore how inhumane the caste system is. Ambedkar's caste life narrative inspired Malvika to use her narrative skills to paint what her consciousness recognized was important, enabling her to dissect the traditional behavior of India's caste-Hindu population.

Photography is another medium through which the stark realities of life can be captured through sustained engagements with the subject of caste. Technical aspects of light and darkness, along with illuminating effects, encompass the formal language of photography. It is important to note the exoticism that gets attached to photographic images. Orientalist attitudes have been a part of photographic engagements in India. Sudharak Olwe, who constantly engaged with a caste subject as part of his social and professional commitment, produced a series of photographs of conservancy workers from the Mumbai Municipal Corporation. His images captured, in stark and contrasting natural light, the dirt, filth, and naked reality of these Dalit workers. He underlined the life of the manual scavenger in the chief metropolis of democratic India. Though political democracy and equality are invoked to celebrate the emergence of the modern nation, the conditions of the "lower castes," as captured through the medium of photography, narrate a different tale. Representation's symbolic nature is subsumed in the realistic capturing in photography, and the subject of caste is used to unfold the nature of the hierarchical structure of society. Similarly, Olwe has made numerous photographic images of Kamathipura, the red light area in Mumbai. Dirt, discomfort, and dinginess are part of Kamathipura, where prostituted people are made to sell their bodies to make a living. Olwe has captured vivid details regarding relationships among people in the red light district, including the relationship of a prostituted woman with her husband as well as with her intimate friend and how both are part of her life, even when she dies. These are emotionally charged images. They diminish perceptions of sexual

Figure 8.16: Sudharak Owle, *Conservancy Workers*, 12 inches x 18 inches, 1999–2000. © Copyright and reproduced courtesy of the artist.

Figure 8.17: Sudharak Owle, *Kamathipura*, 16 inches x 20 inches, 2003. © Copyright and reproduced courtesy of the artist.

desire; instead, the omnipresence of perversity enters through such pictorial representations (Figs. 8.16 and 8.17). When caste becomes an intervening tool in pictorial language, the stark realities of life demand a radical departure from conventional, aesthetic beauty.

Tradition's homogenizing force is a project of nationalist aspirations. This force limits the kind of artwork that is commissioned and exhibited, reducing artistic articulations of what is contained within nationalist imaginations. Works of art become timid and devoid of anyone not celebrated in the national imaginary, particularly the "lower castes." The supposed postcolonial realm hardly produces a capacity to address difference. It does not offer a constructive critique of the hegemonic thinking that most Indians practice and bypasses issues of representation, making the process of knowledge formation a part of "protected ignorance."

Several works have been produced as part of the conceptual framework of the "postcolonial." "Subaltern" has become a generic category within postcolonial frameworks. In "Can the Subaltern Speak?" Spivak argues that articulation is monopolized, and subalterns do not have that kind of power. Caste life narratives are one way in which self-representation is made possible. Experiential realities are represented through an expressive language. Self-representation through narratives about caste is actual representation of the self, rooted in the physical realm of caste life. The self is reconstructed, challenging the perceptions of caste-Hindu society. These experiences, though they are in constant flux, are evidence of the troubling reality of caste-Hindu behavior.

The more pertinent questions here are who are the subalterns and how do we understand and categorize both the subaltern as such and subaltern experiences? In the Indian context, the term has gained considerable currency in the fields of literature, drama, and visual arts. The subaltern is understood as being located in opposition to hegemony. However, "whose hegemony?" is a critical question of analysis. Other serious questions draw our attention to the conceptual category of the subaltern. Subaltern consciousness often does not question graded hierarchy. By applying Ambedkar's definition of caste we can see that the very rubric of subalternity bypasses the existential realm of a direct experience of division of laborers. Caste life narratives, driven by an Ambedkarite consciousness, signify a power of articulation, where the physical realm of existence is categorical in realizing aspirations of equality and liberty. This essay has shown that caste life narratives, as expressed through certain works of art, challenge the social metanarrative of Indian society, interrogate "protected ignorance," implicitly question the ambiguous category of "subaltern," interrogate the "postcolonial," and critique Brahmanical hegemony.

## NOTES

1. For more information, see Alone, "Dr. Ambedkar."
2. The English term close to the word *varna* is "class." *Varna* division in the Brahmanical/Hindu social order consists of four hierarchical divisions of class, mainly the Brahmin (priestly class/community), Kshatriya (warriors), Vaishya (trading class/community), and Shudra (servile class/community).
3. See also Kumar, *Caste and Democracy*; Kumar, "Babashaeb."
4. Gupta was a political dynasty that ruled in North India from 320 to 550 BCE. During this period, many Sanskrit texts were rewritten, new Sanskrit texts were composed, Sanskrit became the language of the court and inscriptions, donations were made to Brahmins, and cow killing resulted in capital punishment. Brahmanical discourse considers the Gupta period as the "golden age" of Indian history.
5. See Kapur and Sundaram; Achar and Pannikar.
6. The entire Ambedkarite community in the state of Maharashtra, as well as outside, never accepted Gandhi, sensing that the life of "untouchables" would have been different had they gotten the separate electorate that Gandhi opposed leading up to independence in what is called the Poona Pact. Eventually, political and employment reservation emerged as a solution, which found a place in the Constitution of India. Their displeasure emerged out of their own caste narratives because the other leaders who mattered to them the most were unrepresented in art.

7. Manu was one of the ancient law givers in India and composed the text Manusmriti in Sanskrit, which dates to the second century BCE. Among other things, the text supports various social codes and punishments based on the four-fold division of *varnas*, including suppressive codes for women and draconian practices.
8. Trivikrama is an incarnation of the Hindu god Vishnu who, according to mythology, goes to King Bali as a tiny Brahmin and expands himself to capture the universe. He places one leg on the head of Bali and buries him. The image of Trivikrama is always shown with a raised leg in space.

## WORKS CITED

Achar, Deeptha, and Shivaji Pannikar. *Articulating Resistance: Art and Activism*. Tulika Books, 2012.

Alone, Y. S. "Dr. Ambedkar's Historicism: Confrontations and Inquiries." *Ambedkar in Retrospect: Essays on Economics, Politics and Society*, edited by Sukhadeo Thorat Aryama, Rawat, 2007, pp. 261–91.

———. "Evoking and Re-Evoking of Past: A Discursive Process." *Kala Traimasik*, vol. 35, 2009, pp. 30–36.

Aloysius, G. *Nationalism without a Nation in India*. Oxford UP, 1997.

Ambedkar, B. R. "Annihilation of Caste." *Dr. Babasaheb Ambedkar: Writings and Speeches*, vol. 1, Government of Maharashtra, 1982, pp. 23–96.

———. "Buddha or Karl Marx." *Dr. Babasaheb Ambedkar: Writings and Speeches*, vol. 3, Government of Maharashtra, 1987, pp. 441–62.

———. *Dr. Babasaheb Ambedkar: Writings and Speeches*. Vol. 3, Government of Maharashtra, 1987.

Bilgrami, Akeel. "Value, Enchantment and the Mentality of Democracy: Some Distant Perspectives." *Democratic Culture: Historical and Philosophical Essays*, edited by Akeel Bilgrami, Routledge, 2011, pp. 23–63.

Coomaraswamy, Ananda Kentish. "Sati: Defense of Eastern Women." *British Sociological Review*, vol. VI, 1913, pp. 117–35.

———. *Transformation of Nature in Indian Art*. Coronet Books, 1994.

Kakkar, Sudhir. *The Inner World: A Psychoanalytic Study of Childhood and Society in India*. Oxford UP, 1978.

Kapur, Geeta, and Vivan Sundaram. "Place for People." Jahangir Art Gallery, Mumbai, Nov. 1981, http://www.aaa.org.hk/Collection/SpecialCollections/Details/5. Accessed 2016.

Kumar, Vivek. "Babasaheb Ambedkar: Conceptualization and Operationalization of Social Justice." *Globalization and Social Justice: Perspectives, Challenges and Praxis*, edited by P. G. Jogdand, Prashant P. Bansode, and N. G. Meshram, Ravat Publication, 2008, pp. 103–55.

———. *Caste and Democracy in India: A Perspective from Below*. Gyan Publishing House, 2014.

Laxman, Mane. *Uparā*. Granthali Prakashan, 1980.

Mills, Charles. "White Ignorance." *Race and Epistemologies of Ignorance*, edited by Shannon Sullivan and Nancy Tuana, SUNY, 2007, pp. 13–38.

Radhakrishnan, S. *A Hindu View of Life*. Macmillan Company, 1954.

Ratan, Parimoo. *Studies in Modern Indian Art*. Kanak Publications, 1975.

Spivak, Gayatri Chakravorty. *A Critique of Postcolonial Reason: Toward a History of the Vanishing Present*. Harvard UP, 1999.

———. "Can the Subaltern Speak?" *Marxism and the Interpretation of Culture*, edited by Cary Nelson and Lawrence Grossberg, U of Illinois P, 1988, pp. 271–313.

Sutar, Sudhanshu. Personal interview. 2016.

Tartakov, Gary Michael, editor. *Dalit Art and Visual Imagery*. Oxford UP, 2012.

Vaijayanti, Shete. "Expressive Theory of Caturvarnya and the *Shilpa* Texts: References to Caste and Gender." *Art of Ancient India: Contextualizing Social Relations*, edited by Shivaji Panikkar and Abha Sheth, Maharaja Sayajirao U of Baroda, 2004.

9

# MANGALA BANSODE AND THE SOCIAL LIFE OF TAMASHA

## Caste, Sexuality, and Discrimination in Modern Maharashtra

SHAILAJA PAIK

The Tamasha (traveling folk theater) legend Vithabai Narayangavkar sang a famous Lavani (folk song) in the 1960s:

> *laaj dhara pavana janachi manachi*
> *potasathi nachatey mee parva kunachi*
> *dava dola jhakun khunavu naka, ho asa tumhi hinavu naka*
> *aathavan dete mee tarnya panachi*
> *potasathi nachatey mee parva kunachi*
>
> [O guest, maintain your shame for others as well as for yourself. I am dancing to earn my livelihood; I do not care for anybody else. Do not make sexual gestures by winking your left eye at me. You are actually mocking me. I am helping you remember your youth. I am dancing for my everyday living. I do not care for anybody else.][1]

Through such pointed and piercing songs, Vithabai interpreted her life as a ritual of "rough music" and cruelty, sharply ridiculing her mixed upper- and lower-caste male audience.[2] Deploying her song as a double entendre to illuminate the tension between her bodily performance of seduction and lyrical refusal of any sexual union, Vithabai productively used her practice of popular song and dance ritual to express her social and economic anxieties as well as to record her resistance and resilience against private and public patriarchy. In so doing, Vithabai exercised her agency, however limited: many times, she used the politics of Tamasha and Lavani to challenge her supposed powerlessness.

In this essay, I deploy the oral history of Mangalatai[3] Bansode (the daughter of Vithabai), a rare and powerful Dalit professional Tamasgir (Tamasha performer) woman and also troupe leader, to examine the ways she repeatedly performed the "obscene" and the "erotic," to earn her livelihood while she also contested and purposefully negotiated patriarchy, public politics, and, most importantly, larger shifting structures of "tradition" and "modernity." How did Mangalatai—a daughter, sister, wife, mother, and grandmother—negotiate double living in her shifting personal and professional life? How did she navigate the image of being a "seductress" in the so-called "dangerous" and "vulgar" practice of Tamasha and Lavani? How did she manage to concentrate on and excel in her art above her rivals? To investigate these questions, I focus on hitherto unexamined "interlocking technologies" of caste, class, community, gender, and sexuality from the position and perspectives of Maharashtrian (Western India) Dalit performers.[4]

Although Mangalatai gradually asserted her power, paradoxically she was also powerless. Her complex life represents her ideas, intentions, and actions, continually entangled in the intersecting webs of her triumphs and tribulations, transformations and tensions, suppression and subversion. I thus attend to deep tensions in her *double living*: the private and public and the personal and professional as well as her triply discriminated life due to the intersectionality of her caste, gender, and sexuality. There were no clean boundaries: the multiple oppressions constantly crept into, challenged, and complicated each other, puncturing her seemingly triumphalist life narrative.

My essay is the first attempt to analyze Mangalatai's life. I examine Mangalatai's everyday living to uncover the hitherto unexplored potentials and problems of intimate and interlocking relations between a Dalit woman artist's "deviant" sexuality, labor, and struggle for survival; the community's social, cultural, and political battles; and folk culture. In so doing, I provide micro-level details of the historical experiences of poverty, hunger, education or the lack thereof, occupation, the strategic deployment of *body politics*, and sexual economy of *erotic excess*. There is no written record of Mangalatai's experiences. Though a celebrity who regularly performed for audiences in Maharashtra and whose website provides photographs of her, her life has remained marginal and obscure.[5]

Methodologically, I aim to open up Mangalatai's lived experiences as epistemic spaces and use the newly produced knowledge to analyze the materiality of caste, class, gender, sexual oppression, local economy, and power relationships, both within and outside of the Dalit community. I delve deeply into personal experiences of Mangalatai's exceptional life to document how she was contained by and at the same time transgressed patriarchy and examine the interlocking technologies of social, familial, political, economic, sexual, and emotional histories of Dalit women. I thus unravel gendered and moral conflicts inside the Dalit community. In contemporary times, Tamasha has emerged as a contested performative practice for the government, social scientists, activists, and Tamasha artists themselves. Mangalatai's individual life narrative offers a unique and unexplored perspective to examine the larger societal, political, cultural, and statist transformations of which she is a part. Mangalatai's life narrative is a social biography that interconnects her past, present, and future with her family, community, and local economy.

## TAMASHA: THE TRAVELING FOLK THEATER OF MAHARASHTRA

Colloquially, the word Tamasha has come to mean fun, play, or even disorder and commotion. Historically, Tamasha actors have preserved and transformed Tamasha and Lavani through the tumultuous changes of time, largely for low- and middle-class caste consumption in contemporary Maharashtra. Maharashtra is home to a rich theatrical history spanning many centuries. As in other parts of Asia, secular theater in Maharashtra brings together skit, song, dance, mime, poetry, and farce. Etymologically, the word Tamasha has roots in Arabic and literally means a show, spectacle, or even a sort of theatrical entertainment. Tamasha as a form of entertainment is thus evidence of the interconnections between Marathi, Persian, and Arab cultures, languages, and societies since the medieval period. It only became associated with being a low-caste folk form at the end of the seventeenth and start of the eighteenth century (Achalkhamb 9).

However, the writer Sadanand Rane favors a different Sanskritic genealogy for Tamasha and suggests that the etymology of the word is *tama* and *asha*, a form that takes us from *tama* (darkness) to *asha* (light) (183).[6] In this alternative etymology, Rane implicitly rejects the idea of an Arabic root. Yet, because the word is rooted in *tama* (ignorance) and ribaldry of supposedly "rural" Bahujans (low-caste people), the ruling elites have expressed their prejudice against the genre's performers. They continually look(ed) down upon Tamasha and sought to sanitize it. Tamasha includes the Maharashtrian local forms of entertainment such as Dashavatar, Gondhal, Lalita, Lavani, and so on (Joshi 121). Lavani is the folkloric singing with *adakari* (gestures) in the Tamasha art form. There are at least five types of Lavanya,[7] including the puranic, devotional, and *shringarik* (erotic). Not all Lavanya are bawdy songs as most writers have suggested; yet, a titillating *shringar* of lovers has become essential to this form of entertainment, especially for the predominantly male audience. Unlike saints, who were relegated to spiritual affairs, *shahirs* engaged with the sensual (Joshi 130).

Tamasha artists, like their Bengali *jatra* and Gujarati *bhavai* counterparts, performed in public squares and open spaces and drew a mixed audience comprised of middle- and low-caste women and men. Traditionally, traders, landlords, local kings, and, most significantly, ordinary people provided patronage to maintain performers and to put on their shows.

Historically, Tamasha constructed close communities of mixed castes as well as religions. It is one of the important *lokakalas*, cultures of the (Bahujan) people of Maharashtra. Traditionally, traveling Tamasha artists largely belonged to nomadic (Kolhati, Asvalvale, Bahurupi, Vasudev), low-caste, and Dalit *bara balutedars* (various artisanal castes) who performed different services for the village, such as Dhobi (washerman), Kumbhar (potter), Mahar, Mang,[8] Sutar (carpenter), Teli (oil presser), and so on, and belonged to both Hindu and Muslim religious communities (Joshi 95). Some Brahman men like Ram Joshi and Patthe Bapurav also performed in Tamasha.

Nonetheless, the wider society and lower and upper castes therein already naturalized the constitution of caste communities within a feudal context. For example, there is a saying in Marathi that crystallizes practices of certain castes: *Brahmana ghari lihina, kunbya ghari dana, ann Mahara ghari gaana* (the top-most caste, Brahmins, are to read and write, peasants to produce grains, and Dalit Mahars to sing and dance). Reinforcing the cultural practices of certain caste communities, the historian Hiroyuki Kotani notes that the ruling classes expected even the headman of Mahars from the Sasvad District (near Pune) to play music during festivals (123).[9] Mahars performed singing, drumming, and music not only to carry out (one of their fifty-two) duties to spread the message of the state to the larger masses but used their skilled performance as a significant medium of entertainment, and moreover deployed this performance as a form of political protest during the twentieth century. Entire villages came out to enjoy these popular Tamasha performances that served as a crucial conduit for the transmission of new ideas.

From the early decades of the twentieth century, Dalit radicals deployed the public culture of Tamasha, Lavani, and street theater in the construction of the vibrant public sphere, and at the same time underscored a new morality and modernity. Dalit radicals like Kisan Phaguji Bansode, Baba Valangkar, Shivram Janba Kamble, and B. R. Ambedkar amply recognized the culture and power of the word and speaking aloud for communicating with an audience that was mostly illiterate. As Bhagavan Thakur elucidates in *Ambedkari Jalse*, by adopting the popular medium of Jalsa (folk drama) in the 1930s, troupes toured remote villages and modern cities and engaged in singing and music to bring about social change.

In this historical conjuncture, the "fun and play" Tamasha emerged as bawdy and risqué. Earlier there was no ban on women watching Tamasha, yet now their participation both as actors and audience members did not fit the new Dalit morality under modernity. Although modernizing, socially mobile Dalit radicals celebrated the Ambedkarite Jalsa. At the same time, they sought to raise their moral status in the eyes of the upper castes and the colonial government. Toward this end, Dalits first colluded with upper castes and the colonial rulers to underscore a "modern" Victorian and Brahmani (brahmanical) morality. As a result, they depict(ed) Tamasha entertainers and entertainment as "immoral," "vulgar," and relegated Tamasha to the realm of "folk art." Most significantly, they now looked upon women actors in Tamasha as a symbol of Dalit degradation. They also banned certain "corrupt" practices in the Tamasha form. In so doing, Dalits refashioned Tamasha by restricting the supposedly "immoral" lives of Muralis (women wedded to the god Khandoba) and Tamasgir women performers because they supposedly represented Dalits' "backwardness." As I point out in my work elsewhere, to elite Dalit women and men, Muralis and Tamasgir women became objects of exploitation, eroticization, and sexual possession for men of all castes, and hence these "lowly," "dishonorable" women had to be "cleansed."[10]

Some Dalit and non-Dalit artists and radical women and men underscored the sensual and sexual overtones of Tamasha and Lavani; yet in both the colonial and postcolonial periods, non-Dalit men artists as well as the state government have sought to sanitize Tamasha performance. The hypocritical state of Maharashtra seems both to provide patronage and at the same time neglect and abandon Tamasha. Most significantly, by making Tamasha a practice of producing Marathamola, robust masculine Marathi identity, the elite upper and lower castes and the state have reappropriated the social and sexual labor of Tamasha artists to serve the state of Maharashtra. As a result, agents of the state have further stigmatized Tamasgirs and also sustained their labor by consistently giving awards to them.

Tamasgir women and men thus engaged the interlocking social, sensual, and sexual realms. Textual and ethnographic evidence illustrates that artists debated deeper social, political, spiritual, ethical, and *shringarik* questions as they emerged in everyday human living. Tamasha songs, skits, and loud music presented dilemmas that people could relate to. On the one hand, some songs and dramas evoked high moral duty, loyalty, devotion, spirituality, and heroic deeds, and on the other hand, tensions and conflicts in the private and public sphere, true and passionate love, and pleasure.

Significantly, both Tamasha *kalakar* (artists) and audiences engaged in the Marathi *kala* (art) to deploy a reiterative body politics of erotic excess: emphasizing bold bodily gestures, that is, winking the left eye to entice one another, accentuating and deploying certain body parts like breasts and hips, openly expressing sensuality and sexual mores, lovemaking, and sexual enjoyment for their predominantly male audience. At the same time, they also sought to solidify a certain normative construction of Marathi masculinity and femininity, that is, a Marathamola man and woman. While they described the man as a brave fighter, tall, with broad shoulders and a thick moustache, the woman was depicted as fair, delicate, doe-eyed, draped in tight *choli* (traditional blouse) and nine-yard sari that accentuated her figure.

## MANGALATAI, TAMASHA, AND LAVANI: FROM MARGINS TO CENTER

In this essay, I break significant historical, societal, intellectual, ideological, and scholarly silences, and bring the so-called "vulgar" Tamasha women to the center of the discipline of History. Historians and anthropologists have seldom considered the life histories of Tamasha artists worthy of systematic analysis. Over the past four decades there has been an increasing academic interest in the field of popular culture and cultural studies. However, in the Indian context, and more specifically in Maharashtra, an elitist focus in the English language on bourgeois forms of "high" art, literature, and entertainment has historically marginalized and even excluded "low" cultures of Tamasha and Lavani, including the performers of these cultural forms. Moreover, elite scholars often writing in an allegedly universal English language have often privileged English as "orderly" and "scholarly." In the process, they have continually marginalized vernacular Marathi materials, Dalit epistemologies, and histories. Further, there is little study about the intersections of popular practices of caste-based cultural forms with sexual labor.

In the broader Indian context, scholars have studied the actions of non-elite groups and popular culture in North and East India.[11] Some have also focused on the lives of Dalit *nautanki* performers and *tawaifs* in North India, and *jogatis* and highly trained, higher-status Devadasis in South India.[12] Unlike Dalit *jogatis*, devadasis performed in the urban temple complexes. In the context of Maharashtra, scholars have also focused on *rashtriya kirtankars* (a nationalist performance combining singing, storytelling, and Hindu philosophical discourse), low-caste and Dalit bhakti saints,[13] music and theatrics of Tamasha and Lavani,[14] and non-Dalit devadasis.[15] Some scholars have worked on elite Marathi theater and other upper-caste initiatives, but they have occluded Tamasha and Lavani art forms.

By contrast, scholars of Marathi literature have mined the literary content and form of Tamasha and Lavani, low-caste art, aesthetics, and culture in the vernacular Marathi language.[16] Some writers have even focused on select leading men *lavanikaars* (Lavani performers), such as Honaji Bala, Saganbhau, Patthe Bapurao, and Ram Joshi, and recorded their lives and Lavanya.[17] More recently, a few artists and activists have sought to understand the complex lives of artists like Vithabai and published their autobiographies and biographies.[18]

However, there are limitations in existing scholarship. Many writers have confined themselves to the textual realm, detailed literary modes and instruments used in the folk art, and thus objectified Tamasha artists. As a result, writers and scholars have rarely stepped outside their middle-class apartments to interact or travel with Tamasha artists to examine their ideas,

Figure 9.1: Mangalatai leading the Lavani performers in September 2004 at Bal Gandharva, Pune. Photo by author.

experiences, and lives. Very rarely have students of Tamasha theater actually engaged with the social life of Tamasha artists, although some journalists, like Sandesh Bhandare and Shirish Shetye, have traveled to open and enclosed Tamasha theaters to produce photographic books on the everyday life of Tamasha artists. Another significant problem is that most writers do not provide detailed information on or analysis of the Marathi sources they procured.

My study departs from the earlier works by turning the gaze onto the hitherto unexamined social life of Tamasha. Moreover, I deploy the oral history of Dalit performers and Dalit epistemologies. Historians have scarcely considered how the actions of the subordinated interrupted polite culture in historical times. Most significantly, there is, thus, little study of the historical and cultural politics of the upper- and lower-caste women and men actors who actualized different literary and theatrical forms as well as continually struggled and negotiated with each other. To date, with the rare exception of two articles by Sharmila Rege and Veena Naregal, there is no systematic study of the role of caste-based cultural performance in the broader social and political history of modern Maharashtra in the English language. Rege significantly delineates the historical shifts in Tamasha and Lavani performances to argue that "shringarik lavani became one of the modes of constructing the bodies of lower caste women as constantly arousing, or satiating male desire" (24).

More recently, Naregal's essay has sought to examine elite ideological and organizational maneuvers to marginalize Lavani and Tamasha and "establish normative categories, institutional networks, and theatrical practices" (81). I build on these works by deepening studies on Tamasha through a focus on the personal life narrative of an individual woman, centering Dalit epistemologies to record the social history of Tamasha.

## HERSTORY: LIFE NARRATIVE, SOCIAL HISTORY, AND EVERYDAY LIVING

Life narratives help us to interrupt and interrogate official history by asking different and difficult questions of the historical, "official," written record. Methodologically, I deploy the life narrative of an individual woman to break boundaries and create conversations between different archives and methods: oral history, folklore, ethnography, and life narrative. In so doing, I not only disrupt the dominant focus on elite actors but also provide strategic spaces for so-called "corrupt" and despised women to verbalize their own ideas, emotions, and lives.

We have to engage seriously in oral history to study Dalit women's own understanding of their history, to write richer and multilayered accounts, including official and non-official history.[19] Dalit histories are not captured in archives, and we need to develop this critical past through the "eyes of the present" (Carr 4). Such a methodology is crucial to hearing voices from within the language of caste, gender, and sexuality. To pursue this methodology, I contacted women performers to collect their life narratives, always paying attention to the uniqueness of each case, not looking merely for abstractions (Atkinson; Portelli, *The Death* 35).

The collection of such life narratives provides a way to put on record the experiences of relatively powerless Dalit women whose ways of knowing and ways of seeing the world are rarely acknowledged, let alone celebrated, in the expressions of a Brahmani hegemonic culture. I underscore Sumitra Bhave's argument: to capture the "life blood and heartbeat of Dalit women oral histories are needed to supplement conceptual knowledge" (xii). Along with conceptual and theoretical analyses, it is essential to examine the real-life experiences of Dalit women to generate theory.

Telling and listening to such stories also created vital links among us—Dalit women—and it could be a powerful and practical instrument of conscientization.[20] In this case, I am an insider/outsider. Dalit women's personal narratives offer them a place from which to reflect upon *our* past and present experiences; to scrutinize *our* stories, which carry agency, meaning, and information about the social and psychological positions we inhabit. The popularity of autobiography and narrativity in feminist research is a measure of the significance attached to experience, reflection, and psychoanalytic understanding as a counterbalance to the kind of public and external evidence that is available from historical and structural analysis and political economy. Many Tamasha women felt very proud to be interviewed and recorded for the first time in their lives. At the same time, some women consciously chose not to speak with me. Through Mangalatai's social biography and oral history, I write a fuller account of Dalit women's ideas, actions, and lives. I represent Mangalatai's experiences, challenges, and corporeal and emotional pressures to put on record her ways of knowing and seeing the world.

### *ENGAGING HISTORICAL FIELDWORK: BREATHING IN DUST FROM THE FIELD*

I first met Mangalatai, a non-literate Tamasha dancer on September 3, 2004, during her performance at the famous Bal Gandharva Rangmandir auditorium in Pune. On October 9 of the same year, I saw her perform in Kada village in Ahmednagar district. In the many hours we spent together, Mangalatai remembered her past and narrated her present while also speculating about her actions in the future. Epistemologically and politically, our listening presence helped Mangalatai evoke forgotten moments, name her anger and discontent with her life situation, and record her resilience and frustrations, both to herself and me (Gay 166).[21] We chatted away that hot afternoon as artists continued with their card games, relaxed or slept before the evening performance, checked their equipment, and ate their meals in the shade of the tents. This was their everyday way of life for eight to nine months every year.

In Mangalatai's words, *our* common background facilitated my entering into sequestered spaces that were often out of bounds to elite scholars:

> I do not take riks [risks], I am a little concerned about who is interviewing, what will they do with my information, and where it will end up? However, I am very happy to talk with you because you belong to *aapla samaj* [our community]. It is because of that that I am sitting with you, or else, we live or die, who cares for us? (Bansode)

Mangalatai did not want to invite trouble from non-caste members. The deeper Marathi caste-community cord is very significant to Mangalatai. She was more comfortable talking with me as a person who belonged to "our" community. Moreover, by deploying her own low-class and low-caste vocabulary of "riks," Mangalatai challenges elite, cultured, sanitized, and sanskritized language practices. Albeit after some persuasion, she talked unhindered and built our common connection.

Mangalatai was a generous host, offering me the best *methichi bhaaji* (vegetable made from fenugreek leaves) and *bhakri* (bread) cooked on a *chool* (open hearth), and I am grateful to her for spending time with me and sharing her life experiences. Other women and men in the troupe viewed me with skepticism. "What is she, a middle-class looking lady, doing here?" they may have thought. I noticed that during our conversation, Mangalatai was very alert and kept a close watch on eavesdroppers who could overhear her story. To be more cautious, we constantly shifted from one location to the other: inside the tent that was a temporary home for artists, outside to the fields, and at times the area around the tent over which we walked. In this manner, she could also keep a watch on workers attending to their duties as she continued to share her experiences of poverty, politics, and titillating performance.

### *POLICING WOMEN, PRODUCING TAMASHA*

Tamasgir women were at the mercy of men in the audience and contractors/managers who policed them in the interest of producing Tamasha. Though of a low status, Mangalatai and other Tamasha artists are hereditary/non-hereditary folk-theater performers; they are not common "prostitutes" or "sex workers." However, they deploy their body politics, their itinerant performativity of their sensual and sexual selves and informal sexual relationships as an economic resource. As a result, women's bodies and especially women's sexuality are a form of wealth for the family. Many women negotiate patriarchal power and bend it to suit their own purposes, engaging the sexual economy of erotic excess and normative societal structures of caste, gender, sexual, and familial labor by manipulating their bodies. Women were (and are) sometimes able to appropriate their own sexuality, selling it, abandoning marriage, and keeping the benefits that they accrue for themselves. In these processes, gender and sexuality emerge(d) as generative activities in a particular way: as source and effect of exchange.[22] However, Mangalatai's modes of life "exceed the logic of capital itself" (Spivak 251) because families increase the value of women by keeping them inside the family and community, and not selling them off as objects of barter and exchange or gifts in the marriage economy.[23]

### *POVERTY AND HUNGER*

We need to challenge critiques located in an East/West or resistance/domination binary that often buries the complexity of women's experiences. Most Tamasgirs concur that they were pushed to perform because of poverty. Yet feminists have asserted that "coercion by poverty" has essentialist connotations and have challenged Orientalist representations of Western women as full of agency and Asian women as powerless victims or "vulnerable to exploitation, in contrast with the promiscuous Western woman who is ruled by the (im)morality of the market" (Kapur 124).[24] Mangalatai recounts her actual days of poverty and hunger: "When I was with my mother, *khaaychi tarambal hoti*," she says, describing how hard it was to procure food. "We had name and fame, but no money to even buy food. My father, uncles both maternal and paternal, looted my mother." Women are often the breadwinners of the entire family, and it is poverty as well as their generational ties to Tamasha that enable them to draw upon their bodies as an economic resource by performing in Tamasha. Mangalatai underscores that although her mother was very famous, as a child Mangalatai did not get food. Moreover, men who depended on women's familial, social, and sexual labor, and at times supported them, also often further oppressed those women.

Seconding Mangalatai, the highly reputed Lavani *samaradni* (Lavani empress) Surekhatai Punekar, a Dalit artist hailing from Pune, recounts her overlapping and complicated struggles:

> My maternal grandparents were in Tamasha. My father was a *hamal* [coolie] at Pune Railway Station. He continued with his *hamali* during the daytime and engaged in *bailgadicha* [bullock cart] Tamasha in the nights. Once the bullock cart met with an accident, and I got a deep cut on my leg. During those times there was only *jhada khalcha* [under the tree] Tamasha. There was no proper stage. Tamasgirs also did not earn the kind of income they do these days. I was introduced to the stage when I was only eight years old. I liked to dance and sing. My father also instructed me to sing well. He did not allow me to sleep and *phatke dyayache avaj chadhavanya sathi* [punished me so I would sing higher]. I stood on a chair and sang. (Punekar)

Thus, Surekhatai endured being physically beaten by her father because she knew without her income there would be no food at home. Hunger was common, she reports:

> We went from village to village to perform. When we got to the village we first begged for *bhakri* and *kalvan* [bread and curry], and then after collecting everything ate together at a *chavadi* [village common hall] and performed in the nights. After three, four months we went home until Divali and worked at *dhoonya bhandyachi kama* [washing clothes and utensils] for 10–12 families. We never had food to eat in our home. I remember *majhe garibiche divas* [days of my poverty], sometimes we got only black tea [because there was no money to buy milk] and *batar* [hard bread]. (Punekar)

Surekhatai was constantly afflicted by hunger and poverty during her childhood. Over the years, however, the larger poverty narrative proved to be complicated and sat uneasily with some non-hereditary young artists who pursued different aims. Mangalatai mentions: "These days girls, college students from even higher castes [Brahmin] at times due to poverty but also to earn easy pocket money participate in my troupe. They want to work with me" (Bansode). For hereditary artists, poverty is further compounded by ignorance and illiteracy.

### *SCHOOLING AND PEDAGOGY OF THE TAMASHA STAGE*

Tamasha artists' first lessons of education are the dance and song training they receive from their parents or family. In the process, the Tamasha stage itself transforms into a school on which parents, like schoolteachers, inflict *phatke* (beatings) to discipline children and instill the pedagogy and body politics of song and dance ritual. Surekhatai was not sent to school because her migratory lifestyle could not allow for this luxury. She reasons:

> My parents were alcoholic. Because my father was *kalechya nadat* [engrossed in the art] he did not send me to school. We were six siblings. I must say that while my parents sent my sisters to school to be educated until the third grade, I was never given such an opportunity. I don't know the reason—my mother said she didn't know. (Punekar)

In a similar vein, Mangalatai continues that her mother initiated her into Tamasha:

> When my mother performed in her Tamasha, there were fewer women performers. She needed more women in her troupe and hence, she discontinued my schooling when I was in class two and pushed me on to the Tamasha stage when I was merely nine years old. Today, I am fifty-five and I am still dancing. My mother is my guru. I am famous because of her. My mother also danced from when she was seven years old. Initially I was scared of the people, but gradually I became bold and could tackle them as I turned fifteen or sixteen. My son Nitin was also introduced to the Tamasha stage when he was only seven years old. We tried our best, but he did not study at all. (Bansode)

Education for Mangalatai was the actual pedagogical training and practice of Tamasha on and off stage. At times, artists hire dance and music experts to train them, but not all women prefer to dance, as Mangalatai's sister Kranti reports:

> I do not like to dance, I always wanted to sing, but my mother only brought me out to dance. I have studied until the fifth class, but I was not interested in school. My mother used to dance and move around, and we were left with some caretaker *bai* who fed us, clothed us, and sent us to school. It was like we were just dancing as a hobby, or since it was in the family, our condition was quite good I feel. After my mother's death, I am now with my elder sister. (Narayangavkar)

Many women were busy earning for their families, and consequently, they could not pay attention to their children. They could barely spend time with them or think about their rearing.

Like classical artists, Tamasha artists spent long hours learning dance moves and in rehearsals. Some also took classical, *kathak* lessons. Mangalatai also learned to dance, sing, perform a variety of skits, and engage in a confident and bold manner with the mixed-caste male audience. The pedagogical goals of Tamasgirs for everyday survival thus contrasted with those of middle-class Dalits who sought education for self-esteem, self-reliance, dignity, self-assertion, and community power (Paik, *Dalit*). Tamasgir parents, kin, and associates educated and trained women to be alert, smart, and attractive, and to engage the audience and cater to men's sensual demands.

### *BODY POLITICS AND EROTIC EXCESS*

The everyday sustenance of Tamasgirs depends on their negotiation, bending, and transgressing of traditional patriarchy through an excessive performance of the erotic and exotic. Although agents of the colonial and postcolonial Maharashtra state, along with upper- and lower-caste women and men, seek to sanitize Maharashtrian society, Mangalatai underscores the necessity of *ashlil* (obscene), erotic excess:

> Some old, traditional Lavanya have *ashlil shabda* [obscene, vulgar words]. We have to dance and make gestures in tune with these words because people in the audience like it. So, we have to also perform *ashlil adaa* [obscene gestures]. For example, the words *choli majhi taatali, kaya majhi bhijali* [my blouse is tight because of full breasts and my body is wet]. How do you show this? How do you show that you have full breasts and hence the choli is tight and the body is covered with water [thus clearly revealing the private body parts]? There's another Lavani: *kiti mee halavu, kiti mee halavu . . . thand garavaa?* [how much do I shake, how much do I shake in this cool breeze?] One has to show everything, enact, and bring to life these obscene words. (Bansode)

Mangalatai indicates that to earn their living, Tamasgir women deploy obscene words and a body politics of erotic excess to entice and fulfill men's desires. It was thus a titillating vicious circle: men in the audience want more sensual and sexual titillation, and women performers provide it because they think that is exactly what audiences want. As a result, women on stage and men in the audience participate in a mutuality of desire through a sexual and erotic body politics of gestures, including winking the left eye, biting lips, continually shaking hips and breasts, accentuating particular body parts, and so on.

Although Mangalatai felt the pains and predicaments of a dancer, at the same time she underscores that artists were dependent on the audience: "Public demands *ashlil* Lavanya. We have to satisfy them, and everybody does it. So, we cannot really help it, or we will lose." As much as in scholarly econometrics, everybody in the Tamasha occupation and business understands the operations of the law of *magani tasa puravatha* (demand and supply). Women, the main breadwinners, easily incorporate family members into the practice of Tamasha. Women and men fight with and support each other. They bend patriarchal rules, partner with each other, and together share the different tasks of singing, dancing, helping with chores, and taking care of the younger children. Yet men also exploit Dalit women's social and sexual labor in various ways.

### *"DEVIANT" SEXUALITY AND THE BRAHMANI PATRIARCHAL POLITICS OF MANGALSUTRA*

The Brahmani patriarchal ruling classes of colonial and postcolonial Maharashtra create(d) a normative hierarchy of caste, gender, and sexuality. As a result, they tightly tie(d) mobile Tamasha dancers to the lowest ladder of sex and sexuality and even depict(ed) their sexuality as "deviant" because, to them, unlike elite women, low-status Tamasha women were not sexually monogamous. Tamasha women engaged in flexible relationships, though some were legally married. Especially during colonial times, driven by social, sexual, and (national) cultural anxiety, ruling elites' engaged with the "woman question" that was rooted in caste structure. To construct a "moral," "respectable" Indian woman they created the binary of "good wife" and "bad prostitute," thus strengthening the connection between chastity and higher caste and excluding low-caste Tamasha performers. As I state elsewhere, upper-caste women and men resignified the "loose" morality of Dalit women to amplify their own upper-caste morality and caste power. Tamasha women are thus in constant and potential danger of being violated physically and face many other *vyap* (difficulties), as Surekhatai and Mangalatai recount.

Tamasha is a highly stigmatized occupation due to the potential for sexual abuse by men. The danger continued for Mangalatai, as she notes:

> In the beginning I was scared to face the public. However, *gradually I learned to handle the public. Hey lok cheshta kartyat, maskari kartyat, pan kunibi haat nhai lavala ajoon . . . mee kadak bai haye* [These people make fun of me, ridicule me, but nobody has so far touched me physically . . . because I am a very strict woman]. *Mee ek lakh deto, don lakh deto, jhopaya ye . . . ashe mhas prasang hote* [I will give one or two lakhs, sleep with me . . . there were many such incidents], but I never gave in and just continued with my Tamasha. My family has been attacked; I have faced caste discrimination in my village . . . but this is life! (Bansode, emphasis mine)

This is the traveling life of a Tamasha dancer: insecure and unstable, oppressed by the intersecting matrix of caste, gender, and sexuality; however, the caravan is always on the move. Due to her engagement with the public and lowly Tamasha, Mangalatai is always already discriminated against as a "promiscuous" Dalit woman by men of all castes. Nevertheless, over the years, she strengthened herself, learned to work with men, and found ways to protect herself.

Mangalatai recounts some significant hazards in the life of Tamasha:

> I remember I was made to dance in what is called a *jhadakhalcha* Tamasha, that is, Tamasha under a tree. There was no stage and we were dancing with all the people around us. I had to walk to the men to take the money from them and at that instance they used to pull the sari or pull us. We were helpless. Sometimes we tried to smile and get away and at times some men from the troupe intervened. What to do . . . *publicach mai baap* [the public is our mother and father, a protector and provider]. I will continue to dance for at least ten years, as long as the public wants me. (Bansode)

Thus, Mangalatai reiterates that men looked at her as a public woman who could be trifled with. She gradually learned to negotiate with men, and to bend and transgress public patriarchy purposefully. Over the years, she also improved her economic status. Mangalatai argues that the government should provide some concession in diesel rates to Tamasha artists who were always on the move. She owned eight trucks. One had a generator and needed a regular supply of diesel. It produced enough electricity for two villages.

Yet life was unstable. Surekhatai recounts her misfortune in finding a trustworthy life partner:

> During my Tamasha life, I fell in love with [a Muslim man] Baba Pathan Contractor. Of course, he never took me to his house because I was a Tamasha dancer [a loathed object nobody wants to associate with]. He used to lock me in a room at a lodge and visit his family, whenever he wanted to. After a few years, I was pregnant and Pathan abandoned me. My family was furious with me over this relationship. And, I still continued to dance. (Punekar)

Surekhatai's silence and discomfort while reflecting on her relationship with her partner suggest how unstable their "affair" was. Unlike Surekhatai, Mangalatai had a stable marriage with a Mahar-Buddhist man.

Most significantly, both Mangalatai and Surekhatai entrenched a new patriarchy and enacted a "different" modernity and robust Dalit "body politics"[25] by donning a thick and long gold *mangalsutra* and creatively refashioning their emotional and corporeal selves.[26] Intimate bodily experiences of intentionally donning *mangalsutra* and full, clean dress emerged as powerful practices of presenting Dalit women's transformed personhood and social and moral status. Yet the body politics of erotic excess are not robust: both women acceded to the modest and moral "traditional" Brahmani patriarchy by donning its marker, the *mangalsutra*. It is through such practices as the politics of *mangalsutra* that Dalits, in their march to modernity from the early decades of the twentieth century, continually disrupt and deprive dominant classes of their norms and powers.

Mangalatai and Surekhatai twist tradition and modernity, and they innovatively redeploy marriage, chastity, and motherhood to forge new moral meanings as wives. Modern *mangalsutra* and marriage offered Mangalatai hitherto denied morality and modesty. Following Ambedkar and Navayana Buddhism, many Dalit women abandoned the black-beaded *mangalsutra* to don a necklace of yellow beads. Many elite upper-caste feminists have also abandoned the Brahmani sign of *mangalsutra*. However, such elite feminist liberatory politics rarely engages with despised Dalit women's practices. By showing off her *mangalsutra*, Mangalatai displays her womanly virtue as well as her moral and modern self. She is not merely imitating married women or seeking complicity with patriarchy as in the case of upper-caste women. She instead negotiates and renegotiates, selectively appropriating certain traditional Brahmani practices, mimicking them, and generating broad possibilities and power for herself.

The tripartite masculine patriarchal actors—the colonial and postcolonial Indian state and upper and lower castes—have looked down upon marriages of Tamasgirs and their alternative practices because they are often "open" contractual relationships that can be made and broken by free will. Hence, to them, Tamasgir women are not bound to the monogamous strictures of marriage and are therefore believed to be lower in the social and sexual ladder. However, many Tamasgir women continue to live with single partners throughout their lives. There are no clean lines. Although *mangalsutra* provides some respectability for monogamy, bodily autonomy, and power to married Tamasgir women, at the same time, women also internalize rigorous disciplining of their subjectivity and perform as second wives with lower status and without honor.

## *TAMASHA IN THE PATRIARCHAL STATE OF MAHARASHTRA*

Along with private patriarchy, Mangalatai was oppressed by public patriarchy. The state and the national government adopted double standards: at times it sought to protect, include, and extend patronage to some artists, and at the same time it neglected them and further exacerbated their vulnerability. After 1960, the newly independent state of Maharashtra sought to carve out its own Marathi identity. To accomplish this task, along with elitist emphasis on "higher cultured" *sangeet natak* (song drama), the state also incorporated the supposedly "degenerate" and "rural" Tamasha art. Both art forms were popular and thrived, however differently. State agents sought to "protect" and "preserve" the so-called "adulterated" art of *lokakala* by setting up committees and boards to collate literature, publish volumes of folk genres, fund events, and even give awards to artists. Although the elite Dalits and non-Dalits looked upon Tamasha as a degraded practice, many non-Dalits along with the state also underscored its essentially Marathi identity and reappropriated the social and sexual labor of Tamasha artists in the service of the state and stigmatized it further.

As a result, some artists sought to work from inside the state machinery and entered the overt political realm. Political parties hired them to perform and disseminate their political agenda. Mangalatai, however, was not keen on entering politics:

> Some people say they are entering politics to serve the needy. However, that is not the case. My mother was also invited to do so. But nothing concrete takes places. The picture is very rosy though. *Mothe lok jagu denaar nhai* [big people will not allow us to survive there]. If we enter the field they will harass us, *chhedtaat amhala* [tease us] as they do here in Tamasha. It is the same when a girl tries to enter the field of modeling or cinema, she has to satisfy everybody [sexually] on her way to success. So it has been my mother's experience and our experience too, so I just do not want it. (Bansode)

Mangalatai was felicitated by politicians; however, that did not stop her from openly criticizing them or taking them to task for troubling artists. She did pay lip service to the state and its agents, but she wanted the state to help artists. She continues:

> I have won the Maharashtra Gaurav Puraskar [Honor Award]. I would like a national award just like my mother received. Then I will feel that my art has acquired its true value. On other fronts I am *troopt* [very contented]. I have no regrets. I am happy. All Tamasha artists are in debt today, so the government should help us a little. It is all the [debt to contractors] so the government should help us a little to repay or do away with that. (Bansode)

Thus, Mangalatai wanted the state to take actions to help its non-elite, hereditary artists. As a result, she negotiated and selectively aligned with some political parties in particular moments. Mangalatai complains that the state's stricter rules were ruining the art of Tamasha; however, she is a thorough businesswoman who controlled her Tamasha empire astutely and wisely. Though Tamasha is an exploitative art form, ironically, it is also financially empowering for the Bansode family—including its male members and other employees.

## DEPLOYING *KHANDANI* AS CULTURAL CAPITAL, WORK, AND OCCUPATION

Tamasha provided many generations of women and men artists with economic capital, as well as *khandani* (literally family occupation and hereditary lineage), which was/is the social and cultural capital they had acquired, accumulated, and cultivated over long years. I am deploying and building on the French sociologist Pierre Bourdieu's conceptualization of "capital."[27] Moreover, I am also gendering this concept. Hereditary Tamasha families deployed the cheap and readily available labor inside the family. As parents and kin, women were always already recruited to serve in roles critical to the integrity of familial labor and household as well as to the sexual economy of Tamasha. Moreover, families gendered *khandani* capital by easily associating women with dance and men with managerial work or playing musical instruments. Family members also competed with each other.

Thus, caste and cultural ideology has not only disciplined the division of labor and laborers, as Ambedkar argues, but also of sexual labor, as I illustrated above. The colonial and postcolonial state of Maharashtra and its agents, as well as upper-caste women and men have constructed Tamasgirs through an erotic gaze and denied them moral gains. Yet, Tamasgirs have repeatedly deployed the obscene and erotic and negotiated with patriarchy to work for economic gains. Hence, unfortunately they have been too easily associated with sex work. Abolitionists and anti-abolitionists have contested the distinctions between free and forced entry into sex work. A critical issue

Figure 9.2: Mangalatai putting on makeup in her makeshift tent and getting ready for her performance. Thirteen years since I first met her in 2004, in April 2017, Mangalatai continued to perform her *khandani* Tamasha at the Tamasha Pandhari, Narayangav, as she had promised. Photo by author.

at local, national, and international levels with regard to the free and forced dichotomy has been the consent and choice of women.[28]

Three generations of Mangalatai's family have performed in Tamasha: her grandparents, parents, and five sisters and three brothers. Mangalatai's family members drew upon and built on the *khandani* Tamasha for their daily sustenance: "We [my mother and I] had no other option. There are other businesses too but Tamasha is our Lakshmi [goddess of wealth]. This is not a business. It is our service to the public. We entertain people, forgetting our own sorrows" (Bansode). In addition to Mangalatai and her family, other families that included one hundred fifty to two hundred women and men depended on Mangalatai for their livelihood. Mangalatai also emphasizes that Tamasha was not for minting money, but to serve the various (especially sensual) needs of the larger public. To serve the audience and to earn their living, the artists often had to give up their own needs.

While other artists depended on her labor, Mangalatai in turn depended on the dictates of politicians and the state:

> The political parties dominant in the village, *sarpanch*, *patil* [headman], the landlord who gives us this place to put up our stage and the police all torture us. Anybody can come and bully us, kick us. We are so helpless . . . *hittha log hagatyat titha amhi khato, nachato* [people defecate *here* and we eat our food in this very place and dance *here*]. Despite all this, I have to continue with this [complicated life], for I have one hundred fifty people to feed. We have to keep everybody happy in this line [of Tamasha], and I have been tolerating these people since I was nine. I just smile at them and get away. Sometimes the public gets mad and political party people are a great nuisance. They start shouting from the gates, *amcha paksha, amhala soda. . . . Vis manasa soda* [ours is the ruling party now, give us free entry. . . . Let our twenty men enter for free]. How do we live in such circumstances? (Bansode)

Thus, Mangalatai argues that Dalit women dancers are at the mercy of everybody: ordinary upper- and lower-caste men as well as big and small politicians.

Nonetheless, Tamasha also emerged as privileged practice because its mobility allowed artists to escape sexual labor under specific patrons as in the case of Lavani or Sangeet-Bari forms. By contrast, Lavani artists from banner shows lacked such agency. Mangalatai comments, "We can also do that [kind of Lavani singing and dancing] by sitting in one place; however, we do not. We move around villages with a troupe of one hundred fifty and perform" (Bansode). Tamasha theater constantly traveled among villages and cities. By contrast, Lavani artists carved out stability by sticking to the city and performing only a few famous songs. Moreover, Lavani troupes were also not as big as those of Tamasha, and hence the financial risks were lower.

Mangalatai further complains that unlike Tamasha, which was in the open and a public performance, some Lavani artists performed in the secluded, private *baithaks* (sittings) for political leaders, *aamdaars*, *mantris*, and *khasdars*, which degraded the art form.

Mangalatai was a thorough entrepreneur. She maintained a thick *hajeri ani pagar pustak* (register) for daily accounting. While we were talking, her son Nitinkumar demanded three hundred rupees. She immediately raised her eyebrows and questioned him: "Why do you need the money?" Nitin responded that it was for diesel for the vehicles. Mangalatai reminded him that she had bought diesel just the day before. However, instead of haggling in my presence, she preferred to give him the money from her *tijori* (locked case to store valuables), which she kept a close eye on. She also insisted that Nitin bring her the receipt.

In actual practice, Mangalatai controlled her finances in a major way. When I first met Mangalatai at Balgandharva and asked about who kept track of her income and expenses, Mangalatai mentioned that her sons and husband took care of everything. However, during deeper conversations in Kada, I found a discrepancy. Given how inconsistent Tamasha income is, Mangalatai was involved in making ends meet. In the middle of a performance, Mangalatai was cramming all the cash collected that evening inside her *tijori*. She sat in her special chamber in the tent donning only a bra and petticoat, calculated all the cash, and put it in the *tijori*. Unlike elite modest women, she did not seem inhibited by her minimal dress among her people. She also asked a male worker how much food grain and vegetables would be required for the entire troupe. She calculated the money to feed everyone and admonished the worker to remember that she was also paying for the grinding of wheat.

Nonetheless, despite her thorough accounting skills, Mangalatai reported that she had incurred a debt of 500,000 rupees and that Tamasha was not as lucrative as it once was. Many Tamasha artists were in debt from taking loans for weddings, schooling, clothing, and family support. Surekhatai seconds this point: "I used to fall sick but I worked undeterred. I got my brother and sisters married. I got my cousins married. Everything is settled now. I have earned up to 80,000 rupees for a show when things were fine. However, I am in debt today and have to start afresh" (Punekar). Mangalatai also laments that Tamasha was losing in the entertainment race because of decreasing audience numbers: "Now is the world of remix, and orchestra, obscene mixes and so there is less public for Tamasha" (Bansode). Other forms of performances and musical medleys pose an immense competition for Tamasha.

While commenting on the change over time and the difference between other popular forms of entertainment and Tamasha, Mangalatai reports: "Earlier the public used to announce prizes, *jalsa* was popular, and men touched women artists' hands, or pressed them as they do at [Sangeet-Bari] of Chauphula and at Aryabhushan theater. But we do not have that kind of physical proximity in Tamasha" (Bansode). Women artists in Tamasha agreed that unlike in folk forms such as Gondhal or Sangeet-Baris where the audience sits closer to the performers, Tamasha is "safer" because women perform on a platform at a distinct distance and even higher than the male audience. It provides some power to women to look down on men. Surekhatai underscores Mangalatai's views:

> Tamasha has changed its form over the recent years and has become more lewd and raunchy, because the public is not the same as earlier. Today, there is a lot of money and less of the art form, clothes and *adakari* [gestures] are changing immensely and if this is the state of the art today, what will happen to future dancers? (Punekar)

Despite this decline in their art form, both Mangalatai and Surekhatai continue to use their talents for the betterment of the community at large. Surekhatai mentions:

> I perform Lavanya. Some of them are very famous. I engaged in a few song-in-drama performances. Along with a *dholakivala* [drum player] and *petivala* [harmonium player] I visited villages and performed *daru bandi*, *hunda bandi* [anti-liquor, anti dowry], AIDS *virodhi* [anti-AIDS] government programmes, and fetched an honorarium. I traveled to villages for this. I performed not only for men but also women [because women never attended and I wanted them to do so]. I also won a prize of two lakhs at the 1998 Lavani Mahotsava [festival]. (Punekar)

Thus, Surekhatai was involved in social activism as well.

She was sensitive to gender discrimination rampant in the society: men enjoyed watching "dishonorable" low-caste, low-status women dance on the Tamasha stage and provide entertainment to men, however, they would not allow "their own respectable" genteel women to watch these shows. Surekhatai thus questioned the double standards of some men who constructed hierarchies in caste, class, and sexuality. Hence, Surekhatai decided to perform "special" Tamasha shows *only* for women. During such events, she herself stood at the doors of the public halls to welcome women who came to watch her dance. Significantly, the Bal Gandharva Theatre has retained the annual "Ladies-Special Lavani Event" as part of the Pune Festival that celebrates Maharashtrian art and culture until today.

Such "ladies only" events were moments of empowerment for all—mixed-caste, elite, and ordinary—women, wherein women enjoyed themselves immensely and transgressed patriarchal and gendered boundaries. For example, they whistled loudly, thrusting their thumb and index finger in their mouths, waved their hands rapidly in the air, and danced in the theater just like men did. In case they could not whistle, many women brought plastic whistles to the auditorium to thoroughly enjoy and participate in the gendered sexual performances. In this instance, for once, the Tamasha theater, typically a masculine space constructed for a male gaze, engendered a liberatory possibility and power for many women.

Despite Surekhatai's positive experience with women audience members, Mangalatai remembers how Tamasha life tortured her mother and family and took everything from them:

> My mother used to dance a lot and she even delivered a baby on the stage. . Our contractor said that the Tamasha had to close down as Vithu [Vithabai] could not dance. So we were put again in a *dharmashala* [temporary rest home]. We had thought that the contractor would at least give us something to survive on for some time, but he never returned to inquire about us. When we visited our mother at the hospital, she had no food or clothes for the newborn. There was no money. So, someone suggested that we could keep the harmonium as collateral and get some money on that. But I refused because the harmonium and *chaal* [ankle bells] are Lakshmi [our wealth]. How can we take a loan on that? I went out and requested the contractor to give us some money and told him that we needed help. But he said that nothing could be done unless the Tamasha started again. There was another *sangeet* party in Jalgaon, and I asked them for some money, saying that I was Vithabai's daughter and that she was in the hospital. That lady agreed to give me 1,000 rupees, but I had to dance every evening. I was very happy. I bought food for everybody and mutton biryani [a delicacy they could rarely afford] for my mother and *angada topada* [clothes] for the newborn. (Bansode)

Poor Tamasha women were dependent for their survival on their performing art. They lacked economic and social resources. While mentioning some unusual *paddhat* (tradition) in a village, Mangalatai says:

> One evening I was made to sit in a vehicle and told that the show was in some other village and I got scared. I took my cousin along and visited that village. There was a typical tradition of dance in that village. The dancers were to dance in a mobile bullock cart. Just imagine this now. We got into the carts, trying to balance ourselves, and started dancing. The crowd shouted and whistled at us; they also threw things at us. It was a dreadful experience. I will never forget it. (Bansode)

Once again, the Tamasha artist was at the mercy of men. Artists also affirmed the hierarchy of wages: the main artist like Surekhatai was paid the highest and the payment decreased as one descended the ladder.

There was/is much borrowing of music, dance, and styles between Tamasha and Marathi and Hindi films. Films provided artists another opportunity to present their art and, moreover, earn an income. Mangalatai also acted in Marathi movies:

> Yesterday we received the actress Alka Kubal's phone call to act in a movie. I have also acted as a special *kalakar* in some movies. But I cannot perform in movies anymore, because I have to take care of the Tamasha business. I have to feed these families.

Thus, Mangalatai reiterated her limitations as a performer. Although Mangalatai entered the film industry, she seemed perpetually troubled by "dishonor" and the blot of her stigmatized life of a *nachee* (low-status dancer):

> People come and go, but the *batta* [blot] of a *nachanarin* [dancing woman] stays forever. *Kunibi changyla najarana baghat nhai* [Nobody looks at us with respect]. Men have their affairs. Their keeps do not move around with their children, but we are not like that. This business is fine.

As a Tamasgir, Mangalatai is aware of the potentials and problems of Tamasha: she has done very well financially; however, she believes she cannot win against her stigma as an "immoral," "disrespectful" public dancer. She is the empress of her empire, married to a man, a "good" wife and mother who bore sons (and daughters) and worked for their success; still, she is successful because she is a *nachee*. Her Tamasha life provides many possibilities, and at the same time, it is a potential threat.

Surekhatai did not want her children to be associated with her world of dance. Uneducated but lucratively employed, this accomplished dancer sent her children away to fancy boarding schools at Panchgani, near Pune. Due to the itinerant nature of her work, she felt that she could not otherwise give them a stable education. She wanted to educate her children and keep them away from the world of Tamasha—of dance and of her life. Yet, ironically, her sons and her family severed ties with her.

Unlike Surekhatai, Mangalatai kept her children with her throughout her life. She celebrated Tamasha and wanted her children to follow their ancestral *khandani* of Tamasha. Yet, not all her descendants are in the practice. Mangalatai believes that Tamasha is an art gifted to them by their *khandan*, and they are following this hereditary art form like other classical arts. But this *khandani* performance is conflicted: it burdens as well as offers Mangalatai financial security. Many elite Dalits still consider Tamasha as a lower form of art, especially because it stigmatizes Dalit women, and instead train their children in classical dance forms of *kathak* or *bharatnatyam*.

Mangalatai continues to live her double life of a Tamasha performer. Mangalatai and her sons are capitalizing on the sexual labor of women and consolidating their hereditary *khandani*, and in the process providing livelihood for future generations of her family. She danced with Nitin—acting like a hero-heroine duo, hugging and performing a sensual song. Their occupation demanded that a non-literate, low-status Dalit woman break social, cultural, and traditional patriarchal norms. The modern, educated, middle-class Dalits certainly disapprove(d) of such sexual labor and entrepreneurial exercises for "genteel" and "respectable" women.

## CONCLUSION

I focused on the social life of Tamasha to unravel particular paradoxes of Dalit Tamasgirs. I represent details of the life experiences of an individual woman—Mangalatai—who was purposefully negotiating the conditions of her life under double patriarchy with the larger society and the historical constraints it had imposed on her. Mangalatai's life narrative presents her very real pain, suffering, and predicaments as well as her conditions as she focuses on the improvement and promotion of her self and her family. It was thus a significant project of shifting structures of historic tradition; new Dalit morality, and modernity; transgressing and consolidating patriarchy; the state's hypocrisy and appropriation of culture; as well as body politics, emotions, and erotic excess. This lucrative but burdensome *khandani* business contains a complex story of a woman working within a community, not merely a triumphant and straightforward rags-to-riches tale.

Deploying life narratives, I have examined both Mangalatai's victimization as well as her agency to pierce the power of double patriarchy and triple discrimination. I have analyzed the precarious materiality of Mangalatai's stigmatized double life that was shaped by her status as a Dalit woman. Mangalatai negotiated and renegotiated with the dominant power of patriarchal, feudal, familial, societal, and state structures. Her experiences of poverty and hunger, pedagogy of Tamasha training, denial of moral womanhood, strategic adherence to Brahmani patriarchy and conventionality, and alignment with particular political parties at significant historical and political conjunctures all prove that her power, however limited, is in how she possesses herself and negotiates with normative apparatuses. She, a despised woman, has thus attempted to piece together whatever is available to sustain her family and troupe.

Together, oral history and ethnographic fieldwork methods help to humanize the life narrative, challenge historical silences, and create critical spaces for Mangalatai to carve out her subjectivity and agency. I engage seriously with oral history neither to "sanitize" nor "preserve" Tamasha, but to engage with Mangalatai's own understanding of her history and community and thus provide meaning and significance to her daily life.

However biased and maybe even incomplete, Mangalatai's life history offers a deep insight into Dalitness that is not publicly well articulated but is still representative of a larger section of Dalits and their predicaments and potentials. Her individual life narrative underscores the vicious paradoxes of empowerment and disempowerment. Mangalatai's life highlights the everyday oppression of structures of caste, gender, sexuality, and her circumscribed ability to dissent and carve out her agency. However fragmented this narrative is, stories like this allow students of history to see the world the way Tamasgir women did, as ever changing, mobile, destabilized, and dangerous. Through engaging with Mangalatai's story, we learn that Tamasha has been a despised form of hereditary performance, and women have had to struggle constantly with it to preserve their honor within and without the Dalit community to enhance their social status and earn their family's livelihood. Ironically, Tamasha continues to be a degraded form of performance that has provided possibilities and power, however limited, to some women.

## NOTES

ACKNOWLEDGMENTS: Special thanks to the editors Charu Gupta and S. Shankar for their critical feedback. I also thank the participants of the "Caste and Life Narrative" workshop conducted at the University of Hawai'i at Mānoa, and audiences at the Nehru Memorial Museum and Library, the American Historical Association Annual Conference on South Asia at the University of Wisconsin, Madison, and the Annual Asian Studies Conference for their questions and comments. I am grateful to David Hardiman, Lucinda Ramberg, Erynn Masi Casanova, and Lisa Bjorkman for timely discussions and critical comments.

1. Vithabai's daughter, Mangalatai Bansode sang the famous Lavani for me, when I interviewed her in the village of Kada, Ahmednagar District, on September 9 and 10, 2004. Throughout this essay, I have translated the interviews and vernacular Marathi sources into English.
2. I am departing from the traditional elite depiction of Tamasha as "rough music" and deploying the term here especially to mark the directed mockery or hostility against certain individuals who offended Vithabai. In another context, English "rough music" rituals correspond with French charivari and denote a rude cacophony (Thompson 467).
3. Instead of calling her by her formal name, I use the Marathi *tai* to address her with affection and respect.
4. I am building on my earlier work here. For details on "interlocking technologies," see Paik, *Dalit.*
5. See http://mangalabansode.com for Mangalatai's website.
6. I thank David Hardiman for this discussion.
7. Lavanya is the plural of Lavani.
8. Traditionally, Mangs made ropes, bangles, wove baskets, and so on. Mahars acted as village watchmen and assisted the village Patil (headman), helped during land border disputes, carried away animal carcasses, swept village streets and other areas, and so on.
9. Kotani unfortunately does not provide full reference with dates or details of the documents he investigated.
10. See Paik, "Forging a New Dalit Womanhood."

11. See Freitag; Hansen; Banerjee.
12. See Mehrotra; Soneji; Ramberg; Oldenburg.
13. See Schultz; Novetzke; Wakankar; Zelliot and Mokashi-Punekar.
14. See Rao; Abrams.
15. See Arondekar.
16. See Vhatkar; Dhond; Moraje; Achalkhamb.
17. See Chandanshiv and Patangankar; Kulkarni and Moraje.
18. See Bagul.
19. See Bhave; Kannabiran and Lalitha; Arnold and Blackburn; Paik, *Dalit*; Hardiman, *Feeding*; Hardiman, "Miracle Cures"; Hardiman, *The Coming*; P. Thompson; Omvedt.
20. "Conscientization" refers to the concept of "critical consciousness." I am also drawing on Jane Thompson's insightful work on working-class women's education in England.
21. Gay has not studied Mangalatai's life but has helped me understand her.
22. I am building on my earlier analysis of caste and gender (see Paik, *Dalit*).
23. For details on the transactions in marriage and sexual economy, see Ramberg.
24. In her feminist-materialist analysis of sexual labor in India, Prabha Kotiswaran argues for the labor paradigm and against abolition by a consideration of legal frameworks and legislative effects in the everyday lives of female sex workers in Andhra Pradesh and Kolkata. See also Kapur.
25. For details on Dalit body politics of modernity and morality in both colonial and postcolonial periods, see Paik, *Dalit* and "Forging a New Dalit Womanhood."
26. *Mangalsutra* is the chain of yellow and black beads worn by married Hindu women as a sign of being married.
27. See Bourdieu; Swartz.
28. Scholars and activists have deeply contested if "sex work" is "work," "entertainment," "economic coercion," and "entrepreneurship." For some details, see Sukthankar.

## WORKS CITED

Abrams, Tevia. "Tamasha: People's Theatre of Maharashtra State, India." PhD diss., Michigan State U, 1974.

Achalkhamb, Rustum. *Tamasha Lokarangbhumi*. Sugava, 2006.

Allman, Paula. *Revolutionary Social Transformation: Democratic Hopes, Political Possibilities and Critical Education*. Praeger Pub Text, 1999.

Arnold, David, and Stuart Blackburn. *Telling Lives in India: Biography, Autobiography, and Life History*. Indiana UP, 2004.

Arondekar, Anjali. "Subject to Sex: A Small History of the Gomantak Maratha Samaj." *South Asian Feminisms*, edited by Ania Loomba and Ritty A. Lukose, Duke UP, 2012, pp. 244–63.

Atkinson, Robert. *The Life Story Interview*. Sage Publications, 1998.

Bagul, Yogiraj. *Tamasha: Vithabaichya Ayushyacha*. Rajhans Prakashan, 2004.

Banerjee, Sumanta. *The Parlour and the Street: Elite and Popular Culture in Nineteenth Century Bengal*. Seagull Books, 1989.

Bansode, Mangalatai. Personal interview. 3 and 9–10 Sept. 2004.

Bhave, Sumitra. *Pan on Fire: Eight Dalit Women Tell Their Story*. Indian Social Institute, 1988.

Bourdieu, Pierre. *Distinction: A Social Critique of the Judgement of Taste*. Harvard UP, 1984.

Carr, Edward Hallett. *What Is History?*. Vintage, 1967.

Chandanshiv, Bhaskar, and Vidyasagar Patangankar, editors. *Sangabhauchya Lavanya*. Sakct Prakashan, 2000.

Dhond, M. *Marathi Lavani*. Mauj, 1988.

Freitag, Sandria B., editor. *Culture and Power in Banaras: Community, Performance, and Environment, 1800–1980*. U of California P, 1989.

Gay, Peter. *The Bourgeois Experience: Victoria to Freud*. Oxford UP, 1984.

Gupta, Charu. "Writing Sex and Sexuality: Archives of Colonial North India." *Journal of Women's History*, vol. 23, no. 4, 2011, pp. 12–35.

Hardiman, David. *The Coming of the Devi: Adivasi Assertion in Western India*. Oxford UP, 1987.

———. *Feeding the Baniya: Peasants and Usurers in Western India*. Oxford UP, 1996.

———. "Miracle Cures for a Suffering Nation: Sai Baba of Shirdi." *Comparative Studies in Society and History*, vol. 57, no. 2, Apr. 2015, pp. 355–80.

Hansen, Kathryn. *Grounds for Play: The Nautanki Theatre of North India*. U of California P, 1991.

Joshi, Vinayak K. *Lokanatyachi Parampara*. Thokal Prakashan, 1961.

Kannabiran, Vasantha, and K. Lalitha. *"We were making history": Life Stories of Women in the Telangana People's Struggle*. Zed Books, 1989.

Kapur, Ratna. *Erotic Justice: Law and the New Politics of Postcolonialism*. Routledge-Cavendish, 2005.

Kotani, Hiroyuki. *Western India in Historical Transition: Seventheenth to Early Twentieth Centuries*. Manohar Publishers and Distributors, 2002.

Kotiswaran, Prabha. *Dangerous Sex, Invisible Labor: Sex Work and the Law in India*. Princeton UP, 2011.

Kulkarni, V. M., and Gangadhar Moraje, editors. *Ram Joshi Krut Lavanya*. 5th ed., Padmagandha, 1998.

Massey, James, and ISPCK. *Indigenous People: Dalits—Dalit Issues in Today's Theological Debate*. Indian Society for Promoting Christian Knowledge, 1994, pp. 4–6.

Mehrotra, Deepti Priya. *Gulab Bai: The Queen of Nautanki Theatre*. Penguin Books, 2006.

Moraje, Gangadhar. *Marathi Lavani Vangmay*. Moghe Prakashan, 1974.

Nair, Janaki. "The Devadasi, Dharma and the State." *Economic and Political Weekly*, vol. 29, no. 50, 1994, pp. 3157–67.

Namdev, Vhatkar. *Marathi Lokanatya Tamasha: Kala Ani Sahitya*. Ajab Prakashan, 1959.

Naregal, Veena. "Performance, Caste, Aesthetics: The Marathi Sangeet Natak and the Dynamics of Cultural Marginalisation." *Contributions to Indian Sociology*, vol. 44, no. 1–2, 2010, pp. 79–101.

Narayangavkar, Kranti. Personal interview. 9 Sept. 2004.

Novetzke, Christian Lee. *Religion and Public Memory: A Cultural History of Saint Namdev in India*. Columbia UP, 2013.

Oldenburg, Veena Talwar. "Lifestyle as Resistance: The Case of the Courtesans of Lucknow, India." *Feminist Studies*, vol. 16, no. 2, 1990, pp. 259–87.

Omvedt, Gail. *We Will Smash This Prison!: Indian Women in Struggle*. Zed Press, 1980.

Paik, Shailaja. *Dalit Women's Education in Modern India: Double Discrimination*. Routledge, 2014.

———. "Forging a New Dalit Womanhood in Colonial Western India: Discourse on Modernity, Rights, Education, and Emancipation." *Journal of Women's History*, vol. 28, no. 4, 2016, pp. 14–40.

Pandian, M. S. S. "Writing the Ordinary Lives." *Economic and Political Weekly*, vol. 43, no. 38, 2008, pp. 34–40.

Portelli, Alessandro. *The Battle of Valle Giulia: Oral History and the Art of Dialogue*. U of Wisconsin P, 1997.

———. *The Death of Luigi Trastulli, and Other Stories: Form and Meaning in Oral History*. SUNY P, 1991.

Punekar, Surekhatai. Personal interview. 20 Sept. 2004.

Ramberg, Lucinda. *Given to the Goddess: South Indian Devadasis and the Sexuality of Religion*. Duke UP, 2014.

Rao, Kristin Olson. "The Lavani of Maharashtra: A Regional Genre of Indian Popular Music." PhD diss., U of California, Los Angeles, 1985.

Rane, Sadanand. *Lokaganga*. Dimple Prakashan, 2012.

Rege, Sharmila. "The Hegemonic Appropriation of Sexuality: The Case of the Lavani Performers of Maharashtra." *Contributions to Indian Sociology*, vol. 29, no. 1–2, 1995, pp. 23–38.

Schultz, Anna C. *Singing a Hindu Nation: Marathi Devotional Performance and Nationalism*. Oxford UP, 2013.

Shetye, Shirish. *Dancing Maidens: The Seduction Called Lavani*. Spenta Multimedia, 2007.

Soneji, Davesh. *Unfinished Gestures: Devadasis, Memory, and Modernity in South India*. U of Chicago P, 2011.

Spivak, Gayatri Chakravorty. "Criticism, Feminism, and the Institution." *The Post-Colonial Critic: Interviews, Strategies, Dialogues*, edited by S. Harasym. Routledge, 1990.

Sukthankar, Ashwini. "Queering Approaches to Sex, Gender, and Labor in India: Examining Paths to Sex Worker Unionism." *South Asian Feminisms*, edited by Ania Loomba and Ritty A. Lukose, Duke UP, 2012, pp. 306–30.

Swartz, David. *Culture and Power: The Sociology of Pierre Bourdieu*. U of Chicago P, 1997.

Thakur, Bhagavan. *Ambedkari Jalse*. Sugava, 2005.

Thompson, E. P. *Customs in Common: Studies in Traditional Popular Culture*. The New Press, 1993.

Thompson, Jane. *Women, Class and Education*. Routledge, 2002.

Thompson, Paul. *Voice of the Past: Oral History*. Oxford UP, 2000.

Vansina, Jan. *Oral Tradition: A Study in Historical Methodology*. Aldine Transaction, 2006.

Vhatkar, Namdeo. *Marathiche Loknatya Tamasha: Kala ani Sahitya*. Jayvant Vhatkar and Yasashree, 1986.

Wakankar, Milind. *Subalternity and Religion: The Prehistory of Dalit Empowerment in South Asia*. Routledge, 2010.

Zelliot, Eleanor, and Rohini Mokashi-Punekar. *Untouchable Saints: An Indian Phenomenon*. Manohar, 2005.

# Law, Society, and Narratives of the Self

# 10

# BRAHMANICAL ACTIVISM AS ECO-CASTEISM

## Reading the Life Narratives of Bindeshwar Pathak, Sulabh International, and "Liberated" Dalits

MUKUL SHARMA

*It is a historic day. From now onward, the liberated manual scavengers of Alwar will call themselves Brahmins. They can become high-caste Brahmins. By being Brahmins, their mind is filled with emotions and their body is shivering. They are getting high.*

—Bindeshwar Pathak (Speech)[1]

*I took the help of sociology and decided to help them to perform rites, rituals and ceremonies of the upper castes people.*

—Bindeshwar Pathak (*Sociology* 20)

Bindeshwar Pathak is a Brahmin who works among "manual scavengers" who are considered to be among the lowest, most polluted, and most degraded "untouchable" castes by birth and are often assigned to the work of cleaning dry latrines and carrying human excreta. In the 1970s Pathak launched Sulabh International, his scheme of Sulabh Shauchalaya, and his organization Rastriya Garima Abhiyan, a national campaign to end manual scavenging. Sulabh International has emerged as one of India's most well-known endeavors for the "liberation" of scavengers and for dealing comprehensively with the problems of scavenging and sanitation.[2] Initially started in certain parts of Bihar, its work has spread to several states in India. Pathak characterizes himself as a sociologist, a social activist, a founder, a pioneer of a social-reform movement, a believer, and a go-getter who utilizes toilets as a tool for social change. And yet Pathak presents himself as a man of contradictions: a Brahmin who gets deeply involved and commits himself to manual scavengers against all odds and yet does not question Brahmanical supremacy, a Brahmin who condemns degrading caste occupation and yet constantly performs "high caste" rituals and customs for liberated scavengers, a Brahmin celebrated for the liberation of scavengers from age-old caste bondages and yet never sheds his "Brahminism" and "casteism" that clothe him and inform his organizational management. This essay is a narrative of Pathak's life, through his writing and that of others who have written about him. At the same time, it is a narrative of how Dalits imagine themselves and describe their lives in comparison to Pathak, whom they admire *and* critique. As this essay will also demonstrate, my interviews with Dalits became a means for them to narrate aspects of their lives.

Pathak has been recognized as a powerful agent for change. However, his agency is largely anchored in an anti-Dalit and dominant Brahmanical discourse. His personal authority, performance, technology, and development have been the key rationales that his organization has deployed for the liberation of scavengers from the 1970s to the 1990s. An emphasis on the inclusiveness of Hindu religion, Brahmin-Harijan[3] unity, pragmatic accommodation and acceptance of political and governmental developments, and power sharing among strategic groups—politicians and political parties, international development agencies, technocrats, retired and serving bureaucrats—has underscored his claim to success and change from 1990 to 2015. Pathak often invokes Gandhi. At the same time, without even mentioning him, he constantly runs Ambedkar down. Pathak never deploys the symbols of Ambedkar and other anticaste reformers, and never invokes them in his program or strategy. His ignoring of Ambedkar and idioms of radical anticaste thought speaks volumes. For example, he states:

> We never tore away Vedas or Puranas, we never burnt the Smriti, we always worked non-violently with folded hands. Powerful and mighty cannot be faulted. Change will come from above. (Speech)

Pathak never uses the term "Dalit" and does not mobilize Dalits as a political-social force. He does the good work for "them." Right from the outset, the Indian State's endorsement and encouragement of Pathak and Sulabh has been a hallmark. Pathak emphasizes that Prime Minister "Modi's dream has become my own" and that he shares the same passions as Amit Shah, the President of the ruling Bharatiya Janata Party (BJP), whom Pathak describes as "a man with a great soul, great thought and great ideology."[4]

The outcomes of Pathak's projects have been mixed. Most initiatives have been relatively successful in liberating the manual scavengers from their occupation. In several cases they have provided alternative Sulabh households and government toilets. However, Pathak is not interested in empowering Dalits socially, radicalizing their individual and collective political consciousness, or instilling in them a language of rights. Significantly, Balmikis still primarily manage Sulabh sanitation systems—public toilets and cleaning.[5] So-called "forward castes," predominantly Brahmins, dominate

Sulabh's organizational structure, and the liberated scavengers mostly occupy "low caste" occupations.[6] At best, Sulabh has rehabilitated liberated scavengers by providing them alternative livelihood, vocational education, and training. However, they have been far removed from any form of Dalit politics, activism, or fight for dignity. Sulabh and Pathak have not sought to synthesize broader social values and support scavengers' solidarity outside their organizational domains.

In this essay, I focus on several of Pathak's writings, especially those published after the launch and success of his initiatives. I also engage with other works, including his biography. In addition, I draw from the fieldwork and interviews I conducted with liberated scavengers living and working in some of Pathak's most well-known project areas in Rajasthan. These interviews provide narratives about scavengers' lives and what Pathak's work and presence has meant for scavengers. While Pathak narrates his life in intense and complex ways, I am concerned with analyzing the ways in which Brahminism creeps into the production and consumption of these narratives. The narrative texts alternate between a romantic remembrance of the past, culture, and religion, and a recognition of the ways that caste crushes people. I also scrutinize Dalits'/Balmikis' narratives, which on the one hand are told in proximity to Pathak's life, but on the other are also self-narrations and presentations of their own lives. As this essay will reveal, interviews with Dalits who are associated with Sulabh reflect fragmentary narrations of their lives and changing perceptions of themselves due to Sulabh's and Pathak's interventions. My argument also illuminates how the making of Pathak in contemporary India through life narratives conflicts with and complements the making of a complex Dalit social world.

Manual scavengers clean excrement from private and public dry toilets and open drains. Based on a centuries-old feudal and caste-based custom, women from communities who traditionally worked as manual scavengers still collect human waste on a daily basis, load it into cane baskets or metal troughs, and carry it away on their heads for disposal at the outskirts of settlements. Manual scavengers are mostly from caste groups customarily relegated to the bottom of caste hierarchy and confined to making their livelihood with work that "high caste" groups consider deplorable or menial. Their caste-designated work reinforces the social stigma of being unclean and untouchable, and perpetuates widespread discrimination against them.

Intense political discussions about and social actions for scavengers have historically centered on their "dirty" job of disposal of human excreta, their work for liberation from this traditional occupation, questions about hygiene and the caste system, the feasibility of low-cost local sanitation systems, and the concepts of purity and pollution. In certain ways, Mahatma Gandhi epitomized these concerns, and his ideas and solutions have been widely quoted, accepted, and critiqued.[7] Vijay Prashad's significant work on the sweepers of Delhi has traced one and a half centuries of their eventful history—including their origins, myths, colonial policies, national debates, early rural organizations, urban migrations, trade unions, strikes, and movements. He shows how the identity of this "untouchable" caste has been historically organized, beginning with the heterogeneous urban "Mehtar" sweepers and followed by the early rural beginnings of the specific caste of "Chuhras," which was then followed by the development of urban-glossed "sweepers," religiously based "Balmikis," Gandhi's "Harijans," and finally the definitive nation-state group of "Citizens." The status of Bhangis as manual scavengers was also a serious point of debate and difference between Gandhi and Ambedkar. While Gandhi believed in manual scavenging as the basis of every service and even suggested specific educational and practical qualities for an "ideal Bhangi," Ambedkar severely criticized such attempts to link a degrading practice with ideals of service, calling it "a cruel joke played on helpless people belonging to this caste" (293). This background provides a wider context for Pathak's life narrative and the narratives of scavengers working with Sulabh.

## SULABH AND BINDESHWAR PATHAK: THE PUBLIC NARRATIVE

Life narratives are both private and public, internal and external. Sidonie Smith and Julia Watson's thesis is that life story, where one gives an account of oneself and also where one listens to the life stories of others, is the stuff of the everyday, taking place in encounters with medical and social service bureaucracies, and performed in talk shows, political campaigns, self-help groups, and personal ads. They acknowledge that "we are not autobiographical subjects at every moment of the day, but we are called on to become autobiographical subjects in a variety of situations, a range of temporalities" (17). Paul John Eakin argues for recognizing the role of life story in everyday life at the level of the social, the political, and the individual's identity. Bindeshwar Pathak's life narrative also has a "public"—an audience, a theater, and a live performance. "Life narratives" can also describe a life that does not constitute a full narrative but is instead fragmentary in nature, describing parts of one's everyday life. These descriptors—Pathak's and Balmikis'—can also be an entry point for providing an ideological critique of life narratives.

Pathak's life and the life of Sulabh have been described publicly and extensively, both nationally and internationally, through their own publications and research and also through publications by a number of environmental writers, practitioners, and organizations. This is how Sulabh International Social Service Organization describes itself:

> A non-profit voluntary social organisation founded in 1970 by Dr. Bindeshwar Pathak and dedicated to Gandhian ideology of emancipation of scavengers. Sulabh has been working for the removal of untouchability and social discrimination against scavengers, a section of Indian society condemned to clean and carry human excreta manually. Sulabh is noted for achieving success in the field of cost-effective sanitation, liberation of scavengers, social transformation of society, prevention of environmental pollution and development of non-conventional sources of energy. ("Meet Sulabh")

Pathak's achievements are manifold, encompassing several regions and issues. The environment friendly two-pit, pour-flush compost toilet known as Sulabh Shauchalaya is claimed to be socially acceptable, economically affordable, technologically appropriate, and does not require scavengers to clean the pits. This toilet has been implemented in more than 1.2 million houses all over India and has helped liberate over a million scavengers. Further, construction and maintenance of public toilets at public places and in slums on a pay-and-use basis is another landmark achievement for Sulabh. According to the organization, so far it has constructed and is maintaining over eight thousand such public toilets and has constructed two hundred biogas plants all over the country ("Meet Sulabh"). Pathak and his organization have received forty-two national and international awards and honors, including the Padma Bhushan and Stockholm Water Prize. The organization is also doing sanitation projects in many developing countries. Sulabh's organizational profile is equally impressive and speaks volumes about its wide spread and structure. Sulabh had 1,075 branches in twenty-nine states and three union territories in 2005, and there were 19,830 full-time associate members working on an honorarium, including social workers, administrators, planners, engineers, scientists, architects, medical doctors, sociologists, and economists (Goyal and Gupta 95).

There have been several rich, celebratory, almost identical accounts of the founding of Sulabh Shauchalaya Sansthan in 1970 (now legally known as Sulabh International Social Service Organisation and registered as an NGO). Pathak, a post-graduate in sociology and English whose doctoral work was on the liberation of scavengers through low-cost sanitation, is the central figure in all such narratives. His experience as a *pracharak* (propagandist) in the Valmiki Mukti Cell of the Gandhi Centenary Celebrations, Patna, in 1969 marked the beginning of Sulabh (S. P. Singh 95).

The popularity of Sulabh's toilets is the result of cost-efficiency and effective funding streams. As compared to ten to fifteen liters required for conventional toilets, Sulabh's toilets require only one and a half to two liters of water to flush, which has made them less expensive to run. Simultaneously, Pathak also thought of maintaining the public toilets out of the money collected from the users (Goyal and Gupta 93). The two concepts—conversion of dry latrines into Sulabh Shauchalayas and the pay-and-use public toilet system—have gone a long way in improving personal hygiene, community health, and the economic well-being of the poor, especially scavengers.

After implementing these toilets, Pathak established the Sulabh International Centre for Action Sociology (SICAS) to launch institutes to train sons and daughters of scavengers in various vocational skills. Sulabh launched Nai Disha, a vocational training center in Alwar, a district town in Rajasthan that is 170 kilometers away from Delhi, to train scavenger women in various vocational skills, including food processing, tailoring, and beauty care. They receive a monthly stipend, and the training center shop sells the goods they make, including pickles, clothes, and bags. These women of Alwar have been called the Alwar ki Nai Rajkumariyan (The New Princesses of Alwar) (*Alwar*). Sulabh also has had success in generating biogas from human excreta by developing appropriate technology. Pathak's technological and institutional innovations have continued. For example, the Sulabh International Institute of Technical Research and Training (SIITRAT) was established in 1984 to provide technological support to the Sulabh sanitation movement. Sulabh also began efforts toward establishing a Sulabh University of Sanitation in early 2000. Pathak's new "dream project," Sulabh International Museum of Toilets, was established in Delhi.

Pathak's life narrative underlines how knowledge of technology and its effective use are intimately interwoven with the liberation of scavengers. Sulabh's technology has been an important mediating link in the interactions between Pathak and scavengers. Underlying Pathak's and Sulabh's understandings of technology, one can discern two interrelated frameworks. First, within Sulabh's professional environment, there is "technical optimism," or a belief in the modeling of sanitation on low-cost, local systems. These systems can be socially and economically engineered for the benefit of scavengers as well as for sustainability, environmental protection, health, hygiene, and rural development (Pathak, "Sulabh" 14). Pathak believes that a growing economy, technology, market, and industry will destroy untouchability. He says, "The Sulabh movement has also played its role by providing a technology and arousing the nation's conscience" (62). A second aspect of Pathak's faith in technology concerns what he has achieved for the Balmikis or Bhangis. Due to technology, Balmikis have been made free from manual scavenging and are receiving vocational training, public toilets are being utilized, and biogas and biofertilizer are being produced in excreta-based plants. Overall, Pathak's life narrative signifies a management-centered fabric of "entrepreneurial success" (Ramachandran 110).

Pathak views the role of technology and management as absolutely positive and constructive: "It goes against no one, no ideology and no shade of life. It benefits all and operates with the spirit of delivering good to all"

(Pathak, *Road* 185).The constructions about technology and management draw support from economics, innovation, services, market, and growth. While this technological and managerial vision of sanitation has helped in abolishing scavenging and has had a bearing on the changing social life of Balmikis, it has not tried to unweave the complex fabric of caste society, and has not disturbed the working of the caste system on the ground, at multiple levels, in and around the Balmikis.

## BEING BRAHMIN: A PERSONAL NARRATIVE

*The need of the hour is to re-discover Hinduism.*

—Bindeshwar Pathak (qtd. in S. P. Singh 490)

Pathak's various life narratives, including the ones he, his biographers, and his organization have written, underscore Pathak's self-awareness and agency in his life. Because Pathak is the founder, central figure, and key driving force of Sulabh, his life narrative is deeply intertwined with Sulabh's. His personality, ideas, experiments, and initiatives play a crucial and abiding role through the length and breadth of the organization. He commands deep respect because of his personal history, caste, culture, performance, and achievement. His persona is associated with courage, commitment, compassion, social skills, status, and religious refinements. He is intensely disciplined and deeply committed to his ideology and mission. Individual agency in life narratives has been a topic of academic discussion. The historian and biographer Jill Ker Conway talks of the cultural scripts that overrun the framing of life writings in the West—the archetypal "secular hero" overcoming odds to emerge triumphant or the "romantic heroine" subjected to the people and circumstances. In feminist and Dalit writings, agency and pathways of resistance are often highlighted. Pathak's "heroic" life and his agency, as perceived by him and others on the one hand, and the limitations and boundaries of that narrative on the other, are underlined in this essay—not just through personal narrative, but also through an ideological critique of that life on questions of caste.

Pathak's narration of his life from his childhood to the present highlights his agency. Born on April 2, 1943, in a "respectable Brahmin family" of the village Rampur Baghel in the Vaishali district of Bihar, Pathak earned a Masters in Sociology and English and a PhD on the liberation of scavengers through low-cost sanitation. Born to an affluent family, he also experienced the decline in his family's economic status when his father, a doctor, gave up his practice and went back to the village to look after extended family. Pathak lived for eighteen years in the village, witnessing a social hierarchy characterized by caste, in which Dusadhs and Chamars were considered impure and Doms untouchable. Once his grandmother saw him touching a

Dom woman, and the whole family got agitated; nobody had food that day and their mood turned grim and somber. A priest was called to conduct a purification ritual, and cow dung, cow urine, and Ganga water was poured into his mouth.

Even though he belonged to an orthodox Brahmin family, Pathak got a job in the Gandhi Birth Centenary Celebration Committee to work for the restoration of human rights and dignity of scavengers. Later, after founding the Sulabh Sansthan, he had to sell a piece of his village land and his wife's ornaments and also take loans from friends to run the organization. He slept on railway platforms and often missed meals because of his shortage of money. At times he thought of committing suicide and was on the verge of collapse and breakdown. When he submitted the Sulabh two-pit-toilet design to the Bihar government, officials were skeptical about the technology. Only after several discussions did they agree to send circulars to the local bodies and municipalities to convert from bucket toilets. In 1991, the Government of India conferred one of the highest civilian awards, the Padma Bhushan, on Pathak for his work in sanitation development and social service. Overcoming several day-to-day challenges in the implementation and expansion of his programs, including "hindrances and obstacles" over his working principles and ideology, also marks Pathak's life narrative. He writes:

> I have been working for the last 40 years but not without opposition, criticism, hindrances and barriers. . . . The factors that hindered my progress were the jealousy of some people. . . . But by the grace of God, till now, I have been able to continue to solve the problem of defecation in the open and manual cleaning of human excreta of scavengers. ("Sulabh Sanitation" 25)

While several ideologies and personalities are flexibly deployed as means and goals in Pathak's work and life, Pathak's endorsement of Gandhian vision and beliefs, particularly his perspective on and work among Bhangis, acquires a special importance in his life. Pathak candidly states:

> To rehabilitate the scavengers, I took the help of one of the tools of Mahatma Gandhi—the tool of non-violence. I did not tear or burn the books of *Vedas* or *Manusmriti.* ("Report" 6)

According to Pathak, Mahatma Gandhi was one of the first to serve the scavengers' cause, as he struggled to liberate the Bhangis from cleaning night soil. Pathak remembers that in 1918, when Gandhi started his ashram at Sabarmati, he advised the inmates of the ashram to tackle the problem of disposal of night soil themselves and not to employ professional Bhangis for their work. Harijan Sevak Sangh, established by Gandhi, did pioneering work, according to Pathak, in this field. He writes:

> The reform movement by Sevak Sangh also aroused the social consciousness among the Harijans themselves, in general, and among the Bhangis in particular, facilitating the process of liberation. (Pathak, *Road* 71)

Gandhi renamed the "untouchable" Harijan, implying thereby that they were God's own people who must be served, just as one served God, as part of one's nationalist duty or dharma. Dalits have increasingly critiqued the term, which they find patronizing since it makes moral claims based on service and care. However, Pathak continues to use the idiom and dismisses the criticism, saying, "there is nothing wrong about the word, it means God's people. It is our prejudiced view that did not allow many of us to so address some amongst ourselves" ("Tool" 23). Pathak's appeal to a Gandhian framework while overtly reinstating his status as a Brahmin working among "scavengers" points to contradictions in the way that Pathak positions himself. One cannot doubt Pathak's sincerity in his commitment to manual scavengers. At the same time, his sympathetic representation of and concern for scavengers retains and adheres to the logic of Brahmanical supremacy. Pathak's life is thus described by one of his supporters, S. P. Singh, Chairman of Sulabh International:

> Dr. Pathak's high birth and indigence also provided the contrary qualities of the Greek tragedy to which pathos is the central emotion. If a Harijan works to help Harijans (like Dr. B.R. Ambedkar), it is not much of news; there is something clannish about it. But, if a Brahmin violates the Brahminical norm of *Chatururvanya* (four castes or Varnas) which has been a major source of oppression in India, and climbs down from his social pedestal to embrace excreta-carrying scavengers, his action is the stuff high dramas are made of. It creates mystique and a personal magic to his leadership, arousing popular loyalty, enthusiasm and a magnetic charm. This is what charisma is all about. Dr. Pathak's ability to empathise with scavengers only heightens his charismatic impact on people. (582–83)

Implicit here is an understanding that the benevolence and kindness that a Brahmin bestows on the scavenger is something for which the latter should always be obliged to the former. It remains an unequal relationship, a relationship between high, "noble" people, feeling for the "low" and not so noble. The "Brahmin Pathak" remains the positive, the constructive, the conclusive standard, and the scavenger retains a dubious identity. S. P. Singh also says in his praise for Pathak: "It is a co-incidence of history that most reformers were Brahmins—Raja Rammohan Roy, Bankim Chandra Chatterjee, Swami Ramkrishan Paramhansa, Ishwar Chandra Vidyasagar, and Dayanand Swami" (571–72). The quote underlines the supremacy of Brahmins historically, emphasizing their leadership in the reform of society. S. P. Singh reiterates that Pathak "condemns Brahminism, but radiates the Brahminical virtues, like the habit of speaking truth, philanthropy, morning prayer, indifference to wealth and encouraging people to respect all religions which, he says, preach good things of life" (575). In such biographical notes, Pathak's compassion for the scavenger is embedded in an understanding that such benevolent paternalism flows from the outstanding status of a sympathetic Brahmin and the superior qualities of Brahmanism. The "Brahmin Pathak" then becomes an agent of reform who nevertheless remains superior to the people he seeks to serve.

The Brahmin becomes an important reference point for the liberation of scavengers, not just for his admirers, but also at times for Pathak himself. Pathak thus explains:

> There has been some impact of liberation on the liberty and social prestige enjoyed by the liberated scavengers, in respect of visit to temples, engagement to *Brahmins* to supervise religious ceremonies, invitation by other caste people on ceremonial occasions, taking water from common places along with other caste people and taking food in hotels and other places. (*Road* 173)

Such narratives of Pathak's life, by him and others, when examined through the lens of radical caste critiques, underline the limitations and boundaries of a life that, purportedly, is centered on the liberation of scavengers. Pathak's life narrative thus cannot be separated from an ideological critique of that life, to which I now turn.

## BRAHMIN HYBRIDITY: CASTE, RELIGION, AND REFORM

> *My strategy for making toilet as a tool of social change consists of a mixed package of Sulabh's low cost sanitation technology and suitable methods of relieving scavengers from the oppressive stronghold of the country's caste system. This holistic approach is radically different from other caste-centred social reform movement in as much as it combines technology with social idealism.*
>
> —Bindeshwar Pathak ("Tool" 28)

Throughout his life, Pathak has attempted to integrate Gandhian social reform, technology, developmental efforts, education, and campaigns to establish "a modern and humane social order based on social justice and equal opportunity" (S. P. Singh 554). Yet, at an ideological level, his discourses are expressed in a deeply ambiguous language, often reflecting elements of eco-casteism. By eco-casteism, I mean environmental and ecological discourses that provide a defense of the caste system.[8] Eco-casteism, an ecological determinant of caste, provides a rationalization and justification of the caste system through nature. Caste identity becomes a key organizing framework for environmental thought and action. Dominant castes can justify their power through such a conception and can even become harbingers of new eco-movements. Eco-casteism, as propagated and practiced presently, does not restrict itself to fixed ideas of hierarchy and division of labor; it calls for a recovery of the traditional. Equally, eco-casteism molds itself from neo-Hinduism, whereby idioms of technology, sustainable development, benevolent paternalism, and reform from above "naturalize" Dalits within a home, community, and nation. Pathak's life deploys some of the frameworks of eco-casteism.

Pathak has often expressed the injustices and indignities meted out by the caste system in India. States Pathak, "The caste system is based on primitive hatred; it is pre-modern, inhuman and thoroughly undemocratic. The time is now to abolish it and restore human rights to the people who have long been denied of them" (qtd. in S. P. Singh 336). However, while Sulabh and Pathak articulate a critique of caste in the present day, in the same breath they often implicitly uphold and justify it in the past, as reflected in some of the writings on Sulabh and Pathak: "Sulabh rejects casteism and says it will lead to social disintegration. The *varna* system might have had some relevance in ancient times by way of, what may be called, specialisation. But, modern science and technology have made this social arrangement irrelevant" (qtd. in S. P. Singh 493). Pathak's denunciations of caste exist in an uneasy tension with descriptions of caste that sound like commemorations, echoing an eco-casteism. Occasionally, he sees in caste "an economic arrangement," which provided social frameworks and institutions for integration and skill building in society at times of war and other social pressures:

> The caste system was also an economic arrangement; carpenter, blacksmith, warriors and teachers provided basic services to make the unit (village) economically viable. The caste system also provided an iron-clad social framework which averted disintegration of the group at the time when the people were conquered and social structure came under great pressure. Education, art, music, theatre, agricultural skill, medicine, etc—all these and much more also developed outside the institutions which have become the rolling mills to produce the so-called experts today. Father trained the son to become dancer, actor, musician, teacher, killer and king. (S. P. Singh 69)

Between caste abolition and an implicit appreciation and rationale for the caste system, where an "esteemed" version of caste and its values is upheld, "caste neutrality" enhances Pathak's and Sulabh's ambiguous discourses on caste. Both Pathak and Sulabh have no hesitation in distancing their endeavors from the reality of caste. For example, in S. P. Singh's text, Sulabh is described as

> a caste-neutral social service outfit with the macro-plan for the entire society with focus on sanitation. Sulabh technology, time-tested and globally approved, is central to its plan for social change. It works as a transmission belt for cross-border knowledge transfer to make its social services competitive and professional. (239–40)

Such sympathetic critiques of caste oppression are often repeated, revealing that Pathak-led Sulabh is simultaneously democratic and indeterminate. It is at times geared toward generating affinity between hierarchical castes, which by its very nature is a fraught proposition. Not surprisingly, we never hear of annihilation of caste in Pathak's life narrative, but rather of a forged "unity" of castes—a seemingly alluring but deceptive slogan that actually fosters "upper caste" hegemony and "lower caste" subordination. This stratification gets reinforced further through an understanding that "a rich Harijan is a Rajput and a poor Rajput is a Harijan. This is the universal truth" (S. P. Singh 61). Pathak's and Sulabh's discourses thus expose the scavengers to models of caste normativity.

In Pathak's understanding, nation is also defined as "natural" (S. P. Singh 517), and a central and steady component of this "natural nation" is perceived as Hinduism. Pathak discursively fashions a Brahmanical Hinduism in his rhetorical, visual, social, and political strategies. Through constant invocations of Vedas and Manusmriti, he reproduces the dominant Hindu order (S. P. Singh 79). For Sulabh, glorious Hindu traditions flow from the Vedas: "The *Vedas*, Dr. Pathak says, are not the book of religion, they are records of profound human thoughts on mysteries of nature" (qtd. in S. P. Singh 59). Sulabh insists on identifying the scavengers as part of the Hindu fold, incorporating them "safely" within a Hindu belief system with its supposed glorious golden past.

In the foreword to S. P. Singh's text, Pathak projects the Sulabh model on Indian values and simultaneously offers a scathing critique of the West, "which tends to view the world as the vast extension of its own culture." In such a situation, Pathak declares a rediscovery of Hinduism, which he states was eroded due to Western ethos and colonialism (490). Sulabh's prescriptions for the protection of the environment through improved sanitation often eulogize ancient Hindu texts, particularly the Manusmriti and the Vishnupuran, which he calls "the most respected Aryan scripture" (S. P. Singh 59). Sulabh International's "Museum of Toilets," Pathak's special project, has a detailed note on the "Aryan Code of Toilets—1500 BC," which draws on the Manusmriti and the Vishnupuran to list elaborate defecation codes, including a "code for married people," an "ablution code," a code "for different classes," and "separate rules for those who are sick or infirm." For Sulabh, these are "Toilet Etiquettes" that fall under the rubric of ancient Hindu scriptures ("Sulabh" 12–14). The scriptures prescribe elaborate drills for defecation practices among these different groups. For example, the *savarna*, or the twice-born, must roll the sacred thread to a smaller size and put it on the right ear. The Vishnu Purana also states that the left hand be cleaned ten times and right seven times ("Aryan Code"). Sulabh's extolling of such defecation practices is ludicrous, given that it was precisely such texts that prescribed slavery for the "low" castes and sanctions for the "upper" castes, and asserted the Brahmin's supremacy as the will of God. It is of course equally well known that a substantial section of Dalits has severely and bitterly condemned such texts and scriptures, which prescribe rituals and social and religious orders to accommodate the very existence of the caste system.

Pathak is also committed to celebrating certain Hindu religious festivals in his work, particularly Mahashivratri and Chhath. Such festivals are elaborately observed at an organizational level among the Balmikis associated with Sulabh, and Pathak observes these holidays publicly. According to Sulabh, Brahmanical rituals and Hindu religious practices are cultivated to develop and foster common ties and smooth pathways to universal brotherhood (Pathak, "Maha Shivaratri" 8). Mahashivratri is an important occasion for Sulabh, with the belief that "Bhagwan Shiva is worshipped right from the north to far south, and from the east to the western parts of our country as supreme deity" (9). Led by Brahmins, its ritual and rites are in fact about believing and perpetuating concepts of sacred and sinful, high and low, purity and pollution, privileges and denial. The festival celebrations mark annual highlights in Pathak's life:

> The great festival is a regular celebration at the campus of Sulabh International in New Delhi. This year the holy day fell on February 27. . . . 1,25,000 *shivalingas* [phallic emblem of God Shiva, symbolizing creative power] were made from the soil brought from the Yamuna *ghats* [landing or bathing place at a riverside]. Dr. Bindeshwar Pathak and Mrs. Amola Pathak with their entire family sat along with the workers of Sulabh International and the liberated scavenger ladies from Alwar and Tonk in Rajasthan as well as Ghaziabad. Chants of Har Har Mahadeva reverberated all along the day. . . .The holy lingams made by all the participants were placed in the rectangular spot meant for placement. Learned Pundits kept on reciting holy *mantras* [sacred verses, especially from the Vedas] and *shlokas* [Sanskrit couplets consisting of several lines] with the offerings of *gangajal* [water of river Ganga], flowers, fruits, *naivedyam* [food consecrated to a deity] . . . on the lingams by all engaged in worship. This was followed by *havan* [oblation with fire] performed in the *kund* [tank] meant for this purpose. (Pathak, "Maha Shivaratri" 19)

A similar celebration occurs around the Chhath festival, an ancient Hindu and the only Vedic festival dedicated to the Sun God:

> Chhath is an important festival dedicated to the Sun God. Chhath puja is mainly observed in Bihar, Jharkhand, Eastern Uttar Pradesh and the Tarai [plains] of Nepal. . . . The four-day festival is celebrated with strict purity and abstinence, for prosperity and well-being, twice in a year, in the months of Chaitra and Karthik. Like every year, the festival was celebrated at the

> residence of Dr. Bindeshwar Pathak, Founder of the Sulabh Sanitation Movement . . . with fast, *puja* [worship] and different types of rituals and offerings. (Pathak, "Chhath Celebration" 9)

Pathak's and Sulabh's much-publicized initiatives to take the liberated manual scavenger women for a dip in the Ganga river at Varanasi and Sangam—which is the confluence of the Ganga, the Yamuna, and the mythological Saraswati at Allahabad, Uttar Pradesh—and the performance of rituals with priests at the Maha Kumbh Mela also inform how Hinduism is naturalized in Pathak's life and becomes a key frame through which religious and cultural practices are conceived and conducted in his life narratives. In June 2011, Pathak took a group of 207 liberated scavenging women from Alwar, Tonk (Rajasthan), and Arrah (Bihar) to Varanasi to take a "dip in the holy river before proceeding to one of the sacred Hindu shrines, Kashi Vishwanath temple, for offering prayers before Jyotirlinga of Lord Shiva" ("Liberated Scavengers on Pilgrimage" 6). In February 2013, around one hundred liberated scavenger women from Rajasthan's Alwar and Tonk districts took a dip in the Sangam and performed puja at the Maha Kumbh Mela. According to Pathak, this action was an "effort towards social upliftment" ("Liberated Scavengers in Kumbh" 21).

Significantly, life narratives of and by the liberated Balmikis who have taken the holy dip also see this moment as a kind of rebirth in Hindu religion and a reaffirmation of their belief in the holiness of sacred places, priests, and divine experiences. Narrating in an interview what was perhaps the most important moment of her life, Guddi Athwal of Alwar says: "The holy dip was like a rebirth for a low caste woman like me. I felt as if I was reborn as part of the Hindu society." In another interview, Shakuntla Chamere too recounts her life thus: "The dip in the holy rivers of Varanasi and Allahabad washed away all our sins of the past and present birth." In her interview, Lalita Nindania says, "It was an unforgettable experience—walking, praying and dining with the Brahmins." These life narratives by the liberated scavengers operate within a dominant Hindu paradigm. Sulabh also upholds this narrative of a "life changing experience":

> "It is an out of this world experience for us. We want to stay here as long as we can. This day will remain most memorable for us. We now feel we have really joined the mainstream led by Dr. Bindeshwar Pathak, who is really an incarnation of god for us. He is leading us to sacred places where even our shadow could not be tolerated in the past. He is making us mingle with the high and mighty," said most of the liberated women as they emerged out of the Vishwanath temple after saying their prayers. (Pathak, "Liberated Scavengers on Pilgrimage" 6)

In the process of actions like this, however, Balmikis' distinct religious traditions often lapse or are coopted under dominant Hindu idioms. The

Balmikis associated with Sulabh habitually become normal appendages to great Hindu cultural traditions. For example, Sulabh is spectacularly silent on Valmiki Jayanti, a festival that cherishes Valmiki as the ancestor and God of Balmikis, and this is frequently reflected even in narratives of the Balmikis of Sulabh. Narrating the role of festivals in her life, twenty-two-year-old Aman Chaumar, daughter of Ushan Chaumar (President of Sulabh International) recounts in an interview:

> We have a significant focus on Mahashivratri and Janmashtmi. We also celebrate normal Hindu festivals like Holi and Diwali. The Balmiki community in Hajuri Gate and other Balmiki colonies have traditionally celebrated Valmiki Jayanti and continue to do so. However, now we, the liberated scavengers, hardly participate in Valmiki Jayanti.

Meera Nindania, who works in Nai Disha, a vocational training center that Sulabh launched in Alwar in 2003 to rehabilitate scavengers, provided a similar account in an interview. A day in her life begins at the center with several *vandanas* (prayers) that worship Hindu deities like Shiv, Ganesh, Lakshmi, and Saraswati, along with a *vandana* for Sulabh. In the Amergarh-based center of the organization, she says, "I am a Hindu because Ram and Balmiki are the same. I have all the Hindu deities in my home. We only celebrate Hindu festivals in the vicinity of Sulabh and Nai Disha." Yet, the majority of the Balmikis at Hajuri Gate and in other Balmiki colonies of Alwar who are not part of the Sulabh program continue to celebrate Valmiki Jayanti as their long-cherished festival. Naresh Lohra describes in detail how the festival is a significant event in their lives, and a collective cultural expression of thousands of Balmikis of Alwar:

> On *Sharad Purnima*, Balmikis of different colonies take out the tableau of Valmiki, with their flags, songs and *bhajans*. The old temple of Valmiki in Lal Khana Arvaipura *mohalla* becomes the nerve-center of our festival. The day-long festival ends in the evening at Teej ki Swarg road, after many rich cultural performances. The community really looks forward to the festival and works hard and long to celebrate it.

These interviews provide windows into Dalit's voices, life narratives, and their self-presentation. In the next two sections, I intertwine Pathak's and Sulabh's understandings of dirt, filth, and pollution with the perceptions of liberated scavengers about their lives. I examine additional interviews with liberated scavengers, whereby they selectively construct their own past, present, and future in light of the role and implications that Pathak and Sulabh have in their everyday lives. Liberated scavengers attempt to make sense of their lives through Pathak's persona, as he is a constant point of reference in their life. While their interviews highlight the "positive" role Pathak has in their life stories, taboos and restrictions also emerge in these life narratives.

## BRAHMIN AND BHANGI LIVES: DIRT, FILTH, AND POLLUTION

*The early Aryan bequeathed to their future generations a dual sense of sanitation. . . .This balanced approach towards sanitation and the science of personal and community health were maintained till the Puranic age. . . . The Manusmriti says that all our organs must be kept clean and in good condition by daily wash and ablution. Men and women shall wash away their dirt with water everyday—this is the means to cleanse their body, but reading the Gita will keep their mind and heart clean of all impurities.*

—S. P. Singh (261–62)

In the Hindu caste system, scavengers—the former "untouchable" castes of Bhangis, Balmikis, and Mehters—were conceptualized as sources of dirt and filth, polluting the "pure" Hindu cultural and social environment. Concepts of purity and pollution have been inherent parts of Brahmanical Hinduism, signifying that something or someone does not belong to them, is an outcaste, and is an untouchable. Moreover, for "Brahmin" and "untouchable" to have any meaning, there has to be a system of belonging, necessitating the assigning of different caste-based roles to separated caste groups. For there to be "order" in Hindu society, there has to be a conceptual and normative assumption about what a "natural" society should look like and what, or who, should be touched or untouched. Pathak traces the existence of scavengers and the system for disposal of "night soil" through Hindu texts, and sums up:

> Scavenging has been existing in India for a long period and the persons engaged in cleaning, carrying and disposing of night soil have been known as scavengers or *Bhangis*. . . .This sub-caste or occupational group was placed at the lowest level and was labelled as "untouchable" in the traditional social system. The scavengers were not included in the caste system; rather they were treated as the polluted out-caste because they clean night soil. They were not allowed to touch the high caste people and, hence, all types of social interactions were forbidden for this sub-caste of scavengers. The demeaning and sub-human occupation of scavenging was their fate under the traditional system and they were not permitted to take up any other job according to their likings, merits and capabilities. (*Road* 159–60)

The paradoxes within Pathak's discourse are, however, soon reflected when the same scavengers are romanticized and their "degraded" occupation upheld as coming "naturally" to them, as they are the "most skilled" in the work of cleaning and sweeping. Mahesh Kumar Singh, a social volunteer with Sulabh, states:

> Broom has been an identity marker of Balmikis. You cannot take away their brooms and traditional skills. That is why, in the public toilets of Alwar, built by Akhil Bhartiya Pariwar Kalyan Parishad, a branch organization of Sulabh, the Balmikis and ex-scavengers are the best skilled workers because of their long tradition.

Similarly, there is rhetoric within Sulabh to teach the art of cleanliness and hygiene to the Bhangis "from above." At the Nai Disha office in Alwar, Rajeev Kumar Singh, a Sulabh volunteer, articulates:

> The Bhangis lived in hell, without any consciousness of a human being. They had no social or political awareness. We have given them lessons in cleanliness, hygiene and purity, and how to come cleanly at the center, how to maintain decorum, and where to find solace, by organizing skill-building and training, and also by creating cultural and religious activities.

Sulabh's power is most visible in the ways that a section of Balmikis internalize these discourses within their own life stories. Balmikis understand and express dirt, filth, and pollution as a crisis of their inner nature ingrained in their bodies and minds; in other words, at the level of their individual identity. At the level of collective identity, too, they not only think that their community is responsible for their age-old degrading status but also blame their own shared habits, customs, and attitudes for their debased standing. Their self-perception and esteem in their narration of their own lives is very low, insofar as they perceive themselves as responsible for their stigma and ostracism. The solution they offer for removal of all dirt, filth, and pollution is deemed to be a simple one—a return to the Brahmin, a Brahmin savior, his values, and purported laws. Naresh Lohra of Hazuri Gate in Alwar, who is a Balmiki associated with Sulabh, says:

> We have had so much of dirt within us—in our living and our working. Take, for example, our relationship with pigs, because of which also we have been seen negatively in the eyes of Hindus. Our language, our habits, our customs—are doomed. We have had no history of our own.

Lakshmi Nindania, another active and vocal figure of Sulabh and who has also traveled nationally and internationally as a liberated and rehabilitated scavenger from Alwar, expresses a similar perspective:

> Since ages we were living in hell. We were dirty. We were in fact not used to bathing regularly or cleaning up our houses properly. We only had a broom to identify ourselves with, and to show it to the world. Nobody else but we only are responsible for our present state.

Such articulations of negative images about themselves and their past lives show that the Balmikis of Sulabh indulge in self-censure and self-condemnation instead of critiquing larger structures of caste oppression. They blame themselves for their own condition, their exploitation, and their marginalization. Sulabh, through its constant references to Hindu idioms, has inculcated in them the idea that they can redeem themselves only through integration within the Hindu society. Blaming oneself for all one's ills serves as an important reference point and helps in justifying Sulabh's Hindu orientation. Balmikis' attempts at acculturation and assimilation into prevailing Hindu concepts suggests that in a sense, Sulabh polices them within a set of boundaries, and they in turn police themselves to remain contained within those confines. The Balmikis of Sulabh are constructed, and they in turn construct themselves as "naturally" Hindu. Such social, cultural, and religious association with Hinduism without a trenchant critique of the political economy and the socio-religious basis of caste is far removed from a radical Dalit discourse. In fact, Dalit is a term that the Balmikis of Sulabh have not heard, a word that is never used in any of Sulabh's literature. Thus says Meera Nindania, "I know what is a Balmiki, I know what is a Bhangi, I know what is a Hindu, but I do not know what is a Dalit."

Pathak and Sulabh have hardly been critiqued from this perspective, and various scholars and environmentalists have constantly eulogized their work. However, we get a rare glimpse of such criticism when Bhasha Singh writes:

> The difference between these [Gandhi's and Ambedkar's] points of views is the same as that between reformation, charity and benevolence on the one hand and revolt for rights, change and liberation on the other hand. . . . It is not that these two points of view are not present today. . . . That's why we have among us today the princesses of Alwar. . . . The people who have liberated them don't tire of proclaiming how they helped these hapless women out of that hell and how they reached where they are now. . . . The other way out—that of liberation through change—doesn't pass through the business of flush toilets. Neither does this second way try to suggest that the practice of manual scavenging will die out if toilets with running water are made available—this is because the people walking this road know that the person cleaning the flush toilets will also be someone from their own community. (xxxvi)

In contrast to Pathak and Sulabh, several organizations and initiatives have emerged in the country since the 1970s, focusing on manual scavengers and working for the eradication of scavenging through campaigns, movements, legislation, and judicial interventions. Safai Karmachari Andolan (SKA), initiated in the early 1990s and led by Bezawada Wilson from the Madiga community, is a national movement committed to the total eradication of manual scavenging and providing all scavengers with dignified occupations. They have taken a multidimensional approach to this issue: demolishing dry latrines, organizing and mobilizing the community against the practice of dry-latrine cleaning, placing evidence before the state on the violation of the Prohibition of the Employment as Manual Scavengers and their Rehabilitation Act of 2013, filing public interest litigation in the Supreme Court against the state, and working against the caste system and for the dignity of Dalits in general (Namala and Divakar 16). While primarily focusing on the rights of manual scavengers, SKA is also committed to working with all those engaged in "unclean" occupations, such as sewage workers, pit workers, and sweepers who fall within the ambit of *safai karmacharis*. SKA has been instrumental in eradicating manual scavenging in hundreds of districts through their campaigns. It works in close cooperation and collaboration with other Dalit and human rights organizations committed to the rights of Dalits and other marginalized communities in general and *safai karmacharis* in particular. From 2015 to 2016, SKA organized a Bhim Yatra (a march in the name of the great Dalit leader Ambedkar) to highlight the continuing practice and plight of manual scavenging in the country. The Yatra began on December 10, 2015, in Assam and concluded in Delhi on April 14, 2016, on Ambedkar's 125th birth anniversary after covering 35,000 kilometers across thirty states in 125 days. Taking on issues of manual scavenging, dry latrines, sewers, and septic tanks under the theme of "Stop Killing Us," the Yatra demanded that the Government of India "tender an apology to the safai karamachari community for the historical injustice and centuries of humiliation of making us manual scavengers" and "eliminate manual scavenging immediately, without any further delay or postponement" (Safai Karmachari). They gave a clarion call: "We, Safai Karmachari Andolan, shall struggle and build solidarity to reclaim our dignity, equality and human personhood. Through eradicating manual scavenging, we will break the link imposed by the caste system between birth and dehumanising occupations" ("Safai Karmachari").

## DALIT: MIRROR IMAGE OF BRAHMIN PATHAK

The constructions of the supposed "superiority" of Brahmanism have disturbingly rubbed themselves off on a section of scavengers as well. These scavengers see their traditional occupation as humiliating and degrading. Yet, it is troubling to see many of those associated with Sulabh speaking in caste-ridden idioms, where the power of the Brahmin is retained and further institutionalized. Their "liberation" at times leads them to want to leave behind the remaining scavengers as they position themselves closer to Brahmins and "high caste" people, justifying their thoughts and actions in the name of pride and prestige. Pathak writes with satisfaction:

> These liberated scavengers declared with a sense of pride and prestige that they were no more engaged in scavenging. . . . Moreover, most of them made it clear that they were not having any interaction with those persons who were still engaged in the scavenging work. (*Road* 174)

Usha Chaumar pointedly expresses this new Brahmanism in her story. Chaumar was a scavenger in Alwar until she became associated with Sulabh. She is now the president of Sulabh International and a visible face of the organization. Residing in the Hazuri Gate colony of Balmikis at Alwar, Usha Chaumar retells her life by idealizing Pathak:

> He is a Brahmin, a Pandit, a God for us. In my future life, I would like to see myself as a Brahmin, a Pandit, a forward caste person like him. I cannot identify myself now as a Balmiki.

"Our saviour and God incarnate" is how Dolly, the youngest liberated girl from Tonk, Rajasthan, characterizes Pathak. Lakshmi Nindania sees Pathak as "a God sent on earth for our lives. We too would like to be a big Brahmin, a big man—travelling on the paths shown by him!"

It may be argued that while attempting to mimic the figure of the Brahmin, the Balmikis of Sulabh also challenge caste structures by expressing the right to inhabit "upper caste" bodies. At the same time, there is a deep expression of loyalty toward Brahmins. Such idealization of the Brahmin figure and the absorption of its epitomized model in Pathak, not only retains a hierarchized caste-Hindu framework but also reinstates the superiority of the Brahmin as the norm. Pathak, functioning through a Brahmanical and sympathetic lens, creates a kind of scavenger he is comfortable with, which he wants and wishes to see, and the scavenger in turn often adopts a similar language when describing his or her life. The Balmikis of Sulabh are forever obliged and indebted to the Brahmin Pathak (the great, the absolute, the chosen representative of God) for feeling compassion for them. The Brahmin continues to maintain a careful watch over his "subjects." It is a relationship between a father and his children and between the learned and the uneducated. Pathak deploys an inbuilt language of charity that combines a hidden, condescending attitude toward the scavenger and a kindness for the Brahmin. With all its goodwill, such empathy preserves and maintains an unconscious Brahmanism. Pathak in a sense symbolizes this ambivalence of caste reform.

The narratives of Pathak, an acclaimed social activist working for the liberation and rehabilitation of scavengers, resonates with such features in complex ways. Elements of eco-casteism crisscross here with concerns for scavengers. The messy collage of Indian environmentalism is underscored in Sulabh and Pathak, where caste-blindness or a tacit endorsement of Brahmanical Hindu faith function in tandem with the belief in the toilet as a tool for social change. Even while attempting to transform hegemonic caste practices, Pathak's life journey ends up reinstating and reaffirming them. The life narratives of the liberated scavengers, revealed through various interviews, often construct and represent their lives in Pathak's shadow, rarely intruding or desecrating the sacred spaces and tastes of the Brahmin world.

## NOTES

1. Pathak delivered this speech at the book release of Mahatma Gandhi's *Life in Color* in New Delhi on October 5, 2016. At this event, Usha Chaumar, President of Sulabh International and a liberated manual scavenger, also announced with chants of Vedic mantras that they all have now turned into "authentic" Brahmins.
2. Pathak and Sulabh use the term "liberation," which is questionable, as it operates within a conservative Brahmin savior model that, arguably, diminishes Dalit's agency.
3. Pathak explicitly deploys this Gandhian terminology, rather than the term "Dalit" for describing scavengers.
4. When Narendra Modi celebrated his sixty-fifth birthday on September 17, 2015, Pathak composed a *qawwali* (a style of devotional music) "Modi ka Sapna Bana Liya Apna" (Modi's Dream Has Become My Own). Pathak composed another song, "Mahima Ganga Kasi Ki" (In Praise of Ganga of Kasi), about how Modi's heart beats for Mother Ganga and Kasi (Varanasi, Modi's parliamentary constituency). He composed a third song, on Modi's Pakistan visit, describing how Modi is spreading the message of peace and brotherhood in the lands of Buddha and Gandhi. After his visit to the BJP president Amit Shah's birthday on October 22, 2016, Pathak described Modi as "a man who's exemplary in his ways, an exceptional thinker and humanist" ("Historical Visit").
5. Balmikis is another name for scavengers, who have been liberated from their traditional, caste-based occupation. Their management of the Sulabh-built toilets and related sanitation systems on the ground reinforces caste-based roles and their status.
6. My fieldwork at worksites and offices of Sulabh in Delhi, Bihar, and Rajasthan supports this claim.
7. See the *Selected Works of Mahatma Gandhi*, vol. 5, which contains Gandhi's views on Bhangis.
8. For a larger discussion of eco-casteism, see my *Green and Saffron: Hindu Nationalism and Indian Environmental Politics* and *Caste and Nature: Dalits and Indian Environmental Politics*.

## WORKS CITED

*Alwar ki Nai Rajkumarian: Nai Manzilen, Nai Raste*. Sulabh Social Service Organisation, 2009.

Ambedkar, B. R. *Dr. Babasaheb Ambedkar's Writings and Speeches*. Vol. 9, Government of Maharashtra, 1990.

"Aryan Code of Toilets (2nd Century AD)." *Sulabh Toilet Museum*, n.d., http://www.sulabhtoiletmuseum.org/history-of-toilets/aryan-code-of-toilets-2nd-century-ad/. Accessed 9 May 2017.

Athwal, Guddi. Personal interview. 18 Aug. 2014.

Chamere, Shakuntla. Personal interview. 18 Aug. 2014.

Chaumar, Aman. Personal interview. 16 Aug. 2014.

Chaumar, Usha. Personal interview. 16 Aug. 2014.

Conway, Jill Ker. *When Memory Speaks: Exploring the Art of Autobiography*. Vintage Books, 1998.

Dolly. Personal interview. 16 Aug. 2014.

Eakin, Paul John. *How Our Lives Become Stories: Making Selves*. Cornell UP, 1999.

Gandhi, Mahatma. *Collected Works of Mahatma Gandhi*. Vol. 5: 1905 to 3 Nov. 1906, Government of India, 1999.

Goyal, Sonu, and Vikas Gupta. "Sulabh International—Social Transformation through Sanitation." *Vikalpa*, vol. 34, no. 1, Jan.–Mar. 2009, pp. 107–09.

"Historical Visit of Hon'ble Shri Amit Shah: National President, Bharatiya Janata Party, at the Sulabh Gram." *Sulabh International*, 20 Dec. 2016, http://www.sulabhinternational.org/wp-content/uploads/2017/05/Historial-Visit-of-Honble-Shri-Amit-Shah.pdf. Accessed 9 May 2017.

Lohra, Naresh. Personal interview. 18 Aug. 2014.

"Meet Sulabh." Sulabh International Social Service Organisation. N.d., http://www.sulabhinternational.org/meet-sulabh/. Accessed 7 July 2014.

Namala, Annie, and N. Paul Divakar. "Battle for Liberation, Then and Now." *Labour File*, vol. 3, no. 6, Nov.–Dec. 2005.

Nindania, Lakshmi. Personal interview. 16 Aug. 2014.

Nindania, Lalita. Personal interview. 16 Aug. 2014.

Nindania, Meera. Personal interview. 18 Aug. 2014.

Pathak, Bindeshwar. "Chhath Celebration." *Sulabh India*, vol. 25, no. 11, Nov. 2013, p. 9.

———. "India of the Past Was a Golden Bird." *Sulabh India*, vol. 26, no. 1, Jan. 2014, p. 2.

———. "Liberated Scavengers in Kumbh Mela Rituals." *Sulabh India*, vol. 25, no. 2, Feb. 2013, p. 20.

———. "Liberated Scavengers on Pilgrimage." *Sulabh India*, vol. 23, no. 7, July 2011, p. 6.

———. "Maha Shivaratri Festival at Sulabh Campus." *Sulabh India*, vol. 24, no. 3, Mar. 2012, pp. 8–9.

———. "New Princesses of Alwar." *Sulabh India*, vol. 24, no. 10, Oct. 2012, p. 23.

———. "Report on National Conference on Sociology of Sanitation." *Sulabh India*, vol. 25, no. 1, Jan. 2013, p. 6.

———. *Road to Freedom: A Sociological Study on the Abolition of Scavenging in India*. Sulabh Foundation, 1991.

———, editor. *Sociology of Sanitation: Environmental Sanitation, Public Health and Social Deprivation*. Kalpaz Publications, 2015.

———. Speech for the Book Release of Mahatma Gandhi's *Life in Color*, Mawalakar Hall, New Delhi, 5 Oct. 2016.

———. "Sulabh Sanitation and Social Reform Movement." *International NGO Journal*, vol. 6, no. 1, Jan. 2011, pp. 14–29.

———. "Tool of Social Change." *Sulabh India*, vol. n.a., no. n.a., Aug. 2009, p. 28.

Prashad, Vijay. *Untouchable Freedom: A Social History of a Dalit Community*. Oxford UP, 2000.

Ramachandran, R. "Satisfying Solution for a Compelling Need Makes Sulabh an Entrepreneurial Success." *Vikalpa*, vol. 34, no. 1, Jan.–Mar. 2009, pp. 109–11.

Safai Karmachari Andolan. "Day 1: 10th December 2015, Inauguration of Bhim Bus Yatra." 2015, http://safaikarmachariandolan.org/Bhim-Yatra-10Dec-InaugralDay.html, 22 Jun. 2017.

———. "Safai Karmachari Andolan." *Safai Karmachari Andolan*, 2010, http://safaikarmachariandolan.org/. Accessed 1 Nov. 2016.

Sharma, Mukul. *Caste and Nature: Dalits and Indian Environmental Politics*. Oxford UP, 2017.

———. *Green and Saffron: Hindu Nationalism and Indian Environmental Politics*. Permanent Black, 2012.

Singh, Bhasha. *Unseen: The Truth About India's Manual Scavengers*. Penguin Books, 2012.

Singh, Mahesh Kumar. Personal interview. 16 Aug. 2014.

Singh, Rajeev Kumar. Personal interview. 16 Aug. 2014.

Singh, S. P. *Sulabh Sanitation Movement: Vision—2000 Plus*. 4th ed., Sulabh International Social Service Organisation, 2005.

Smith, Sidonie, and Julia Watson, editors. *Getting a Life: Everyday Uses of Autobiography*. U of Minnesota P, 1996.

"Sulabh." *Sulabh International*. 2017, http://www.sulabhinternational.org/. Accessed 27 Jan. 2017.

# 11

# INVISIBILITY OF "OTHER" DALITS AND SILENCE IN THE LAW

SUMIT BAUDH

*"An ounce of illustration is worth more than a pound of theory."*

—B. R. Ambedkar (qtd. in Rodrigues 20)

## INTRODUCTION

For the first time, the 2011 census of India counted a population "other" than male or female. This essay takes a cue from the census and traces the invisibility of "other" Dalits, while attempting to break the silence about them in the law through life narratives. Formerly considered "untouchable" in the deeply unequal and hierarchical caste system of India, Dalits are also known as Scheduled Castes (SC) in the legal parlance.[1] The invisibility of "other" Dalits and the silence about them is located in an emerging legal moment in which transgender persons are compared with "untouchable" Dalits, but there is no legal understanding of persons who are *both* transgender and Dalit.

In addition to the usage of "other" in the census, the use of this term in this essay includes sexual orientations, identities, and expressions, such as lesbian, gay, bisexual, and queer. The use of "other" Dalits follows a consciously inconsistent terminology: while "other" is borrowed from its official legal usage in the 2011 census, the corresponding legal term for Dalits would be SC. There is an ideological significance of the word Dalit that does not carry well in SC's legal terminology.[2] This essay is conscious of and recognizes that Dalit ideology.

Other definitions and concepts need to be laid out and clarified. Usages of "upper caste" and "lower caste" in formal legal literature implicitly reinforce caste hierarchies. This essay makes a departure from this legal reiteration of caste hierarchies. In the place of "upper caste" this essay uses "dominant caste" and instead of "lower caste" it uses "subordinate caste" in recognition of the systemic domination and subordination within caste hierarchies.

Compared to more settled areas of the law in India, legal understanding of sexual orientation, gender identity, and expression (SOGIE) is relatively new and emerging. This essay is timely, situated in the aftermath of the recriminalization of same-sex sexual acts by the Supreme Court of India in 2013, wherein the court upheld the constitutional validity of a colonial-era sodomy law (*Koushal* 97). Though seemingly contradictory, in another judgment merely four months later, the Supreme Court directed the Government of India to consider transgender persons as a "socially and educationally backward class" and to extend "reservations" to them (*NLSA* 2). This emerging judicial understanding of gender and sexuality is contradictory: on the one hand, it creates a protected category for transgender persons, but on the other hand, it implicitly places some of the same transgender persons—for example, hijras—within the purview of criminality for their perceived sexual acts. In 2009, four years prior to this recriminalization, the Delhi High Court decriminalized consensual same-sex sexual acts on constitutional grounds, specifically rights to privacy, human dignity, equality, and non-discrimination (Articles 21, 14, 15, Constitution of India; *Naz* 105). The Delhi High Court also drew comparisons with other colonial-era laws, for example, the Criminal Tribes Act of 1871 that had historically imposed criminality upon transgender persons (*Naz* 41–42). This judicial analogy of the criminalization of "unnatural offences" with erstwhile "criminal tribes" was brief and made in passing. A one-paragraph reference did not develop the analogous comparison in any detail. Later, in another case, the Supreme Court of India drew a similarly passing analogy between transgender persons and "untouchable" Dalits in the following words:

> Our society often ridicules and abuses the Transgender community and in public places like railway stations, bus stands, schools, workplaces, malls, theatres, hospitals, *they are sidelined and treated as untouchables,* forgetting the fact that the moral failure lies in the society's unwillingness to contain or embrace different gender identities and expressions, a mindset which we have to change. (*NLSA* 2, emphasis mine)

Some of the transgender community are not just "sidelined and treated as untouchables," some of them *are* "untouchables," as the narratives in this essay testify. If the Supreme Court decision paid attention to this overlap of transgender and Dalit status, it may have resulted in a different decision with a better understanding of SOGIE and the law in India. At the stage of completing this essay, the Supreme Court has agreed to reconsider the decision of 2013 and a Special Bench of five unnamed judges are slated to hear the case afresh in a "curative petition."

What is the scope and significance of the invisibility of "other" Dalits and the silence about them? Is it an identity claim, and does this essay have relevance only for an understanding of the law in relation to this subgroup? The absence of explicit legal remedies against violence and discrimination based on the intersection of caste and SOGIE is compelling, especially given the abundance of legal remedial measures on caste alone (with varying degrees of success). This essay's attempt to uncover the invisibility is not just a claim to identity or of recognition for "other" Dalits (although there is no harm in making that claim). A study of this invisibility is a deeper critique of the law, and it portends greater consequences for more than just this particular group. An understanding of the production of invisibility of "other" Dalits through the narratives expounded in this essay can help in developing an insight that could at least broaden the legal remediation based on SOGIE beyond the decriminalization of sodomy. At a broader level of law and legal scholarship, such narrativizations can aid in tracing other invisibilities that are part of the law and social fabric of domination (for example, with regard to Dalit women and Dalit religious minorities).

This essay is structured in three parts. The first part starts with a self-narrative, an anecdote about this author that shows the lack of protective legislation against homophobic and transphobic violence in India. This lack of legal protection is contrasted with a surfeit of formal legal remedies that are based on caste. While developing this combined understanding of caste and its intersection with SOGIE, this anecdote also foregrounds the author's personal positioning. Next, the essay goes on to tell a personal narrative of a disabled trans person, which shows the law's inability to grasp multiple identities and statuses based on disability, ethnicity, caste, and SOGIE. The following part grapples with theoretical ideas about standpoint epistemology, personal narratives, experiences, and situated knowledges, thus developing a critical understanding of law and legal theory. It underlines that an insufficient understanding of caste in the legal scholarship is puzzling (and unacceptable to me) because of the salience of caste to inequalities in India.

The task of showing something that is invisible and of breaking silences is challenging. To do this, this essay relies on and deploys personal narratives and experiences. Further, it draws upon other eclectic sources from feminist scholarship, critical race theory (CRT), and Dalit scholarship. The final part of the essay brings the theoretical understanding to application, and "breaks the silence" in a composite area of the law and social movements, illustrating some of the probable factors that generate the silence and the invisibility.

## I. TRACING INVISIBILITY

### *THROUGH AN EXPERIENCE OF INSULT—NIGGER, FAGGOT, CHAKKA, CHAMAR*

I was about to enter the Haus Khas Park, and as usual I had workout music blasting in my earphones. I saw two men on their way out staring at me.

There was a gap of a few seconds between the music when I heard one of them say, *chakka-re-chakka* (faggot-o-faggot). This happened so fast that it took me a moment to grasp. These men had left the park by then and the next track had started blasting. I was running and thinking to myself:

> *Did that man really say what I heard?*
> *Did he say that about me?*
> *Why?*
> *Was it my clothes?*
> *Was it my gait?*

A fellow queer runner has said to me often that I run like a girl. It was harmless banter. Yet in this moment, that harmless banter came back to me. I checked my gait. I wondered if my short shorts were too short (see Fig. 1).

I felt insulted, humiliated, and furious all at the same time. The verbal abuse echoed in my ears louder than the blasting music. I tried to pacify myself by thinking that it was just two obnoxious men and no one else heard them. It was early morning and there were very few people in the park at the time. Even then, this brief moment of abuse had changed the whole atmosphere and experience of the park for me. True, no one other than me had heard these men, but the park did. In my fertile imagination, every little leaf of every tree was now whispering this incident. The foliage of the park had heard the insult, some of this foliage was mocking me, some of it was sympathetic, some just did not care. It vitiated the whole atmosphere of the park, which is otherwise very dear to me.

Venting my rage by writing about this incident on social media, I wanted to make collective sense of it with the help of my friends and acquaintances, a group including lawyers, scholars, activists, and a judge (Baudh, Status). A Judicial Magistrate in India noted that Section 504 of the Indian Penal Code (IPC) of 1860 would apply. Section 504 identifies insult and insulter in these words:

> Intentional insult with intent to provoke breach of the peace—Whoever intentionally insults, and thereby gives provocation to any person, intending or knowing it to be likely that such provocation will cause him to break the public peace, or to commit any other offence.

Did the men intend "to provoke breach of the peace"? I do not know their intention. If I were to speculate, I would think their intention was to entertain themselves with a kind of commonplace humor. If I were to dig deeper into their intention, I might speculate that they were motivated by prevailing ideas of masculinity. My skimpy clothes and my gait might have been contrary to such ideas. Consciously or unconsciously, these men were social agents in enforcing a certain unwritten code of masculinity. I am not about to psycho-

Figure 11.1: Illustrative self-portrait, May 2015, New Delhi.

analyze these men any further. It is sufficient to note that the language of Section 504 does not seem to apply to this incident.

That said, Section 504 could well include an insult based on caste, and yet there is an additional and special legal remedy for that. The Scheduled Castes and the Scheduled Tribes (Prevention of Atrocities) Act of 1989, referred in short as the SC/ST Act or PoA, is a remedial legislation for the prevention of "atrocities" against the members of the SC and the Scheduled Tribes (ST). The SC and the ST are two different legal categories: SC connotes caste status—that is, it is associated with the practice of "untouchability"—and ST connotes tribal status. In a listing of practices and circumstances in which caste-based violence is commonly inflicted, Section 3 of the SC/ST Act provides a list of offences that are legally considered an "atrocity." In this list, Section 3 (1) (x) states:

> Whoever, not being a member of a SC or a ST, intentionally insults or intimidates with intent to humiliate a member of a SC or a ST in any place within public view, shall be punishable with imprisonment for a term which shall not be less than six months but which may extend to five years and with fine.

I am a member of an SC, and I think these men intended to humiliate me. That would be insufficient to invoke the SC/ST Act because it penalizes only certain kinds of insults that are inflicted by non-SC or non-ST persons upon SC or ST persons. Presuming that these men were non-SC/ST, for Section 3 (1) (x) to apply, they should have insulted me on the basis of my caste. For example, if they were to say, *chamar-o-chamar*, that would qualify as an insult based on caste.

Judicial decisions have confirmed the use of caste names as a means of insult. Drawing upon an analogy with abusive name-calling like "nigger" or "negro" for African Americans, the Supreme Court of India has stated:

> [U]ses of the words "pallan", "pallapayal" "parayan" or "paraparayan" with intent to insult is highly objectionable and is also an offence under the SC/ST Act. It is just unacceptable in the modern age, just as the words "Nigger" or "Negro" are unacceptable for African-Americans today. (*Arumugam* 2)

This analogy of racialized slurs like "nigger" with caste names in India presents a combined understanding of insults based on caste and race. In a similar vein, there could be a combined understanding of insults based on caste and gender. Although *chakka-re-chakka* is not an insult based on caste, the intention to insult is analogous to insults based on caste. Aside from broad analogies such as these, I ask myself, would I have felt any more or less insulted if I were called *chamar* instead of *chakka*? The answer is no. I would have felt equally insulted at being called either of the two. The former is a slur based on caste, while the latter is a slur based on misogyny and patriarchal ideas of masculinity. They are both intended to secure a certain systemic compliance of subordination, casteist and patriarchal.

The next morning when I was about to get into my running gear, I wondered if I should cover up more of my body. It was the month of May and the cruel Delhi summer was setting in. I looked at my running gear and I asked myself:

> *Should I wear this?*
> *Is it too skimpy?*
> *Will people stare?*

This self-scrutiny was a direct result of my experience of slur and humiliation. I understood this and I decided to wear what I wanted to: I put on the same running gear as the previous day. I am aware of the privilege of a male body that allows me to make this decision. It would be far more risky, with imminent threat of physical violence, for women runners to wear what I wear in a public park in Delhi.

Reflecting on my experiences of running in Haus Khas Park is an example of how self-narrative can demonstrate the invisibility of "other" Dalits in the law. It underlines the significance of tracing this invisibility for understanding the law more broadly. Equally, this personal narrative shows the need for remedial action against violence and discrimination based on SOGIE.

Now, let us consider a personal narrative of a disabled ST trans man to further trace some of the outlines of invisibility and to illustrate the intersection of disability, ethnicity, caste, and SOGIE in the law.

### *THROUGH A PERSONAL NARRATIVE: SO MANY IDENTITIES BUT THE GOVERNMENT WANTS JUST ONE*

Kiran is a disabled trans man. He says, "I was born female and I was disabled so my family thought, 'What is the point of educating a disabled girl?'" Born in a "subordinate caste," Lambani, Kiran fell in love with a "dominant caste" woman, and they decided to live together. "Radhika's family was upset because they thought I was a girl and how could two girls be married and live together?" Kiran explains. Radhika's family considered Kiran someone with whom they wouldn't even drink water. "How could you have a relationship with someone like that?" they said.

Because of this hostility in their hometown in Andhra Pradesh, Radhika and Kiran moved to the neighboring state of Karnataka. Their problems did not end. Kiran could not avail "reservations" because Lambani is categorized differently in the two states: as ST in Andhra Pradesh and as SC in Karnataka. Sometimes these categories are registered differently in different states, as in Kiran's case; and because of this difference, Kiran lost his legal status of ST in Karnataka. On the other hand, Kiran could not avail of the SC status because he did not have the corresponding SC legal certification. Even if he had had this certification, Kiran could not have availed of "reservations" in Karnataka because SC status is often state specific and it applies only within that state.

Figure 11.2: Kiran Nayak at the Roundtable "Law at the Intersection of Caste, Gender, and Sexuality" held on August 6, 2014. Reproduced courtesy of Tathagata Mandal. Used by permission.

Aside from falling between the cracks of legal categories, Kiran is now the subject of another legal category, called the "Backward Class" (BC). In April 2014, the Supreme Court granted legal recognition and protection to transgender persons as BC (*NLSA*). The legal category of BC is based on social and educational "backwardness," and it is different from both SC and ST.

These multiple legal categories now make Kiran SC, ST, BC, transgender, and disabled, but in different legal registers. Kiran continues to jostle with overlapping forms of discrimination in a legal administration that is fraught with ambiguities. "I have so many identities but the government wants just one," he says. To secure his disability pension, Kiran had to show several certificates related to his gender, disability, and caste. "The government is very confused about what pension to give me. It took six months to negotiate [with the government] and get my due."

This conflation of legal categories is not unique to Kiran. There are more than one hundred thousand SC and ST transgender persons who are apparently invisible to the law. As noted, transgender persons in India were counted for the first time in the 2011 census. The census had a category "other" than male and female. In principle, this category could have included all those who are "other" than male or female, including indigenous gender transgressive persons like hijra, *kinnar*, *kothi*, *aravani*, *jogappas*, and *jogtis*. The census found that there are almost half a million of this "other" population; of these, more than 16 percent (78,811) are SC and about 7 percent (33,293) are ST. In other words, almost one quarter (23 percent) of this "other" category are SC and ST.

While we consider these numbers, it is important to note the strong likelihood of undercounting of this "other" category. This new category had to be explained to the surveyors and the surveyed at various stages of data collection. There is anecdotal information about the failure of the surveyors to understand this new category and a resulting failure to collect the full data. Scholar and transgender activist Reshma Prasad reflected on the misconceptions associated with the word transgender and the popular understanding of hijras. Speaking as a panelist at the second Men Engage Global Symposium in 2014, Prasad narrates her life thus:

> Indian transgender, especially transgender women, are associated with the hijra identity, although the transgender community includes everyone. When I step out, most people think of only one thing—that I am a hijra, ignoring that I am an activist and I work for the community. They think that I beg for alms.

It is true that the word transgender is commonly understood as hijra, and it is likely to have prevailed during the census, too. In addition to this common misunderstanding, there is little or no understanding about trans men. This lack of understanding implies a virtual invisibility of female-to-male trans men in the census.

Yet, 112,104 is the official census figure for the "other" category, which means that this category is numerically visible. In spite of this numerical visibility, there is no understanding of "other" SC and ST persons in the law. An example of this legal invisibility shows in the Supreme Court judgment in *National Legal Services Authority (NLSA) v. Union of India* in 2014. While granting legal protection to transgender persons as BC, the Supreme Court did not clarify the resulting legal status of SC/ST transgender persons. Do they constitute an additional legal category of BC? The Government of India has petitioned the Supreme Court to clarify this (Anand). Thus, the composite character of Kiran's gender expression and ethnicity, as noted above, is rendered invisible, and for legal purposes, he becomes a non-ST disabled person.

## II. PERSONAL NARRATIVES, EXPERIENCES, AND SITUATED KNOWLEDGES IN THE LAW AND LEGAL THEORY

How do personal narratives and experiences, as above, inform the law, legal scholarship, and theory? Contemporary legal theory in India is informed mostly by Western theorists and philosophers. H. L. A. Hart, Lon Fuller, John Rawls, and Ronald Dworkin are the core readings in jurisprudence that are applied mostly to the subject areas of Constitutional Law and Criminal Law. Some theorists in India have read these theorists and combined their ideas with a reading of ancient Hindu scriptures like Vedas, Shastras, and Smritis (Singh). Other theorists have devoted their efforts to proving and disproving the works of Western legal theorists, though they remain silent on the question of caste.

In an important work of legal scholarship, Kalpana Kannabiran presents an understanding of "Intersectional Jurisprudence" and offers a critical engagement with the law in the context of the routine perpetration of atrocities on entire communities. Kannabiran foregrounds colonization as the dominant form of historic oppression, while making no reference to other forms of oppression, such as patriarchy and casteism, that operate along with colonialism. However, these intersecting forms of oppression would be relevant to a foundational understanding of intersectional jurisprudence. With this partial understanding of oppression, Kannabiran then makes a cursory commentary about Ambedkar's contributions and the specific context of caste, but overlooks the existing understanding of discrimination in India. Most important, the author does not offer any explanation of the text of Article 15 (1) of the Constitution that ought to include intersectional grounds of discrimination (Atrey). A fundamental lapse in Kannabiran's articulation of intersectional jurisprudence is that she explores her argument with reference to distinct groups: persons with disabilities, Dalits, Adivasis, religious minorities, women, and sexual minorities, in that order. Kannabiran does not consider intersectional groups like "other" Dalits.

Another leading scholar, Upendra Baxi, situates Ronald Dworkin in contemporary Indian jurisprudence and offers a critique of Dworkin's legal theory and its application to the law in India (Baxi).[3] Baxi refers to the works of postcolonial theorist Gayatri Chakravorty Spivak to challenge Dworkin and promptly distances himself from Spivak, leaving some ambiguity about his own position.[4] Baxi unquestioningly defers to the makers of the Constitution of India, namely their effort to prohibit "untouchability" (via Article 17), as well as the legislative defense against the judicial unconstitutionality of reservations. He extols the Indian judiciary without interrogating the dominant-caste composition and subjectivities of the judges. Baxi does not make anything of Dalits' experiences or of the value of personal experiences to theory and knowledge production. Although Baxi acknowledges that it was the subordination of colonization that fueled the freedom struggle in India, which in turn became the guiding spirit for the Constitution, he does not make any sense of the casteism that was, at the least, parallel to colonialism.

Contemporary legal theory has not sufficiently attended to the relationship between caste and the law in India. In contrast, the social sciences have an extensive body of literature on caste. Well-known social-science scholars have "positioned" their work from Dalit perspectives (to name just a few: Gopal Guru, Kancha Ilaiah, and Anand Teltumbde). And yet there is an intriguing silence about caste in contemporary legal scholarship; there are no legal scholars who "position" themselves as Dalit in their writings. This part of the essay thus develops a combined understanding of positionality, situated knowledges, experience, personal narratives, and their potential relevance to contemporary legal theory and scholarship.

What could be the significance, if any, of Dalit positioning in legal scholarship? Given the universalist nature of the law, in the sense that it applies universally to all its subjects, there is a seeming objectivity in the functions of legislature, judiciary, police, and other law-enforcement agencies. Those at the top of power hierarchies assume a standard of objectivity and deliver a universalist character of the law. These agencies of the law are invisible and unmarked in their empowered positions of dominant caste, class, gender, sexual orientation, physical abilities, and other power systems. The body of legal knowledge emerges from these empowered positions that remain unmarked. According to Donna Haraway, "Knowledge from the point of view of the unmarked is truly fantastic, distorted, and irrational" (587). This is a starting point for "situated knowledges" and "standpoint epistemology" in feminist scholarship. An assumed objectivity and a resulting claim to universality—of those at the top—pose a problem to the subjugated and marginalized lives of Dalits and other subordinate groups. Positioning is thus crucial to "situated knowledges" and to generating stronger standards for the "objectivity" of the law.

However, vantage points and positioning of Dalits are not conclusively authoritative and impossible to challenge. Haraway clarifies, "The positionings of the subjugated are not exempt from critical reexamination, decoding, deconstruction, and interpretation; that is, from both semiological and hermeneutic modes of critical inquiry" (584). Thus, the view from a body is distinguished from the view from above. Haraway argues "for politics and epistemologies of location, positioning, and situating, where partiality and not universality is the condition of being heard to make rational knowledge claims" (588). Often, the law projects this view from above; in contrast, Dalit location, positioning, and situating are views from below, from a body that could make rational knowledge claims to this authority and implementation of the law from above.

In addition to their location from below, vantage points of the subjugated are correlated with communities. As Haraway argues, "Situated knowledges are about communities, not about isolated individuals" (590). It would stand to reason that subjugation and subordination along the lines of race, caste, ethnicity, and gender are group inequalities that are communities' collective experiences. This correlation of situated knowledges and communities would apply very differently to subjugation and subordination that is experienced through, and partially because of, isolation. For example, lesbian, gay, bisexual, transgender, intersex, and queer (LGBTIQ) narratives often testify to prolonged experiences of isolation in which individuals might feel they are alone and there is nobody else like them. Their situated knowledges would necessarily start from the subject position of isolation that might later acquire the character of shared community experiences. Further, located within experiences of "intersectional subordination," individuals could have conflicted memberships in two or more communities. For example, I could experience rejection by Dalit communities because of my queerness, and I could experience rejection by queer communities because of my Dalitness. In this "intersectional subordination" my subject position would start essentially from my situation as an isolated individual who might connect with subject positions of other Dalits and queers over time. Even if that were not to happen, I remain an individual subject of the law in the sense that the law applies to me individually and to the groups of which I am part. Therefore the correlation of situated knowledges and communities needs to be reviewed in relation to isolated individuals, nascent communities, and "intersectional subordination."

In other parts of the world, and within legal scholarship, critical race theory has looked to the "bottom" for substantive outcome, authenticity, credibility, and voice. Proponents of authenticity have argued that voices at the "bottom" present an authentic, albeit diverse, voice. Looking to the "bottom" is an effective way to capture the narratives of people of color, providing them with meaningful opportunities to be heard. Critical race theorists like Mari Matsuda, Patricia Williams, and Robert Chang have expounded and relied upon the use of "personal narratives" in their works. Notwithstanding this extensive deployment of "personal narrative," there is an insufficient theorizing within critical race theory about the so-called "bottom" (Carbado 1312). With an insufficient yet useful theorizing in legal scholarship, I look toward understanding the law and its relationship with caste in India.

The disciplines of philosophy and sociology have expounded on the ethics of theorization (Guru and Sarukkai). In making this leap across disciplines and geography, I correlate the use of "personal narrative" in critical race theory in the US and the use of "experience" in Dalit theorizing in India. Dalit scholar Gopal Guru starts with an understanding that the existing treatment of theoretical concepts is discursive, and that experience can dispute this treatment. According to Guru, "reference to experience is important for disputing efforts that seek to assign discursive treatment to theoretical concepts" (Guru and Sarukkai 115). The philosophical foundations of emancipatory movements are lacking the experiences of victimhood, and this experience of victimhood provides the necessary vocabulary for a philosophical understanding. Guru makes a case for understanding the external world by starting with one's own experience. He underscores the narrativization of humiliation and degradation with the hope that this might invoke the sympathetic understanding of those who inflict these humiliations and degradation:

> For understanding the external world, one has to start from one's own experience. The connection between the abstract and the immediate takes place primarily through theoretical mediation between the particular and the universal. The description of a particular experience in the form of an autobiographical account may not be sufficient condition to radically connect the particular to the universal . . . while autobiography is important to open up dialogue with those who are not part of the experience, they can merely share that experience through sympathy with the authors. This is sufficient. Moreover, humiliating, degrading experience narrativized through autobiographies might prompt some to notice the details of the painful experience and develop the moral stamina not to repeat the act that would produce such a morally objectionable experience for others. (Guru and Sarukkai 119)

Elsewhere, Guru places moral responsibility upon those who are the recipients of torment to vocalize their experience of past silence. In conceiving of this moral responsibility, Guru formulates a binary of the "recipients of torment" and the "tormentor," and an implicit homogeneity of Dalit experiences that places moral responsibility upon the "recipients of torment" to vocalize the experience of past silence (Guru and Sarukkai 117–19). Although this binary supports the use of experience and personal narratives in this essay, I would distance myself from any "moral responsibility." Rather than my responsibility, moral or otherwise, it is a collective responsibility of everybody to vocalize and amplify the experiences of being silenced.

Rethinking standpoint epistemology and elaborating new subjects of knowledge, Sandra Harding states:

> Such a project requires learning to listen attentively to marginalized people; it requires educating oneself about their histories, achievements, preferred social relations, hopes for the future; it requires putting one's body on the line for "their" causes until they feel like "our" causes. (458)

This call to action presumes a neat distinction between marginalized people and those who create knowledge. The distinction fades when marginalized people create knowledge about themselves. Even if the distinction were neat, clear, and true, what would it mean to put "one's body on the line for 'their' causes until they feel like 'our' causes"? How adept could anyone be to "feel" anyone else's cause? My limited experience of deploying Dalit positioning has evoked intense anxiety, anguish, grief, and anger within me. Occasionally I have found myself at loggerheads with some of my friends and former colleagues. There have been times when I have confronted senior and more accomplished people who could jeopardize my career prospects. Recollection of personal memories of humiliation and a pursuit of confrontations has yielded some of the content of my narratives—at the cost of my psychological wellbeing. In the process of developing these narratives, I started getting bizarre nightmares that became routine: I would be placed on a guillotine, sometimes consensually, and I would watch my beheading with indifference. This was deeply disturbing and mystifying because I have never seen a guillotine in real life or witnessed anyone's beheading, much less my own. I would wake up disturbed and disoriented. These subconscious feelings of fear, despair, and anxiety began to creep into my consciousness, and I started getting uncanny thoughts of killing myself. For no reason, I would think of throwing myself in front of running trains in subway stations. Around this time, there was also the disturbing news about Dalit research scholar Rohith Vemula's suicide by hanging. My eerie thoughts of killing myself now started to include death by hanging. I recovered from this turmoil through a combination of coping mechanisms, including regular running and meditation, personal resilience and will, but the intensity of this protracted experience took me to dark spaces within that were previously unknown to me. All this gave me a sense of what it might mean to put "one's body on the line for 'their' causes until they feel like 'our' causes." Only that in my case there is a thin line between "their" and "our." My self-identification as Dalit is a conscious subject positioning and vantage point through which I have developed this essay.

A word of caution: the use of personal narrative as a heuristic tool should be done with a preparedness to undergo intense anxiety, anguish, grief, and anger, especially when these narratives uncover personal experiences of humiliation and subordination. *The Essential Writings of B. R. Ambedkar*, edited by Valerian Rodrigues, presents commentary about Ambedkar's writings on "untouchability" and the intimacy, grief, and anger in those writings. According to Rodrigues:

> Ambedkar's engagement as a researcher, an intellectual and activist, is much more nuanced, hesitant but intimate as compared to his viewpoint on caste, where he is prepared to offer stronger judgements and proffer solutions. However with untouchability, there is often a failure of words. *Grief is merged with anger.* (27, emphasis mine)

As researchers and writers, we should be aware of the possibility of experiencing grief and anger when we revisit personal memories of humiliation, subordination, and discrimination—especially when our research requires us to break the silence by confronting our systemic oppressors.

At times, my deployment of personal experience, borrowing from Joan W. Scott's words, becomes "evidence for the fact of difference, rather than a way of exploring how difference is established, how it operates, how and in what ways it constitutes subjects who see and act in the world. . . . We know they exist, but not how they have been constructed" (25). Readers may note that my focus is more on the law and less on difference and identity formation. Questions about identity formation are there in my experiences for anyone to analyze, critique, disagree with, or debunk. My experiences are not so much about how difference is established; they are more about tracing the invisibility of "other" Dalits and breaking the silence about them in the law. Even just a partial visibility exposes some of the inadequacies and failures of the law in one part, and in another part, it exposes the existence of repressive laws. That is the limited purpose of my deployment of experience and personal narrative in this essay: to start a critical conversation about the law, legal scholarship, and theory.

Borrowing again from Scott's words, "Making visible the experience of a different group exposes the existence of repressive mechanisms, but not their inner workings or logics; we know that difference exists, but we don't understand it as constituted rationally" (25). Some of my experiences and analyses attempt that exploration in the realm of law. In part, the law animates and enacts some of the repressive mechanisms. How and in what ways does the law constitute subjects who see and act in the world? At this stage of my writing and in this essay, I do not answer this question to any satisfaction. It is the start of an understanding, not a conclusive end.

## III. BREAKING THE SILENCE

After tracing the invisibility of "other" Dalits in the law in the first part of this essay, and considering the theoretical understanding of situated knowledges, standpoint epistemology, and personal narrative and experience in the second part, I break the silence about "other" Dalits in a composite area of the law and social movements. I end now in the way I began—with a personal narrative.

As part of a civil society coalition that pursued an "intersectional approach" in its demand for decriminalization of sodomy in India, I led a campaign for the ongoing litigation in the Delhi High Court. This effort achieved some success in the judicial ruling of *Naz Foundation v. Government of NCT Delhi*, but the success was narrow and short lived. It was narrow because the resulting decriminalization was only for sexual acts "in private," ignoring the realities of working-class, Dalit, and Adivasi queer persons, many of whom did not have the privileges of private spaces. Indeed, many of the arrests under the law originated from public spaces. Despite awareness about this on-the-ground reality within social movements and campaigns, the legal demand for decriminalization was limited to private spaces. The Delhi High Court ruling of 2009 conceded this demand. It was short lived because the Supreme Court of India overturned the High Court ruling in 2013.

In 2014, a roundtable seminar titled "Law at the Intersection of Caste, Gender and Sexuality" discussed this wrinkle in the decriminalization campaign regarding public and private spaces. The roundtable also raised pertinent questions about my silence and inaction at the time of the campaign. While I was open about my Dalit and gay status within this campaign, my understanding of an "intersectional approach" in our demand for decriminalization was limited to multiple identity formations, devoid of any understanding of how intersectional identity formations played out in our demands for law reform. Later, and in response to questions posed in the roundtable, I reflected on the formal and informal mechanisms that produce silence and invisibility. Perhaps knowingly or unknowingly, dominant cultures within social movements can be sometimes hostile toward and alienating of subordinate groups like Dalits. I use the following narrative as an anecdotal example of the dominant class and caste composition of social movements that exclude and silence the working classes and Dalit groups, resulting in invisibility.

The following happened to come to my attention by chance. It is neither typical nor definitive of "other" Dalit experiences. I was browsing my Facebook newsfeed and I stopped at the sight of my grandfather's name. Someone had posted a business card with the name Phool Singh, and this card said: "please contact for gardening work." The person who posted this photo was formerly part of the civil society coalition that had demanded decriminalization of sodomy on "intersectional" grounds.

*Phool* translates as flower, and so my Facebook friend had captioned her post as: *Jaisa naam waisa kaam* (a name that matches one's occupation). Make no mistake, my friend was not endorsing the services of Phool Singh. She was mocking both his name, Phool, and his occupation, gardening.

This mockery continued in the comments section. The first comment mocked the mailing address that had the word palace in it. This was making fun of the menial occupation of gardening and the contrasting regalia of palaces. Someone else said, "going by this formula, what should our names be?" My friend replied, "*Sevika*??? [female servant] <vomit>." My friend was disgusted with the word servant in the description of her white-collar work. Someone else pointed to the phonetic similarity between Phool and fool.

There were no comments about this being a real business card, and that Phool Singh was a real person—who was trying to make a humble living. Although my father's father was not a gardener, I still found this post and its surrounding conversation especially poignant. My grandfather Phool Singh had a small business of selling *baans* and *balli* wood. On my mother's side, her father was a gardener, yes, and his name was Lal Chand.

At the time of Lal Chand's birth around 1929, in the distant peripheries of Lutyens's Delhi, there was a consciousness in naming. Dignified names were reserved for persons of "higher" stature and caste, and such names were denied to persons of "lower" stature and caste. Even today, certain names are set apart for people who are born *savarnas* ("dominant caste" Hindus) and those who are born *avarnas* ("untouchable" Dalit). Lal Chand was Dalit and his name had to be commonplace, modest, and nothing grand. He was called Lala and this is not the kind of *lala* that we know in a colloquial sense, typically a rotund merchant or moneylender. *Lal* is a term of endearment for male children and perhaps Lala was a derivative of that, a childhood pet name that stuck for life.

There is also something distinctive about surnames. The practice of using surnames came to India with British colonization. These surnames were crafted from a combination of a person's community, place of origin, and occupation, and all of this had caste underpinnings. Caste had anyhow played a decisive role in the allocation of occupations. The practice of surnames provided easy and open means of caste identification, especially in cosmopolitan urban locations, where caste was becoming relatively obscure. These surnames have remained proud declarations of family lineage and occupation, except in the cases of Dalits who are compelled to carry lineages of poverty, deprivation, and shame.

As a Dalit who was unable to complete his primary education, Lala had very few options for work. Lala's father sat him down to serve at a *piau* (drinking-water facility) at the age of twelve. Around this time, he was married to a five-year-old girl Kela (this name Kela translates as banana). At some point, Lala stopped serving at the *piau* and was assigned the work of a gardener. Lala took care of gardens in Lutyens's Delhi,[5] and subsequently gained formal employment in the Government Department of Horticulture. He also moonlighted as a gardener in private residential houses of another locality called Jangpura in Delhi.

Back to my friend and her Facebook post. She was mocking a genuine business card, and this mockery dismissed the personhood of Phool Singh and attacked his human dignity. This kind of ridicule is common in dominant cultures that mock certain occupations and names. I added my comment and said that "the caste system doesn't allow people to choose their occupations and names, and do you think that's funny?" I was confronting my friend and all the others who were mocking this Phool Singh.

My friend did not answer me but she deleted her post almost immediately. Her deletion did not undo the personal offense that was caused to me. It reminded me of the times when, knowingly or unknowingly, my peers would mock me, my caste, my ancestors, and I would have to keep quiet. My silence was complicit in my shaming.

Now I break the silence. I talk back.

Lala's firstborn child, my mother, was named Vidyavati, a name that translates as "bearer of knowledge." Vidyavati was born in the same month as the Constitution of India, in January 1950. True to her name and true to the constitutional aspirations of equality, perhaps, Vidyavati became the first woman in her family to complete higher secondary school, and she became the first person in her family to get a white-collar job. With a name that matches her occupation indeed, Vidyavati taught for forty years in the primary schools of the Municipal Corporation of Delhi. And I am proud to be this Vidyavati's child.

Sometimes my dominant-caste and class-activist colleagues cannot understand what keeps Dalit groups away from the "intersectional" civil society groups. It is presumed but rarely said out loud that Dalit groups are ignorant, uneducated, and less sophisticated than more elite women and LGBTIQ groups. This dominant caste and class subjectivity of the social movements needs to be understood, because this subjectivity renders some of the social movements inhospitable, unwelcoming, domineering, and non-intersectional. This dominant class and caste subjectivity is counterproductive to the supposed "intersectional approach," and it alienates subordinate groups like Dalits.

## CONCLUSION

My personal narratives in this essay have shown the need for developing legal scholarship on caste and a need for legal theory in the composite areas of caste and its intersections with SOGIE. This essay has elevated SOGIE issues in the context of caste, and it has interrogated caste in the growing discourse around SOGIE politics and equality. The knowledge that comes from examining overlapping vulnerabilities would help strengthen tools, instruments, and rhetoric designed to address violence, discrimination, and social disempowerment globally. More particularly, given the background from which this essay has emerged, the ongoing campaign for decriminalization of sodomy in India and the upcoming "curative petition" in the Supreme Court could be informed by an "intersectional" understanding of caste and SOGIE presented in this essay. Only a part of the law, as it comes into being, is formulated within legislatures, executives, and judiciaries. There is a part of the law that originates in the very demands for law reform from social movements. Decriminalization of sodomy is one such demand that is currently being formulated within social movements in India. There needs to be a greater self-awareness and anticaste consciousness within these movements for them to imagine and formulate the demands from an understanding of "intersectionality." Only in the narrowest sense is the decriminalization about "privacy"; in a wider and more intersectional sense, the demand for decriminalization is about equality and human dignity. Histories of discrimination, oppression, and indignities originating in the caste system in India could be pivotal to informing the broader agenda of liberation and human rights for all.

The seemingly contradictory and puzzling outcome of the judicial process in *Koushal* and *NLSA* could be considered an inadvertent folly of a judiciary that is anyway subject to an impending "curative" process. At the same time, it would be a folly to consider this judicial outcome a folly. There could be some rationale to the outcome that might be obscure. Even a cursory reading of the comparative advancement of transgender rights—over sexual orientation—in the neighboring jurisdictions of Pakistan and Nepal would reveal a pattern that is worthy of mentioning. In *Pant v. Nepal,* the Supreme Court of Nepal issued a decision in recognition of "third gender" in 2007 (Bochenek and Knight) and in 2009, the Supreme Court of Pakistan recognized the rights of "eunuchs" to inherit property, vote, and receive education, among other things (*Khaki v. Rawalpindi*). It cannot be inadvertent that multiple jurisdictions in South Asia have yielded a greater advancement of transgender rights over sexual orientation. Another example of this advancement can be seen in the legislative process in India that accepted the Transgender Bill in the Upper House of the Parliament, while rejecting an initiative for the decriminalization of sodomy proposed by Member of Parliament Shashi Tharoor (Express News Service). There needs to be a separate and combined understanding of the two axes of sexual orientation and gender identity (SOGI) that is otherwise lumped into one category. SOGI is an "intersection" of two different categories; and these two categories can yield contradictory outcomes. The legal process is rendered less puzzling with an "intersectional" understanding of SOGI.

Further, SOGI and its intersections with other axes, such as caste and ethnicity, contains unexplored opportunities for understanding some of the analogous grounds. The passing analogies between transgender status and "untouchability" in *NLSA*, and similar passing analogies between British colonial criminalization of sodomy and the former "criminal tribes" in *Naz*, are helpful for understanding the legal and judicial processes at hand. It almost seems like the judges are nudging lawyers and social movements to present their arguments based on analogous grounds: caste, tribal status, and SOGI. And if so, "other" Dalits are suitable candidates for examining these analogous grounds. Embodied experiences of SOGI and its intersection with caste would shed more light on a subject that is otherwise rendered obscure in a seemingly contradictory legal moment. The challenge is to trace the invisibility and break the silence about "other" Dalits with greater force—including through the deployment of personal narratives and experience.

## NOTES

Acknowledgments: This essay is informed by the author's enrollment in the Doctor of Juridical Science (SJD) program at the University of California, Los Angeles (UCLA) School of Law and the guidance from my SJD dissertation committee: Professors Kimberlé Crenshaw (Chair), Devon Carbado, and Purnima Mankekar (Cochairs). Part of this essay borrows from a roundtable seminar entitled "Law at the Intersection of Caste, Gender and Sexuality" in New Delhi in 2014, which I jointly organized with the Indian Institute of Dalit Studies in my role as University of California Human Rights Fellow. This essay has also benefitted from input from the UCLA Graduate Writing Center consultants Eric Newman and Mercedes Douglass, and from the workshop at the University of Hawai'i at Mānoa in 2016 on "Caste and Life Narratives". The author is grateful to everyone for their input and remains solely responsible for all errors and omissions.

1. Dalit translates into English as broken, downtrodden, or crushed. It is a figurative usage that calls out centuries of subordination based on caste. Dalits are considered polluted and unclean, and deemed "untouchable" in the caste system. Some of these practices of untouchability and discrimination flourish to date. Cleaning tasks are typically assigned to Dalits. "Manual scavenging" is a euphemism for cleaning sewers and latrines by hand. Residential areas in rural India remain segregated along caste lines. Although urban India allows some anonymity of caste, dominant caste identities are only too apparent in caste-oriented surnames, like Sharma, Menon, Iyer, Gupta, and Kapur. These are just a few examples of caste-oriented surnames, not an exhaustive list. Dalit status is implied or presumed in lesser-known obscure surnames—or no surnames at all.
2. At the same time, not all SCs self-identify as Dalit because the literal meaning of the word Dalit (as "downtrodden") is considered demeaning and derogatory by some persons who might prefer to self-identity as SC or their specific caste categories and names. I have written about this elsewhere, in an opinion piece entitled "I Am Dalit, Not SC."

3. The following critiques are illustrative of several others that Baxi raises: Dworkin does not have an explicit theory of state (Baxi 562–63); there is an insufficient conception of democracy and the "normless ways in which minuscule citizens somehow become apex justices" (Baxi 565); Dworkin's corpus gives insufficient attention to "global economic constitutionalism" (567–69); it appears resolute in non-post-modernism (569–70); it is silent about "the conceptual distinction (or indistinction) between 'interpretation' and 'amendment' [of the constitution]" (578); and it is insufficient in its understanding of the "constitutional" and "social pasts" as it might apply to the "subaltern" and "the rightless people" (578–81).
4. Spivak "insists that the 'regulative political concepts' of the actually existing postcolonial constitutions are symptomatic of 'catachreses,' that is, 'concept-metaphors without an adequate historic referent' outside the 'supposedly authoritative narrative . . . in the social formations of Western Europe'" (Baxi 575). According to Baxi, "besides overlooking histories of the Indian struggle for independence and conceptions of equal concern, justice, and political decency," Spivak's general description of postcolonial constitutionalism as catachresis "also fails to note the ways in which justices need to enunciate 'preconditions of legitimate democracy'" (581).
5. Lutyens's Delhi is a lasting colonial legacy that marks the grandeur of the capital city of British India, with distinct architectural buildings, mansions, and sprawling gardens. My grandfather was placed in this colonial site and ironically it was in this heart of colonialism that he imbibed progressive values that allowed his daughter (who was to later become my mother) access to education.

## WORKS CITED

Anand, Utkarsh. "Government Objects to SC Empowering Third Gender." *The Indian Express*, 11 Sept. 2004, http://indianexpress.com/article/india/india-others/government-objects-to-sc-empowering-third-gender/. Accessed 23 May 2017.

*Arumugam Servai v. State of Tamil Nadu*. Supreme Court of India. 2011, http://123.63.242.116/devakkottai/Vimalavidya-SC_judgement-Suspend_SPs_Dt%20Collectors%20if%20fail%20to%20prevent%20atrocities%20agaibst%20SC%20ST.pdf. Accessed 23 May 2017.

Atrey, Shreya. "Through the Looking Glass of Intersectionality: Making Sense of Indian Discrimination Jurisprudence under Article 15." *The Equal Rights Review*, vol. 16, 2016, pp. 160–85.

Baudh, Sumit. "I Am Dalit, Not SC: Why Personal, Social and Political Self-Identification of Dalits Must Count More than the Legal Nomenclature." *Indian Express*, 6 Oct. 2016, http://indianexpress.com/article/opinion/columns/rohith-vemula-dalit-scheduled-caste-treatment-suicide-opinion-2998129/. Accessed 6 Oct. 2016.

———. "I am about to enter the Haus Khas Park . . . ." *Facebook*, 4 May 2015, https://www.facebook.com/photo.php?fbid=10153911477190942&set=a.464334640941.258583.626895941&type=1&theater. Accessed 27 June 2017.

Baxi, Upendra. "'A known but an indifferent judge': Situating Ronald Dworkin in Contemporary Indian Jurisprudence." *International Journal of Constitutional Law*, 2003, vol. 1, no. 4, pp. 557–89.

Bochenek, Michael, and Kyle Knight. "Establishing a Third Gender Category in Nepal: Process and Prognosis." *Emory International Law Review*, vol. 26, http://law.emory.edu/eilr/content/volume-26/issue-1/recent-developments/establishing-a-third-gender-in-nepal.html. Accessed 23 May 2017.

Carbado, Devon W. "Critical Race Studies: Race to the Bottom." *UCLA Law Review*, vol. 49, 2002, pp. 1283–313.

Chang, Robert. *Disoriented: Asian Americans, Law, and the Nation-State*. New York UP, 1999.

Express News Service. "Lok Sabha Votes Against Shashi Tharoor's Bill to Decriminalise Homosexuality. Again." *The Indian Express*, 12 Mar. 2016, http://indianexpress.com/article/india/india-news-india/decriminalising-homosexuality-lok-sabha-votes-against-shashi-tharoors-bill-again/. Accessed 23 May 2017.

Guru, Gopal, and Sundar Sarukkai. *The Cracked Mirror: An Indian Debate on Experience and Theory*. Oxford UP, 2012.

Haraway, Donna. "Situated Knowledges: The Science Question in Feminism and the Privilege of Partial Perspective." *Feminist Studies*, vol. 14, no. 3, Autumn 1988, pp. 575–99.

Harding, Sandra. "Rethinking Standpoint Epistemology: What Is 'Strong Objectivity?'" *The Centennial Review*, vol. 36, no. 3, Fall 1992, pp. 437–70.

Kannabiran, Kalpana. *Tools of Justice: Non-discrimination and the Indian Constitution*. Routledge, 2012.

*Khaki v. Rawalpindi. Sexual Orientation, Gender Identity, and Justice: A Comparative Law Casebook*. International Commission of Jurists, 2011, https://www.icj.org/sogicasebook/khaki-v-rawalpindi-supreme-court-of-pakistan-12-december-2009/. Accessed 23 May 2017.

Kiran, Usha. Personal interview. Translated by Shubha Chacko, India International Center, 6 Aug. 2014.

*Koushal v. Naz Foundation and Others*. Supreme Court of India. 2013, http://judis.nic.in/supremecourt/imgs1.aspx?filename=41070. Accessed 23 May 2017.

Matsuda, Mari J. "Looking to the Bottom: Critical Legal Studies and Reparations." *Harvard Civil Rights-Civil Liberties Law Review*, Spring 1987, pp. 1–55.

*National Legal Services Authority (NLSA) v. Union of India*. Supreme Court of India. 2014, http://judis.nic.in/supremecourt/imgs1.aspx?filename=41411. Accessed 23 May 2017.

*Naz Foundation v. Government of NCT Delhi*. High Court of Delhi. 2009, http://lobis.nic.in/ddir/dhc/APS/judgement/02-07-2009/APS02072009CW74552001.pdf. Accessed 23 May 2017.

Prasad, Reshma. Beyond the Gender Binary: Working with Genders and Sexualities Symposium Session. The 2nd Men Engage Global Symposium 2014, India Habitat Centre, New Delhi, India, 10–13 Nov. 2014.

Rodrigues, Valerian, editor. *The Essential Writings of B. R. Ambedkar*. Oxford UP, 2004.

Scott, Joan W. "Experience." *Feminists Theorize the Political*, edited by Judith Butler and Joan W. Scott, Routledge, 1992, pp. 22–40.

Singh, Chattrapati. "Dharmasastras and Contemporary Jurisprudence." *Journal of the Indian Law Institute*, vol. 32, no. 2, 1990, pp. 179–88.

Williams, Patricia. *The Alchemy of Race and Rights: Diary of a Law Professor*. Harvard UP, 1992.

# Out of India

# 12

# STORIES OF DALIT DIASPORA
## Migration, Life Narratives, and Caste in the US

SHWETA MAJUMDAR ADUR AND ANJANA NARAYAN

### INTRODUCTION

Nayyirah Waheed's poignant and visceral words "you broke the ocean in / half to be here. / only to meet nothing that wants you. —immigrant" (4) animate the lived realities of countless nameless and faceless immigrants whose struggles to exist and belong cross time and space. Every day and in myriad ways the diaspora has survived and performed the pain of leaving; some find home in their destinations while others endure the trauma of remaining perpetual foreigners; their narratives are rarely recorded and, when recited, easily overlooked. Yet they persevere and rise to tell their stories because stories, as Thenmozhi Soundararajan has reiterated, are "the most important unit of social change" especially for groups whose lives have appeared dispensable and less worthy of documenting ("Thenmozhi Soundararajan").

This paper focuses on the *story* of a similar group of immigrants—the Dalit diaspora in the US told through the narratives of three Dalit activists.[1] S. Kumar and B. Singh (names altered) are first-generation male immigrants while Thenmozhi Soundararajan is a second-generation woman and well-known Dalit feminist activist. The life narratives of these three people reveal experiences of Dalit migrants in the US who comprise the "new" stream out of India.[2]

Dalits' lives are rarely at the center of discussions of South Asian diaspora, and the dearth of scholarship on Dalit lives and activism in the US is a testament to that marginalization. As we demonstrate in this paper, this struggle to belong is multifaceted; as double minorities, their bid to assimilate is thwarted not only by racism in the mainstream US but also by casteism within their own ethnic communities. As a "diaspora within a diaspora," their alliances are multilayered and more nuanced than those of their "upper caste" coethnics whose voices are reified and lives mirrored in the ethnic culture they construct to recreate a "home away from home." By centering Dalit lives in the diaspora we specifically fill two crucial gaps in 1) South Asian American scholarship and 2) mainstream diaspora studies.

While prominent South Asian American scholars such as Bandana Purkayastha, Khyati Y. Joshi, Monisha Das Gupta, and Pawan Dhingra have produced prolific scholarship on questions of race, ethnicity, class, religion, gender, and intergenerational dynamics there is little that investigates the role of caste in diaspora even though caste has been a central unit of analysis in Indian scholarship due to the ubiquitous role caste politics have played in shaping the social dynamics of the subcontinent. Even when scholars like Namita Manohar and Anjali Gera Roy have studied the impact of caste in the US, they have typically focused on twice-born castes, such as the Patels and the Jats. Further, our study also contributes to an emerging branch of scholarship in diaspora studies. In earlier scholarship, "diaspora" has been treated as a homogenous whole, and studies have overwhelmingly documented negotiations with the host society. More recently, scholarship has been sensitive to the internal dynamics of belonging (for example, in *Unruly Immigrants*, Das Gupta examines the role of class, gender, and sexuality to the internal dynamics of belonging within the South Asian American diaspora).[3] Our paper builds on that branch by examining Dalits, who demonstrate a significant axis of marginalization within the Indian immigrant community in the US.

This paper is divided into three sections: section one provides a brief assessment of existing literature on diaspora and describes gaps in the study of diasporic lives; section two establishes the importance and contribution of life narratives in studying diasporic life; and section three focuses on describing the making of a Dalit diaspora and Dalit experiences and activism. In this final section we discuss the structural underpinnings of Dalit migration to the US, the multilayered negotiations with the broader ethnic community, and finally the activism that pushes back against marginalization. We conclude this paper with some observations about possible future directions in the study of Dalit lives in the US.

## I. CRITICAL PERSPECTIVES ON DIASPORA

For this essay, we primarily engage with the field of diaspora studies as an epistemological and empirical framework to understand better the Dalit diaspora in the US. The interdisciplinary work in diaspora studies that Homi K. Bhabha, Robin Cohen, James Clifford, Paul Gilroy, Stuart Hall, Khachig Tölölyan, and Steven Vertovec have produced provides important insights to explore the complex and multilayered identities of contemporary migrants whose lives span national boundaries. The term diaspora is derived from the Greek word *diaspeirein*, which means dispersion. While the historic conceptualization of diaspora that Stéphane Dufoix, Jana Evans Braziel and Anita Mannur, and Robin Cohen utilize speaks to the phenomenon of scattering of people like that of exiled Jews, scholars like Steven Vertovec continue to contest the term by broadening definitions of diaspora.

Drawing on the exile and dispersion of Jews, Benedict Anderson, Robin Cohen, and William Safran have embedded classical definitions of diaspora within the framework of a strong collective identity with emphasis on roots and a deep connection to the ancestral homeland. As Yasemin Nuhoglu Soysal highlights, "the dominant conceptualizations of diaspora presumptively accept the formation of tightly bounded communities and solidarities (on the basis of common cultural and ethnic references) between places of origin and arrival" (2). Rogers Brubaker identifies three core characteristics of diaspora: 1) geographical dispersion or scattering of people from a territory of origin to settlement in societies around the globe; 2) loyalty toward a real and imagined homeland and the idea of eventual return to the homeland; and 3) boundary maintenance, which means that diasporic groups resist total cultural assimilation and maintain a distinct identity which continues through successive generations (5–7). Similarly, Tölölyan argues that Jews form the archetypal diasporic group and the characteristics of a diaspora include "a culture and a collective identity that preserves elements of the homeland's language, or religious, social and cultural practice" (649). Finally, William Safran enumerates a series of qualities in his definition of the term diaspora in his seminal essay, "Diasporas in Modern Societies: Myths of Homeland and Return," where he describes groups who reside "outside the homeland" and "retain a collective memory, vision or myth about their original homeland" (83).

The second approach, named "the postmodern version of diaspora," challenges the centrality of the homeland in traditional definitions of diaspora (Anthias 560). According to Floya Anthias, the postmodern conceptualization of diaspora denotes "a condition rather than being descriptive of a group" (565). This version, upheld by scholars as diverse as Pnina Werbner, Stuart Hall, Paul Gilroy, James Clifford, Avtar Brah, Homi Bhabha, and Gloria Anzaldúa suggests that fixed and static notions of identity have been replaced by hybrid, syncretic, and fluid identities. Emphasizing heterogeneity and diversity, Cohen states that contemporary diasporas "bridge the gap between the individual and society, between the local and the global," blurring boundaries and syncretizing cultures (196). The postmodern perspective views hybridity and Gilroy's conception of double consciousness as distinctive attributes of postmodern diasporic communities because their identities are multifaceted, occupying multiple cultural and geographic spaces that include the homeland and countries of settlement.

The concept of transnationalism also addresses the growing debate among scholars about the relevance of essentialized notions of belonging. While Thomas Faist has argued about the distinction between transnationalism and diaspora, many migration scholars have used the terms interchangeably. Scholars like anthropologists Nina Glick Schiller, Linda Basch, and Cristina Szanton-Blanc, who discuss both diaspora and transnationalism in *Nations Abound*, argue that globalization causes technological advancements, massively increasing cross-border communications and exchanges while reducing the emotional distance between homeland and diasporic communities in the host society. The focus of contemporary transnational and diasporic literature has shifted from minority groups within nation-states to the ethnicity of groups within a global arena. Scholars like Peggy Levitt and Rafael de la Dehesa have begun to document how increasing numbers of groups are constructing lives spanning home and host countries to analyze ways in which technology aids this process and to examine how multiple nations attempt to incorporate migrants simultaneously. These scholars argue that ethnic identities are developed not solely in response to the structure of the host country but also with reference to the home country.

While these recent discussions on diaspora and transnationalism deconstruct and problematize the notion of homeland, Tariq Jazeel registers an essential but frequently neglected focus in diaspora studies when he emphasizes "how the diaspora experiences are embedded in the complexities of class, race, gender, generation and other social divisions" (19). It is important to acknowledge that diasporic communities are not homogenous entities but are characterized by enormous social, economic, cultural, and political diversity. According to Brah, members of diasporas occupy "differentiated, heterogeneous, contested spaces, even as they are implicated in the construction of a common 'we.'" She explains, "A multi-axial performative conception of power highlights the ways in which a group constituted as 'minority' along one dimension of differentiation may be constructed as a 'majority' along another" (189). In other words, the diasporic space must be understood through different axes of differentiation in terms of class, gender, race, sexual orientation, generation, and religion. Accordingly, we draw upon this theorization of diaspora to understand the complex positionality of Dalits who form a minority within the Indian diasporic space in the US. What are the experiences of Dalits in the diaspora? How have Dalits in the diaspora emphasized continuing caste discrimination in contemporary times?

Critics have also argued that surprisingly little attention has been paid to the gendered nature of diasporic experiences. Anthias questions an exclusive focus of diaspora studies on essentialist and primordialist approaches and calls for a concept of diaspora that pays full attention to the significance of gender. The academic scholarship on women in ethnic groups, including Naila Kabeer's *The Power to Choose: Bangladeshi Women and Labor Market Decisions in London and Dhaka*, has demonstrated how women in minority groups become subject to new controls that are reflective of their positions as racially marginalized groups in the West. Floya Anthias and Nira Yuval-Davis, along with Valentine M. Moghadam, have also argued that marginalized groups try to construct "affirming" identities to disengage from the identities assigned to them by the mainstream. This scholarship has demonstrated that women frequently become the sign and the marker of political goals, cultural identity, and signifiers of the collectivity's honor. Representations of women assume political significance, and certain images of women define and demarcate ethnic identity. However, diasporic literature has, as of yet, used few of these insights to assess if gender is a key component and, if it is, in what ways.[4] Accordingly, this paper explores the ways in which Dalit women comprehend their situations of marginality in the diaspora.

Finally, critics like Faiza Hirji, Russell King, and Anastasia Christou also note that the classical understandings of diaspora that William Safran and Robin Cohen put forth are not well suited to analyzing the experiences of second- and third-generation immigrants. According to Hirji, post-immigrant generations relate differently to their origin than do the first generation—at the same time, they appear to understand "what it means to be inhabitants of diaspora" (1). That is, despite not having gone through the dislocation and trauma that earlier kin suffered, most second- and third-generation immigrants feel a "sense of difference and an uncertainty in terms of belonging, that does gives them a diasporic consciousness" (3). Bandana Purkayastha's *Negotiating Ethnicity* and Purkayastha's coauthored text with Anjana Narayan, *Living Our Religions*, indicate that this "sense of not belonging" in mainstream societies together with the increasing global interconnectedness may fortify their commitment to diaspora. Drawing on this literature, our study also analyzes the experiences of second-generation Dalits in the US diaspora to understand how children of migrants navigate the complex intersections of caste, generational, and diasporic identities.

## II. LIFE NARRATIVES, MIGRATION, AND CASTE

This paper uses the methodological framework of narrative inquiry to study the Dalit diaspora in the US. While life narratives have earned prominence over the last several years as a powerful tool to document both Dalit oppression and agency, little attention has been paid to the analysis of Dalit narratives in the diaspora.[5] Using a narrative approach, we aim to unpack a diverse, layered, and nuanced perspective of Dalit migrants. Although this study examines the experiences of Dalits within the US, we adopt a transnational perspective to examine how Dalits position themselves across historical, social, and cultural contexts. Specifically, the narrative approach draws attention to barriers and opportunities that Dalit groups encounter in the US and explores how they voice their expressions of home and belonging. Our intent is to demonstrate the value of narrative analysis to examine how caste, race, nationality, class, culture, and age intersect to shape the way Dalit migrants make meaning of their social positioning in the US.

Previously, migration studies as a discipline was largely dominated by positivist scientific methods that reduced the experiences of migrants to a series of abstract variables and a priori assumptions.[6] The "narrative turn" in social sciences began in the 1980s, which led to a shift from objective and formulaic methods in migration research to methodological approaches that capture how migrants make sense of their lived experiences. The interdisciplinary field of narrative inquiry has largely been influenced by social-constructionist and interpretive paradigms such as phenomenology, ethnomethodology, symbolic interactionism, and feminism. As discussed in Catherine Kohler Riessman's *Narrative Methods for the Human Sciences*, narrative inquiry is an approach that pays attention to how people construct their understandings of social reality through the stories they tell about it.

The life narrative approach provides an excellent way to study contemporary migrants, as this method draws attention to lives that are woven through the histories, politics, and cultures of social location within transnational contexts. According to Ursula Apitzch and Irini Siouti, life narratives allow the recognition of a wide variety of spaces across countries of origin, settlement, and beyond, thereby offering an alternative way of looking at the migration process. They argue that it has proven particularly productive in overcoming the trap of "methodological nationalism" (576), which refers to the tendency to conceptualize social phenomena like migration around the boundaries of the nation-state.[7] Overall, narrative inquiry offers a unique methodological strategy to capture the growing complexity, heterogeneity, and dynamism of migration phenomena.

Within narrative research, the most widely adopted method of data collection consists of narrative biographical interviews, which are characterized by semistructured and in-depth conversations. These interviews allow for a more fluid interaction between the researcher and interviewees with the objective of gaining an empathetic understanding of their world. Life narrative interviews have also gained currency within migration research as a useful way of studying the transnational lives of migrants. For this project, we conducted two biographical life narrative interviews with Dalit leaders in the diaspora.

We also distilled a life narrative of a third Dalit leader in the diaspora from published materials and digital platforms such as websites and blogs by and about her.[8] Researchers like Ken Plummer increasingly recognize blogs or online personal journals as a rich source of qualitative data. Rebecca O'Connell and Julia Brannen contend that virtual spaces are "widely prevalent forms of knowledge and identity construction, largely personally narrated, concerned with everyday lives and with wide socioeconomic, cross-gender and intergenerational reach" (2). As G. Thomas Couser has said, digital forms of communication have opened up new platforms and audiences for life writing. Couser argues that online blogs are not constrained by traditional gatekeepers of publishing and have had a "powerfully democratizing effect on life writing" (13). Furthermore, as Carmela Bosangit, Juline Dulnuan, and Miguela Mena have stated, the anonymity and lack of researcher influence make the virtual platform an ideal space for people to narrate their personal experiences, thoughts, and opinions honestly and candidly. As Paul Longley Arthur claims, "whether they are perceived as exciting or threatening, these innovations open up opportunities for new biographical forms and understanding to emerge" (76). Overall, virtual platforms are altering how we view life narratives, making them a fluid and dynamic medium to capture the stories and lived experiences of people.[9]

Finally, we used brief stories reported in the news media as sources of data. Alexandra Georgakopalou argues that narrative inquiry has primarily focused on longer narratives such as biographical interviews and memoirs. She contends that researchers should consider small and fragmented stories such as those reported in online spaces and mainstream news platforms because they are part of what Elinor Ochs and Lisa Capps call "living narratives." According to Ochs and Capps, though living narratives are seemingly diverse and disjointed, they are part of everyday storytelling, conversations, and interactions, making them a rich source of data.

## III. DALIT DIASPORA IN THE US

### *THE "NEW" DALIT DIASPORA: DALIT MIGRANTS IN THE US*

In "Cataracts of Silence: Race on the Edge of Indian Thought," Vijay Prashad argues that "India's powerful independence movement (1885–1947) produced perhaps the world's most extensive system of affirmative action for oppressed peoples like the Dalits" (3). The mandated reservations in educational opportunities and jobs facilitated the emergence of an educated and upwardly mobile group of Dalits. Even though the sweeping changes and de jure protections did not lead to the end of casteism, they equipped and empowered Dalits to organize against the caste system and fight for their rights. Around the same time as the Dalit movement was picking up pace in

India, the US overturned its race-based immigration quotas through the Hart Cellar Act of 1965. This comprehensive act, also known as the Immigration and Nationality Act of 1965, explicitly prohibited discrimination on the basis of race, sex, and national origin and reversed the earlier limits on migration from Asian countries. The act represented a turning point for Indian migration to the US. While on the one hand the US postwar economy and the government's investment in expanding STEM-related fields created more opportunities than the US-born labor force could fill, on the other hand India, with a globally competitive yet highly subsidized higher-education system, was producing more high-skilled professionals than its own economy could viably absorb. Put together, the conditions coalesced to create a fortuitous pipeline responsible for the emigration of Indians to the US. For the educated Dalit elite, many of whom, according to Vivek Kumar, were "first generation literates and professionals," beneficiaries of the affirmative action policy, this also meant an opportunity of leaving behind the draconian caste system to live in a caste-free society (114). This dream was already discernible in Dalit leader B. R. Ambedkar's experience during his time as a student at Columbia University in New York City where he earned an MA in 1915 and a PhD in 1927. Famously, Ambedkar is said to have described his time in New York as his first experience of social equality ("Bhimrao Ambedkar"). The circumstances outlined marked the migration trajectories of a number of Dalit professionals in the US as well as the interviewees featured in this study. The following pages provide snapshots of the lives of the three interviewees, their migration histories to the US, and their occupations.

S. Kumar was born in a small town in North India, but with the aid of the new government programs and sheer determination he completed his MA from a prestigious university in Delhi before moving to an equally renowned school in the US to complete his PhD. At the time of the interview, he was employed as a faculty member in a US university. Yet his path to success was littered with painful reminders of an unequal birth and memories of being shunned by the twice-born Hindus, some of whom were figures of authority during his formative years. Speaking of one such incident, he describes the violence he endured at the hand of a teacher:

> When I was a student in India, higher-caste teachers used to put four pens [between my fingers] and squeeze my hand because my [hand]writing was good. I have gone through those kinds of experiences since my childhood, still I am standing and I am fighting for my community and I am doing my job.

The memory he describes proves that the de jure goodwill toward inclusion did not always translate into equality in everyday life. The recollection demonstrates an "upper caste" teacher's prejudice toward a "low caste" student and his inability to accept that a Dalit boy could have good handwriting. The punitive measures, such as putting pens between his fingers and squeezing them to presumably alter the shape of his fingers and thereby his handwriting, prove that de facto discrimination and violence continued to mark the lives of Dalits.

B. Singh remembers similar experiences. He, too, was born in a small town in India where he encountered and overcame numerous adversities to find his way to the US in the 1970s. He would often be reminded not to aim high and to remember his place in life. He says:

> When I was young, each step [in] my life I was told who I was. My identity was defined by somebody else. I was told that "you are a low caste, you are chamar, you are dalit, you are achyut [untouchable] you are a scheduled caste." And I said . . . what is this . . . I am not an equal with anybody else? I used to fight in the high school. My mother used to tell me we are lower caste.

B. R. Ambedkar's life and visionary contribution empowered both men to persevere and move beyond the limitations imposed on them by a society entrenched in caste bigotry. Recounting the indelible impact of Ambedkar in his life, B. Singh says, "I read the biography of Dr. Ambedkar and his biography was remarkable and I was looking for a role model for myself, somebody whose achievements I could copy." Later, after completing his MBBS from a premier institution in India, B. Singh moved to the US for further specialization. At the time of the interview, he was practicing medicine in the US.

Thenmozhi Soundararajan is a prominent Dalit rights activist and a second-generation Dalit immigrant born of Dalit doctors who migrated to the US in the 1970s also from a small town, though in Tamil Nadu.[10] Though she found out her caste when she was in fifth grade, Soundararajan describes herself as "coming out" as Dalit only in college. "Coming out," a phrase typically used by queer communities, refers to making one's authentic self known to the world, embracing and declaring an aspect of one's identity that is otherwise shamed and shunned by mainstream society. "Coming out," then, becomes a political and subversive act of reclaiming the self in its entirety. Soundararajan has collaborated with All Indian Dalit Women's Rights Forum to raise awareness about caste-based sexual violence against Dalit women ("Dalit Diva").

## *EVERYDAY LIVES IN THE US*

Dalits like S. Kumar and B. Singh have faced comparatively fewer stringent social norms against upward mobility in the US. India's caste system is inconsequential to the American mainstream. Dalits are unidentifiable from the other Indians, as caste identifiers such as last names and traditional occupation mean little to other Americans. Thus, in the US, Dalits are perceived and racialized simply as Indians. Yet within the coethnic community, negotiations are multilayered and complex. Immigrant coethnic communities and cultures develop as responses to racism in the mainstream; what is advanced as "authentic" Indian culture within these spaces is shorn of heterogeneity and is coded instead to reflect the voice of the dominant majority—which, as South Asian American scholars like Vijay Prashad (*Karma*), Monisha Das Gupta, and Shweta Majumdar Adur and Bandana Purkayastha demonstrate, is distilled through a Hindu, first-generation "upper caste" male point of view. Consequently, the tone of the hegemonic Indian cultural discourse—for migrant and postmigrant generations—becomes, implicitly even if not always explicitly, casteist (in addition to being patriarchal and elitist). While casteism can indeed exist and flourish in secular contexts, the growing dominance of Hindutva among Non-Resident Indians (NRIs) imbues the construction of Indian culture in significant ways. Prema A. Kurien, Arvind Rajagopal, and Anjana Narayan and Bandana Purkayastha have documented the presence of numerous organizations in the US that actively assert a "Hindu identity" imagined through the uncritical glorification of an "ancient India" steeped in Brahmanical Hindu values, resulting in the consequent downplaying, if not the disawoval, of the evils of the caste system. In other instances, caste becomes routinized in everyday performances of ethnic belonging and identity. Thenmozhi Soundararajan argues,

> For second-generation NRIs, flashing caste becomes a part of their cultural street cred with other communities. Some do it intentionally to elevate their identity while others operate from a misunderstanding of their own roots and blindly accept the symbols of their culture. Punjabi rappers throw down lyrics about being proud Jats. Tam-Brahms show off their sacred thread, recreate Thiruvayur in Cleveland, and learn Bharatanatyam while using their powerful networks to connect and succeed in the diaspora. ("Black Indians")

Similarly, speaking of the enduring legacy of caste in the diaspora, S. Kumar confirms:

> Here in North America we have people who don't practice caste system but there are some, but there are some people who still live in India though they live in America . . . they permanently live in India [in terms of mindset]. I hate to say they practice casteism or untouchability in North America.

These everyday experiences may vary from erasure, invisibility, or a lack of acknowledgment of the oppressive caste system, to outright experiences of caste discrimination centered on petty acts governed by the contingencies of purity and pollution. For example, as recently as 2015, the California State Board of Education sought to revise its curriculum for purposes of diversity to incorporate the history of South Asia. While the decision by the Board was an unprecedented move, it also laid bare the fractures within South Asian ethnic communities. The Hindu American Foundation (HAF) argued against the inclusion of casteism in the textbooks on the pretext that it was a negative portrayal of Hinduism and Hindu culture and would only fuel American stereotypes of Indians as being backward.[12] The desire to conceal centuries of repression and violence perpetrated against Dalits in the name of caste is tantamount to expunging the history of an entire community. HAF's move was rightfully met with vociferous protests by more progressive South Asian groups. In addition to demonstrating the friction within the community around questions of caste, this incident sheds light on the everyday lives of many in the diaspora. Consider, for example, S. Kumar's experience and his conversation with a second-generation Indian student:

> I gave her an assignment to find out about Dalit diaspora. After spending two weeks in the library she told me, "There is nothing on the Dalit diaspora, what can I do?" I said, "No, there is a lot of material and you have to find it." She came with the hypothesis that Dalits are not very professional or they don't represent professional backgrounds in North America. I asked why. She said, "*bechare woh to gareeb hai* [they are very poor]. After they come to North America they don't have money. They don't have power." And I said, "No, no, this is not true. There are Dalits who are professionals, who are engineers, doctors, you can find Dalits everywhere in every city." She said, "No, no, no, it's not true." When she insisted, I said, "There is one sitting in front of you." And she said, "*You*." . . . She burst into tears and said, "I can't imagine a Dalit can be a distinguished professor. This is a shock to me." I said, "This is not shocking and there are many people who have received education and are doing good jobs like others."

The student's misinformation about the absence of Dalits in the US or, specifically, her inability to conceive of the possibility that Dalits could occupy elite positions in the US demonstrates the stereotypes associated with Dalits and general lack of visibility of casteism in the US. Yet this lack of awareness among the second generation in part may also be indicative of the reluctance of some Dalit migrants who moved to the US to identify themselves as Dalits. To rid themselves of caste oppression, they may have intentionally distanced themselves from the institution by changing their names or passing as twice-born in the company of others. Alternatively viewed, this strategic move also results from the need to survive as a minority in an otherwise alien country wherein outing one's caste/Dalit identity impacts the level of support one receives from the coethnic community. Consider Thenmozhi Soundararajan's experience. In her blogs, she candidly remembers her parents' maneuverings around their Dalit identity and their desire to remain closeted for the fear of being ostracized by the Indian community. When she finally came out as a Dalit woman, she experienced the firsthand vitriol that her parents might have protected her from by simply "passing" as non-Dalits:

> Friends stopped talking to us. I had plates and utensils switched on me. I even received hate mail and death threats. . . . All of the Indian professors on campus were upper caste as well, and all, except one, refused to advise me on projects and blacklisted my work. I stopped getting invited to South Asian events. These are some of the structural manifestations of caste in the diaspora. ("What It Means")

Soundararajan's experience in the so-called liberal bastion of the academic ivory tower is not isolated. S. Kumar remembers a similar incident during his own doctoral studies:

> There was a professor when I was doing my PhD who came [to] realize that I come from [a] certain background . . . he told me clearly that I'll make sure that you don't go through. Luckily I was supported by my committee members and I got through and he was very disappointed.

Thus, in routine interpersonal negotiations silencing and disavowing caste become operative bases for survival for a significant portion of the diaspora in the US. For the hegemonic ethnic community (that mirrors the voices of the "upper caste"), concealing one's caste reveals a desire to be seen as less backward by the mainstream American society, and for many Dalits, like Soundararajan's parents, not revealing their caste identity offers a modicum of belonging to the hegemonic ethnic community in an otherwise alien country. Despite the pretenses of casting out caste, casteism insidiously shapes the workings of the ethnic community.

Perhaps nowhere are caste proscriptions more transparent than in intimate spaces. Consider matrimonial websites, which not only state caste preference but often break down into subcaste categories for closer matches. Commenting on the trend, S. Kumar says,

> When you see matrimonials in the US seeking bride or groom, they say "caste no bar except from Dalits or untouchables." What does that mean? Do they mean that Dalits are not human beings?

Clearly, caste is an important consideration when contracting marriages, and violent reprisals have been known to follow infractions. In 2007, a man was arrested on charges of killing his pregnant daughter, his son-in-law, and his three-year-old grandson. He set their apartment on fire to punish the daughter for what he perceived to be a "cultural slight"; his daughter had married without his approval and to someone of a "lower caste" (Davey).

While it is not known whether the daughter married a Dalit, the example shows how the caste system can survive migration.

### *DALIT ACTIVISM IN THE DIASPORA*

While many first-generation Dalit immigrants, like Soundararajan's parents, made a conscious decision to conceal their Dalit identities and assimilate into the dominant coethnic Indian community, others like B. Singh and S. Kumar refused to assimilate. Instead of leaving the fight behind, they invested themselves in social activism. S. Kumar was a Dalit activist even while he was a student in India and remembers his delight and surprise in finding a network of Dalit activists in the US. He says:

> When I came to the US I was eager to find Dalit activists. I was surprised to find out that there was a huge movement going on in the United States. I found that there were so many professionals who had an organization called VISION. The organization was headed by Dr. Shobha Singh and there are some activists in Washington DC, like Dr. Laxmi Berwa. He is a known physician of that area. There is a strong movement in the US, not only in the US but all over North America.

As we detail below, Dalit activists in the US contribute to networks of Dalits in two main ways. First, by founding and investing in Dalit spaces and communities in the US, they have created alternative networks of support. The Ravi Dassi network, followers of Guru Ravidas, which we detail below, is one such platform. Second, by using global media platforms, Dalit activists have advanced their movement for rights beyond the confines of the nation-state. With multipronged activism, they have pushed back against casteist politics, especially that of the Hindu Right in the diaspora, while simultaneously raising awareness on the global stage about the human rights violations that Dalits endured in India. Vivek Kumar writes that the politically conscious New Dalit Diaspora has also "influenced politically subdued 'old' dalit diaspora as well" (114).

The Ravi Das temples have opened up an indomitable space of support for Dalits and Dalit rights in the US. With a global presence and approximately fifteen temples in North America, Ravi Dassis have done it all—from everyday mundane acts of support (such as offering a newly arrived immigrant food and a place to sleep) to organizing politically against casteism and untouchability.

The rise of the information economy and the resultant space-time compression in disseminating news of rampant caste-based violence in India—the homicides, rapes, and beatings—have connected aggrieved activists and allies in the diaspora. For example, as mentioned earlier, diasporic Dalits led by Shobha Singh formed Volunteers in Service to India's Oppressed and

Neglected (VISION) in 1975. Over the years, Dalit activists have staged multiple protests in major cities of the US. B. Singh remembers:

> Families and friends from California, New Jersey, and New York area came together, and we protested when Ms. Indira Gandhi was visiting President Reagan. We met K. R. Narayan, the ambassador, and asked to meet Ms. Gandhi to express our concern about the killings of Dalits in Bihar and many other parts of India. But we were not given an opportunity to express our concerns. So we protested in front of the White House.

Peaceful protests became a way to raise awareness and discredit Indian dignitaries who uncritically endorse the urban IT economy of India as its success story. Civil protests against these double standards are a reminder to Western audiences and the upwardly mobile Indian immigrants that, as B. Singh says:

> There is slavery in the largest democracy in the world; we have a shining India campaign by BJP government; we export the highest number of software engineers. But you go to rural India, untouchability is still practiced. The upper caste have their separate teacups; lower castes have separate wells. Even in my home town of [name removed] there is big water tank which says "tank for harijans." We are living in the twenty-first century or in the eighteenth-century medieval times?

More recently, in September 2015, Dalit activists protested India's Prime Minister, Narendra Modi's, visit to the US. A month before that, noted US scholars engaged in South Asian studies circulated a petition expressing their concern over the "uncritical fanfare being generated" over his visit given that Modi's electoral platform was mired in allegations of vitriolic Hindu fundamentalism and Islamophobia that threatened both religious and caste minorities in India ("Faculty Statement").

Since the 1990s, liberalization of the Indian economy has amplified the political importance of supranational institutions of governance, such as the UN, the World Bank, and the IMF. Concomitantly, these transnational spaces have also become crucial sites for Dalit activism. The first international conference of Dalits was held in Malaysia in October 1998. Since then, the Dalit issue has slowly become a reckonable force at the level of the UN and the European Union. The participation of Dalit activists in the United Nations World Conference Against Racism, held in Durban, South Africa in 2001 (WCAR 2001), was a major turning point in Dalit transnational activism. For a Western audience, Dalit activists have raised consciousness about the reprehensible treatment meted out to them by using the language of human rights and by equating casteism to racism—a frame useful in conveying an otherwise "local" issue to the "global" audience.[13] Though both interview participants recognized the similarities as well as differences between racism and casteism, they regarded an equation between the two salient to contemporary transnational justice movements. Both emphatically argued that casteism is worse than racism. Illustrating his notion, B. Singh says:

> In America a black woman used to breastfeed a white infant. They used to clean and maintain the house, maintain laundry . . . but the Dalits in India are not allowed to even come close to upper caste. The Dalits of Peshawa in Pune have to carry a broom on their backs so that they clean the place of any pollution that they may create . . . yet again, when you have two tumbler system, you have two graveyards, two temples, two waterwells . . . when your barber refuses to cut your hair it is nothing but racism.

In the US, Dalit activists have also been vocal about alliances with other people of color. In doing so, they set themselves apart from the dominant Indian American ethnic community, especially the first-generation immigrants who have characteristically remained aloof from progressive race-based politics and have gone out of their way to repudiate any similarities with Black people in hopes of capitalizing on their model-minority status.[14] Even at its outset, VISION, which was formed by first-generation Dalit immigrants of the 70s, aligned with the Black Panthers and proudly became a sign of Black and Dalit unity, while the conservative Indian American hegemony remained invested in the rhetoric of the model minority. The progressive alliances endure as second-generation Soundararajan demonstrates: "I found my home within other communities of colour—women from these communities welcomed my experience and we found sisterhood in our shared intersections of sorrow" ("What It Means"). The participation of Dalit women in Incite's Color of Violence 4 Conference 2015 testifies to the presence of transnational feminist alliances. Thus Dalit activism in the US contests Dalit marginalization in multiple spaces and demonstrates a worldview that is distinct from "upper caste" Indian immigrants in the US.

## CONCLUSION

Despite their upper-class, seemingly assimilated lives, Dalit immigrants in the US continue to remain on the fringes of dominant and conservative Indian American culture. To many this marginalization is a painful reminder that culture—the good and the bad—moves with immigrants. While some migrants (in this case, the "upper caste" immigrants) seek to recreate and maintain caste hierarchies with a mixture of nostalgia and longing, others—like Dalits—wear it as an albatross around their necks, waiting to free themselves from its oppressive weight. Indeed, Dalits have pushed back. In their refusal to be erased and forgotten, they push back to demand that wrongs be righted, and they push back by reaching out to their less privileged community—Dalits in India and elsewhere—across the seas.

Based on this study we can make two interrelated arguments about the use of diaspora as a theoretical framework. First, the narratives of Dalit migrants in the US suggest that diaspora as a conceptual framework needs to take into consideration the more fluid and complex identities that characterize today's migrants. We argue that beyond the recognition of homeland connections, diaspora as a framework needs to take into account power inequalities and gendered, racialized hierarchies that shape the lives of diasporic groups in host societies as well. By shifting the emphasis in diaspora studies away from the homeland, we can begin to understand the experiences of second- and third-generation Dalits as racialized minorities in countries like the US, where there is a widespread lack of understanding of caste practices.

We also draw two sets of conclusions on the use of life narratives to study the lives of Dalit immigrants in the US. Sociologist C. Wright Mills uses the term "sociological imagination" to argue that "neither the life of an individual nor the history of a society can be understood without understanding both" (5). Mill's main point is that a person's biography provides an insight into broader sociohistorical realities. He argues that larger structural forces and individual agency are inextricably linked, and as researchers, seeing the connections between the individual and the social is important.

Life narratives provided us the ideal tool to exercise our sociological imagination by demonstrating how the personal stories of Dalit migrants offer us a window into the historical, political, social, and transnational contexts that shape their lived experiences. Second, the use of life narratives as a methodological tool also enabled us to do justice to the diversity and multiplicity of identities within the Dalit diaspora. Specifically, the use of alternative data sources such as virtual blogs and online news stories allowed us to document experiences of Dalit women and postimmigrant-generation Dalits in the US, whose voices are often hard to access through conventional biographical interviews. The virtual data helped demonstrate how marginalized groups like Dalits use cyberspace not only to speak openly about issues important to them but also to mobilize support for members of their communities.

## NOTES

1. See the editors' introduction to this volume, which includes a more detailed note on caste and the caste system in India (Shankar and Gupta).
2. Vivek Kumar divides the Dalit diaspora into two streams. The "Old Dalit Diaspora" refers to the movement of indentured laborers to service the plantation economy during the colonial era while the "New" comprises the migration approximately

after World War II to countries such as the US, UK, and Australia. Here we focus on the Dalit diaspora located in the US.

3. See also Brah; Manekar.
4. See also Yuval-Davis.
5. See Charu and Shankar; Ganguli.
6. See Iosifides and Sporton; Apitzch and Siouti.
7. See Wimmer and Glick Schiller; Levitt and Khagram.
8. Indian American Dalit activist Thenmozhi Soundararajan created www.dalitwomenfight.com to document stories of human rights violations against Dalit women. She is also the author of the blog *Dalit Nation*, which provides a platform for both her own writings as well as work of other Dalit scholars and activists.
9. See Plummer.
10. Her name has not been altered because the narrative we assess here has been distilled from writings by and about and interviews with Soundararajan that are already available online.
11. See Golden; Shankar.
12. For more on this framing, see Majumdar, which was published before the author took on the surname Adur.
13. See Prashad, *Karma of Brown Folk*.

## WORKS CITED

Adur, Shweta Majumdar, and Bandana Purkayastha. "On the Edges of Belonging: Indian American Dalits, Queers, Guest Workers and Questions of Ethnic Belonging." *Journal of Intercultural Studies*, vol. 34, no. 4, 2013, pp. 418–30.

Anderson, Benedict. *Imagined Communities: Reflections on the Origin and Spread of Nationalism*. Verso, 1983.

Anthias, Floya. "Evaluating 'Diaspora': Beyond Ethnicity?" *Sociology*, vol. 32, no. 3, 1998, pp. 557–80.

Anthias, Floya, and Nira Yuval-Davis. *Woman-Nation-State*. Macmillan, 1989.

Anzaldúa, Gloria. *Borderlands/La Frontera: The New Mestiza*. Aunt Lute Books, 1987.

Apitzsch, Ursula, and Irini Siouti. "Biographical Analysis as an Interdisciplinary Research Perspective in the Field of Migration Studies." *Research Integration*, 2007, https://www.york.ac.uk/res/researchintegration/Integrative_Research_Methods/Apitzsch%20Biographical%20Analysis%20April%202007.pdf. Accessed 15 Oct. 2016.

Arthur, Paul Longley. "Digital Biography: Capturing Lives Online." *a/b: Auto/Biography Studies*, vol. 24, no. 1, 2009, pp. 74–92.

Bhabha, Homi K. *The Location of Culture*. Routledge, 1994.

"Bhimrao Ambedkar." *Columbia250*. Jan. 2004, http://c250.columbia.edu/c250_celebrates/remarkable_columbians/bhimrao_ambedkar.html. Accessed 3 Mar. 2017.

Bosangit, Carmela, Juline Dulnuan, and Miguela Mena. "Using Travel Blogs to Examine the Postconsumption Behavior of Tourists." *Journal of Vacation Marketing*, vol. 18, no. 3, 2012, pp. 207–19.

Brah, Avtar. *Cartographies of Diaspora: Contesting Identities*. Routledge, 1996.

Braziel, Jana Evans, and Anita Mannur. "Nation, Migration, Globalization: Points of Contention in Diaspora Studies." *Theorizing Diaspora: A Reader*, edited by Jana Evans Braziel and Anita Mannur, Wiley Blackwell, 2006, pp. 1–22.

Brubaker, Rogers. "The 'Diaspora' Diaspora." *Ethnic and Racial Studies*, vol. 28, no. 1, Jan. 2005, pp. 1–19.

Clifford, James. "Diasporas." *Cultural Anthropology*, vol. 9, no. 3, Aug. 1994, pp. 302–38.

Cohen, Robin. *Global Diasporas: An Introduction*. U of Washington P, 1997.

Couser, G. Thomas. *Signifying Bodies: Disability in Contemporary Life Writing*. U of Michigan P, 2009.

"Dalit Diva." *Rauschenberg Foundation*. N.d., http://www.rauschenbergfoundation.org/grants/dalit-diva. Accessed 3 Mar. 2017.

Das Gupta, Monisha. *Unruly Immigrants: Rights, Activism, and Transnational South Asian Politics in the United States*. Duke UP, 2006.

Davey, Monica. "Father Says He Set Fire That Killed Three." *New York Times*, 3 Jan. 2008, https://nyti.ms/2m9kAS8. Accessed 26 Jan. 2017.

Dhingra, Pawan. "Hospitable to Others: Indian American Motel Owners Create Boundaries and Belonging in the Heartland." *Ethnic and Racial Studies*, vol. 33, no. 6, 2010, pp. 1088–107.

Dufoix, Stéphane. *Diasporas*. Translated by William Rodamor, U of California P, 2008.

"Faculty Statement over Narendra Modi Visit to Silicon Valley." *Academe Blog*, https://academeblog.org/2015/08/27/faculty-statement-on-modi-visit-to-silicon-valley/. Accessed 19 May 2017.

Faist, Thomas. "Diaspora and Transnationalism: What Kind of Dance Partners?" *Diaspora and Transnationalism: Concepts, Theories and Methods*, edited by Rainer Bauböck and Thomas Faist, Amsterdam UP, 2010, pp. 9–34.

Ganguli, Debjani. "Pain, Personhood, and the Collective: Dalit Life Narratives." *Asian Studies Review*, vol. 33, no. 4, Dec. 2009, pp. 429–42.

Georgakopoulou, Alexandra. *Small Stories, Interaction and Identities*. John Benjamins Publishing Company, 2007.

Gilroy, Paul. *There Ain't No Black in the Union Jack: The Cultural Politics of Race and Nation*. U of Chicago P, 1989.

Glick Schiller, Nina, Linda Basch, and Cristina Szanton-Blanc. "From Immigrant to Transmigrant: Theorizing Transnational Migration." *Anthropological Quarterly*, vol. 68, no. 1, Jan. 1995, pp. 48–63.

———. *Nations Unbound: Transnational Projects, Postcolonial Predicaments, and Deterritorialized Nation-States*. Routledge, 1994.

Golden, Daniel. "New Battleground in Textbook Wars: Religion in History." *The Wall*

*Street Journal*, 25 Jan. 2006, http://wsj.com/articles/SB113815619665855532. Accessed 26 Jan. 2017.

Hall, Stuart. "Cultural Identity and the Diaspora." *Identity: Community, Culture, Difference*, edited by Jonathan Rutherford, Lawrence and Wishart, 1990, pp. 222–37.

Hirji, Faiza. "The Next Generation: Diaspora, Youth and Identity Construction." *Surrey*, June 2009, https://www.surrey.ac.uk/cronem/files/conf2009papers/Hirji.pdf. Accessed 20 Jan. 2017.

Iosifides, Theodoros, and Deborah Sporton. "Biographical Migration Research." *Migration Letters*, vol. 6, no. 2, 2009, pp. 175–82.

Jazeel, Tariq. "Postcolonial Geographies of Privilege: Diaspora Space, the Politics of Personhood and the 'Sri Lankan Women's Association in the UK.'" *Transactions of the Institute of British Geographers*, vol. 31, no. 1, Mar. 2006, pp. 19–33.

Joshi, Khyati Y. *New Roots in America's Sacred Ground: Religion, Race, and Ethnicity in Indian America*. Rutgers UP, 2006.

Kabeer, Naila. *The Power to Choose: Bangladeshi Women and Labor Market Decisions in London and Dhaka*. Verso, 2002.

King, Russell, and Anastasia Christou. "Cultural Geographies of Counter-Diasporic Migration: Perspectives from the Study of Second-Generation 'Returnees' to Greece." *Population, Space and Place*, vol. 16, no. 2, Mar./Apr. 2010, pp. 103–19.

Kumar, S. Personal interview. 2006.

Kumar, Vivek. "Understanding Dalit Diaspora." *Economic and Political Weekly*, vol. 39, no. 1, Jan. 2004, pp. 114–16.

Kurien, Prema A. "Being Young, Brown, and Hindu: The Identity Struggles of Second-Generation Indian Americans." *Journal of Contemporary Ethnography*, vol. 34, no. 4, 2005, pp. 434–69.

Levitt, Peggy, and Rafael de la Dehesa. "Transnational Migration and the Redefinition of the State: Variations and Explanations." *Ethnic and Racial Studies*, vol. 26, no. 4, 2003, pp. 587–611.

Levitt, Peggy, and Sanjeev Khagram, editors. *The Transnational Studies Reader: Intersections and Innovations*. Routledge, 2007.

Majumdar, Manekar, Purnima. "Off-Center: Feminism and South Asian Studies in the Diaspora." *At Home in Diaspora*, edited by Jackie Assayag and Véronique B'énéï, Indiana UP, 2003, pp. 52–65.

Majumdar, Shweta. "Challenging the Master Frame through Dalit Organizing in the United States." *Living Our Religions: Hindu and Muslim South Asian-American Women Narrate Their Experiences*, edited by Anjana Narayan and Bandana Purkayastha, Kumarian Books, 2009, pp. 265–80.

Manohar, Namita. "'Sshh . . . !! Don't Tell My Parents': Dating among Second-Generation Patels in Florida." *Journal of Comparative Family Studies*, vol. 39, no. 4, Autumn 2008, pp. 571–88.

Mills, C. Wright. *The Sociological Imagination*. Oxford UP, 1959.

Moghadam, Valentine M., editor. *Identity Politics and Women: Cultural Reassertions and Feminisms from an International Perspective*. Westview Press, 2004.

Narayan, Anjana, and Bandana Purkayastha, editors. *Living Our Religions: Hindu and Muslim South Asian-American Women Narrate Their Experiences*. Kumarian Press, 2009.

Ochs, Elinor, and Lisa Capps. *Living Narrative: Creating Lives in Everyday Storytelling*. Harvard UP, 2002.

O'Connell, Rebecca, and Julia Brannen. "Children's Food, Power and Control: Negotiations in Families with Younger Children in England." *Childhood*, vol. 21, no. 1, 2014, pp. 87–102.

Plummer, Ken. *Documents of Life 2: An Invitation to a Critical Humanism*. 2nd ed., Sage Publishing, 2001.

Prashad, Vijay. "Cataracts of Silence: Race on the Edge of Indian Thought." United Nations Research Institute for Social Development Conference on Racism and Public Policy, 5 Sept. 2001, Durban, South Africa, http://www.unrisd.org/80256B3C005BCCF9/(httpAuxPages)/60C50AEDD6AEE2CE80256B6D00578609/$file/dprashad.pdf. Accessed 1 Sept. 2016.

———. *The Karma of Brown Folk*. U of Minnesota P, 2001.

Purkayastha, Bandana. *Negotiating Ethnicity: Second-Generation South Asian Americans Traverse a Transnational World*. Rutgers UP, 2005.

Rajagopal, Arvind. "Hindu Nationalism in the US: Changing Configurations of Political Practice." *Ethnic and Racial Studies*, vol. 23, no. 3, 2000, pp. 467–96.

Riessman, Catherine Kohler. *Narrative Methods for the Human Sciences*. Sage Publishing, 2008.

Roy, Anjali Gera. "Celebrating 'The Sons of Jat': The Return of Tribes in the Global Village." *South Asian Diaspora*, vol. 3, no. 1, 2011, pp. 89–102.

Safran, William. "Diasporas in Modern Societies: Myths of Homeland and Return." *Diaspora: A Journal of Transnational Studies*, vol. 1, no. 1, Spring 1991, pp. 83–99.

Shankar, S. "Being Hindu in America: An Atheist's Perspective on the California Textbook Controversy." *S. Shankar: Writer*, 11 May 2016, https://sshankar.net/2016/05/11/being-hindu-in-america-an-atheists-perspective-on-the-california-textbook-controversy/. Accessed 26 Jan. 2017.

Shankar, S., and Charu Gupta. "'My Birth Is My Fatal Accident': Introduction to Caste and Life Narratives." *Caste and Life Narratives*, ed. S. Shankar and Charu Gupta, Primus Books, 2019, pp. 1–15.

Singh, B. Personal interview. 2006.

Soundararajan, Thenmozhi. "The Black Indians: Growing up Dalit in the US, Finding Your Roots, Fighting for Your Identity." *Outlook India*, 20 Aug. 2012, http://www.outlookindia.com/magazine/story/the-black-indians/281938. Accessed 29 Jan. 2017.

———. "What It Means to be an 'Untouchable' in 2017: How a Dalit Woman Came to Accept Her Identity, and Then Embrace It." *Elle India*, 29 July 2014, http://elle.in/magazine/still-i-rise/. Accessed 29 Jan. 2017.

Soysal, Yasemin Nuhoglu. "Citizenship and Identity: Living in Diasporas in Post-War Europe?" *Ethnic and Racial Studies*, vol. 23, no. 1, 2000, pp. 1–15.

"Thenmozhi Soundararajan." *A Room of Her Own Foundation*, n.d., http://aroomofherownfoundation.org/thenmozhi-soundararajan/. Accessed 24 May 2017.

Tölölyan, Khachig. "Rethinking Diaspora(s): Stateless Power in the Transnational Moment." *Diaspora: A Journal of Transnational Studies*, vol. 5, no. 1, Spring 1996, pp. 3–36.

Vertovec, Steven. "Three Meanings of 'Diaspora,' Exemplified among South Asian Religions." *Diaspora: A Journal of Transnational Studies*, vol. 6, no. 3, Winter 1997, pp. 277–99.

Waheed, Nayyirah. *Salt.* Kindle ed., CreateSpace Independent Publishing Platform, 2013.

Werbner, Pnina. "Introduction: The Materiality of Diaspora—Between Aesthetic and 'Real' Politics." *Diaspora: A Journal of Transnational Studies*, vol. 9, no. 1, Spring 2000, pp. 5–20.

Wimmer, Andreas, and Nina Glick Schiller. "Methodological Nationalism, the Social Science and the Study of Migration: An Essay in Historical Epistemology." *The International Migration Review*, vol. 37, no. 3, pp. 576–610.

Yuval-Davis, Nira. *Gender & Nation.* Sage Publishing, 1997.

# 13

## CASTE IN JAPAN
## The Burakumin

JUNE A. GORDON

The narrow street is lined with people squatting on small stools tending steaming pots of boiled innards; behind them hang hunks of raw meat. Children joyfully run loose, kicking up dust as they shuffle back and forth, hiding in between the crevasses of the wooden walls that demarcate one space from another. Weaving in and out of upturned bicycles, plastic furniture, and odd wares for sale, dodging adult cries to calm down, are the mischievous faces of youth, testing their limits. While I am a stranger in this community, we muster little attention because my host, Professor Hideo Aoki, is known in the area, a longstanding human rights advocate and scholar and, more importantly, a trusted friend. To him a nod is offered, a greeting, a smile, or a brief wave of the hand. This is a community unlike most others in contemporary Japan. Here there is interaction and open communication, a village within an urban space. While all the stereotypes of a *buraku* that are common in Japan are confirmed within a few blocks of our route, within this space they take on a different meaning. How can laughter and cries of contestation across a dusty city street be viewed as vulgar and non-Japanese? How can suppression of feelings, emotions, and thoughts be seen as more acceptable? Do the Burakumin, people of the *buraku*, in fact represent an echoing back to a traditional Japanese past when the distinction between *tatemae* (what is displayed) and *honne* (what is felt) was not so rigidly enforced?

Hiroshima's *buraku* neighborhood of around six thousand members has been transformed over the past twenty years from a slum of rundown shacks into respectable newer housing, thanks to the pressure exerted on the government by the Buraku Liberation League, the principal organization for advancing the cause of the Burakumin since the end of the Asia-Pacific war. The area has become far more diverse in the process, not only because it lies next to the local Korean community and public housing for victims of the A-bomb, but also due to the influx of newly arrived immigrants, in particular the Chinese. Resting alongside the river and newly developed park, the community buzzes as people move in and out of small shops and eating places. The leather factory is now gone, along with many jobs, though the meat industry still thrives, providing a good living for individuals well positioned in the local hierarchy. Older people who live in the neighborhood tend to stay within its confines. As a result, it is difficult to measure accurately the changes in the degree of discrimination, since contact with the outer world is limited. A Buddhist temple in disarray stands as testimony to one priest's attempt to lift the community and fight discrimination from the prewar days. Now abandoned, it quietly bids the visitor to enter.

As a white female *gaijin* conducting research in Japan, I brought both personal and professional perspectives to a study of the Burakumin. My prior work with racial minorities in the US, as well as with working-class and non-working communities in the UK,[1] created an expectation that extending this research to Japan would take me into the low-income and troubled schools of urban Japan.[2] What I didn't realize at that time, even though I had lived and worked in Japan prior to this research, was that the people of Japan equated low-income status with the Burakumin (where *buraku* is equated with hamlet or village; and *min* is equated with people). While my awareness of "low-caste" communities in Japan was limited, I knew that there were Japanese who struggled both economically and educationally who did not identify as Burakumin. When I discussed this apparent conundrum with my Japanese colleagues, it became clear that the majority of Japanese cling passionately to the view of themselves as middle class, an identity shaped by the contrast between prewar and postwar conditions. By relegating Burakumin to an outcaste status, meaning that the discrimination they face is based on inherited status outside of the four traditional Confucian caste labels (samurai, farmers, artisans, merchants), other Japanese absolve themselves of holding to prewar social hierarchies and inequalities. The caste system goes back hundreds of years to the Edo period (1603–1867) when one's status was defined not by money but by birth, which could not be altered. At the end of WWII, liberation came in many forms but it did not remove the harsh, inequitable conditions of most Burakumin, which tainted the image of modern Japan. By not acknowledging the existence of the Burakumin, Japanese were able to continue to believe themselves to be middle class or class-less.

In accepting the advice of my colleagues to focus on the Burakumin, I quickly became aware that I was moving into a space, both psychological and physical, that few people know much about and that is claimed as a "taboo" topic of conversation, not to mention as a topic of research. Over the next five years of fieldwork on schooling, immigration, and changing attitudes toward teachers in Japan,[3] the study of Burakumin became the major narrative of my professional life. Since I could not directly experience the lives of the people in the *buraku*, I relied on teachers, community leaders, and fellow scholars for introductions to schools, teachers, organizations, and neighborhoods that engaged children stigmatized by Burakumin identity.[4] In the process, my professional life joined with the scholars and activists of postwar Japan who had devoted and risked their careers to the amelioration of caste discrimination in their nation. The resulting work presented here combines the lives of the Burakumin, the work of teachers, activists, scholars, and my own experience in Japan.

## HISTORICAL CONTEXT

While most writing on caste emanates from South Asia, my research explores caste in Japan as expressed in the lives of those known as the Burakumin, Japanese citizens who for generations have lived as outcastes based on the professions and neighborhoods of their presumed ancestors.[5] Modern Burakumin history must be viewed in four broad eras: prewar (1920–40s), early postwar (1945–1960s), the antidiscrimination movement (1969–2002), and post-Special Measures (2002–present).

Prewar Japan saw the development of progressive efforts to address discrimination against the Burakumin. However, due to the fascist government's need to focus on national solidarity during military expansion, leftist groups attempting to address particular social problems, such as the housing, health, and educational deficiencies in *buraku* areas, were outlawed.[6] Early postwar Japan brought US occupation but also the liberalization of unions, voting rights for women, and a resurgence of social movements. One of these movements, led by a broad coalition of activists, focused on social inequalities and in particular the Burakumin.[7] The Buraku Liberation League (BLL) pressured the government not only to acknowledge the plight of the Burakumin but to find ways to compensate them for historical degradation. Such compensation came in the form of the Special Measures, an antidiscrimination program that lasted from 1969 to 2002, and included educational efforts to increase support and success for youth living in various *buraku* communities throughout Japan.[8] Dōwa Kyōiku, as it was called, took the form of what might be considered affirmative action in that additional teachers were sent to *dowa* schools, students were provided with extracurricular education, and resources were increased. However, in 2002 the national government officially terminated the Special Measures and announced that discrimination no longer existed; the "problem" of the Burakumin had been solved. In reality, due to numerous outside pressures, the programs and special services offered to the Burakumin were now to be expanded to include women, Korean Zainichi, those with disabilities, immigrants and other minorities. The Burakumin were now subsumed within the more inclusive human rights, or Jinken movement, in order to appease the demands of other marginalized groups while still allowing the BLL to remain a dominant voice in advancing human rights in Japan.[9]

## WHO ARE THE BURAKUMIN?

During Japan's long history of nation-building, various individuals and families lived on the margins of society due to their social standing, occupations, or location.[10] These people served the essential interests of the host society by carrying out undesirable tasks and performing services considered demeaning and/or polluting, such as animal butchering, human burial, and gardening, as well as waste removal and guard duty. Families who lived in certain areas were assigned to this work and came to be identified with the labor that was viewed as contaminated; they were called the *eta* (impure), a term replaced in postwar Japan by the term Burakumin, which I use throughout this paper.

Organized along a traditional hierarchy with an elder, or head chieftain, in charge of claiming rights to certain trades and involved in internal policing of the group, Burakumin had a degree of autonomy and protection as long as they accepted their outcaste status. They were not marginal in the sense of being dispensable; they were valued and necessary contributors to society, doing work that was essential for the functioning of Japan's villages and towns. Other groups, such as itinerate performers, beggars, and prostitutes were known as *hinin* (nonhuman). These two major groups, the *eta* and *hinin*, were combined in various ways and at various points in time to constitute what has been viewed by many as outcaste, meaning that they operated outside the traditional hierarchy of warriors (samurai), farmers, artisans, and merchants. At varying points in time, the nobility, centered in the imperial court, or the Shogunate, a ruling military regime, ruled over the system and saw to its enforcement.

During the eighth to twelfth centuries Japan's outcastes formed a category called *senmin*, or "lowly people," and were not allowed to intermarry with *ryōmin*, the "good people," within the Confucian hierarchy. Still, some *senmin* were able to move out of stigmatized labor into farming or other skilled trades as power shifted between feudal warlords. While previously a rather fluid group of individuals whose status depended on demand for services and the political necessities of the period, the relative calm and tightening hold of the Tokugawa regime (the Shogunate period, 1603–1867) increasingly fixed and legitimated their marginal status and segregated habitat. Shintoism provided further justification for discrimination insofar as it prohibited contact with the unclean, including the diseased, the dead, and women during childbirth. Buddhism followed with prohibitions against the slaughtering and eating of animals. Segregated Buddhist temples and Shinto shrines were set aside for outcastes and reinforced their difference. Caste distinctions were expressed in costume, hair styles, footwear, and, most famously, in the two swords of the samurai that could be used against the lower castes with impunity.

With the Meiji restoration of the imperial dynasty (1867–1889), a new national government created the concept of a national citizenry, legally eliminating the caste system. The obvious embarrassment of a caste-like minority group within a modern nation, as well as the desire for the new government to eliminate any intermediate contenders for power, such as the elder chieftains, led to the official emancipation of the *eta* and *hinin* and resulted in their new designation as Shinheimin, or "new commoners" in 1871. However, the unofficial social standing of the Shinheimin did not change; local custom dictated a continuation of their traditional tasks as the proper livelihood of the "new commoners." While primarily identified by separate neighborhoods and villages to which they were restricted, the people who have come to be known euphemistically as Burakumin continued to dominate the work of butchering, leather making, sanitation, and refuse collection. Living in isolated communities, often along riverbanks or on undesirable land, the Burakumin developed some degree of identifiable diets, manners, dialects, and local loyalties different from their commoner neighbors who resented the emancipation of the Burakumin. Resentment turned to mindless violence in several cases following the Emancipation Edict, resulting in protests and, in a few incidences, the burning of Burakumin villages.

While discrimination toward the Burakumin previously had legal sanction, after the edict, discrimination was not protected by the rule of law in the newly constituted society. The emancipation edict, in officially removing the stigma of caste, also eliminated prior protections provided for the Burakumin and the monopolies that they held on certain trades.[11] Rather, the land from their villages was often redistributed, leaving them landless and without a tax base to draw upon for social services, including the education of their youth. These actions left the Burakumin to struggle for survival in a society that had not forgotten their historical standing as a contaminated caste, often in urban ghettos shared with other deprived citizens. Due to effective housing segregation and other cultural practices, in spite of the emancipation, edict discrimination in marriage, employment, and residence continued on both government and nongovernment levels into the early years of the twentieth century.

In 1922, in the midst of socialist and communist movements taking place around the world, the Burakumin and their allies found organized form in the Suiheisha, or Levelers' Society. The main tactic of the Suiheisha was denunciation (*kyūudan tōosōo*), which forced perpetrators of hate speech and injurious acts toward Burakumin to apologize publicly. The next decade brought political victories on a variety of fronts, including the improvement of the status of women, Shin Fujin Kyoukai, and the large-scale Burakumin liberation movement, Buraku Kaihōo Undōo. In pursuit of a unified nationalist cause and military manpower, the Japanese government in 1942, during a wartime period of growing fascist rule, passed legislation banning social protest and stressing a common citizenship. Suiheisha was forced to disband and the momentum it had gained was consumed by the militarization of the nation and its imperial project. To further the perception, if not the reality, of a cohesive nation, the term used to refer to *buraku* issues shifted from *yūwa*, meaning appeasement, to *dōwa*, meaning "same" or "harmony." Given that the original use of the word *dōwa* came as part of the Imperial Edict in 1926 to maintain order and assimilate those elements of the populace that could potentially destabilize the country, some activists chafe at its application to contemporary liberation causes. The continued use of *dōwa* to refer to Burakumin issues, in particular education, in postwar Japan seems a bit puzzling given its close association with the imperial system, but in fact this term came down to a point of convenience and respect. Throughout the Suiheisha period (1920–40s) many teachers who worked with Burakumin youth identified themselves as *dōwa* educators and formed various associations, including the National Dowa Education Association (Zendōkyo).

As people began to respond to the phenomenal changes pressed upon them in postwar chaos combined with international movements around the world, basic philosophical differences began to emerge regarding how to reengage and reconceptualize "the movement." Suiheisha, which had transformed into the Buraku Liberation Committee in 1946, now became the Buraku Liberation League (Buraku Kaihoo Domei, BLL) in 1955. The first two decades of postwar Japan brought an alliance between the country's two leftist parties, the Japanese Socialist Party (JSP) and the Japanese Communist Party (JCP), in support of the BLL and their efforts to improve the economic, social, and educational welfare of Burakumin. The National Teacher's Union was another strong voice for Burakumin and other human rights. Leftist efforts in Japan were generally suppressed in the 1950s as the occupying US administration joined with conservative business and imperial interests in facing the threats of North Korea and its Soviet and Chinese support.

After BLL's years of struggle and perseverance, a government review of conditions in the nation's several hundred *buraku* made recommendations for improvement in 1965 that led in 1969 to national legislation known as the Special Measures. The programs put forward attempted to address disadvantages in housing, health care, transportation, education, and employment. Except for the funding used for educational enhancement, the implementation was largely left to local governments. The school projects that were developed to remediate and open access to Burakumin youth who had been blocked for generations were part of what came to be known as Dōwa Kyōiku, loosely defined as "education for liberation." Specific schools with significant populations of Burakumin youth and who agreed to the appellation were designated as *dōwa* schools.[12] Some districts and schools that could have accepted *dōwa* designation refused it in order to minimize their reputation as *buraku* and the stigmatization that followed.

## BURAKUMIN IN MODERN JAPAN

Crucial to our topic is the understanding that the Burakumin identity is legally a matter of residence; anyone living in a known *buraku* can be seen and accept identity as Burakumin. One's home village, *furusato*, is of great importance in Japanese life; it is traditionally where one's identity was registered in the *koseki*, an official document held in the local temple. Even today one can find these local census records and historical maps to affirm the location of *buraku* communities (Amos 62–67). According to Aoki,

> The last official survey of the national Burakumin population organizes the data according to region: 533,000 people in the 781 *burakus* in the Kinki region, 261,000 in the 1,052 *burakus* in the Chyūgoku region, 454,000 in the 835 *burakus* in the Kyushu region, 260,000 in the 670 *burakus* in the Shikoku region, 319,000 in the 572 *burakus* in the Kantō region, and 329,000 in the 532 *burakus* in the Chūbu region. The Kinki region has a lot of large urban *burakus*. The Chugoku region has a lot of small fishing and agrarian *burakus*. The Kyūshū region has a lot of urban and agrarian *burakus*. Its (former) coal mining areas have a lot of *burakus* that formed in the modern era. The Kanto region has a lot of small urban *burakus*. Meanwhile, the Chūbu region has a lot of small agrarian *burakus*. Many of the jobs in the urban *burakus* are in the manufacturing, construction, and service industries. (164)

US firebombing of Japan's major cities at the end of WWII, especially Tokyo, destroyed the identity of most prewar urban *buraku*, although investigations easily uncover businesses and community organizations with Burakumin participation (Amos 58–62). Advocacy groups now estimate the number of Burakumin as approximating three million; however, since the end of the Special Measures, the government claims that the number has decreased to one or two million. It must be said that any discussion of *buraku* and their residents, past and present, is fraught with historical and legal ambiguity; all estimates are based on a fluid and complex accounting of residence. There is no doubt, however, that there has been a focused and determined effort by a series of organizations to resist discrimination directed at assumed Burakumin, even if everything else is open to interpretation.

In the 1970s and 1980s while communities and schools with large populations of Burakumin were infused with resources, a negative stigma remained, as did numerous forms of social marginalization.[13] Improvement in physical structures of the community did not alter private employment practices or the relative socioeconomic status of the group; neither did it significantly impact the academic engagement of Burakumin students as had been anticipated.[14] The historical legacy of discrimination has left many parents illiterate, unemployed, on social benefits, and unsure of the connection between education and success.[15] One effort to reclaim a space for personal, educational, and economic development took place in a community where I conducted about half of this research. Located in a longstanding *buraku* in the southern part of Osaka, a new school was proposed to provide children with the opportunity to attend a school within their own community, closer to their homes.[16] Discussions that were underway as early as the 1960s faced particularly strong resistance from elderly non-Burakumin who did not want their grandchildren studying alongside *buraku* youth. Sensitive to this possibility and needing the cooperation of all concerned, the individuals who resisted were not openly accused of discrimination but rather brought along over the years to see the value of having a beautiful new school located in their neighborhood. When the school finally opened, only ten percent of the students were identified as Burakumin. Other students were either low-income Japanese or immigrants, both voluntary and involuntary, in particular Zainichi, people of Korean descent, or individuals of Chinese ancestry. While the school remains as a beacon of hope for Burakumin in the area, it retains a negative image as a *dōwa* school in the wider community.

A significant transformation over these last thirty-five years relates to the composition of the *buraku* communities. While there have always been low-income non-Burakumin living in these areas, the number has increased, including recent and long-standing immigrants. The migration of people into such communities to live in cheap, government-subsidized housing—a result of the Special Measures and open to all—has attracted non-Burakumin to areas where the gains were won by those now in the minority again. The majority of people now living in places previously known as *buraku* are not Burakumin by their own or any known authority. However, the new migrants pay a high price for low-cost housing, as those within the community are subject to informal discrimination in marriage and employment due to their residential status. Those who make a point of denying any Burakumin identity end up being subject to the scorn of their neighbors, while others accept the situation along with the lower-status identity.

In contrast to immigrant groups, the Burakumin have no alternative country of origin from which they can claim roots or through which they can create a real or fictitious positive identity. To borrow at length from Hideo Aoki, who hosted me in Hiroshima and is the colleague with whom I walked the local *buraku* that I described at the beginning of this essay:

> Burakumin are discriminated against based on their descent as real or *imagined* "descendants of outcastes." De Vos and Wagatsuma (1966) understand the Burakumin through concepts of race or caste. They apply racial and caste concepts on the Burakumin as they believe that the mentality of the discriminators and Burakumin response to discrimination is identical to that of American and Indian minorities. However, racial concepts tend to place an emphasis on our physical characteristics. Even when this escalates to create a *social* race, the basic principle still applies. Another theory believes that the Burakumin are of a different race. The use of racial concepts will inevitably support this view.
>
> Secondly, caste refers to people who have been classified based on "endogamy," "hereditary status," and "class based hierarchy." Caste concepts are also often applied to similar groups in countries other than India. For example, African Americans are referred to as the American caste. However, Burakumin in the modern age are not living within a system of social hierarchy as seen with the Indian castes. Religiosity is also negligible. The concept of uncleanness lies at the root of discrimination both against the Burakumin as well as caste discrimination. Today, however, the concept of uncleanness is no longer expressed directly in acts of discrimination against the Burakumin. Buddhist notions of metempsychosis, karma, and the like have also receded. Discrimination against the Burakumin is generally *conceived* as the "remnants of the feudal status system." This gives rise to the *belief* that discrimination against the Burakumin will (supposedly) disappear with the advent of modernization. However, discrimination against the Burakumin as it exists today was reconstructed after the start of the modern age and has not disappeared since it started. The Burakumin are also different from African Americans. The Burakumin are both racially and culturally invisible. The Burakumin are a (modern) social status group who are discriminated against based on a *belief about their descent* that they are real or imagined "descendants of outcastes." (172)

## THE RESEARCHER

My research has been a unique process during several years in an attempt to understand existing Japanese communities proscribed as "low caste," unwanted, and even, for political expediency's sake, denied an existence. The process has been complex and at times painful for all involved. Discussing these matters is difficult for those willing to claim Burakumin identity or who work within organizations committed to ameliorating the apparent and clearly irrational stigma still applied to anyone or any neighborhood given the Burakumin identity—whether or not they accept that identity. No recent or reliable statistics provide data on the number of Burakumin, where they live, or the level of discrimination they currently face, since the subject is itself taboo within Japanese society and government. Complicating this situation is the fact that first-person accounts by Burakumin are rare. One of the most famous firsthand accounts of prewar *buraku* life is by Sumii; however, this text is only partially available and the author is someone who lived in the same village but did not identify as Burakumin. Other material in Japanese with Burakumin authors has long been available but largely unexamined by non-Japanese scholars. Efforts to publish texts either by or about the Burakumin are suppressed by a combination of those attempting to support the Burakumin by avoiding critical work and by unwritten rules within the general society that such accounts are undesirable.[17]

Most contemporary Japanese claim to know nothing about the continued existence of Burakumin and those who do are afraid to speak of them, either in using their present-day appellation, Burakumin, or their former, *eta*. Access to *buraku* is extremely difficult for outsiders because the interpretation of findings about this community is scrutinized for political correctness. Discussion of the Burakumin, not to mention research, is caught within webs of complexity both political and social. One clear example of such an attempt to block dissemination of information was the termination of a contract to publish my research on the education of Burakumin after it had been published in English as *Japan's Outcaste Youth* and translated into Japanese. Turning the research into a book was not my idea but rather that of many Japanese educators and community activists with whom I had explored the limitations of Burakumin access to schooling over several years. Their view was that the publication of my work would not only reveal that discrimination continues but also clarify the complexity of the conditions that the Burakumin community face in its present state, which was as the Special Measures were coming to an end. While the book was being prepared for publication in English, I was asked by a leading scholar if he could translate it into Japanese. His reputation of working with and allying with the causes of the Burakumin is strong, so it seemed like a good match. I was aware of the complicated protocols of translation in Japan, meaning that an invitation has to come by someone of comparable status to do a translation. Akashi Shoten, the leading human-rights publisher in Japan, had already published two of my prior books on marginalized communities in the US after they had been translated into Japanese by two other Japanese scholars.[18] They have been used in graduate courses in the sociology of education in Japan ever since. However, discussing infringements on social justice in the US or the UK is radically different from exposing the underbelly of Japanese society. Yet, even though the *Outcaste* book was more contentious within the Japanese context, I was assured by Mr. Ishii,[19] whom I had met previously and spoken to extensively, that this new book would be a valuable addition to his distinguished catalog of books on marginalized communities around the world. A contract was drawn up and plans went forward. However, at the last minute, without any reason offered, I received an email from the translator that the book could not move into production. I learned unofficially that there had been resistance on the part of some Burakumin advocates to a Japanese translation of a book on this taboo subject. A complete explanation has never been offered and, given the importance of the relationship with my colleagues in Japan, I have never asked.

The termination of the work affected many people who had labored over the years to illuminate the complexity of this topic. Much of the writing on the Burakumin, particularly that which is written in English, regurgitates historical sources of discrimination, such as family lineage or traditional occupations relegated to the Burakumin dealing with the dead or contaminated, such as tanning, butchery, burials, and gardening. According to Osaka City University Professor Noguchi in the text *Burakumin Mondai no "Paradigm" Tenkan*,[20] focusing on these issues creates misunderstanding and blinds people to the far more complex issues Burakumin face today, which are a result of changes that have rapidly been unfolding since the 1980s. But as seen above, even with the support of a leading publisher, Mr. Ishii, who is himself Burakumin, and his company, Akashi Shoten, scholarship on the Burakumin requires more than a courageous champion as political considerations may limit publication in translation. Meanwhile, research and debates on the origins and continuity of injustices continue apace among both Japanese- and English-language scholars.[21]

## RESEARCH

My research involved several years of engagement with numerous schools and community organizations throughout Japan in areas that had been historically identified as having large populations of Burakumin. I focused in particular on the teachers and scholars who had committed their lives to working with Burakumin youth and their families while they simultaneously interrogated and educated the larger society in an attempt to alter the feudal mindset that held prejudices in place.[22] This research also required, both directly and indirectly, engagement with members of the longstanding advocacy group, the Buraku Liberation League (BLL).

My journey into a world usually closed to outsiders and avoided by the vast majority of Japanese required face-to-face introductions from people whom the Burakumin not only trusted but who had proven their worth through significant self-sacrifice within their own communities.[24] This process began when I met Professor Noguchi, a longtime researcher and activist within the struggle for Burakumin liberation. Accepting an invitation to their home, I listened as Noguchi's wife, a retired teacher and a member of the Burakumin community, shared her experiences of trying to organize teachers in the 1970s. She informed me that "Twenty-five years ago most teachers did not want to work with or teach Burakumin; they hated them." To move them beyond fear and resistance, she invited them to come to the local community center, a settlement house for Burakumin located in each community. Her mission was two-fold: (1) to educate teachers about the history of the Burakumin, their identity, and concerns, and (2) to ask teachers to provide additional support for students in identifying learning problems while collaborating with parents in an attempt to better prepare their children for life at school. Her initial efforts at organizing proved futile; teachers would not come, claiming that such requests were beyond the call of duty and asking, "Why should we take our free time to visit such a center?" Ironically, she claimed, "Once the students learned of their teachers' refusal to attend, several students, enraged by the insult, committed themselves to the idea of becoming a teacher so as to prevent the next generation of Burakumin children from receiving similar treatment."

Professor Noguchi suggested I meet Mr. Maruyama, a teacher at nearby Abiko Minami (a junior high school) who served as the Dōwa Kyōiku coordinator, a complicated position that negotiated the needs of the community within the legal constraints of the government, both local and national. Little did either of us know at that time that this would become a long-term relationship with my returning year after year for ten years as I expanded my network and created allies, enabling me to ask questions and gain insights into this historically complex topic fraught with trap doors. Maruyama had taught in low-income *dōwa* schools for more than twenty years. Not of Burakumin ancestry himself, it had taken him some time to gain the trust of the community as someone to whom parents could send their children. When asked the reason for his lifelong commitment, he would launch into a discussion on "worker consciousness"; he enjoyed "working with deviant, trouble-making youth," finding them refreshing and insightful (Maruyama). Critical of himself and others, and aware of the interplay of history with contemporary demands on marginalized youth, he often would fret over not having reached a certain student or not having understood their needs. Never the flashy radical, he worked in the background, supporting those who spoke more eloquently or were willing to take more controversial stands. But he endured where others did not or could not.

Arriving at the door of Abiko Minami adjacent to a longstanding *buraku*, Asaka, are the children whose lives are complicated not only by identity, poverty, and discrimination, but also a historical legacy of low academic performance. Interviews with teachers in several *dōwa* schools show that the stigma felt by and the mark left on family and community patterns due to hundreds of years of oppression play a significant role in the degree to which young people engage with schooling. A major part of the Dōwa Kyōiku agenda, especially in schools and communities as mixed as Asaka, was to educate non-Burakumin about this history so that they might move beyond the stories and gossip that keep families separated and communities divided.[24] It was an awesome task.

In the 1960s and 70s it was not uncommon for some activist teachers to take the stance that the success of the Burakumin liberation movement was largely based on embracing one's identity and openly revealing past and present discrimination. These teachers encouraged, sometimes quite forcibly, their colleagues to confront their own prejudice openly and to invite Burakumin youth to share their experiences in class.[25] As a result, some young people whose parents may have hidden their identity from them were as shocked to find out that they were Burakumin as were their schoolmates. In some schools such acknowledgement or "outing" could serve as a route to empowerment, while in others it became a vehicle for shame and bullying. The teachers who worked in schools like Abiko Minami walked a fine line between exposing and representing issues that some families would rather not have disclosed or discussed.[26]

My school visits and interviews with teachers began during the last few years of the Special Measures and the educational programs that included *dōwa* programs at schools like Abiko Minami. It took me a few minutes to gather the pieces of the puzzle to understand why one such teacher, Ms. Yamamoto, had become a teacher at a *dōwa* school. She spoke effortlessly, which was a tribute to her trust in Maruyama that he would not subject her to an interview with a foreigner who was unfamiliar with the issues she faced. Her father died when she was twelve due in part to alcoholism and in part to despair; he had been unemployed for some time prior to this death. As she continued to lay out her journey into teaching, glances went around the room: did I get it? Did I know yet? Had the clues been sufficient? Ten minutes later she spoke even more plainly and declared that she was Burakumin. I looked over to Maruyama and he nodded; it was okay to go further, and the scripted interview questions shifted in direction as I inquired more fully about attitudes toward Burakumin and the ways in which she saw "her culture" as "different."

Leaving Abiko Minami, we later met in the Osaka office of Ms. Nakamura, who agreed to share her experience as a teacher and scholar devoted to understanding and undoing discrimination of the Burakumin. Wanting to learn from her expertise and gain from her study and personal journey, I asked her to describe how she conceived of Burakumin culture as different from Japanese culture. She was silent for a while before she began musing on the reality that there was no difference, but then she ventured, "If the culture comes out publicly, sometimes it is praiseworthy but sometimes it is abominable." She went on searching for explanations for the stereotypical images that people cling to in order to maintain social hierarchies. One of the most common is a difference in dietary culture. The Burakumin are known to eat the entrails of animals, parts that supposedly cultured people wouldn't eat but poor people would have to. Though years have passed and there have been great gains since the liberation movement, Nakamura reminded us, "There are still many people who believe that the Burakumin are fierce. They have an image of *buraku* people that they do dreadful things."

Maruyama conceded that the problem is most prevalent in the case of marriage. When I inquired how people would know if someone was Burakumin, he alluded to the Kōshinsho, an investigation that occurs prior to marriage based on the *koseki* or equivalent records. Results of such an inquiry lead to a document that is given at the marriage ceremony. Apparently when people do not produce it, sometimes because they don't believe that such forms of discrimination are acceptable, it is assumed that they are hiding something, usually that they are not "real" Japanese. Even the threat that a person could be Burakumin has terminated many a marriage. An official survey distributed in 2000 asked thousands of residents in Osaka if discrimination against *buraku* people was still a part of daily life.[27] The majority answered "yes, but only in marriage and work," probably the two most significant areas of one's life. Although largely banned, the use of *koseki* records in the form of a notorious "black book" was common and still surfaced as late as 2002 among Japanese companies seeking to discriminate against applicants.[28] The next survey question was "When choosing a place to live, would you agree to live near *buraku* people?" Most people answered, "I would not." So, this takes in the third most important issue, housing.

When I returned to Osaka in 2003, the situation in *dōwa* schools had changed radically. The termination of the Special Measures legislation in 2002 meant that additional funding and support would no longer be granted to schools simply because they had large Burakumin populations. Schools were officially not allowed to know the identity of their students, nor could they single out youth for extra assistance. Activist teachers connected to the BLL were moved out of predominantly Burakumin schools. Teachers who had been trained in and worked under the directives of the BLL suddenly found themselves without a singular mission.[29] Added to policy changes that directly impacted *dōwa* schools were new national educational reforms demanding alterations in the length of the school week, the implementation of a new integrated curriculum, and a movement toward pedagogical practices that few teachers understood.[30] The complexity of this context offered me the opportunity to see how schools, educators, students, parents, and communities were responding to the changes.

Arriving at a formerly designated *dōwa* school, Maruyama and I were put at ease immediately as Principal Mizuno settled us into overstuffed chairs and enthusiastically began offering a profile of his students; it clearly is not a picture typically conjured up in Western images of Japan: "The divorce rate of the parents in this school is over 50 percent. About 30 percent live with one parent; some live with only their mother and some their father. Altogether the rate of students living with real [both birth] parents is 50 percent. The rate of students with a stepparent because of remarriage is 20 percent." Maruyama, who was listening attentively, to whom I assumed all this would be familiar given his years working in *dōwa* schools and the community, inquired if this breakup of the family is a recent tendency. Mizuno clarified that it was not; in fact, there had long been a situation of what he called "fatherless families" in this school. According to him, and verified by other interviews, there was a tradition of intermarriage among members of the same community. Mizuno went on to say, "This is largely due to discrimination. They divorce easily and after divorce, they live in the neighborhood. And then they remarry to another person. So, their blood becomes thicker."[31]

In other interviews a different but related set of issues emerged, such as early pregnancy and marriage. When the average age of marriage for young women in Japan was about twenty-six or older, some were getting pregnant and/or married as young as sixteen. Burakumin seem to be overrepresented in these outliers. They also tend to take on adult responsibilities earlier, in part because they are not staying in school. This situation was exacerbated by the economic crises of the 1990s as well as by the elimination of financial support to the Burakumin in 2002. There is, however, an underlying policy as well as a philosophy in the districts where *dōwa* education is taught that lack of funding should not be a reason to give up on schooling. If students want to continue on to high school, scholarships can be found to pay for tuition fees. Junior high school teachers in these schools have therefore faced a particularly difficult challenge to convince parents that the cost of high school, which is not free or compulsory for anyone, is worth the effort. At a time of economic instability, this argument has been muted as parents have been laid off and income from working young people has been seen as a potential for economic survival. Youth who may not be engaged at school, academically or socially, may be more than willing to seek immediate gratification over perseverance, especially if the likelihood is that discrimination will ultimately thwart their employment efforts anyway.

Usually it is only through *kateihōmon* (home visits) that teachers find out the real situation that a child is confronting. As one teacher said, "In daily talk, children never tell us that the factory where their father or mother was working became bankrupt or that someone has been injured or is ill" (Komin). The economic crisis of recent years has affected many low-income families as the employees of subcontractors have lost their jobs in the wake of bankruptcies among larger companies that they supplied. The end result is that many families in low-income communities turn to public assistance.

But, in Japan, admitting that one is in need of aid is not easy and the desire to appear self-sufficient is strong. Yet for Burakumin the situation is slightly different. Few Burakumin families work in factories; most are employed in small shops and businesses within their community, often related to leather goods. Much of the work is part time and often conducted in their homes. And while this might be viewed as a dated stereotype, I am told repeatedly that Burakumin are butchers or do work that involves the transportation of the dead, including humans, animals, and their byproducts. Such work has contributed to the treatment of the Burakumin as Japan's "untouchables." But the fact that this stigma, more than two hundred years old, continues into modern Japan with the power to impede access to housing, marriage, and employment is bewildering to say the least.

Mr. Sasaki, a small, intense, wiry, enthusiastic man of about forty-five years of age, was introduced to me as the Chief Dōwa Kyōiku Coordinator for the city of Osaka. Glancing back and forth between Maruyama and me, he waits for a sign, a benchmark from which to begin this outflow, this interview, set up by his trusted friend, a far more radical activist teacher than himself, to a stranger, a foreign woman. Knowing that his school has recently seen an influx of non-Burakumin individuals and wanting to secure his engagement, I begin with a neutral inquiry: How has the composition of students over the last few years changed in your school? He chooses as a response a finely grained analysis of the ways in which the consciousness of Burakumin parents has changed. According to Sasaki, during the time of the Buraku Liberation Movement, parents were very active in organizing for the improvement of their children's education. Teachers often went into the *mura* (village) and talked with parents about education. This activity has now changed drastically. Sasaki claims, "The organization which parents formed for their children's education doesn't work anymore. So parents don't say to children, 'Since you are *buraku* children, you have to be strong.'" He worries that the children don't realize that they are Burakumin. This might seem like an issue of assimilation, but lack of identity with the *buraku* movement and community seems to have affected the academic success of these children as well, not only by the termination of scholarship money but also by the assumption by non-Burakumin that the problems, if not the Burakumin themselves, have disappeared. Sasaki claimed that one of the biggest problems now is that the government does not allow for identification of Burakumin. Since schools are more mixed in population and teachers do not know clearly how to teach about *buraku* issues or which students need more support in terms of their identity formation, they are at a loss. The sadness in his voice was obvious, as was the confusion around how to respond to student needs, which remain serious, even though officially they have disappeared. I wondered if the government believed that equity will arise simply by wishing it so. Having interviewed a significant number of Japanese teachers in dozens of schools across Japan who have expressed negative views of the Burakumin and supplied me with a host of supposedly unique characteristics that demarcate Burakumin from other Japanese, I asked Sasaki if teachers are allowed the time and safe space to talk about *buraku* problems among themselves. He responds:

> Teachers are very sensitive to discrimination. [Harkening back to leftist tendencies and social justice agendas held by the teachers' union.] So, when they encounter a scene of discrimination, they talk about it and teach students about discrimination, regardless of whether those who are discriminated against are disabled, Zainichi, or *buraku* students. But there is a problem about who will tell *buraku* children that they are from the *buraku*: parents or teachers? Parents may hide the fact; so teachers try to make contact with parents to understand their views. Many years ago, *buraku* students came to school with a cloth on their chest which read, "I am from Asaka and a member of *buraku* liberation alliance." So teachers could talk about *dōwa* education openly, but now there is no such alliance.

I inquired about the potential stigma that this forthright insignia might cause. He was aware of the complexity of this issue, how things have changed, and unsure of how he should respond to me or if he would even continue the conversation. He knew that I was not looking for definitive answers, but he seemed to wish he had them, for himself if not for me. Today is not thirty years ago. Back then such an emblem did create a stigma, but one of resistance and pride. This was true as long as the liberation movement remained strong and enabled people to draw upon it for sustenance and power. When the movement began to fracture, in part due to its success, assimilation for some became more desirable than identification. Stories abound, regardless of how true or how many, that as the Burakumin gained economically from government compensation, movement out of the *buraku* became inevitable. The desirability to pass in a society in which meeting the group norm is paramount cannot be faulted.

## CONCLUSION

This paper finds its place amid accounts of issues facing the Dalits of India, including their efforts for expression and liberation. India's *varna-jati* system is similar to, but different from, the Japanese social hierarchical traditions that call on issues of contamination to define access to society, creating categories such as Burakumin. Both systems have ancient origins that have been reinforced with legal and official designations. Dalits can seek liberation in many forms, both as a collective and as individuals, but they do so with forms of recognition lacking for the Burakumin of Japan (Amos 18–32).

The uncertainty and ambiguity of the Burakumin identity and how one claims it, or is ascribed to it, allows for "passing" as well as prejudice and discrimination without formal challenge or retribution, mostly in the areas of marriage, residence, and employment.[32] While some escape these constraints, "passing" can be treacherous within Japanese society, which is still fraught with concern for maintaining the purity of the imagined Japanese "race" and its grounding in the traditional village.[33]

Who is defined as Burakumin has altered over the centuries as Burakumin services have been in more or less demand, as well as when certain groups were removed from the category. Similarly, a range of programs has been implemented over the years to ameliorate the conditions within the various *buraku* throughout Japan. Some of these programs were terminated during the height of Japan's militaristic and nationalistic period of the early 1920s and 30s only to resurface in new forms along with the Occupation. In the 1960s yet another attempt took form, the Special Measures, in large part due to pressure from radicals within the Buraku Liberation League and those supporting its aims, who pressed for government compensation for enduring discrimination.

Since the termination of this policy, what was once seen as a liberation movement for Burakumin has now found itself included among many other groups who claim marginality, such as women, the disabled, Korean Zainichi, and immigrant groups, in a broad Human Rights Education (Jinken Kyōiku) movement. This inclusiveness has altered the focus of *dōwa* education and, as some would say, diluted the original intention from ending discrimination against Burakumin to embracing human rights for everyone.[34] Some may see this as a move toward a more multicultural orientation, but in Japan the prejudices against Burakumin are unique and deeply rooted. If knowledge of historical underpinnings of discrimination against the Burakumin disappears, will they continue to be viewed as a contaminated caste or simply be relegated to the bottom rung of Japanese society without any explanation or context other than self-inflicted isolation? My view is that an end to the prejudices apparent in Japanese society toward alleged Burakumin or residents in *buraku* communities will be slow in coming and largely impervious to research or legislation now designed to promote the human rights of Japan's many minority and disadvantaged peoples.

In an effort to work against these ongoing prejudices, this essay employs stories of and about Burakumin, as narrated by them, and by the educators and teachers who work among and along with them. They together weave a complex narrative of Burakumin lives as they grapple with denying or undermining their marginalized identity while continuing to face discrimination in inexplicable ways. The many interviews I undertook with students and teachers constitute fragmentary pieces of a kind of life narrative of the Burakumin. These interviews are a rich source through which to explore caste consciousness in Japanese society and to uncover a story that has been suppressed and evaded. Life narratives as a *form* and *method* enrich our understandings of the Burakumin. The "unwritten rules" regarding first-person accounts work as they play a "witnessing function." It is in this context that I offer excerpts from my fieldwork and ethnographic interviews—excerpts that capture aspects of the lives of Burakumin and non-Burakumin who engage with them—as forms of life narratives.

## NOTES

1. See Gordon, *The Color*; "A Shoelace."
2. See Komine; Kudomi.
3. See Gordon, "Inequities"; "The Crumbling."
4. In her contribution to this volume, Shailaja Paik offers a similar methodology for the study of a marginalized group in India.
5. See Aoki; Amos.
6. See Neary.
7. See Reber.
8. See Buraku Mondai Kenkyusho; Akashi.
9. See Nabeshima, et al.
10. See Fujitani; Groemer.
11. The samurai class during this same period, who were also relieved of their prior obligations and status, received loans to supplement their income and reestablish themselves; the Burakumin did not.
12. See Hawkins.
13. See Ikeda, "Buraku"; Kiyonori.
14. See Nabeshima, "Invisible."
15. See Okuda.
16. See Executive Committee.
17. See De Vos and Wagatsuma.
18. See Sumii.
19. Throughout this essay, first names for contacts such as Mr. Ishii and all interviewees are not given in recognition of the Japanese custom of using last names in most forms of communication, even among colleagues.
20. See M. Noguchi.
21. See Shimahara; Kawamoto and Shimizu.
22. See Akashi.
23. See Y. Noguchi; M. Noguchi and Y. Noguchi.
24. See Kanegae.
25. See Shimizu.

26. See Ikeda, "Theoretical"; "Buraku."
27. See Okuda.
28. See Okuda.
29. See Gordon, "From Liberation."
30. See H. Fujita, "Education"; "Whither."
31. The idea of blood becoming thicker is a euphemism for marriage within one's own clan or caste.
32. See Buraku Kaihō Kenkyūsho.
33. See Befu.
34. See Gordon, "From Liberation"; Nabeshima, "*Dowa* Education"; Nabeshima, "Invisible Racism."

## WORKS CITED

Akashi, Ichiro. "Teachers' Commitment to *Dowa* Education." *Dowa Education: Educational Challenge toward a Discrimination-Free Japan*, edited by Yasumasa Hirasawa, Yoshiro Nabeshima, and Minoru Mori, Buraku Liberation Research Institute, 1995, pp. 15–23.

Amos, Timothy D. *Embodying Difference: The Making of Burakumin in Modern Japan*. U of Hawai'i P, 2011.

Aoki, Hideo. "Buraku Culture." *Globalization, Minorities and Civil Society: Perspective from Asian and Western Cities*, edited by Koichi Hasegawa and Noaki Yoshihara, Trans Pacific Press, 2008, pp. 154–72.

Befu, Harumi. *Hegemony of Homogeneity: An Anthropological Analysis of Nihonjinron*. Trans Pacific P, 2001.

Buraku Mondai Kenkyusho. *History of Burakumin and Emancipation Movement*. Buraku Mondai Kenkyusho, 1970.

Buraku Kaihō Kenkyūsho. *Konnichi no buraku sabetsu: kakuchi no jittai chōsa kekka yori*. Third edition, Buraku Liberation Publishing House, 1997.

De Vos, George A., and Hiroshi Wagatsuma. *Japan's Invisible Race: Caste in Culture and Personality*. U of California P, 1966.

Executive Committee for Comprehensive Planning of Buraku Liberation in the Asaka Area. *A Guide for Asaka Buraku*. Asaka Buraku Liberation Center, 1995.

Fujita, Hidenori. "Education Reform and Education Politics in Japan." *The American Sociologist*, vol. 31, no. 3, 2000, pp. 42–57.

———. "Whither Japanese Schooling?: Educational Reforms and Their Impact on Ability Formation and Educational Opportunity." *Challenges to Japanese Education: Economics, Reform, and Human Rights*, edited by June A. Gordon, Hidenori Fujita, Takehiko Kariya, and Gerald LeTendre, Teachers College P, 2010, pp. 17–53.

Fujitani, Takashi. "Modern History of Buraku." *Burakumin History and Emancipation Movement*, edited by Kiyoshi Inoue, Buraku Mondai Kenkyusho, 1954.

Gordon, June A. *The Color of Teaching*. Falmer, 2000.

———. "The Crumbling Pedestal: Changing Images of Japanese Teachers." *Journal of Teacher Education*, vol. 56, no. 5, 2005, pp. 459–70.

———. "From Liberation to Human Rights: Challenges for Teachers of the *Burakumin* in Japan." *Race, Ethnicity and Education*, vol. 9, no. 2, 2006, pp. 183–202.

———. *Henkaku Teki Kyoikugaku Toshite*. Translated by Kokichi Shimizu, Akashi Shoten, 2010.

———. "Inequities in Japanese Urban Schools." *The Urban Review*, vol. 37, no. 1, 2005, pp. 49–62.

———. *Japan's Outcaste Youth: Education for Liberation*. Paradigm Publishers, 2008.

———. *Mainoritei to Kyooiku*. Translated by Mamoru Tsukada, Akashi Shoten, 2004.

———. "A Shoelace Left Untied: Teachers Confront Class and Ethnicity in a City of Northern England." *Urban Review*, vol. 35, no. 3, 2003, pp. 191–215.

Groemer, Gerald. "The Creation of the Edo Outcaste Order." *Race, Ethnicity and Migration in Modern Japan: Volume II: Indigenous and Colonial Others*, edited by Michael Weiner, RoutledgeCurzon, 2004.

Hawkins, John N. "Educational Demands and Institutional Response: *Dowa* Education in Japan." *Japanese Schooling: Patterns of Socialization, Equality, and Political Control*, edited by James J. Shields, Jr., Pennsylvania State UP, 1989, pp. 194–212.

Ikeda, Hiroshi. "Buraku Students and Cultural Identity: The Case of a Japanese Minority." *History of Burakumin and Theory of Emancipation*, edited by Kiyoshi Inoue, Hatada Shoten, 2001.

———. "Theoretical Considerations of the Self-Concept and the Academic Achievement of the Buraku Children." *The Bulletin of the Faculty of Human Sciences*, vol. 20, 1995, pp. 435–55.

Kawamoto, Yoshikazu, and Hidetada Shimizu. "Burakugaku: A Paradigm Shift for Education." *Mid-Western Educational Researcher*, vol. 17, no. 4, 2004, pp. 27–33.

Kanegae, Haruhiko. *Dowa Kyoiku He No Shakaiteki Shiza*. Akashi Shoten, 1999.

Kiyonori, Konishi. *50 Years of Dowa Education*. Human Rights Organization, 2002.

Komin. Personal interview. 15 Sept. 2003.

Komine, Naofumi. "Kyoiku Konanko Ni Okeru Kyoshi No 'Identity' Ni Kansuru Kenkyu." Kanto Educational Society, 2000.

Kudomi, Yoshiyuki. "Teachers Facing the Confusion and Conflicts in Today's Japan." *Hitotsubashi Journal of Social Studies*, vol. 31, no. 2, 1999, pp. 69–83.

Maruyama. Personal interview. May 1999.

Mizuno. Personal interview. 12 Sept. 2003.

Nabeshima, Yoshiro. "*Dowa* Education as Human Rights." *Dowa Education: Educational Challenge toward a Discrimination-Free Japan*, edited by Yasumasa Hirasawa, Yoshiro Nabeshima, and Minoru Mori, Buraku Liberation Research Institute, 1995.

———. "Invisible Racism in Japan: Impact on Academic Achievement of Minority Children." *Challenges to Japanese Education: Economics, Reform, and Human Rights*, edited by June A. Gordon, Hidenori Fujita, Takehiko Kariya, and Gerald LeTendre, Teachers College P, 2010, pp. 109–31.

Nabeshima, Yoshiro, Mariko Akuzawa, Shinichi Hayashi, and Koonae Park. "Human Rights Education in Japanese School System." *Dowa Mondai Kenkyuu*, vol. 22, 2000, pp. 101–25.

Nakamura, Minako. *Chiiki no Seikatsu to Bunka*. Educational Center, 1994.

———. Personal interview. May 1999.

Neary, Ian. *Political Protest and Social Control in Pre-War Japan: The Origins of Buraku Liberation*. Humanities P, 1989.

Noguchi, Michihiko. *Burakumin Mondai no "Paradigm" Tenkan*. Akashi Shoten, 2000.

Noguchi, Michihiko, and Yoshiko Noguchi. *Han Sabetsu No Gakkyuu Shudan Zukuri*. Akashi Shoten, 1997.

Noguchi, Yoshiko. *Ikikata o Tuskuru Hansabetsu no Kyoiku: Kagirinaku Yasashii Kodomotachi*. Akashi Shoten, 1990.

———. Personal interview. 14 May 1999.

Okuda, Hitoshi. "Posuto 'Tokusohō' Idai no Shuppatsuten: Dēta Kara Kangaeru Kekkon Sabetsu Mondai." *Hyūman Raitsu*, vol. 166, 2002, pp. 4–17.

Paik, Shailaja. "Mangala Bansode and the Social Life of Tamasha: Caste, Sexuality, and Discrimination in Modern Maharashtra." *Caste and Life Narratives*, ed. S. Shankar and Charu Gupta, Primus Books, 2019, pp. 173–201.

Reber, Su-lan E. A. "Buraku Mondai in Japan: Historical and Modern Perspectives and Directions for the Future." *Harvard Human Rights Journal*, vol. 12, 1999, pp. 297–359.

Sasaki. Personal interview. 7 Nov. 2003.

Shimahara, Nobuo K. "Toward the Equality of a Japanese Minority: The Case of *Burakumin*." *Comparative Education*, vol. 20, no. 3, 1984, pp. 339–53.

Shimizu, Hidetada. "Two Courses of Identity Development among *Burakumin* Children: The Impact of 'Open' vs. 'Closed' Education Policies." Youth at the Margins: Schooling and Identity Negotiation in Japan. American Educational Research Association, 2006, San Francisco.

Shibata, Michiko. *Hisabetsu Buraku no Denshō to Bunka: Shinshū no Buraku Korō Kiki Gaki*. San-ichi Shobō, 1972.

Sumii, Sue. *My Life: Living, Loving, and Fighting*. U of Michigan P, 2001.

Yamamoto. Personal interview. May 1999.

# SELECT BIBLIOGRAPHY

This list is not meant to be comprehensive. We have included a range of perspectives on caste and on life narratives in India, and though this list focuses on scholarship, it also includes a few examples of actual life narratives.


Ambedkar, B. R. *Annihilation of Caste: The Annotated Critical Edition*. Edited by S. Anand, Navayana, 2014.

———. *The Essential Writings of B. R. Ambedkar*. Edited by Valerian Rodrigues, Oxford UP, 2002.

Arnold, David, and Stuart Blackburn, editors. *Telling Lives in India: Biography, Autobiography, and Life History*. Indiana UP, 2004.

Bama. *Karukku*. 1992. Translated by Lakshmi Holmstrom, Macmillan, 2000.

Bayly, Susan. *Caste, Society and Politics in India from the Eighteenth Century to the Modern Age*. Cambridge UP, 1999.

Berreman, Gerald. "Caste in India and the United States." *American Journal of Sociology*, vol. 66, no. 2, 1960, pp. 120–27.

Bhave, Sumitra. *Pan on Fire: Eight Dalit Women Tell Their Story*. Indian Social Institute, 1988.

Brueck, Laura R. *Writing Resistance: The Rhetorical Imagination of Hindi Dalit Literature*. Columbia UP, 2014.

Carroll, Lucy. "Caste, Community and Caste(s) Association: A Note on the Organisation of the Kayastha Conference and the Definition of a Kayastha Community." *Contribution to Asian Studies*, vol. 10, 1977, pp. 3–24.

Cox, Oliver Cromwell. *Caste, Class, and Race: A Study in Social Dynamics*. Monthly Review, 1959.

Dalit Panthers. "Dalit Panthers Manifesto." *Untouchable!: Voices of the Dalit Liberation Movement*, edited by Barbara Joshi, Zed Books, 1986, pp. 141–47.

Dangle, Arjun, editor. *Poisoned Bread: Translations from Modern Marathi Dalit Literature*. Introduction by Arjun Dangle, Orient Blackswan, 2009.

Dirks, Nicholas. *Castes of Mind: Colonialism and the Making of Modern India*. Princeton UP, 2001.

Dumont, Louis. *Homo Hierarchicus: An Essay on the Caste System*. Translated by Mark Sainsbury, U of Chicago P, 1970.

Fernandes, Leela. "Reading 'India's Bandit Queen': A Trans/national Feminist Perspective on the Discrepancies of Representation." *Signs: Journal of Women in Culture and Society*, vol. 25, no. 1, 1999, pp. 123–52.

Gajarawala, Toral Jatin. *Untouchable Fictions: Literary Realism and the Crisis of Caste.* Fordham UP, 2013.

Ganguli, Debjani. "Pain, Personhood and the Collective: Dalit Life Narratives." *Asian Studies Review*, vol. 33, no. 4, 2009, pp. 429–42.

Geetha, V., and S. V. Rajadurai. *Towards a Non-Brahmin Millenium: From Iyothee Das to Periyar.* Samya, 1998.

Ghurye, G. S. *Caste, Class and Occupation.* 4th ed., Popular Book Depot, 1961.

Gooptu, Nandini. *Swami Achhutanand and the Adi Hindi Movement.* Critical Quest, 2009.

Gupta, Charu. "Dalit 'Viranganas' and Reinvention of 1857." *Economic and Political Weekly*, vol. 42, no. 19, 2007, pp. 1739–45.

———. *The Gender of Caste: Representing Dalits in Print.* U of Washington P, 2016.

Guru, Gopal, and Sundar Sarukkai. *The Cracked Mirror: An Indian Debate on Experience and Theory.* Oxford UP, 2012.

Heering, Alexandra de. "Oral History and Dalit Testimonies: From the Ordeal to Speak to the Necessity to Testify." *South Asia Research*, vol. 33, no. 1, 2013, pp. 39–55.

Human Rights Watch. "Caste Discrimination: A Global Concern." Sept. 2001, http://hrw.org/reports/2001/globalcaste/.

Human Rights Watch and Center for Human Rights and Global Justice. *Hidden Apartheid: Caste Discrimination against India's "Untouchables."* Feb. 2007, www.hrw.org/reports/2007/india0207/.

Iliah, Kancha. *Why I Am Not a Hindu: A Sudra Critique of Hindutva Philosophy, Culture and Political Economy.* Samya, 1996.

———. *The Weapon of the Other: Dalitbahujan Writings and the Remaking of Indian Nationalist Thought.* Pearson, 2010.

Hunt, Sarah Beth. *Hindi Dalit Literature and the Politics of Representation.* Routledge, 2014.

Joshi, Barbara R., editor. *Untouchable!: Voices of the Dalit Liberation Movement.* Zed Books, 1986.

Karlekar, Malavika. *Voices from Within: Early Personal Narratives of Bengali Women.* Oxford UP, 1991.

Kshirsagar, R. K. *Dalit Movement in India and Its Leaders (1857–1956).* MD Publications, 1994.

Kumar, Raj. *Dalit Personal Narratives: Reading Caste, Nation and Identity.* Orient Blackswan, 2010.

Kumar, Udaya. *Writing the First Person: Literature, History and Autobiography in Modern Kerala.* Permanent Black, 2016.

Liddle, Joanna, and Rama Joshi. *Daughters of Independence: Gender, Caste and Class in India.* Zed Books, 1986.

Limbale, Sharan Kumar. *Toward an Aesthetics of Dalit Literature*. Translated by Alok Mukherjee, Orient Longman, 2004.

———. *The Outcaste: Akkarmashi*. Translated by Santosh Bhoomkar, Oxford UP, 2003.

Menon, Dilip M. *The Blindness of Insight: Essays on Caste in Modern India*. Navayana, 2006.

Nagaraj, D. R. *The Flaming Feet and Other Essays: The Dalit Movement in India*. Permanent Black, 2010.

Narayan, Badri. *The Making of the Dalit Public in North India: Uttar Pradesh, 1950–Present*. Oxford UP, 2011.

———. *Women Heroes and Dalit Assertion in North India: Culture, Identity and Politics*. Sage, 2006.

Narayan, Badri, and A. R. Misra. *Multiple Marginalities: An Anthology of Identified Dalit Writings*. Manohar, 2004.

O'Hanlon, Rosalind. *Caste, Conflict and Ideology: Mahatma Jotirao Phule and Low-Caste Protest in Nineteenth-Century India*. Cambridge UP, 1985.

Omvedt, Gail. *Dalits and the Democratic Revolution: Dr. Ambedkar and the Dalit Movement in Colonial India*. Sage, 1994.

Orsini, Francesca. *The Hindi Public Sphere, 1920–1940*. Oxford UP, 2002.

Pandey, Gyanendra. *A History of Prejudice: Race, Caste, and Difference in India and the United States*. Cambridge UP, 2013.

Pandian, M. S. S. "On a Dalit Woman's Testimonio." *Gender and Caste*, edited by Anupama Rao, Kali for Women, 2003, pp. 129–35.

———. "Writing Ordinary Lives." *Economic and Political Weekly*, vol. 43, no. 38, 2008, pp. 34–40.

———. *Brahmin and Non-Brahmin: Genealogies of the Tamil Political Present*. Permanent Black, 2007.

Ramaswamy, Vijaya, and Yogesh Sharma, editors. *Biography as History: Indian Perspectives*. Orient Blackswan, 2009.

Rao, Anupama. *The Caste Question: Dalits and the Politics of Modern India*. Permanent Black, 2009.

Rawat, Ramnarayan S. *Reconsidering Untouchability: Chamars and Dalit History in North India*. Permanent Black, 2012.

Rege, Sharmila. *Against the Madness of Manu: B. R. Ambedkar's Writings on Brahmanical Patriarchy*. Navayana, 2013.

———. *Writing Caste/Writing Gender: Narrating Dalit Women's Testimonios*. Zubaan, 2006.

Satyanarayana, K., and Susie Tharu, editors. *No Alphabet in Sight: New Dalit Writing from South India, Dossier 1—Tamil and Malayalam*. Penguin, 2011.

———. *Steel Nibs Are Sprouting: New Dalit Writing from South India, Dossier 2—Kannada and Telugu*. Harper Collins, 2013.

Shankar, S. *Flesh and Fish Blood: Postcolonialism, Translation, and the Vernacular.* U of California P, 2012.

———. "Spitting at Power: The Boom in Dalit Literature and Questions of Agency." *Journal of Contemporary Thought*, vol. 39, Summer 2014, pp. 145–54.

———. "Thugs and Bandits: Life and Law in Colonial and Epicolonial India." *Biography: An Interdisciplinary Quarterly*, vol. 36, no. 1, Winter 2013, pp. 97–123.

Sharma, Pradeep K. *Dalit Politics and Literature.* Shipra Publications, 2006.

Srinivas, M. N. *Social Change in Modern India.* U of California P, 1966.

Valmiki, Omprakash. *Jhoothan: A Dalit's Life.* Translated by Arun Prabha Mukherjee, Columbia UP, 2003.

Viramma, Josiane Racine, and Jean-Luc Racine. *Viramma: Life of an Untouchable.* Translated by Will Hobson, Verso, 1998.

Zelliot, Eleanor. "Dalit: New Cultural Context for an Old Marathi Word." *From Untouchable to Dalit: Essays on the Ambedkar Movement*, edited by Eleanor Zelliot, Manohar, 1992, pp. 267–92.

Zelliot, Eleanor, and Rohini Mokashi-Punekar, editors. *Untouchable Saints: An Indian Phenomenon.* Manohar, 2005.

# EDITORS AND CONTRIBUTORS

S. SHANKAR is a novelist and critic. He is the author, editor, or translator of eight books, the most recent of which is the novel *Ghost in the Tamarind* (U of Hawai'i P, 2017). His critical works relate to postcolonial literature, translation studies, and debates over World Literature, as seen in his two most recent critical essays, "Literatures of the World: An Inquiry" (*PMLA*, 2016) and "The Languages of Love: An Essay on Translation and Affect" (*Comparative Literature*, 2017). He is a professor of English at the University of Hawai'i at Mānoa.

CHARU GUPTA teaches in the Department of History, University of Delhi. She has been a visiting professor and ICCR Chair at the University of Vienna, a visiting faculty member at Yale University, Washington University, and the University of Hawai'i. She has also been a fellow at the Nehru Memorial Museum & Library, Delhi; the Social Science Research Council, New York; the Asian Scholarship Foundation, Thailand; the Wellcome Institute, London; and the University of Oxford. She is the author of *Sexuality, Obscenity, Community: Women, Muslims and the Hindu Public in Colonial India* (Permanent Black, 2001; Palgrave, 2002), and *The Gender of Caste: Representing Dalits in Print* (Permanent Black and U of Washington P, 2016). She is also the editor of *Gendering Colonial India: Reforms, Print, Caste and Communalism* (Orient BlackSwan, 2012).

SHWETA MAJUMDAR ADUR is an assistant professor of sociology at California State University, Los Angeles. Before this, she was as an assistant professor of women and gender studies at California State University, Fullerton. She completed her PhD in sociology from the University of Connecticut, earned a master's in international development from the University of Pittsburgh, and a master's in sociology from Jawaharlal Nehru University, New Delhi. Her research interests include gender, sexuality, human rights, and immigration. She is the co-author of *As the Leaves Turn Gold: Asian Americans and Experiences of Aging* (Rowman and Littlefield, 2012), the author of several publications in peer-reviewed journals, and a contributor to edited collections.

Y.S. ALONE is a professor in visual studies at the School of Arts and Aesthetics, Jawaharlal Nehru University, New Delhi. His research interests are ancient Indian art, Ajanta Caves and Buddhist caves in western India, the interpretative framework of Ambedkar, modern Indian art and popular visual culture, critics of postcolonial paradigms, neo-Buddhist visual culture, and general social sciences. Alone is currently involved in developing the conceptual formulation of "protected ignorance." He has presented research papers at national and international art history and social sciences seminars, and at conferences within India and abroad. He was nominated as an Indian Council for Cultural Relations (ICCR) chair visiting professor in Shenzhen University, China, and was also invited to be a visiting professor at Autonoma University Madrid, Spain, and Renmin University of China, Beijing. He has been engaged in popular lectures as part of social movements. Kaveri Books published his text, *Early Western Indian Buddhist Caves: Forms and Patronage* in 2016.

TAPAN BASU taught at the Department of English, Hindu College, University of Delhi, for more than twenty-eight years before joining the Department of English, University of Delhi, as an associate professor. His teaching and research interests include American literature (especially African American literature) and Indian literature (especially Dalit literature). His publications include *Khaki Shorts, Saffron Flags: A Critique of the Hindu Right* (co-authored, Orient Longman, 1993); *Translating Caste: A Critical Anthology of Writings on Caste* (edited, Katha, 2001); *Listen to the Flames: Texts and Readings from the Margins* (co-edited, Oxford UP, 2016); and *Crossing Borders: Essays on Literature, Culture and Society in Honor of Amritjit Singh* (coedited, Fairleigh Dickinson UP, 2017). He has received several academic awards, including a Fulbright fellowship; a South Asia Research Program fellowship from the Social Science Research Council, New York; and a fellowship at the Ferguson Centre for African and Asian Studies, the Open University, Milton Keynes, UK. Last year, he was a fellow at the Salzburg Global Seminar.

SUMIT BAUDH received his Doctor of Juridical Science (SJD) from the UCLA School of Law. He is a former research fellow of the Center for Intersectionality and Social Policy Studies at Columbia Law School; consultant to the Arcus Foundation; University of California Human Rights Fellow; and Michael D. Palm Fellow of the Williams Institute, UCLA School of Law. All of these associations have contributed to formulating the ideas and content of the essay included in this volume. Sumit Baudh is currently an associate professor at the O. P. Jindal Global University in Sonipat, Haryana.

LAURA R. BRUECK is an associate professor of South Asian literature and culture at Northwestern University in Evanston, IL. She is the author of

*Writing Resistance: The Rhetorical Imagination of Hindi Dalit Literature* (Columbia UP, 2014) and has translated several short stories by Ajay Navaria in a volume called *Unclaimed Terrain* (Navayana, 2013).

SWARNAVEL ESWARAN is an associate professor in the Departments of English and Media and Information (MI) at Michigan State University. He is a graduate of the Film and Television Institute of India and the University of Iowa. His documentaries include *Thangam* (1995), *INA* (1996), *Villu* (1997), *Unfinished Journey: A City in Transition* (2012), *Migrations of Islam* (2014), *Hmong Memory at the Crossroads* (2015), and *Nagapattinam: Waves from the Deep* (2016). His research focuses on the history, theory, and production of documentaries, the specificity of Tamil cinema, and its complex relationship with Hollywood as well as popular Hindi films. His recent books are *Cinema: Sattagamum Saalaramum* (Nizhal, 2013) and an anthology of essays on documentaries and experimental films in *Tamil and Madras Studios: Narrative, Genre, and Ideology in Tamil Cinema* (Sage Publications, 2015). His essay, "Cinematography and the Poetics of 1950s Tamil Cinema: Maruthi Rao and Visual Style," is published in the spring 2017 issue of *Screen.*

JUNE A. GORDON, professor of international comparative education at the University of California, Santa Cruz, conducts ethnographic research on the impact of economic, political, and social contexts of schooling both in the US and internationally—in particular, in Japan, China, India, Southeast Asia, Bhutan, and Northern England. Her recent work has included education in various Muslim countries as well as educational change in post-Soviet regions such as the Balkans and Caucasus. She has authored four books and numerous chapters and publications related to educational access.

BINDU MENON is presently a fellow at the Indian Institute of Advanced Study at Shimla. She teaches mass communication and journalism at Lady Shri Ram College, Delhi University. She has authored essays on early film history, media studies, and music cultures in peer-reviewed journals in English and in her native language of Malayalam. She is currently at work on her book about a history of early twentieth-century cinema publics and media archaeology in south India.

PARTHASARATHI MUTHUKKARUPPAN teaches in the Department of Cultural Studies in the English and Foreign Languages University, Hyderabad. He has completed his PhD dissertation, titled "Caste Violence in Contemporary India: Theory and History in the Field of Dalit Studies." He has published essays in various journals, including *Social Scientist*, *Economic and Political Weekly*, and *Critical Quarterly*. His areas of interest include cultural theory, literature, Ambedkarism, and Marxism.

ANJANA NARAYAN is an associate professor of sociology at California State Polytechnic University, Pomona. Her areas of interest include ethnicity, gender, and migration. She is the co-author of *Living Our Religions: Hindu and Muslim South Asian-American Women Narrate Their Experiences* (Kumarian Press, 2008) and co-editor of *Research Beyond Borders: Interdisciplinary Reflections* (Lexington Books, 2011). She received her doctorate in sociology from the University of Connecticut and a postgraduate degree in social work from the Tata Institute of Social Sciences (TISS), Mumbai.

SHAILAJA PAIK, an associate professor of history at the University of Cincinnati, is the author of *Dalit Women's Education in Modern India: Double Discrimination* (Routledge, 2014) and several articles that focus on the forging of a new Dalit womanhood in colonial Western India, the education of Dalit women, patriarchy within Dalit communities, the history and politics of naming Dalits, and building solidarity between Dalit and African American women. Her work has been funded by the National Endowment for the Humanities, the Ford Foundation, Yale University, Emory University, the Indian Council for Social Science Research, and the Charles Phelps Taft Center, among others. She is currently on the National Endowment for the Humanities–funded American Institute of Indian Studies Long-term Senior Fellowship conducting research on her second book, which examines the politics of caste, gender, sexuality, art and aesthetics, and community and nation in popular culture in modern Maharashtra.

MUKUL SHARMA is a Delhi-based writer specializing in environment, human rights, and media issues. Since 1984, he has worked for *The Times of India* newspaper group, Amnesty International, Action Aid International, the Heinrich Böll Foundation, Climate Parliament, and the Indian Institute of Mass Communication (IIMC) as a journalist, development professional, and academician. Presently, he is a professor of development communication at IIMC, New Delhi. He has published several books in English and Hindi, the latest being *Green and Saffron: Hindu Nationalism and Indian Environmental Politics* (Permanent Black, 2012). His forthcoming book is *Caste and Nature: Dalits and Indian Environmental Politics* (Oxford UP, 2017). He has received twelve national and international awards for his writings on environment, labor, and human rights issues.

# INDEX


*Achhut* 49–50
"Achut Ki Shikayat" 48
Adi Dharma 49–50
*Adi Hindu* (newspaper) 50, 63
Alexander 106
Ali 107
Ambedkar, B.R. 2, 9, 13, 19–20, 28, 32–4, 36, 40–1, 49–51, 53–4, 62–3, 67–8, 79–85, 88–91, 104, 110, 144–5, 147–51, 153–5, 157–8, 163–4, 167, 170, 176, 188, 190, 206, 208, 213, 222–3, 228, 236, 241, 260–1
  Annihilation 19, 33, 35, 50, 81–2, 84, 88
  *Annihilation of Caste* 19, 33, 50, 81–2, 84, 88
  *Bhagwan Baba Bheemrao Ambedkar* 50
  *Bhagwan Baba Saheb Ka Jeevan Sangharsh* 50
  *Dr Babasaheb Ambedkar* 104
  interventions in constitutional politics 53
  plea for separate electorates 54
*Ananda Vikatan* 109
*Antarjatiya* 34, 37–9
*Apne Apne Pinjre* 54, 56–7, 59, 61–2
*Arthvaninche Pakshi* 55
*Arya Gazette* 31
Arya Samaj 19–21, 23–4, 26–8, 30–2, 34–5, 38, 40–1, 49–50, 61
Autobiography(ies) 2, 4, 6, 9–10, 19–23, 26, 28, 32, 35, 40, 54–5, 58, 60–2, 70, 72, 86, 87, 128, 130, 178, 180, 239
  black 22

*Bahuta* 55
Baker, Houston A. 2
Balmikis 31, 206–8, 210–11, 217–22, 224
Bama 4–5, 67–71, 76
*Bandit Queen* 11, 98–9
Bharathi 73, 99, 112
*Bharat Ke Adi-Nivasiyon* 50
Biographies 4, 6, 9–10, 50–1, 79, 82–4, 88, 98–9, 107, 130, 175, 178, 181, 207, 261, 268
Biopics 2, 4, 6, 11, 98–9, 101–2, 104, 107–8, 112, 130
*Brahmacharya* 27, 39
Brahmanical leanings 31
Brahminical hegemonic order 52
Brueck, Laura 2, 5–6, 22, 24–5, 80
*Buraku* 274–6, 279–81, 283, 285, 287, 289–91

Caste-gender dynamics 21
Caste-Hindu 146, 150, 154, 158–60, 163–4, 167, 169–70, 224
  society 146, 154, 163, 169
Casteism 26, 69, 73, 99–100, 104, 114, 205–6, 214–15, 224, 236–7, 253, 259, 262–7
*Caste Must Go* 29, 35
Caste order, hegemonic 2
Castes
  counter-narrative of 21
  critiques of 28, 35, 81, 216
  definition of 3, 170
  discrimination 13, 24, 186, 256, 262, 276, 282
  hierarchies 21, 25, 39, 228, 267
  interventions on 22
  life 2, 8, 144, 146–8, 150–1, 153, 157, 159, 163–4, 167, 169–70

low/lower 2, 26–7, 29–30, 48–50, 63, 98, 104, 128, 131, 134–5, 148, 155, 159, 168–9, 177, 179, 188, 216, 228, 261, 264, 266, 278
oppression 2, 48, 60, 114, 216, 221, 263
persistence of 56, 72
practices 34
purity 35
radicals 2, 9, 19–20, 30, 214
reality of 4, 170, 215
relations 121–2, 136
resistance and critique of 21
respectability 32
socialities of 21
stigma 26
taboos 21, 35
"twice-born" 35
untouchable 47–8, 55, 80, 146, 205, 220
upper 2, 7–8, 10–11, 26–7, 33, 41, 48, 51, 53, 59, 62, 67–8, 71–2, 74–5, 83–4, 89–90, 98, 104, 108, 114, 123, 127, 133–5, 176, 205, 216, 224, 228, 253, 260, 262, 264, 266–7

Celibacy 27

*Celluloid* 121, 130–4

*Census of India, 1911* 27

*Census of India, 1931* 29

Child/Children 12, 35, 37–8, 40, 47, 49, 59, 61, 90, 99, 101–4, 107, 112, 123, 183–4, 186, 195, 211, 224, 243–4, 257, 260, 274, 276, 281, 285, 288–90
education 289
girl 61
male 243
marriage 102
school 112
widowed 103
younger 186

Christianity 30, 69, 74, 123, 125–6

Christians 49

Cinema 6–7, 98, 101–3, 105–6, 109, 111, 114, 120–2, 124, 126–7, 129–37, 189
commercial 131

*Cinemayude* 121

Citizenship 37, 125, 128, 279
rights 37, 128

Civil rights activism 21

Class boundaries 126

Conflicts 27, 31, 57, 60–1, 72, 116, 126, 145, 147, 153, 174, 177, 207
gendered 174
moral 174

Contestation 23, 28, 75, 274

*Copying Beethoven* 107

Critical Race Theory (CRT) 3, 230

Cultural nationalism 148, 150

Dalit Art and Visual Imagery 153

Dalitbahujans 2, 9, 11, 24

*Dalit Pissing on Manu* 158

Dalits 1–4, 6–13, 20, 22–6, 32, 37, 41, 47–55, 57–63, 66–76, 79–86, 88–91, 97, 114, 116, 120, 122–3, 125–8, 130–7, 151, 153–60, 163, 168, 173–4, 176–81, 183, 185–9, 191, 195–7, 205–7, 211, 213, 215, 217, 219, 222–3, 228–30, 233, 236–44, 246, 253–4, 256–68, 290; see also Untouchable
activism 8, 265
autobiographies 26, 55, 58
awakening 53
consciousness 53, 71, 73, 80
counterpublic 51, 53, 62
diasporic 6
heroes 51
identity 10, 54, 57, 62, 68, 134
intellectuals 25–6, 134
leaders 50
life narratives 2, 11, 23, 76, 137, 156
literature 22–3, 53, 55, 58, 60, 62–3, 66–8, 70, 73–6, 79–80, 84, 91
lives 9
movements 32, 54, 128
narrations 8
oppression 257
organizations 32
personal narrative 47, 49
poems 49
politics 24
positionality of 256

print culture 48
role models 50
status of 2
struggles 53–4
urban 54
women 9, 48, 61, 69, 97, 126–8, 130–1, 136, 160, 174, 177, 180–1, 186–8, 191, 195
writings 2, 50–1, 54, 60, 68, 73, 132
Dalit women 9, 48, 61, 69, 97, 126–8, 130–1, 136, 160, 174, 177, 180–1, 186–8, 191, 195
histories of 174
narratives 48
social and sexual labor 186
*Dampati Mitra* 39
*Dasi* 38
Deprivation 61, 243
Desire 35, 39–40, 85, 110, 126, 134, 147, 158, 169, 179, 185, 263–4, 278, 289
*Devadasi Ani Nagnapujā* 160
*Dhammachakra* 160
Dharm 20, 26–8, 31–2, 40
*Dinakaran* 111–12
Disability 230, 233, 235
Discriminations 13
caste 13, 24, 186, 256, 262, 276, 282
gender 193
social 209
*Dowa* 279–81, 285–8, 290–1
*Downcast Eyes* 137
*Dr Kotnis Ki Amar Kahani* 98

Economic
anxieties 173
arrangement 215
boycotts 3
capital 190
commonalities 24
crises 288, 298
discrimination 56
instability 288
interests 150
interpretations 144, 148
reform 149
resource 183, 194
survival 288
well-being 210
*Elakku* 73–4
Elizabeth 104
Employment 79, 244, 278–9, 281, 288–9, 291
formal 244
interventionist employment 79
practices 281
private 281
Endogamy 3, 21, 34, 36, 38–9, 41, 282
Equality 27, 37–8, 40, 88, 91, 98, 125, 128, 149, 168, 170, 223, 229, 244–5, 260
aspirations of 170, 244
concepts of 125
social 88, 128, 260
universal 91
Ethnicity 8, 10, 230, 233, 236, 238, 246, 254, 256
Exclusions 3, 21, 34, 62, 102, 129, 132, 145
Exploitation 81, 88, 177, 182, 221

*Foundation of India* 158

*Gandhi* 107, 110–11
*Gandhi after Pune Karar* 154
*Gandhi: My Father* 98
Gandhi, M. K. 2, 4–5, 10, 20, 28, 32–3, 37, 40, 53, 79–91, 98, 107, 110–11, 149–52, 154–6, 206–9, 212–13, 222, 266
Ambedkar and 20, 28, 32, 40, 83, 90, 150
attitudes toward caste 91
global icon of Gandhi 83
greatness of 85
life narratives and representations of 149
moralistic authority 88
perceptions of morality 150
*Gazetteer of the Hoshiarpur District, 1883–4* 25
Geetha, V. 3, 37
Gender 1–2, 5–7, 10, 21, 35, 39, 41, 53,

126–8, 130–1, 134, 136–7, 149, 174, 180, 182, 186, 193, 197, 229, 233–8, 242, 245, 254, 256–7, 259
asymmetry 127
discrimination 193
identity 229, 245
relations 127, 137
Gilroy, Paul 22, 37, 254–5
*Guardian, The* 106

Hagiographies 9, 50
*Hans* 85
Harihar, Swami Achhutanand 47–50, 52–5, 59, 62–3
"How Long Will the Dalit Lie Dormant?" 48
"Manusmriti Is Burning Us" 47
*Swami Achhutanand Harihar: Jivan Aur Krititva* 50
Harijans 208, 213
"Hello, Premchand!" 85, 89–90
Hijra 235
Hindu American Foundation (HAF) 263
Hinduism 19–21, 28, 31–3, 35, 41, 47, 49, 116, 211, 215–16, 218, 220, 222, 263
retrogressive 35
Hindu orthodoxy 21, 31
Hindu Samaj Sudhar Karyalaya 50
Hindus 27, 30, 35, 38, 47, 49, 98, 146–8, 150–1, 155–7, 163, 221, 243, 260
mobilization 50
narrowmindedness of 30
*Hindu, The* 31, 263
Homogeneity 37, 147, 239
Human Rights Watch 3
*Humara Samaj* 23, 31, 36–7, 39

Identity 5–6, 8–12, 20, 22, 25, 32, 37, 54–5, 57, 60, 62–3, 67–8, 79, 86–7, 89–91, 134–6, 156, 177, 188–9, 208, 213–14, 220–1, 228–30, 234–5, 241–2, 245, 254–7, 259, 261–5, 268, 275–6, 280–2, 285–7, 289, 291
collective 22
dalit 10, 54, 57, 62, 68, 134
formation 11, 135, 241, 289
gender 229, 245
politics 54, 79
Ilaiah, Kancha 24
*Why I Am Not a Hindu* 24
*Independent, The* 83
India
colonial 21, 25, 29, 150
contemporary 207
dalit struggles in 53
life narratives in 7
north 1, 5, 21, 48–9, 51–2, 54–5, 57–8, 61–3, 178
social movements in 245
*Indian Social Reformer* 35
Indian society 7, 53, 144, 146–7, 158, 161, 164, 170, 209
Inequality 1–3, 5, 11
embodied allegories of 11
political 2
structures of 5
Intimacy 6, 11, 21, 28, 40–1, 241
Islam 30, 74, 110, 126

Japan 3, 5–8, 11, 13, 274–7, 279–80, 283–4, 288–91
social order of 13
*Jati* 3–4, 11, 13, 41, 149, 290, see also Castes, *Varna*
*Jatibhed* 33
*Jat-Pat Torak* 28–9, 35
Jat-Pat Torak Mandal (JPTM) 19–21, 27–36
social history of 28
*Jevha Mi Jaat Chorali Hoti* 55
*Joothan* 54, 83
*Jore* 105
Juergensmeyer, Mark 26–7, 30, 32
Justice 37, 214, 267–8, 283, 290
social 214, 283, 290
transnational 267

Kakkarissi theater 123
*Kalachuvadu* 109
*Kamshastra* 39
*Kappalottiya Thamizhan* 99

*Karukku* 4, 67, 69–72
Kerala 5, 9, 120, 122, 128, 131, 134, 163
*Kinnar* 235
*Kranti* 23, 27–8, 33, 184

Labor 40, 69, 74, 84, 127, 131, 145, 158, 174, 177–8, 182–3, 186, 189–91, 195–6, 215, 260, 277
  agricultural 74
  cheap 74
  Dalit 131
  division of labor 145, 170, 190, 215
  familial 182, 190
  industrial 74
  mental 69
  physical 69
  productive and reproductive 40
  sexual 177–8, 183, 186, 189–91, 195–6
  skilled 158
Languages 2, 4–5, 10, 13, 20–2, 25, 27, 32, 40–1, 49, 51, 58, 68–73, 79–80, 84, 86, 101, 103, 105–6, 109, 122, 125–6, 135, 144–5, 147, 149–50, 153, 160, 168–9, 175, 178–81, 206, 214, 221, 224, 232, 255, 266, 284
  English 10, 27, 39, 48–9, 58, 70–1, 83, 89, 120, 178–9, 209, 211, 283–4
  Gurmukhi 49
  Hindi 1–2, 5–6, 20, 22–3, 25, 27–8, 31, 33, 39, 47–51, 53–5, 57–9, 62–3, 79–81, 85–7, 91, 102, 194
  Japanese 5, 274–6, 279–84, 286–7, 290–2
  Malayalam 5, 104, 120, 122, 126, 131, 133
  Marathi 2, 5, 27, 54–5, 63, 153, 160, 175–9, 181, 188–9, 194
  Tamil 1–2, 5–6, 19, 33, 66–7, 69–70, 72–6, 98–9, 101–3, 105–7, 109–14, 120, 126
  Urdu 27, 33, 49, 80, 85
Lesbian, gay, bisexual, transgender, intersex, and queer (LGBTIQ) 238, 244
Life narratives 1–2, 4–11, 13, 19, 21–3, 28–9, 41, 66–72, 76, 79, 120–2, 125, 130, 135–7, 144–51, 153, 156–7, 160, 163–4, 167, 169–70, 174–5, 180, 196, 207–8, 210–12, 214, 216, 218–19, 224, 228, 253–4, 257–9, 268, 292
  caste and 2, 7–8, 10, 144–51, 153, 163, 169–70
  dalit 2, 11, 23, 76, 137, 156
  forms of 2, 136, 292
  Indian 7
  study of 1, 8, 10, 130
  use of 268
  women's 10
*Lincoln* 104
Literature 1, 6, 22–3, 52–3, 55, 57–8, 60, 62–3, 66–70, 72–6, 79–80, 84–5, 91, 99, 170, 178, 189, 222, 228, 237, 254, 256–7
  dalit 22–3, 52–3, 55, 58, 60, 62–3, 66–8, 70, 73–6, 79–80, 84, 91
  Tamil 1, 66, 69–70, 74
Lubin, Alex 21

*Madhuri* 39
*Madhur Veena* 35
*Mahaprabhu Ravidas Ka Chamatkar* 50
Maharashtra 5, 47, 51, 53, 55, 67, 153–4, 173–9, 185–6, 188–90
*Malayala* 123
*Malcolm X* 107
Mangalatai 6, 173–5, 179, 181–97
Mani, Kunnukuzhy 121–3, 135–6
  tragic Heroine in search of History 135
Manusmriti 47–8, 212, 216, 220
Marginalization 88–9, 221, 253–4, 267, 281
  social 281
Marriages 3, 21, 28–9, 30–41, 60–1, 100, 102–3, 113, 116, 126, 129, 167, 182, 187–8, 264, 278, 281, 287–9, 291
  child 102
  intercaste 21, 28–9, 31–41, 113
  interregional 37
*Mary Kom* 98

Media 11, 58, 63, 83–4, 111–12, 115, 122, 132, 149, 166, 231, 259, 265
social 11, 122, 132, 231
Memoirs 4, 259
*Mera Bachpan Mere Kandhon Par* 54
*Mere Jeevan ke Anubhav* 19–20, 23–32, 35–40
Middle classes 53, 57
Migration 254, 256–8, 260, 265, 281
Missionaries 30, 126
*Mississippi Masala* 107
*Mo' Better Blues* 107
Modernity 21, 28, 34, 36, 38, 40, 125, 127–8, 130–1, 135, 146, 148–50, 153, 156, 163, 174, 176, 187–8, 196
Moral 121, 130–1, 134, 144, 161, 174, 176–7, 186–8, 190, 196, 213, 229, 239
conflicts 174
*Mother India* 112
Muslims 30, 49, 56, 155
broadmindedness of 30

*Nashtanayika* 121
*National Legal Ser vices Authority (NLSA)* 229, 234–5, 245–6
Naz 229, 242, 246
*The New York Times* 105
*Nixon* 107
*Nokkadu: Tamil Dalit Sirukathaikal* 72
Non-Resident Indians (NRIs) 262
Norms 40, 60, 116, 146, 156, 158, 188, 195, 290
aesthetic 156
Brahminical 213
group 290
patriarchal 195
sexual 40, 156
societal 158, 261
North Indian Dalit movement 50

Oppression 2, 9, 48, 59–60, 72, 98–9, 103–4, 114, 153, 155, 174, 197, 213, 216, 221, 236, 245, 257, 263, 285
caste 2, 48, 60, 114, 216, 221, 263
sexual 174
Outcaste 4, 47–8, 50, 220, 275, 277
*Outcaste* (name of a book) 283
*Outlook India* 82

Pamphlet 51, 124
*Panchakonankal* 73
*Panchamar* 73
Pandian, M. S. S. 2, 20, 70, 111
*Parasakthi* 101
Pathak, Bindeshwar 205–34
Personal narratives 54–5, 62, 180, 230, 236–9, 244, 246
Phule, Mahatma Jyotiba 2, 9, 41, 50–1, 150–1, 159, 163
Pirs 30
Poems 48–9
dalit 49
*Poi + Abatham = Unmai* 74
Political engagement 84, 90
Political inequality 2
Politics 6, 8, 10, 12, 21, 24, 33–4, 53–4, 68, 74–6, 79–81, 83–5, 90, 97, 99, 101–2, 107, 109–13, 115–16, 121, 132, 134, 144, 147, 163, 173–4, 177, 179, 182, 184–9, 196, 207, 238, 245, 254, 258, 265, 267
constitutional 53
dalit 24
Gandhian 21
identity 54, 79
patriarchal 186
social 90
Poverty 9, 25, 28, 86, 156, 174, 182–4, 196, 243, 285
Premchand, Munshi 53, 85, 60, 79–81, 83–6, 88–91
narratives 53, 60
Punjab 5, 19–20, 24, 26–7, 29

Race 2–3, 5, 8, 83, 107, 144, 192, 230, 233, 238–9, 254, 256, 258, 260, 267, 282, 291
Rajadurai, S. V. 3, 37
*Rativilas* 39
Religion 7, 10, 29, 34, 49, 52, 74, 98, 100, 104, 107–8, 113, 115–16, 125–6, 128, 148–9, 206–7, 214, 216, 218, 254, 256

Religious conversions 30
Rights
    citizenship 37, 128
    collective 22
    transgender 245
Rosy, P. K. 6, 120
    biographical essay on 122–3, 135
    disappearance 121, 130
    family 123
    life 7, 120, 130, 137
    life narratives 121–2, 130, 137
    memory 121
    passage from theater to cinema 127
    print and visual traces 125
    Rosy Memorial Arts and Sports Club 121
    stage and film career 131
    violence on 134
    writings on 133
*Roti-beti* 21, 34
*Round Table India* 83, 132

Santram BA 6, 8, 19–41
    arguments 38
    articles 31
    as editor 28, 35
    autobiography of 19, 21–3, 28, 35, 40
    between Gandhi and Ambedkar 32
    *Caste Must Go* 29, 35
    *Contraception* 39
    critiques of castes 28, 35
    family 28
    glimpses of 21
    *Jat-Pat* 19, 28–9, 35, 81
    life and writings 21, 41
    life narrative 19, 41
    love for Hindi 27
    *Married Love* 39
    narrative 38
    personal narrative 20
    responses to caste 21
    thought 21
    *Vivahit Prem* 39
    writings 21, 41
*Sardar* 104
Sawarkar 158
Self-consciousness 47
Self-expression 52, 54, 58
Selfhood 38
Self-knowledge 37
Self-liberation 23
Self-sufficiency 37
Sex 30, 39–40, 160, 182, 186, 190, 229, 260
Sexism 60
Sexual economies 69
Sexuality 10, 35, 40, 69, 127, 134, 160, 173–4, 180, 182, 186, 193, 197, 229, 234, 242, 254
Sexual labor 177–8, 183, 186, 189–91, 195–6
Sexual norms 40
Sexual oppression 174
Sexual orientation 229, 237, 245, 256
Sexual orientation, gender identity, and expression (SOGIE) 229–30, 233, 244–5
Sexual pleasure 39
Sexual relations 38
Short story 55, 73, 85
*Shuddhi* 27, 30
Singh, Satnam 23–4
*Sivagangai Seemai* 99
Skills 167, 192, 210–11, 220
    social 211
Slave 2, 71
    narrative 2
Slavery 30, 37, 125, 217, 266
Social
    activism 193, 265
    behavior 149
    castigation 63
    change 116, 135, 149, 176, 205, 214–15, 224, 253
    consciousness 213
    difference 3
    discrimination 209
    disintegration 215
    divisions 256
    equality 88, 128, 260
    exploitation 81
    hierarchies 275, 286

history 21–2, 28, 40, 180
idealism 214
implication 149
inequalities 275–6
injustices 148
interactions 220
interventions 22
justice 214, 283, 290
liberation 72
life 21, 41, 173, 179, 196, 211
marginalization 281
media 11, 122, 132, 231
movements 230, 242, 244–6, 276
norms 261
objectives 147
order 13, 47, 126, 214
organization 3, 209
ostracism 3
politics 90
position 52, 68, 91
positioning 11, 258
practices 6
pressures 215
prestige 214
problems 276
race 282
realism 74
reform 20–1, 29, 35, 41, 100, 111, 128, 149, 214
reformer 114
reform movement 111, 205, 214
relations 126–7, 130, 240
service 212
skills 211
spaces 125–6
status 3, 27, 197, 282
structure 8, 215
struggle 128
system 81, 128, 148, 220
tension 123
transformation 125, 151, 209
upliftment 218
Sodomy law 229
South Asia 3–4, 10, 245, 263, 276
*Sreemoolam Prajasabha* 121
*Sri Ravidas Bhagwan Ki Prabhuta* 50
Stigmatization 3, 6, 23, 280
Sulabh International 205–34
Sulabh International Institute of Technical Research and Training (SIITRAT) 210
Subalternity 23, 170
*Sudha* 38
Suffering 19, 22–3, 47, 135, 196
Sympathy 60, 81, 239

Tamil Nadu 5
*The Essential Writings of B. R. Ambedkar* 241
*The Inner World* 161
*The Notorious Bettie Page* 98
*The Story of My Experiments with Truth*? 4, 86–7
*Tiraskrit* 55
*Transformation of Nature in Indian Art* 147
Transgender 228–9, 234–6, 238, 245–6
rights 245

Undercastes 48–51
United States (US) 2–3, 7, 265
social positioning in 258
Untouchability 25, 37, 49, 59–60, 69, 148, 163–4, 209–10, 232, 237, 241, 246, 262, 265–6
Untouchables 2, 4, 27, 30, 37, 47–50, 54–6, 67–8, 71, 73–4, 76, 80, 82, 86, 90, 125, 146, 148, 156–9, 161, 205, 207–8, 211, 213, 220, 228–9, 243, 261, 264, 289; see also Dalit
castes 47–8, 55, 80, 146, 205, 220
citizenship rights to 37
education of 146
job reserved for 86
lowliness of 74
poverty of 156
*varna*-less 4
*Untouchables under the Black Sun* 156
*Upara* 55, 157
*Usha* 23
*Uttar katha* 89
Uttar Pradesh 51, 53–4, 61, 217–18

*Varanashramdharm* 31

*Varna* 3–4, 11, 13, 35, 38, 40, 47, 49, 146, 148–51, 158, 215, 290; see also Castes, *Jati*
*Varna-jati* 3, 11, 13, 290
*Varna-jati* complex 3, 11, 13, 41
*Varnavyavastha* 31–2, 38
*Veerpandiya Kattabomman* 99
Vegetarianism 27, 30
*Vetrivel Shakthivel* 105
*Viduthalai* 33
*Vigatakumaran* 120–3, 125, 131, 132
Violence 3, 6, 22, 34, 74–5, 121–2, 124, 127, 130–1, 133–6, 146, 157–60, 212, 230, 232–3, 245, 260–1, 263, 265, 278
*Vishwajyoti* 27

Widow 36, 102–3, 147
Women 9–10, 28, 34–5, 38–40, 48, 55, 59–61, 69, 75, 97–8, 101–4, 115, 123, 126–31, 134, 136, 160, 163, 174–97, 207, 210, 218, 220, 222, 230, 233, 235–6, 244, 257, 261, 267–8, 276–7, 279, 288, 291
  dalit 9, 48, 61, 69, 97, 126–8, 130–1, 136, 160, 174, 177, 180–1, 186–8, 191, 195
  Indian 186
  life narratives 10
  transgender 235

*Yugantar* 27–8, 30

www.ingramcontent.com/pod-product-compliance
Lightning Source LLC
Chambersburg PA
CBHW020743020826
48980CB00019B/806/J
* 9 7 8 9 3 5 2 9 0 8 7 6 9 *